Sportscard Counterfeit Detector

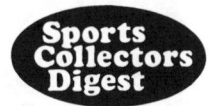

Sports Collectors Digest

By Bob Lemke and Sally Grace

Acknowledgements

The authors wish to thank the many manufacturers, dealers, collectors and other hobbyists who provided information and examination specimens for the compilation of this book. Hobbyists who provided special assistance include: Karnig Adrian, Steve Barcus, Rob Berg, David Berman, Guy Blasco, Gary Brison, George Brown, Carl Burger, Cardtime Wholesalers, Brian Cole, Dan Cook, Lou Costanzo, Richard Culp, Greg Czerkies, David Denenberg, Terry Diener, Don Dorwart Jr., Dan Fergot, Joe Filas, Ned Fishkin, Mike Friedlen, Gary Gagen, Tony Galovich, Jim Goodfriend, Howard Gordon, Michael Gordon, Vince Grisi, J.J. Guiliano, David Hakes, Kent Hakes, John Inouye, Joe Irmen, Ted Isham, Mike Jurist, Carl Kahn, Lowell Katz, John Lockwood, Roger Marth, Jim McLauchlin, Blake Meyer, New Lenox Baseball Cards, Jim O'Brien, Mike O'Brien, Bud Obermeyer, Wally Opyt, Dale Pinney, Bill Rodman, Bob Rose, Rut's Baseball Cards, Ed Ryan, Jim Schierhorn, Bob Snyder, Ferdi Tan, Randy Thompson, Ed Tsang, Ira Weiss, Richard Weiss and Henry Yee.

ISBN: 0-87341-252-4
Library of Congress: 91-77563

Published by

Printed in the United States of America

Update service available through pages of SCD

Keeping ahead of the sportscard counterfeiters is a never-ending challenge. New forgeries have been discovered at an average rate of at least two per month for the past several years. There is no reason to believe that pace will slacken in the near future.

Only through the provision of timely information to dealers, collectors and investors can the sale of counterfeit cards be halted. With the market diminished, the incentive to issue counterfeit cards may also disappear.

The addition of several newly discovered counterfeits as this edition went to press points up the need for a continuing source of fast, accurate information.

For this reason, updated information on newly discovered counterfeits will be compiled on a continuing basis and presented in *Sports Collectors Digest*, the hobby's weekly trade paper.

As new counterfeits are discovered, information and photographs will be assembled in format similar to the listings within this book and be presented in a special format within the pages of SCD, allowing the hobby to benefit from up-to-the-minute data on current counterfeits.

A one-year (52-issue) subscription to *Sports Collectors Digest* is normally $49.95. As a special service to purchasers of this book, a one-year subscription may be purchased at a $10 discount.

Use the coupon below or a reasonable facsimile to sign up now. Remember, the information in just a single new listing can save you several times the cost of the entire year's subscription.

_____ Yes, I want to keep informed on new counterfeit discoveries, please enter my subscription to *Sports Collectors Digest*. I enclose $39.95.

Make checks payable to **Krause Publications** and mail to:
Sports Collectors Digest
700 E. State St.
Iola, WI 54990

Name _____

Address _____

City _____ State _____ ZIP _____

Table of contents

Minor league baseball

Football

Basketball

Hockey

Preface

The detection of counterfeit sportscards — while it can and should employ some scientific procedures — is not an exact science. To be consistently correct requires a unique combination of training and experience.

Foremost is exposure to sportscards themselves. When a person has long or intensive exposure to all types of cards — new and old; baseball, football, basketball and hockey — he quickly develops a sense (perhaps even subconsciously) of the characteristics of each card. When a card comes along that is not quite "right," in terms of printing quality, weight and feel of the cardboard or surface texture, an experienced card handler often hears alarm bells.

Too often, however, the viewer of such a card cannot specifically pinpoint what is wrong with the card that identifies it as a counterfeit rather than just a printing variation or abnormality. It is here that training and/or experience in the printing methods by which cards are produced — and illegally reproduced — is necessary. A successful counterfeit detector must have an understanding of today's complex computerized printing technology as well as the literally stone-age lithography techniques by which cards were produced for the tobacco companies 80 years ago.

Finally, formal training in the field of counterfeit detection is beneficial. Knowing the specific methods by which a counterfeit is created from a genuine item defines the perimeter of the battleground where this war is fought. Understanding the physiology of the counterfeit and the psychology of the counterfeiter is essential to detection.

I began collecting sportscards in 1954 and have been involved daily in the sportscard hobby on a professional basis for more than a decade. Nearly 20 years in the publishing business have imparted a thorough working knowledge of the graphic arts and printing technology. A graduate of the American Numismatic Association's counterfeit detection training program, I have written numerous articles on counterfeit currency and counterfeit sportscards.

While this book is the result of dedicated work on the part of many persons in the hobby/industry, I alone must accept the responsibility for the final product. While I am confident that what is presented here is accurate, if there are mistakes in the attribution of counterfeit status or within the specific descriptions of counterfeit cards, they are my errors. It is fervently hoped that the reader will assist the on-going work by providing correction to my mistakes and by filling the many informational and photographic gaps within these pages.

Bob Lemke
April, 1993

A special note about this edition . . .

You hold in your hands the second edition of the *Sportscard Counterfeit Detector*. It must be recognized that this edition is not "complete." In a larger sense, this book will never be complete because it is the publisher's intention to keep the volume perpetually in print and updated on an annual basis as new counterfeits are discovered.

Your assistance is vital

The assistance of all readers is particularly sought to help narrow the gap toward completeness on this project. Specifically, if any reader can assist in providing information and/or specimens of counterfeit cards not listed in this book, or for listings which are incomplete in this edition, or information on errors which might be promulgated in these pages, they are urged to contact: Bob Lemke, Sports Collectors Digest, 700 E. State St., Iola, WI 54990.

Remember, it was the assistance of your fellow dealers and collectors that made possible the creation of this book. One day the information which they unselfishly provided could prevent you from making a mistake worth several hundred or several thousand dollars. Please be as generous with your information for the greater benefit of the entire hobby/industry.

The scope of this book

Comprehensive coverage within the pages of this book is limited to counterfeit versions of genuine sportscards. The scope of this edition does not allow for the inclusion of detailed data concerning reprints (other than those made for the specific purpose of defrauding buyers), fantasy cards or unauthorized collector issues ("broders"), although those areas are covered in brief chapters in this volume.

All counterfeits known to the editor at presstime are presented in this book, including some cards for which few details are currently available. It is the intention of the publisher to continually update the body of this work as new information becomes available.

A cautionary note . . .

Just because a card is not listed in this book does not mean it is not a counterfeit. This book lists all counterfeits which were known to a relatively small group of hobby professionals, and for which definitive data could be worked up within a tight production schedule. There are undoubtedly counterfeit cards in the hobby market that are unlisted here. It is hoped the reader will be able to use the methodology learned here and apply it to the examination of other suspect cards.

How to use this book

This book cannot detect counterfeit sportscards for you. It does indicate which counterfeits were known to the publisher at the time of printing, and how the editors determined the cards were counterfeit. The final determination of whether a suspect card is good or bad rests in your hands.

You can count on this — if a card you hold displays the characteristics for that specific counterfeit, it *is* a counterfeit. It cannot be genuine, no matter how much you paid for it, nor how much you wish it to be genuine. Conversely, just because a card you suspect does not display the specific characteristics shown in this book does not mean it cannot be a counterfeit. The fakers will continue to produce new counterfeits of cards which had not previously been reproduced, and they will continue to produce new versions of cards which have already been counterfeited. Hopefully, by studying the methods by which existing counterfeits have been identified in this book, you can apply that knowledge to a suspect card you might be faced with that is not currently covered in this volume.

To have any chance at all of matching a suspect card with the known fakes in this book, it is essential that you get a good magnifying glass. Virtually all of the counterfeits in this book can be identified with a lens no stronger than 5X (producing an image five times actual size), since we have already pinpointed the areas in which to conduct a close-up examination. For a few cards, a lens in the range to 10X might be desirable, but for the average dealer or collector, nothing stronger will ever be needed. While the initial efforts to identify characteristics of many of these counterfeits included the use of a stereo microscope, scales which weigh to tenths of a gram and other laboratory-quality instruments, the expense of such equipment is totally unnecessary to fully utilize the information in this book.

Each known counterfeit is exposed in this book through written descriptions and — where available — comparative photographs. Some examples, however, are not completely presented due to a lack of either actual specimens of the counterfeits, of the genuine cards, or both. Unless otherwise marked, the full front and back card photos are of the specific counterfeit being profiled. Where possible, microphotographs of both genuine and counterfeit cards are presented. Generally these detail photos provide the easiest clue to identification. Other characteristics of the counterfeits will appear in the text. It should be noted that not all of the identified characteristics of the counterfeits have been presented. This was done both to conserve space and to avoid letting the counterfeiters know all of the mistakes they made in attempting to reproduce the genuine cards.

We have generally avoided the use of subjective signposts to positively identify counterfeits. Such things as shade and intensity of color and ink coverage, clarity of photo, texture of the cardboard stock and composition of the color printing dot structure are subject to the interpretation of the viewer and cannot be easily imparted in the written word nor even in the finest of photographs. For that reason, we have concentrated on presenting, wherever possible, tell-tale clues that can be found on each and every specimen of a particular counterfeit card and on no known specimens of the genuine card.

The emphasis in this book's presentation has been on ease of use for the reader. Suggestions for improvement are invited by the authors.

A word about weight . . .

With few exceptions, of the more than 200 types of counterfeit sportscards covered in this book, none weigh in within the tolerances to be expected for the genuine cards they purport to be.

In most cases, a broad approximation of the paper stock on which the genuine cards were printed is the best that a counterfeiter can provide for his product. In virtually all cases, this cardboard, when imprinted and cut to the size of the real thing, will be so significantly heavier or lighter that it provides the first clue to a card's counterfeit status. That difference in weight is seldom less than 3-4%, most often 5-10%, but occasionally as much as 20% or more.

Unfortunately, it takes a very sensitive (and very expensive) scale, weighing differences as little as one-tenth of a gram, to provide this data. For this reason, we have not, in most cases, included weight information as the basis for identifying the counterfeits in this book.

Other, more pragmatic reasons mitigate against quoting specific weights either for genuine or counterfeit cards. First and foremost, a weight recorded on a scale at the publisher's office may be different than a weight recorded at your location. Differences in the calibration of scales and the interpretation of the reading by the person doing the weighing are sure to exist. Outside of laboratory conditions, most scales will weigh the very same item differently at different times, depending on such variables as drafts within the room, atmospheric and other physical conditions. Too, except for the most recent cards in Mint condition, wear and aging factors have to be considered in the weight of genuine cards, as well as the possibility that slight differences in "batches" of cardboard may have existed at the time of printing. Counterfeits, because of the less exact nature of their manufacture are sure to vary in weight more from card to card than genuine examples. Because our investigation was not conducted on large numbers of specimens of any given counterfeit, any weights quoted would not be sufficiently representative.

In the real hobby world, the weight of a card can almost never be used in and of itself to determine whether a card is genuine or counterfeit. It should only be considered as a relative measure. Rather than keeping detailed files of genuine card weights, it is better to compare the weight of suspected counterfeit cards with known genuine examples by actually weighing each card in the same session. When possible, always weigh several genuine cards to determine a range of weights against which the suspected counterfeit can be compared.

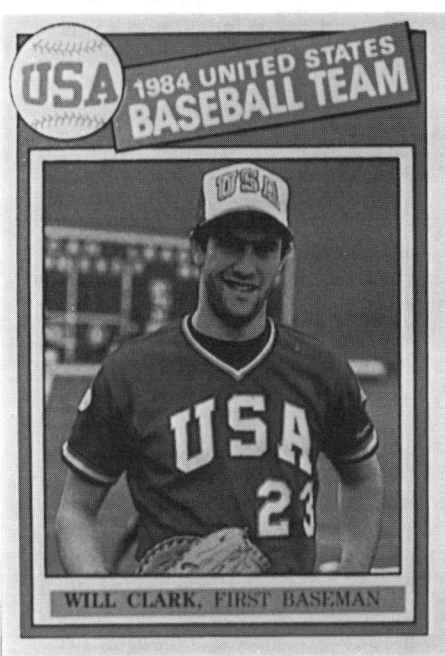

WILL CLARK, FIRST BASEMAN

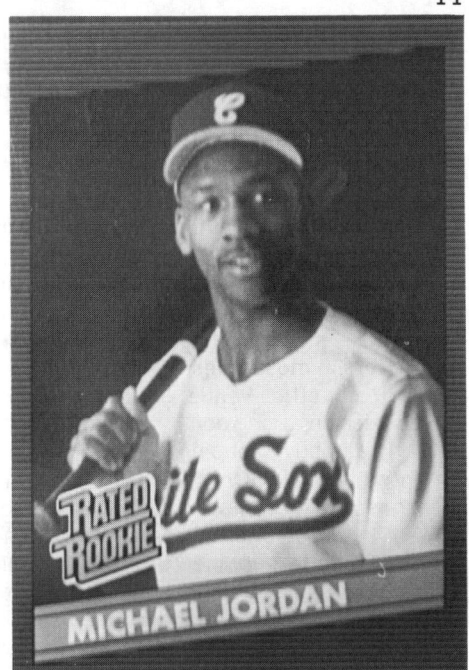

MICHAEL JORDAN

Fantasies and "broders"

Only a few of the cards which fit the broad category of "collectors' issues" could even remotely qualify for inclusion in the main body of this book.

Instead, a few words about the genre will probably be sufficient.

While there were dozens of collectors' issues produced in the 1970s, they were principally team sets of non-current players, done in designs that had no resemblance to contemporary cards.

A phenomenon of the 1980s was the emergence of current-player cards that have come to be known by the generic term of "broders," in honor of the person who was responsible for the issue of the majority of such cards through the middle years of the decade.

By definition, broders are cards that are not licensed by the player depicted, the players' association or the league. With no licenses to restrict them, there is no control over the number of cards issued. Theoretically, if a particular broder sells well, the card could be reprinted — either by the original issuer or anybody else. This means that such cards have no true collector value. In general, however, until recent years many of the broder cards were of better design and better quality printing than the cards of the major legal manufacturers. Selling for 25¢ to $1 apiece, they were (and still are) attractive alternatives to high-priced "real" cards of currently hot superstars — at least among children and beginning collectors.

In the mid-1980s, Krause Publications became the first hobby entity to take a stand against broders, refusing to accept advertising for the cards. Other publications have followed suit in recent years.

Until very recently, the persons who should have shouldered the responsibility for controling the spread of these pirate cards were totally indifferent to the problem. The players' unions and leagues, to whom legitimate card manufacturers pay royalties for the use of player pictures and team logos, should have been tracking down the makers of these cards and halting their printing presses. Led by the National Basketball Association, beginning in 1990, some effort is now being made to crack down on the illegal cards. In 1993, California enacted legislation making it illegal to manufacture or sell unlicensed sportscards and providing criminal penalties for violations.

Still, new broders appear each month and it is not uncommon at card shows to find dealer tables occupied entirely by unauthorized issues. These cards will not disappear until other elements of the hobby take action. If card shop owners refused to handle such merchandise and if card show promoters would refuse to allow broders to be displayed or sold, the market for such cards would disappear. In today's ever-competitive hobby market, however, shop owners and show promoters in most cities cannot afford to do anything that will drive paying customers to another venue, so it is unlikely that broders will become an endangered species anytime soon.

The hobby's leading dealers' organization, the Sports Collectibles Association International (SCAI) does not allow broders to be sold at shows which it sanctions, and its by-laws prohibit its members from dealing in unauthorized issues.

A recent trend among the producers of broders has been to issue cards in similitude to genuine card designs. Michael Jordan's well-publicized visit to the Chicago White Sox batting cage resulted in Michael Jordan baseball cards being produced in the designs of the 1986 Topps and Donruss cards, and even a card shared with Bo Jackson in the design of the 1986 Fleer "Major League Prospects" design.

Similarly, Nolan Ryan, who originally shared his 1968 Topps card with Jerry Koosman, can be found on a recent broder all by himself in a design that

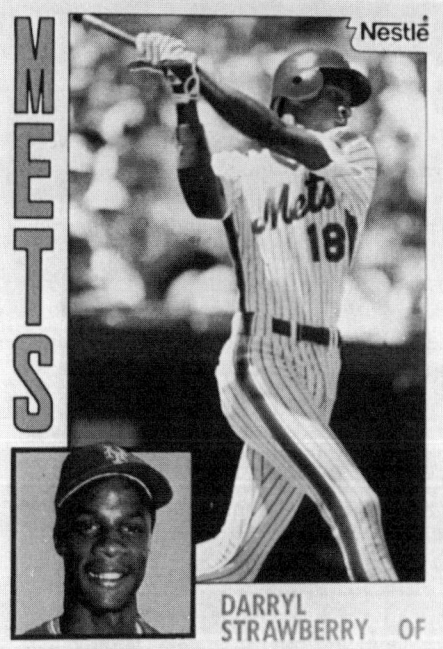
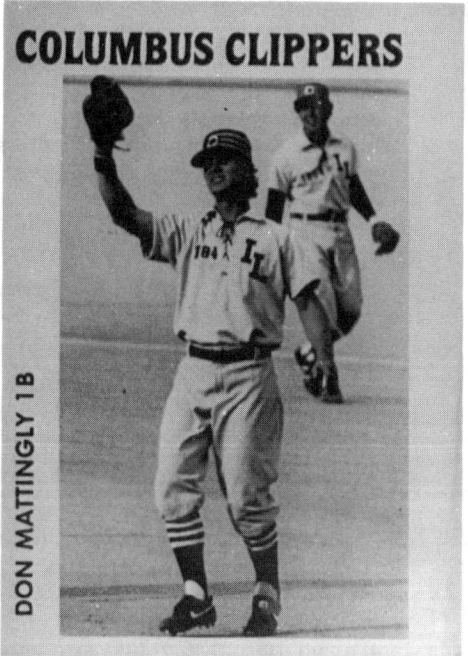

(Left: Black-and-white versions of the star cards from the 1984 Topps/Nestle's issue can be found purporting to be rare proof cards. Right: Don Mattingly in a 19th Century uniform is found on this common fantasy issue.)

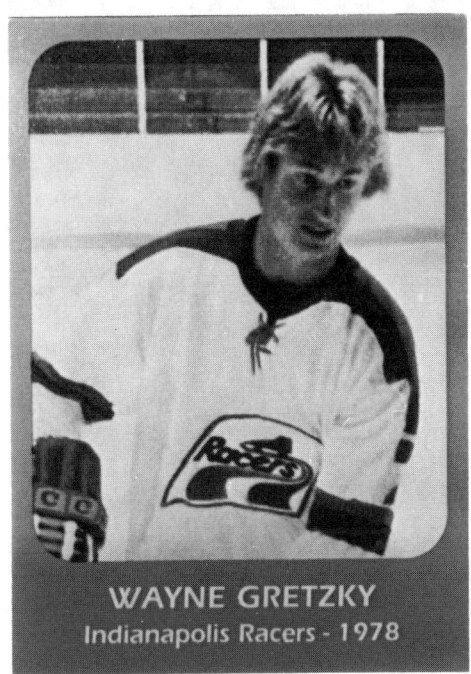

WAYNE GRETZKY
Indianapolis Racers - 1978

The makers of this Wayne Gretzky fantasy sent out a mailing trying to convince dealers it was a genuine 1978 issue.

reproduces the burlap look of the '68 Topps. Other oft-seen cards of this type depict Will Clark in the 1984 U.S. Olympic team uniform, and done in the style of the 1985 Topps cards which depicted eligible players from that squad, and a Darryl Strawberry card done in the style of a 1984 TCMA Tidewater Tides issue.

The class of unauthorized cards which comes the closest to fitting the scope of this book is the fantasies. These are cards that are generally, but not always, produced several years after the originals in an attempt to induce the belief that they are real cards that have somehow been overlooked by the entire hobby.

Don Mattingly has been a frequent victim of these fantasy cards. There have been fantasy cards depicting him as an Evansville High School player and as a member of the Greensboro Hornets minor league team. One widely circulated card is done in a style roughly similar to a 1982 TCMA card; it depicts Mattingly in a 19th Century uniform used for a special game.

A recent fantasy card was offered depicting Wayne Gretzky in the uniform of the Indianapolis Racers, and purporting to have been issued in 1978, and carries the copyright line of "National Sports Cards".

Still another type of fantasy card that was popular a couple of years back was the phony "proof card" and "test issue". Done in black-and-white (it's much cheaper to print than a color fake), these cards attempt to portray rare pre-production versions of valuable cards. Such fantasies are usually found with notations of "TEST" or "PROOF" overprinted on them, along with some meaningless code combinations of letters and/or numbers. The producers of such cards are apparently unaware that genuine card manufacturers would never have cause to make such proof cards — or at least they hope the suckers to whom they're trying to sell the phony proofs are ignorant about actual printing methods.

Two frequently seen types of this fakery are black-and-white versions of the 1984 Topps-printed Nestle's cards, and the infamous 1989 Fleer card of Billy Ripken which features a vulgarism visible on the knob of his bat.

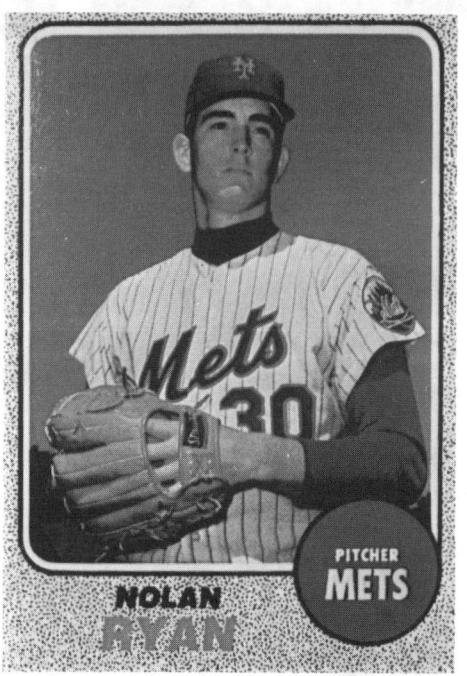

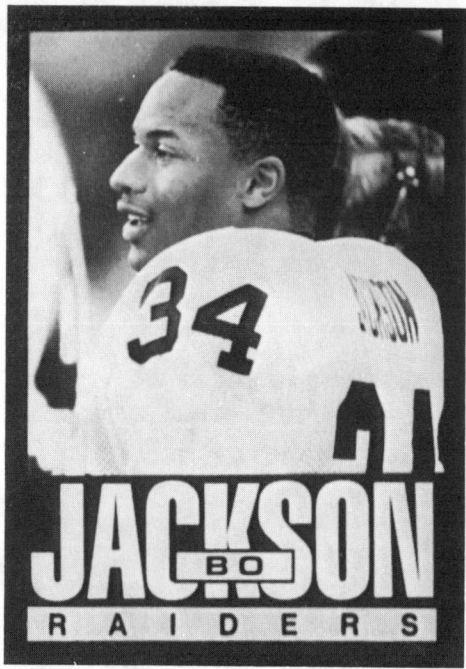

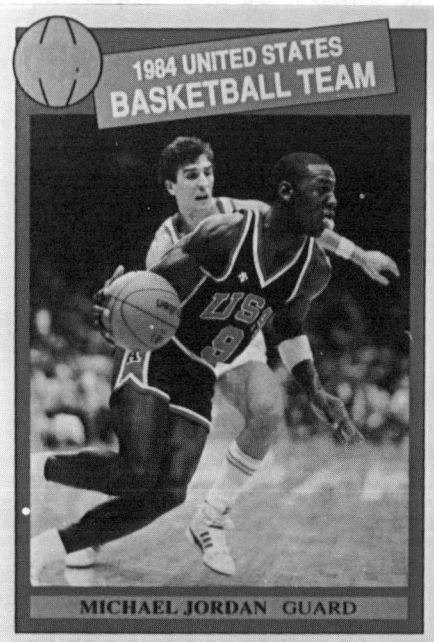

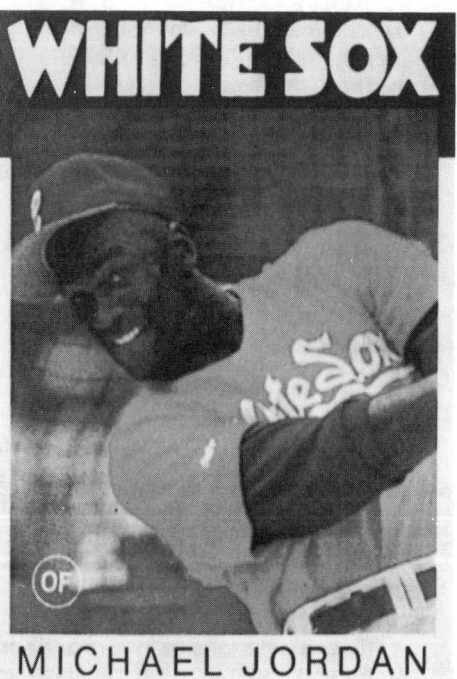

Each new superstar that emerges in big time sports can expect to find his image pirated by makers of illegal "broder" cards. First it was Don Mattingly and Wade Boggs, then Jose Canseco and Bo Jackson, then Michael Jordan and Nolan Ryan; now it's Shaquille O'Neal and Eric Lindros.

Reprints

It is a fine line indeed which separates a reprint from a counterfeit.

Both are reproductions of a genuine sportscard produced for profit. It is largely the degree of profitability being sought by the second-generation manufacturer that marks the difference. The reprinter seeks to create a replica card of sufficient similitude to the genuine to entice purchasers who cannot find or afford the real card. Generally the selling price of a reprint is set based upon the actual costs of the manufacturer. The counterfeiter seeks to create a replica card that is so similar to the genuine as to entice purchasers into believing they are purchasing the original. The selling price of a counterfeit is generally based on the current hobby market value of the genuine card.

Intent, therefore, seems to be the key to differentiating an innocent reprint from a sinister forgery.

That is the criteria upon which decisions were made to include or exclude certain unauthentic cards from the body of this work. Usually, a person who intends his replica cards to be sold as reprints builds into his creation at least one significant difference between the reproduction and the original. It may be as dramatic and indisputable as varying the size of the reproduction, or the color of ink with which the card backs are printed. It may be as simple as adding the word "Reprint" in tiny — easily removed — type on the back of the card. Often the differences are more subtle variances from the original's cardboard stock and surface finish.

The counterfeiter, by contrast, does everything possible to make his product as much like the genuine as possible.

The reader will notice several cards listed in this book that are clearly marked as reprints. It is the editor's contention that these cards — despite the reprint disclaimer — were produced with the intention of defrauding the hobby. As often as not, specimens of these cards that are seen in the marketplace have had the word "Reprint" erased. The similarity of paper stock and printing quality,

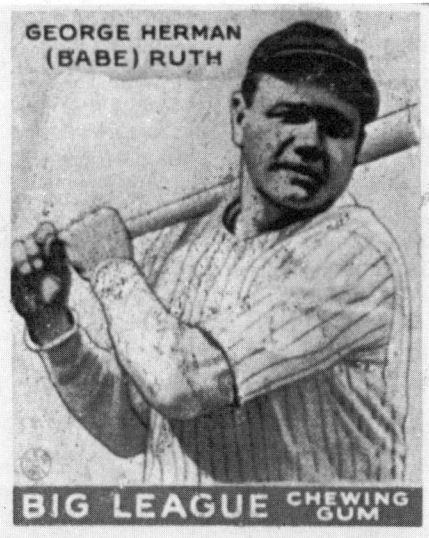 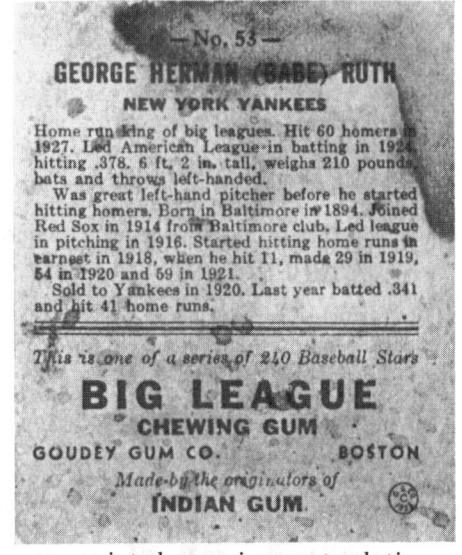

This 1933 Goudey Babe Ruth reproduction was printed as an innocent substitute for the collector who could not afford the real thing. It was subsequently altered by having the "Reprint" notation erased, and being artifically aged with dirt and stains to give it the appearance of a 50-year-old card. It was passed as genuine.

at least as viewed by non-expert hobbyists, to the genuine cards makes this series of reprints a danger that warrants their inclusion here.

Conversely, a veteran hobbyist may note the absence from these listings of some early reprint cards which bore no notation of their status. While those who know well the Michigan dealer who was responsible for the production of many such cards in the early 1970s may question his motivations in producing unmarked reprints, it is clear that within the hobby — such as it existed at that time — the reproductions were not a danger. As is so often the case with unmarked reprints, however, these early replicas soon found their way into the hands of the "public," being passed as genuine. They continue to surface today in "old-time" collections, much to the consternation of the would-be seller.

Obviously, that is the principal danger of sportscard reprints — that they will be altered by unscrupulous persons who will attempt to sell them to the unwary as originals. This is usually accomplished by erasing or covering up the reprint notation, if any, which appears on the back of the card, and by artificially aging the card through the judicious application of dirt, or even weak solutions of tea or coffee. The altered reprints are usually offered for sale with a convincing story about how they have been in the family for generations. The price is almost always quoted at a great discount from current catalog value, hoping to prey on the greed of a buyer who thinks he is getting a real steal of a deal.

The reprinting of sportscards was unknown until about 20 years ago. After all, until that time, cards had little or no monetary value. They were children's toys that were seriously collected by only a handful of adults who preferred trading the cards to buying and selling.

Since the floodgates of reprinting were opened in the early 1970s with the reproduction of a handful of Hall of Famers from the 1933 and 1934 Goudey sets and a few others, the torrent has not yet subsided. A large percentage of the major baseball card issues from the pre-World War II years have been reprinted in whole or in part, along with a significant sampling of the national, regional and local issues of the late 1940s and 1950s. Only the existence of copyright laws has prevented major reprintings of more recent cards. Until very recently, football, basketball and other sportscards were ignored by reprinters; again, because of lack of collector value of the originals.

Reprints are usually sold as complete sets. A price of 10¢ per card is not uncommon, and some sets that have utilized high-gloss finish cost even more. In the 1970s and 1980s, many reprints were sold in books, which had the cards perforated for easy removal. Many of the cards are still found with perforated edges, though they can also be found with the ragged edges trimmed. It is from these books that many of the reprints of single Hall of Famer cards originated.

It is beyond the scope of this book to fully detail all of the reprints which have been produced in the past two decades, though perhaps future editions may be more complete in that respect.

For now, we will provide an outline of the more commonly encountered baseball card reprints, along with a few notes. This list should not be considered complete, as some earlier issues may have been overlooked, and new reprints of older sets are appearing at the rate of one every couple of months or so.

The parenthetical designations are the *American Card Catalog* numbers of the original issues, where appropriate.

1869 Cincinnati Red Stockings team card
1887 Lone Jack cigarettes
   All 13 cards of the 1886 champion St. Louis Browns have been reprinted.
1887-88 Allen & Ginter (N28, N29, N43)
1888 Goodwin Champions (N162)
   All of the baseball players from the multi-sport composition of these sets have been reprinted; some by more than one manufacturer.

1887-1890 Old Judge/Gypsy Queen (N172)
All of the Hall of Famers and many other players from this landmark set have been reprinted in one of several replica reissues.

1895 Mayo Cut Plug (N300)
The major league baseball player cards and the college football player cards from this issue have all been reprinted.

1904 Fan Craze (WG2)
The 51-card American League and 48-card National League game card sets have been fully reprinted.

1909 American Caramels (E90-1)
Sixteen of the 118 cards in this set were reprinted in 1992; all Hall of Famers plus Joe Jackson.

1909 Philadelphia Caramels (E95)
Complete set of 25 reprinted in original 1½x2⅝" size.

1909 Ramly (T204)
The complete set of this elegant 121 card issue has been reprinted.

1910 Plow Boy Tobacco
Downsized to standard 2½x3½" in reprint form, the originals were issued in cabinet size (5¾x8"). Forty-two of the 50 White Sox and Cubs cards were reprinted in 1992.

1909-11 American Tobacco Co. (T206)
Single cards — including the "King of Baseball Cards," Honus Wagner — have been oft reprinted. Two different companies have offered reprints of the entire set — 524 cards.

1910 American Tobacco Co. (T205)
The complete set of 208 cards has been reprinted, as have been selected single cards.

1911 Mecca doublefolders (T201)
The complete set of 50 cards has been reprinted.

1911 Turkey Reds (T3)
The 100 baseball player cards from this large-format set (the originals were 5¾x8") have been reprinted in modern 2½x3½" size. These Turkey Red "minis" are sometimes seen with the reprint notice on the back erased and the cards artifically "aged," being sold as rare prototypes.

1911 General Baking (D304)
The complete set of 25 cards has been reprinted in the original 1¾x2½" size.

1912 Hassan triplefolders (T202)
The complete set of this issue has been reprinted.

1913 Fatima team cards (T200)
All 16 major league team cards have been reprinted.

1913 Tom Barker National Game (WG6 - green back)
1913 Base Ball The National Game (WG5 - red back)
Each of these 52-card game sets were reprinted.

1914-15 Cracker Jack
Single cards of the 1914 (set of 144) and 1915 (set of 176) have been reprinted, as has the complete 1915 set.

1915 Sporting News
This 200-card set has been reprinted in its entirety.

1916 Collins-McCarthy (E135)
All 200 cards reprinted.

1921 American Caramel Co. (E121)
Selected star cards reprinted.

1922 American Caramel Co. (E120)
A complete reprint of the 240-card set has been produced.

1922 strip cards (W551)
Selected Hall of Famers reprinted.

1925 strip cards (W504)
16 Brooklyn Dodgers players and a team card reprinted.

1926 strip cards (W512)
Selected Hall of Famers reprinted.

1927 Middy Bread
The 42 St. Louis Cardinals and Browns cards from this die-cut set were reprinted in 1992 in smaller (2½x3½'') size, not die-cut.

1927 playing cards (W560)
A complete 64-card set reprint.

1928 Tharp's ice cream
Various star cards reprinted.

1928 Babe Ruth candy
Card #2 of the six-card set reprinted.

1931 Babe Ruth Sportoscope flip book

1933 Tattoo Orbit
Selected Hall of Famers reprinted.

1933 DeLong
Complete set of 24 cards reprinted.

1933 Goudey premium
Four large-format cards reprinted.

1933 Goudey
1933 Goudey Sport Kings
1934-36 Diamond Stars
1934 Goudey
1935 Goudey four-in-one
1935 National Chicle (football)
1936 Goudey game
1938 Goudey heads-up
1939 Play Ball—America
1940 Play Ball
1941 Play Ball
1941 Goudey
Each of the above 12 sets has been reproduced in their entirety; some more than once. In addition, most of the Hall of Fame players from these sets have been reproduced as individual reprints.

1946-50 Remar bread
Selected star cards from this Pacific Coast League series reprinted.

1947 Tip Top
Complete 163-card reprint.

1947-48 Jackie Robinson ad cards
Cards from a Montreal clothier and Old Gold cigarettes have been reprinted in postcard size.

1947-66 Exhibit cards
Selected star cards reprinted.

1948 Sport Thrills
Complete set reprint.

1948 Bowman
The black-and-white baseball card set of 48 cards has been reprinted in its entirety, along with the 108-card football issue and 72-card basketball set.

1948-49 Leaf
Selected star player cards reprinted.

1949 Bowman
Both the 240-card set of major league players and the rare 36-card Pacific Coast League player issue have been reprinted in their entirety.

1950 Bowman

The complete 252-card baseball and 144-card football issues have been reproduced.

1951 Bowman
1952 Bowman

The above two sets have been reprinted both as individual cards and as complete boxed sets with modern glossy surface finish.

1952 Topps

Virtually the complete 407-card set was reprinted in the current smaller 2½x3½" format as a boxed set by Topps.

1952 Red Man ad poster

Features Ralph Kiner card on front.

1953 Bowman color
1953 Bowman black-and-white

Both sets have been reprinted in their entirety.

1953 Topps

The complete set, along with some cards that weren't part of the original issue, was reprinted by Topps in 1991 in a smaller-format glossy version.

1953 Red Man ad poster

Features Enos Slaughter card on front.

1954 Red Man ad poster

Features picture of Johnny Mize on front.

☆　☆　☆

The following regional baseball card sets have been reprinted in their entirety. Most of them have been altered in format from their original sizes to conform to the now-standard 2½x3½" size.

1952 Red Man tobacco
1953 Johnston cookies Milwaukee Braves
1954 Red Heart dog food
1954 Dan-Dee potato chips
1954 Wilson Franks
1954 Johnston cookies Milwaukee Braves
1955 Johnston cookies Milwaukee Braves
1955 Rodeo meats Kansas City A's
1956 Rodeo meats Kansas City A's
1957 Spic-and-Span Milwaukee Braves
1959 Home Run Derby
1960 Lake to Lake milk Milwaukee Braves
1968 Dexter Press/Coca Cola

Star cards reprinted in 2½x3¼" sticker format.

1970 Flavor-est milk Milwaukee Brewers

A reprint of an unauthorized collectors issue!

☆　☆　☆

Even minor league cards have not been safe from reprinting. More than a dozen of the original TCMA minor league cards of the 1979-1985 era were reprinted and sold as part of 100-card collector packages. The reprints are distinguishable from the originals by the existence on the back of Major League Baseball logos and/or on the front by the existence of white borders which are not found on the originals. The reprinted minor league cards are:

1979 Kelvin Chapman, Tidewater
1979 Ron Hassey, Tacoma
1980 Tom Foley, Waterbury
1980 Matt Galante, Columbus
1981 Michael Cole, Wisconsin Rapids
1983 Jack Fimple, Albuquerque
1983 Kirk McCaskill, Redwood
1983 Spike Owen, Salt Lake City
1984 Rufino Linares, Richmond
1984 Frank Wills, Omaha
1984 Kurt Stillwell, Cedar Rapids
1985 Paul Assenmacher, Durham
1985 Jeff Dedmon, Richmond
1985 Tom Filer, Syracuse

Alterations

Counterfeits are not the only bogus cards that hobbyists must be wary of. The alteration of genuine cards to make them appear to be a more valuable variation is also a danger.

That threat became reality in the summer of 1990 when altered versions of two of the hobby's most expensive cards began appearing. The cards were the "MAGIE" spelling error and the "DOYLE, N.Y. NAT'L" variation from the T206 American Tobacco Co. set of 1909-11.

The Magie card has a long history as one of the most desirable cards in the "old-time" hobby's most popular set. A misspelling of the name of Phillies outfielder Sherry Magee was quickly corrected when the T206 cards were first issued, creating a scarce variation. In the summer of 1990, a "Magie" error card in Excellent condition was valued at $7,500.

Even more valuable was the Doyle "Nat'l" variation. Uncovered nearly a decade ago, but kept secret while the discoverer attempted to find additional speci-

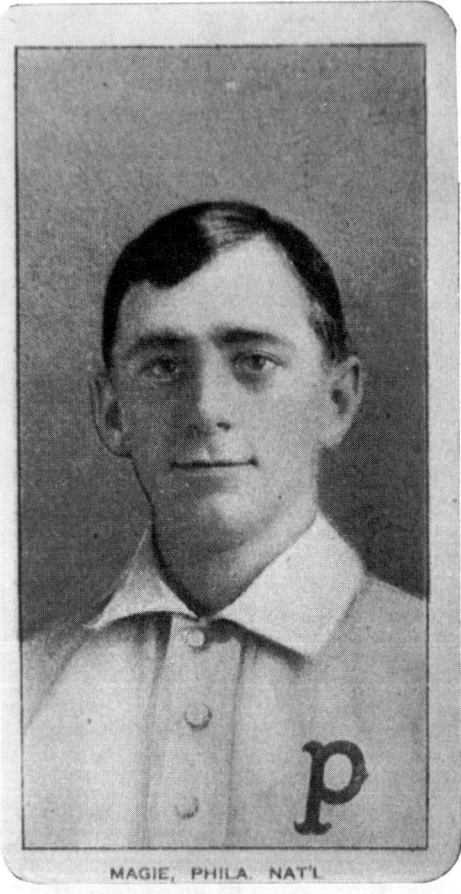

MAGIE, PHILA. NAT'L

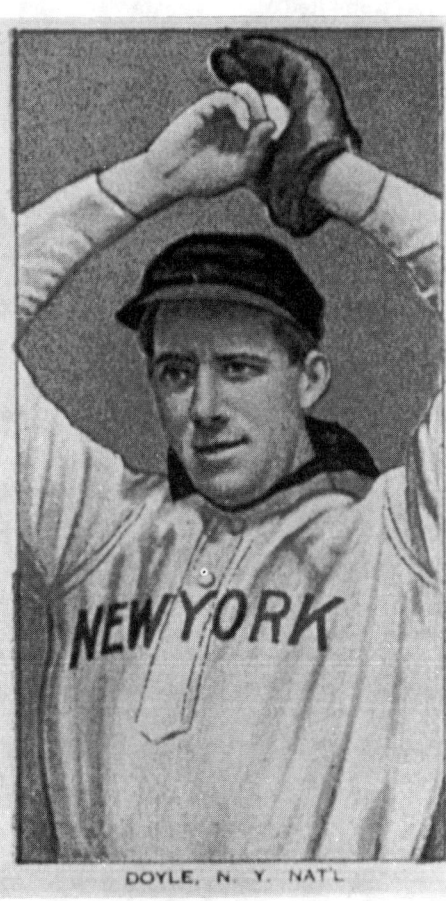

DOYLE, N. Y. NAT'L

By altering the line of type at the bottom of these cards, a $200 pair of common versions was fraudulently transformed into $20,000 worth of fake rarities.

mens, fewer than a handful of genuine examples were known in the summer of 1990, making it numerically much rarer than even the famed Honus Wagner card from the same set.

There were four Doyle card types issued in the T206 set. Three were of N.Y. Giants second baseman Larry Doyle in portrait, batting and throwing poses; the fourth was of Giants pitcher Judd "Slow Joe" Doyle, shown winding up to pitch. Virtually all of the known cards of Judd Doyle omit the league designation in the line of type at the bottom of the card, leaving just "DOYLE, N.Y.".

In the summer of 1990, the few known examples of the leagueless variation were valued at $15,000 in Excellent condition.

The value of these variations was too much temptation for one sharp operator who began buying up specimens of the genuine, lower-valued variations of these cards. In Excellent condition, a Magee or a Doyle, Nat'l T206 would sell for under $100. The genuine cards were then altered by erasing the line of type at the bottom and replacing it with an entirely new line, creating a bogus example of the rare variations. The style of type chosen and the color of ink were virtual perfect matches, but the fakers made one fatal flaw in not exactly copying the style of league designation on the cards.

On all genuine T206 National League cards, the "N" of "NAT'L" is significantly larger than the other three letters, and the top of the apostrophe is flush with the tops of the letters "ATL". On the altered cards, the "N" was reproduced the same size as the other letters, and the top of the apostrophe was allowed to rise above the tops of the letters.

By the time the story of these fakes was printed in *Sports Collectors Digest*, two of the Doyles and one of the Magies had been sold to unsuspecting collectors. As of mid-1993, no further examples have been found.

Thankfully, there are few similar rare cards in the hobby which can be simulated by altering a genuine less-expensive specimen. Also, the recent trend among collectors away from paying big dollars for variations works against the possibilities of more forgeries of this type being created.

Collectors and dealers, however, must be wary of the potential for such fraud.

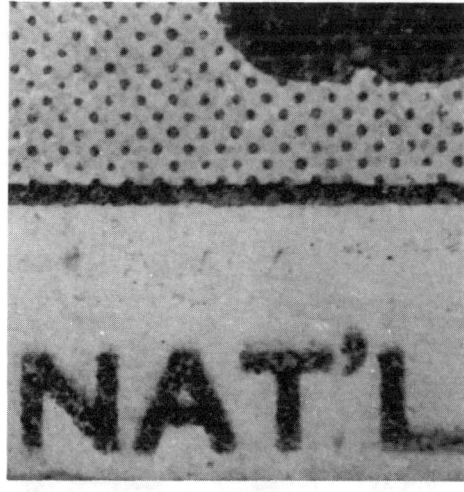

Genuine   **Altered**

On a genuine T206 National Leaguer's card, the "N" is larger than the "ATL" and the apostrophe is level with the tops of the last three letters. The altered cards show the "N" the same size as the other letters, and the top of the apostrophe floats above the tops of the letters.

The manufacturers

Between the early 1980s, when a pair of Southern Californians was prosecuted for selling counterfeit 1963 Topps Pete Rose rookie cards, and 1991, when both Topps and Leaf-Donruss launched major investigations into counterfeiting rings, there was not a single known case of a person being arrested for either counterfeiting or selling counterfeit cards, and only a couple of instances on record in which persons were required to make restitution for selling fakes.

The plain fact was that the legitimate card companies did not seem interested in protecting the hobby from counterfeiters. The attitude among the manufacturers seemed to be that they had made their profit from the cards' sale originally, and they were no longer concerned with those cards in the aftermarket.

Perhaps the investigations launched in 1991 were a sign that at least some of the card companies were willing to participate in cleaning up this problem.

The first indication that a major card company recognized the counterfeiting problem and was willing to do something about it came in the summer of 1988, when Upper Deck announced its forthcoming 1989 premiere baseball card set. One of the principal characteristics on which Upper Deck pre-sold their new premium card concept was that the card would be counterfeit-proof. The application of a hologram to each card was intended to insure that Upper Deck cards could never be illegally duplicated. The expense of creating and printing a duplicate hologram is theoretically too great for counterfeiters to shoulder.

So far, Upper Deck's technology seems to be working. There are no known cases of Upper Deck cards having been counterfeited.

In late 1991, two other major manufacturers announced their own anti-counterfeiting measures.

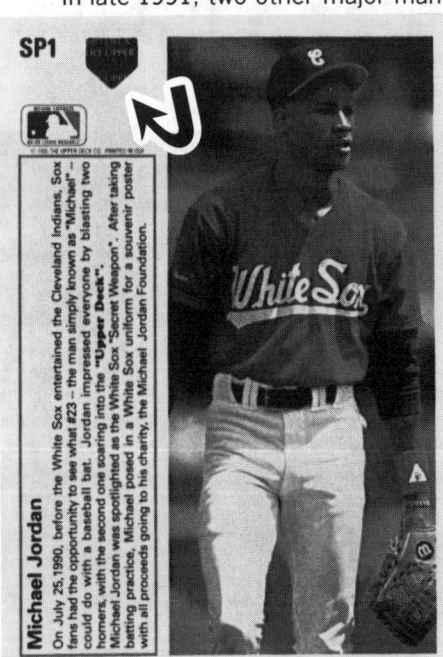

With the introduction of its Pinnacle football set, Score debuted a small optical variable device on the back which they claim cannot be reproduced by the techniques employed by counterfeiters. The specially designed strip shows one image when it is viewed through a special ribbed plastic tool laid horizontally on the card, and a different image when the tool is laid vertically on the card.

Score continued to incorporate this technology on its later premium card issues.

Donruss also premiered an anti-counterfeiting measure on its 1992 baseball card issue. A special application of a fifth-color ink on the back of the card creates another optical variable device that would be difficult or impossible to duplicate. The printing thus applied can only be seen when the card is held at a very specific and narrow range of angles.

The hobby can only hope that other card companies will invest the time, technology and money necessary to protect their products' integrity — and more importantly — their customers.

Hot-stamped holograms on the backs of its cards have so far protected Upper Deck from counterfeiters.

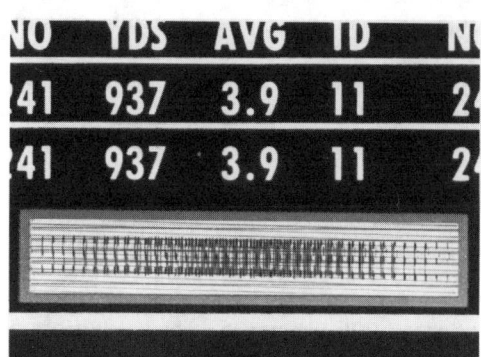

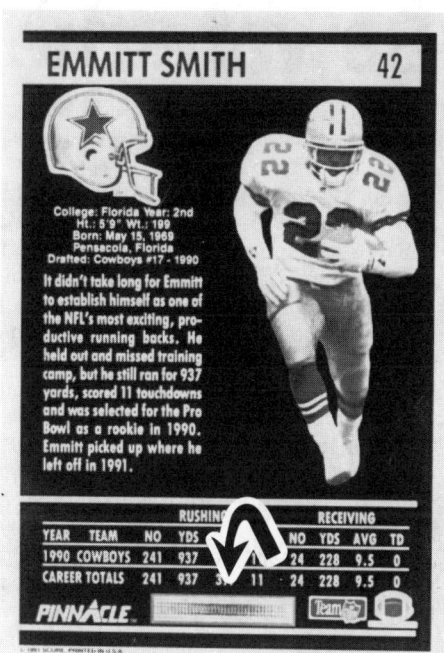

Beginning on its 1992 baseball cards, Donruss has employed a "fifth-color" overprint on the backs of its cards to foil counterfeiters. Visibile only at certain angles, the technique cannot be easily duplicated by counterfeiters.

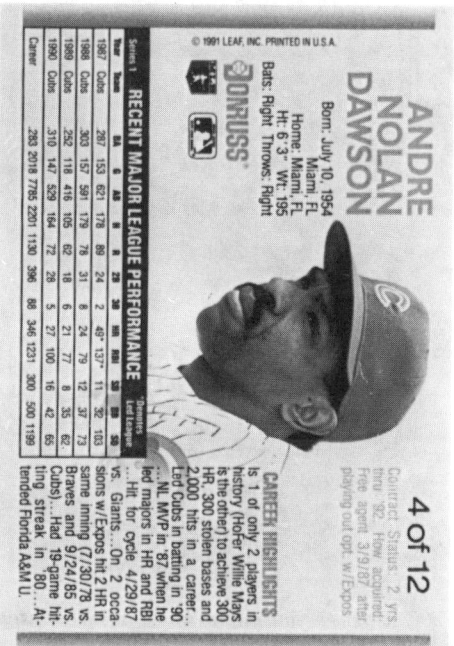

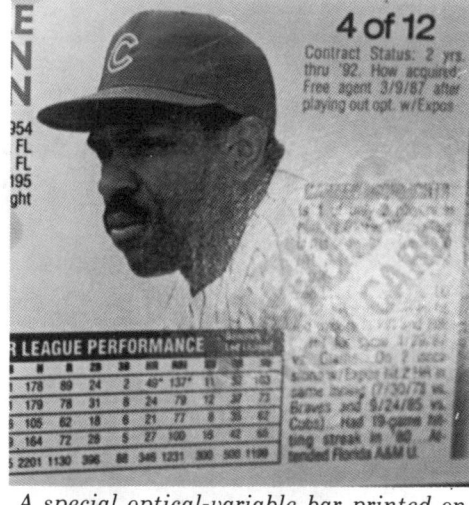

A special optical-variable bar printed on the backs of Score's 1991 Pinnacle football cards, and continued on later Pinnacle releases is said to be impossible to counterfeit with the technology available in the fakers' arsenal.

Beware the bogus Honus

With the current price of T-206 Honus Wagner cards in the $40,000-450,000 range, it should go without saying that a buyer should exercise the utmost care in filling that particular hole on a wantlist.

Even to rely on the information in this book when contemplating such a purchase would be foolhardy. Nonetheless, we have heard of one collector who recently paid $15,000 for a counterfeit Wagner and there was another being offered around at card shows around the nation in the past year or two.

Besides outright counterfeits of the treasured Wagner card, there are numerous specimens being offered as genuine which consist of altered reprints and fakes which have been made by sandwiching a reprinted Wagner front onto a genuine T-206 back. Many of these concoctions are creased, yellowed and otherwise "aged" to give the appearance of legitimacy. They all come with a good story.

The best defense against purchase of a phony T-206 Wagner is to buy only from a well-known hobby dealer and to thoroughly examine the card's pedigree. Virtually all of the known examples of this card have been bought and sold several times within the past 20 years and the previous owner or sales agent will most certainly be able to verify whether the card being sold is the same specimen. If you buy a Wagner from a flea market dealer who claims to have just found it in an old cigar box or being used as a bookmark in the family bible, you deserve whatever hit you take in the wallet for letting your greed override your common sense. Before plunking down $10,000 or $100,000 for a Wagner, seek the advice of an acknowledged expert in older cards, and pay him for his opinion.

Any dealer or collector who takes the time to familiarize himself with original T-206 cards can prevent himself from being victimized by every fake Wagner seen to date. Remember, while this card is worth six-figures today, when it was produced in 1909, it was produced in exactly the same manner as the other cards in the issue and stuffed

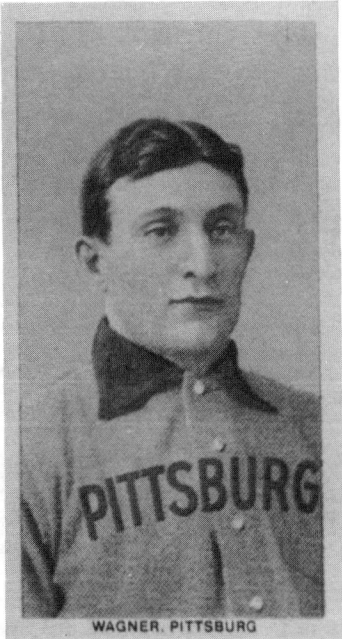
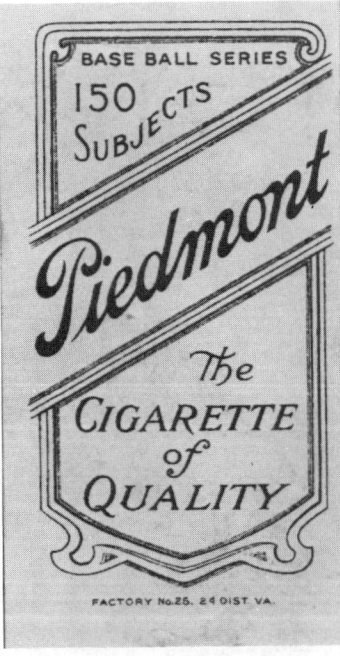

WAGNER, PITTSBURG

Please do not attempt to authenticate any T-206 Wagner you might be comtemplating the purchase of based on what you read in this book. It's a job for the experts.

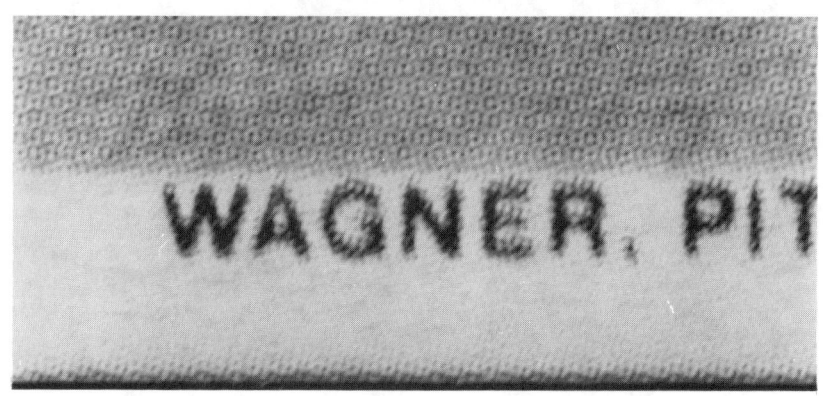

The player and team name on every T-206 card is printed in solid, dark brown lines, not fuzzy dots.

into cigarette packages. That means the paper has a soft, somewhat porous texture, the player's name and position at bottom are printed in solid, deep brown letters, and there is a solid black pinstripe around the colored picture of the player. All of the reprints show the letters and stripe as a composition of color dots, rather than solid lines. That does not mean, however, that if the letters and lines are solid, the card in genuine; it just means that up to now nobody has taken the time and gone to the expense of faking the line art and the player picture separately and stripping them together to create a fake.

Always pay more attention to the front of a Wagner than the back, because, as mentioned, many fakes are made by gluing a reprint front to a genuine back. It is worth memorizing that every known genuine Wagner is from the original 1909 "150 SUBJECTS" issue. Something like 90-95% of the real Wagners have Sweet Caporal backs, though a couple of genuine examples are known with the Piedmont ad on back.

To re-emphasize, if you're contemplating the purchase of a T-206 Wagner, don't attempt to authenticate it yourself based on anything you've read here. You must have an expert evaluate the card. Any seller who balks at your selection of a third-party authenticator should be viewed with great apprehension.

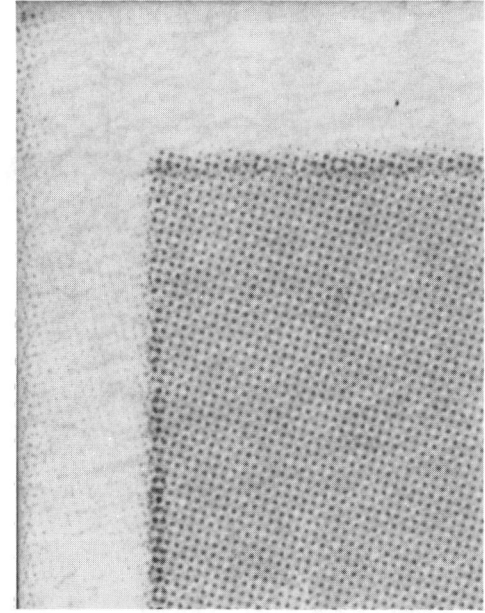

All genuine T-206 cards have a solid black pinstripe separating the white border from the colored player photo. This counterfeit shows the line as a string of dark dots.

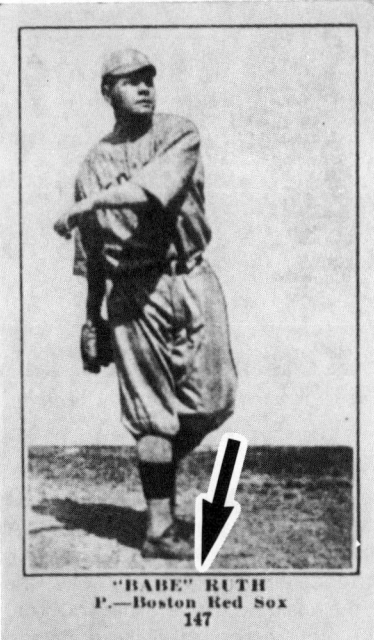

"BABE" RUTH
P.—Boston Red Sox
147

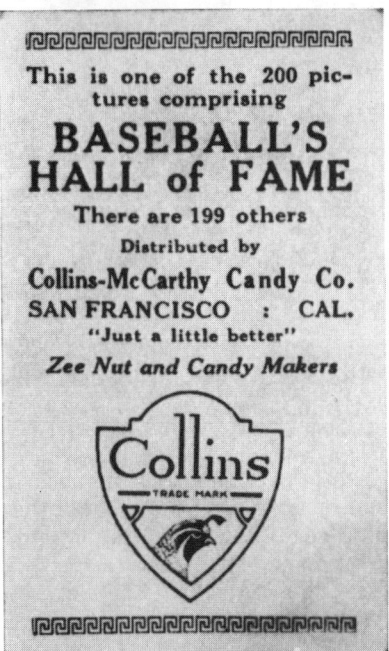

This is one of the 200 pictures comprising

BASEBALL'S HALL of FAME

There are 199 others

Distributed by

Collins-McCarthy Candy Co.
SAN FRANCISCO : CAL.
"Just a little better"
Zee Nut and Candy Makers

Because so few dealers or collectors have ever seen a genuine Collins-McCarthy card (set E135 in the *American Card Catalog* designation system) the physical appearance of this counterfeit might not arouse immediate suspicion.

This fake, however, differs from a genuine E135 in that it is printed on thinner — much thinner — cardboard than a genuine card. Besides having a semi-gloss surface on the front that genuine E135s do not possess, the stock on which the counterfeit is printed is so thin that when held up to any light source, the printing on the opposite side of the card can be easily seen.

Other evidence branding this card a counterfeit can be seen under magnification. The lettering on the front of the counterfeit — the player's name, position, team and card number — is formed of many tiny black dots. On a genuine card, these letters are formed of solid lines.

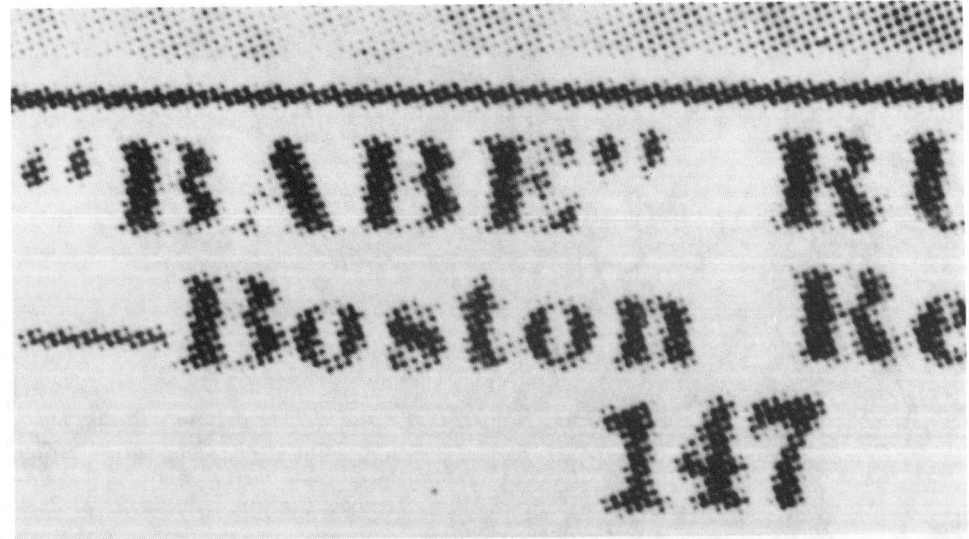

Counterfeit

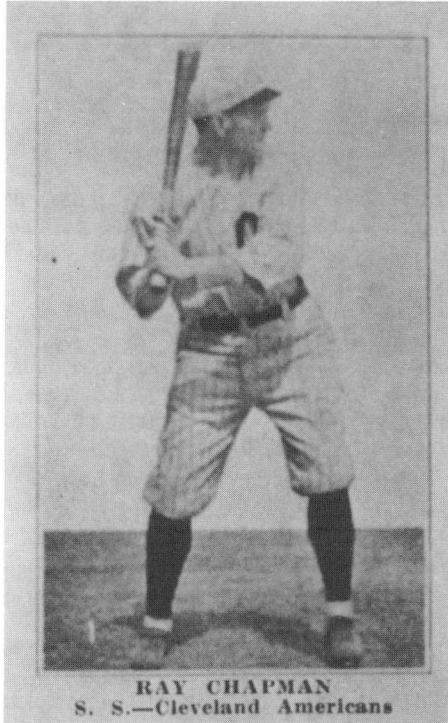

RAY CHAPMAN
S. S.—Cleveland Americans

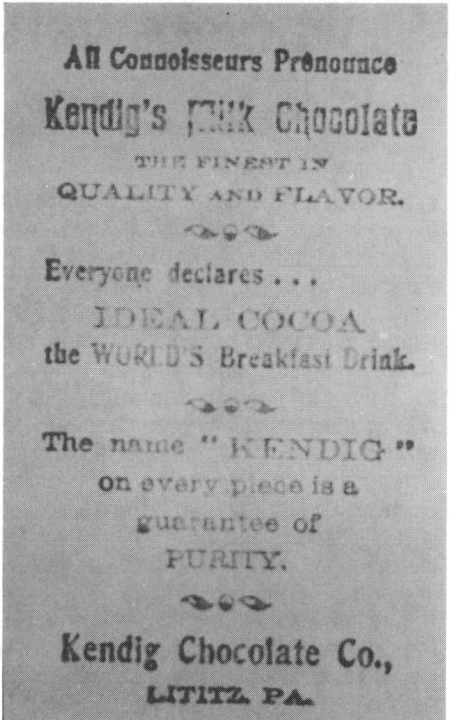

These cards should more accurately be classified among the fantasies than true counterfeits because the company never issued baseball cards. However, since Kendig's did issue trading cards, and since most collectors and dealers are not all that familiar with legitimate issues of the 1910s, it seems appropriate to include these cards within the body of the book.

These fantasies/counterfeits were first reported in late 1989, having surfaced at East Coast flea markets. Two players were reported seen on the cards, Babe Ruth and Ray Chapman; others most certainly exist.

Card fronts were apparently copied from the 1916 Collins-McCarthy "Base-ball's Hall of Fame" issue of 200 cards (E-135 in the *American Card Catalog*), with the exception that the card number from the originals was not included on the fakes. This might account for the fantasy cards' measuring only 3⅛" in length, rather than the 3¼" of genuine E-135s.

Backs of the phony baseball cards appears to have been rubber-stamped, reproducing the typography and layout found on genuine Kendig's "Flags of the World" cards which were roughly contemporary with the Collins-McCarthy.

Genuine E-135s have a semi-gloss surface on the front. The purported Kendig's baseball cards are printed on porous paper which has been artificially aged.

Still no answers on Fro-joy Ruths

By Bob Lemke

Certainly one of the greatest "crimes" ever perpetrated on the baseball card hobby was the reprinting of the 1928 Fro-joy uncut sheet of six Babe Ruth cards. Hobby lore holds that the sheets were first faked in the late 1970s. I can personally attest to having seen unmarked reprints at least a decade ago at flea markets.

Like all reprints, the original motivation was likely innocent enough: to provide collectors with an inexpensive alternative to a rare item which was out of most persons' fiscal reach. Unfortunately, the original reprinter (is that an oxymoron?) did not mark the reproduced sheets as reprints and the result has been total chaos in the marketplace for Babe Ruth Fro-joy cards.

In fact, except among the gullible or gamblers, there is no market for Babe Ruth Fro-joys. It's been estimated by hobby experts that 99% of the Fro-joys seen in the hobby are fakes. That has totally destroyed the value for whatever genuine cards are out there. While the popularity of the respective sets cannot be compared, look at the differences in price guide values for contemporary Babe Ruth cards. The lowest-priced among the four different types of Ruths in the 1933 Goudey set is listed at $4,500 in Near Mint condition. A Ruth card from the 1921-22 American Caramel E120 or E121 issues lists for $1,500-2,000. Perhaps more analogous, the six cards in the 1928 George Ruth Candy Co. issue are listed at $800 apiece. By contrast, the Fro-joy Ruths are listed at $125, tops.

As co-author of the *Sportscard Counterfeit Detector* book it has been especially frustrating not being able to provide any guidance to help the hobby differentiate between genuine and reprint Fro-joys.

Recently, with invaluable assistance from a few very dedicated hobbyists, I put some serious time into studying this issue.

Unfortunately, the results are incomplete, possibly inconclusive. This is being written in an attempt to share what is known, and to seek further assistance.

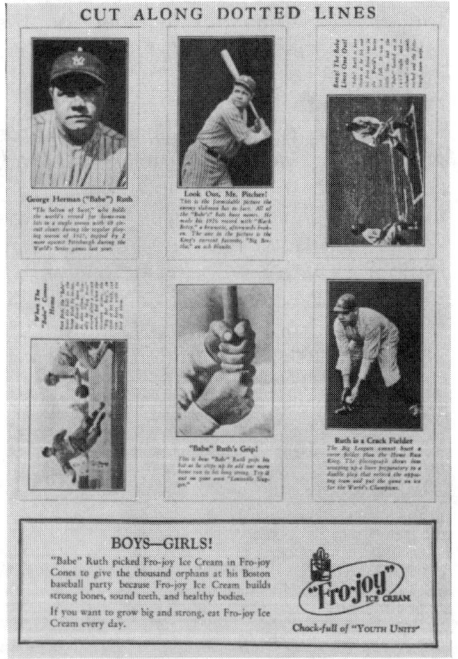
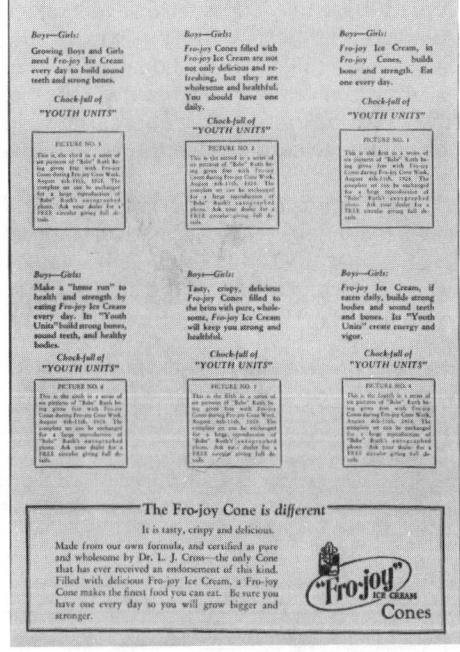

It has been reliably estimated by hobby experts that more than 99% of the Babe Ruth Fro-joy cards and sheets in the hobby are unmarked reprints.

Much of the hindrance to making positive identification of counterfeits can be traced to the methods by which the cards were originally issued.

Each day of "Fro-joy Cone Week," Aug. 6-11, 1928, purchasers of a cone were given one of the six Babe Ruth cards. By collecting and sending in all six individual cards, kids could receive a "large reproduction of 'Babe' Ruth's autographed photo," plus get back their six cards.

Actually, the six individual cards submitted were not returned, but rather an uncut advertising sheet. This raises the possibility — actually the probability — that there were two distinct printings of Fro-joys; one to create the single cards and one to create the six-card sheets. It is, however, also possible that only the six-card sheets were produced, and that the individual cards had their genesis thereon. It is my personal opinion this latter scenario is unlikely because of the relatively higher cost of printing 65 years ago. By actual measurement, nearly 44% of each uncut sheet would be scrap if the cards were cut out.

This raises the issue of whether there were detectable differences in the cards issued singly and those on the uncut sheet, and with the card stock on which each was printed. And that makes the most rudimentary steps of counterfeit detection — comparison of known genuine with suspect cards — extremely difficult in this case.

Until recently, my examination of Fro-joys was hampered by the fact that I never could be sure whether I was looking at genuine single-issued cards, genuine cards cut from sheets, genuine sheets or counterfeits of any of the three. Another wrench in the works is the fact that over the years reprints have been made of the reprints, creating several generations of fakes. When comparing one of the later reprints with one of the early reprints, it is easily possible for a person to believe the earlier version is genuine, based on its perceptibly visible superiority of printing quality.

As mentioned, recent efforts by a quartet of concerned hobbyists has given me the resources to partially solve some of the puzzle. With their assistance I was able to acquire two Fro-joys — a Babe Ruth and a Gene Tunney — which were undoubtedly genuine. The legitimacy of the Ruth card could be traced to the fact that it has been owned by a knowledgeable dealer since before the reprints surfaced. The Tunney is unquestionably genuine

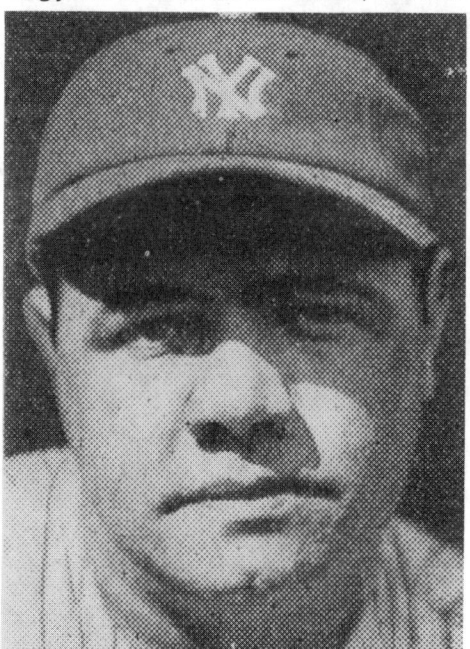 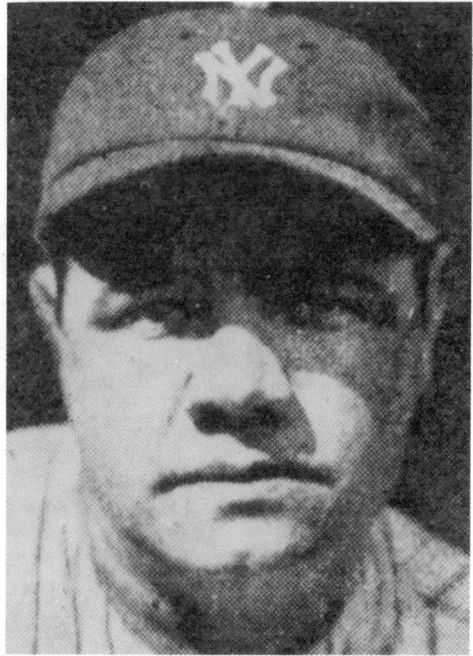

Note the existence of highlight dots in the N.Y. cap logo and on Ruth's nose and cheekbones on a known genuine card (left), and their absence on the card (right) from a suspected reprint sheet.

because the boxer's cards — issued in a promotion identical to the Ruth — have never been reprinted.

With undeniably genuine cards available, I was able to authenticate another pair of Ruth cards as genuine, finally creating enough of a "data base" of good cards from which to begin spotting the bad cards.

With the materials at hand, however, only limited observations can be made, along with some informed recommendations.

The principal difference which has been observed between the known genuine Fro-joy cards examined and a handful of suspected sheets is that the genuine cards all exhibit a complete pattern of printing dots throughout the photo area of the card. Even on the whitest and brightest sections of a genuine Fro-joy, examination with a magnifying glass will show tiny black highlight dots.

In making printing materials for the reprints, the smallest of these dots were burned out, leaving tell-tale spots of pure white on the reprints. These white patches will show up on those areas of the photos that were the brightest. Examples would be:

Card 1: *George Herman "Babe" Ruth*. The logo and button of the cap; his cheekbones and nose.

Card 2: *Look Out, Mr. Pitcher*. The upper portion of the bat, and the uniform collar behind his neck.

Card 3: *Bang! The Babe Lines One Out!* The forearms and shoulders of Ruth's uniform, the front of the batter's box between his legs.

Card 4: *When The "Babe" Comes Home*. The sky directly above Ruth's head.

Card 5: *"Babe" Ruth's Grip!* Thumbnail and the background to the right of the right hand.

Card 6: *Ruth is a Crack Fielder*. Cap logo and left side of baseball.

It must be stressed that the differences noted are between known genuine single cards and suspected reprinted sheets. Only the comparison to a known genuine sheet will ultimately answer all of the questions about this issue.

How can a person know if a Babe Ruth Fro-joy sheet is unquestionably genuine? Hobby experts say the only way to be sure is to buy a sheet that comes with its original mailing envelope and/or the premium "autographed" photo. If the trio survived together, you can be sure it's genuine. Some experienced dealers say they will buy a Babe Ruth Fro-joy sheet no other way.

The premium picture is about the same size as the uncut sheet, approximately 8x10-1/2" and in printed in blue in the debossed center portion of a sheet of cream-colored stock. The

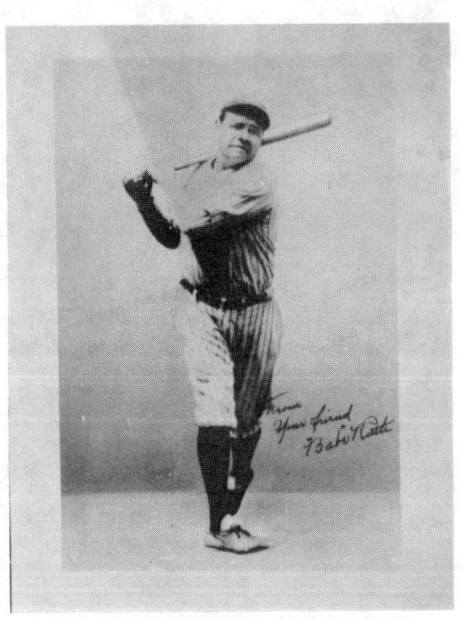
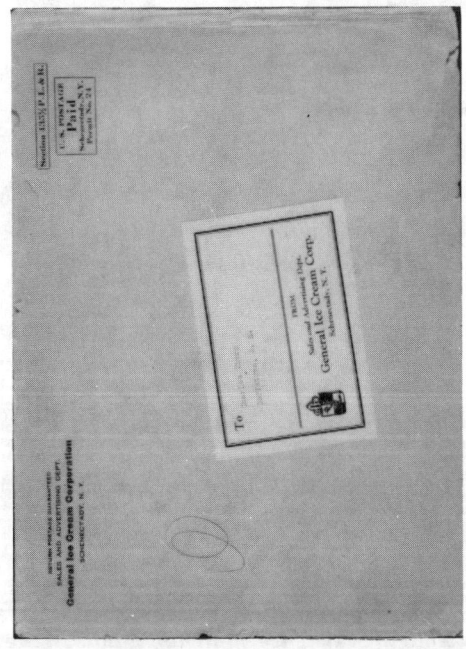

Unless it is accompanied by the premium photo and/or the original mailing envelope, the purchase of a Babe Ruth Fro-joy sheet is best left to the gullible and the gamblers.

"autograph" on the picture is, of course, pre-printed rather than hand-signed.

Both the premium photo and the card sheet were mailed in a brown kraft envelope bearing the advertising of the General Ice Cream Co., of Schenectady, N.Y.

Any person who can provide a certifiably genuine Fro-joy sheet, preferably with the original envelope and premium photo, is encouraged to contact me. With just a bit more help we may be able to finally issue definitive guidelines which will help the hobby protect itself from these ubiquitous reprints while allowing the genuine cards to achieve the market value their scarcity calls for.

* * *

What about color Fro-joy sheets? In my estimation, they are all fraudulent. While they usually come with a good story about being test sheets or printer's proofs, two facts mitigate against their genuineness.

First, nobody ever saw a color Fro-joy sheet until 1991, when they started popping up all over.

Second, in 1928 as today, most of the cost of four-color printing was incurred in the pre-press work. If a company had gone to that expense, it is extremely unlikely that the cost of the color ink to print all of the cards in color would have been a deterrent.

Avoid all color Fro-joy sheets and cards.

Special thanks!

As mentioned, this presentation could not have been accomplished without the assistance of Rob Lifson, who provided the genuine single cards for study; Ron Oser and David Spivack, who provided examples of the premium photo and mailing envelope, and Robert Temeyer, who provided examples of uncut sheets.

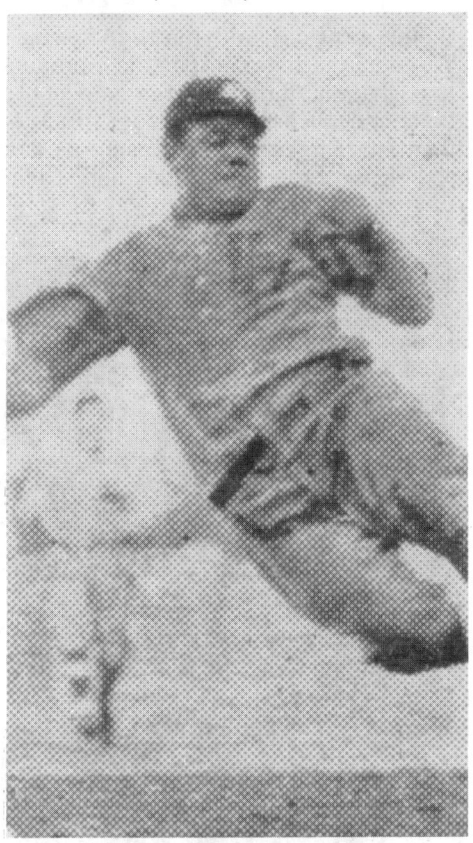 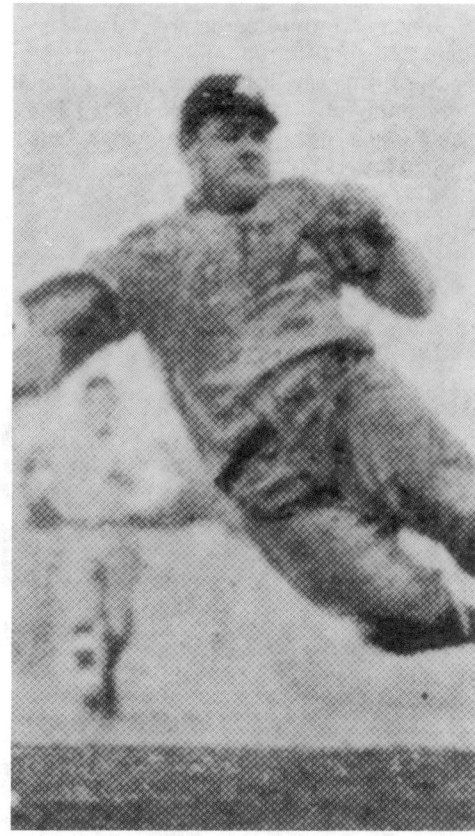

On card No. 4, "When The 'Babe' Comes Home," the genuine card (left) shows tiny black dots throughout the entire sky above Ruth's head. The suspected counterfeit (right) has a white halo over Babe's head and in the sky immediately around.

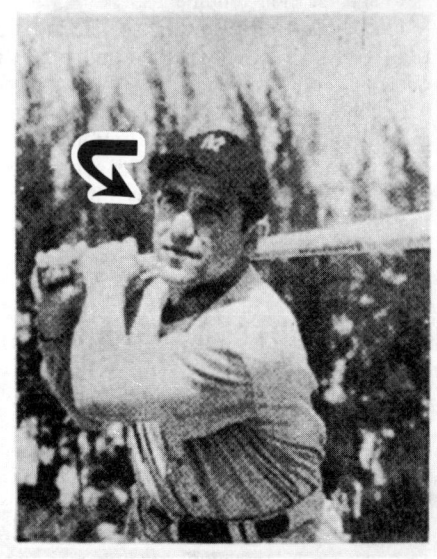

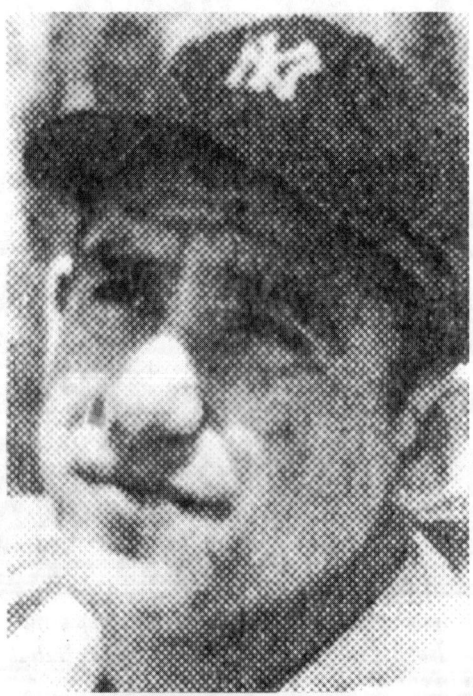

Black-and-white cards are much easier and cheaper to counterfeit than color cards. Ironically, it is much more difficult to identify and describe counterfeit characteristics on a black-and-white card, even though it is fairly easy to spot a fake.

Such is the case with the 1948 Bowman Yogi Berra card. In creating the reproduction, the counterfeiters created a photo that has a much larger black dot structure than a genuine card. This gives the picture a darker overall appearance and a ten-

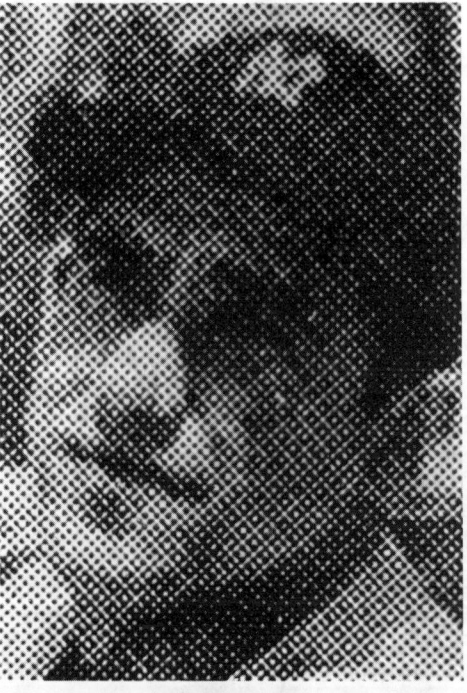

Genuine   **Counterfeit**

dency toward a lack of fine detail. However, without a genuine '48 Berra card for comparison, these subjective observations are not useful in the detection of a counterfeit.

One feature seen on the counterfeit examined may or may not be diagnostic, as it may or may not appear on other copies. On the specimen photographed, there is a vertical hairline of black ink about ¼" long running from the top-right border of the card into the photo. Under magnification, this appears to be a printing flaw, rather than a design problem. Obviously, if a suspect card features an identical ink line, it is a counterfeit. Just because a card may not exhibit such a line, however, does not make it genuine.

The best place to determine the status of a '48 Berra card is on the back. Because the counterfeiters photoreproduced black type from the gray cardboard background on an original card, the type on the fake is much lighter than normal. There are also two flaws in the back printing — areas where the bottoms of several contiguous letters are not printed. The most noticeable is the very bottom line of type, which on the counterfeit features incomplete letters "N" and "G" in "BOWMAN GUM". A similar flaw can be observed in the last complete line of the biography. The counterfeit lacks the bottom details of the letters "gam" in "games".

The counterfeit '48 Bowman Berra card is also considerably (about 25%) heavier than a genuine card.

Genuine   Counterfeit

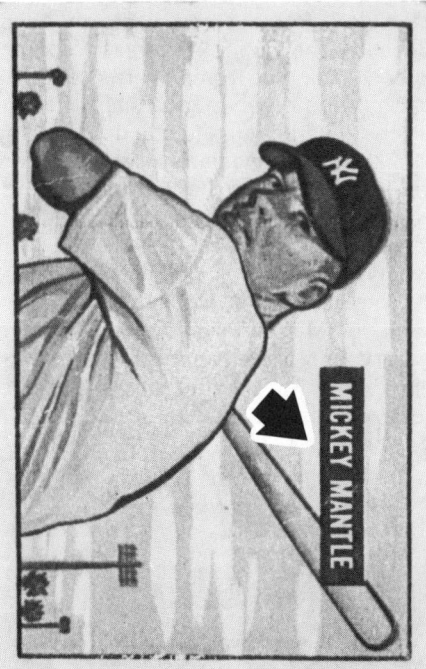

MICKEY MANTLE

Outfield—New York Yankees
Born: Commerce, Okla., Oct. 20, 1931
Height: 5-10   Weight: 175
Bats: Switch   Throws: Right

Mickey is the Yankee rookie of whom so much is expected in 1951. Everyone was talking about him during spring training in which he batted over .400. Kept on clicking when the regular season got under way. Spent most of the 1950 campaign with Joplin of the Western Association. In 137 games, hitting .383, and driving in 136 runs. Got 199 hits which included 30 doubles, 12 triples, 26 homers.

No. 253 in the 1951 SERIES

BASEBALL

PICTURE CARDS

©1951 Bowman Gum, Inc., Phila., Pa., U.S.A.

The back of the card is the key to detecting this counterfeit of Mickey Mantle's rookie card.

Genuine 1951 Bowman cards have the back printing in blue and red. The player's name and "BASEBALL" are printed in red on both genuine Bowmans and on this counterfeit. On the real cards, however, all other printing on the back is in blue ink. This counterfeit has the biographical details, career summary, etc., printed in black.

The front of this counterfeit shows the evidence of rescreening in the black border around the picture and the black box containing the player's name. On a genuine card these black elements will be solid, with sharp edges where they meet the white border and the letters. Under magnification, the counterfeit shows black dots intruding into the white areas.

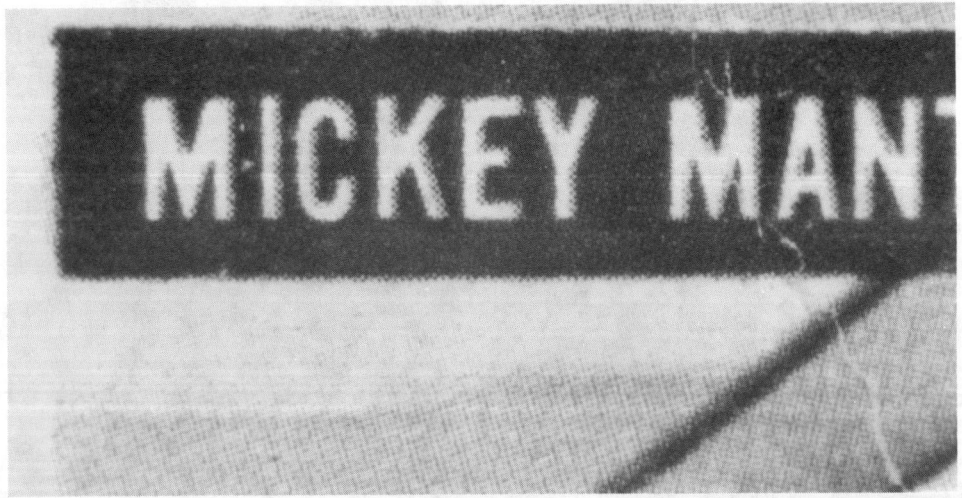

Counterfeit

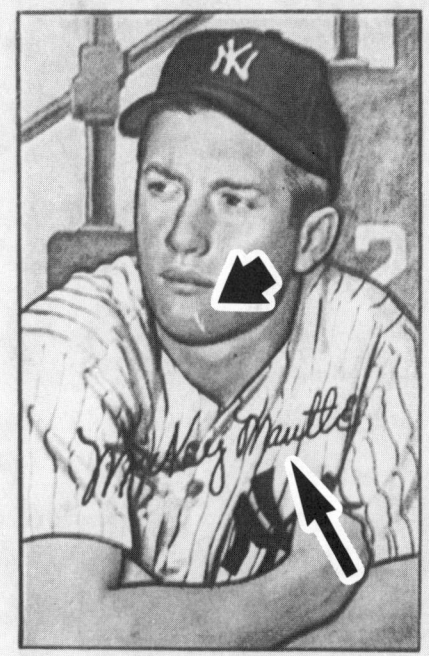

MICKEY MANTLE

Outfield—New York Yankees
Born: Spavinaw, Okla., Oct. 20, 1931
Height: 5-11   Weight: 175
Bats: Switch   Throws: Right

Began the 1951 season with Yanks' Kansas City farm. Had batted in 50 runs in 40 games, and was sporting a .361 average, when called up by the parent club. In 96 games for the Bombers. Got 91 hits, including 13 home runs. Batted .267, and drove in 65 runs.

No. 101 in the 1952 SERIES

BASEBALL®

PICTURE CARDS

Get a $1.00 value Baseball Cap of your favorite major league team by sending 5 wrappers and 50 cents to BOWMAN Baseball, P. O. BOX 234, New York 23, N. Y. State size: small, medium or large.

© 1952 Bowman Gum Division, Haelan Laboratories, Inc., Phila. 44, Pa.—Ptd. in U. S. A.

Visually a fairly deceptive counterfeit, the back of this fake is particularly well executed.

Fortunately, the front of the counterfeit offers easily seen evidence of its bogus status. All examples seen of this counterfeit show a green "scar" on Mantle's left jaw. Other diagnostics include the autograph, which on a genuine card is printed in solid black, but which on this counterfeit can be seen to be made up of black, red and blue dots.

Similarly, the black border around the picture is a solid line on a genuine card, but is made up of tiny black dots on the counterfeit. All specimens seen of this counterfeit exhibit out-of-register printing, but as this condition is fairly common on genuine '52 Bowman Mantle cards, it cannot be used as a definitive indicator of counterfeit status.

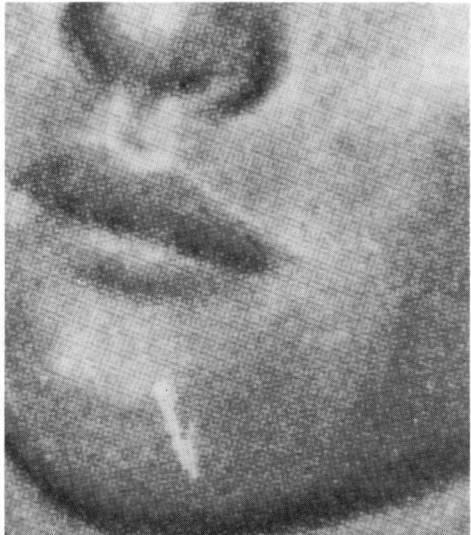

Counterfeit

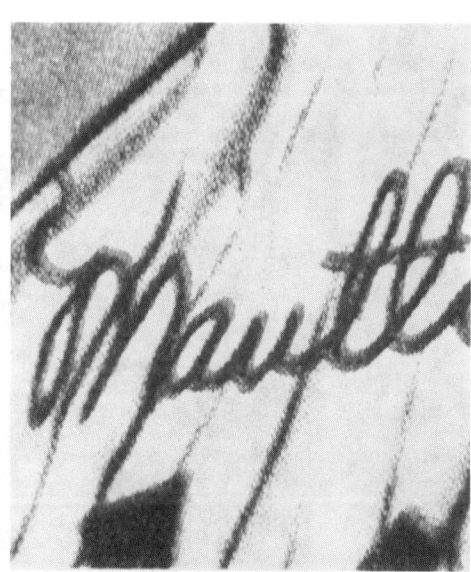

Counterfeit

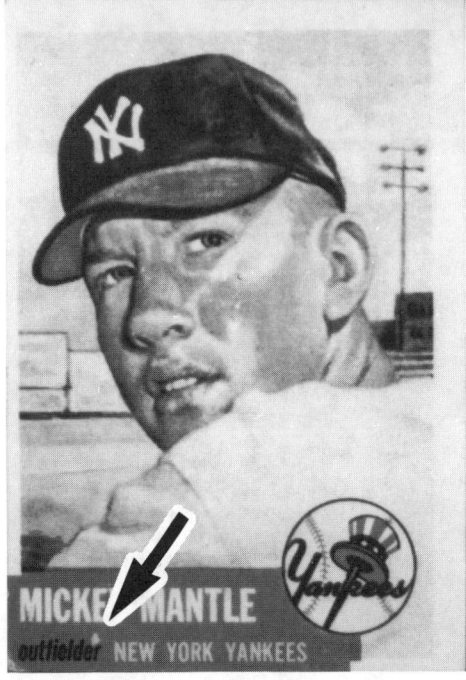

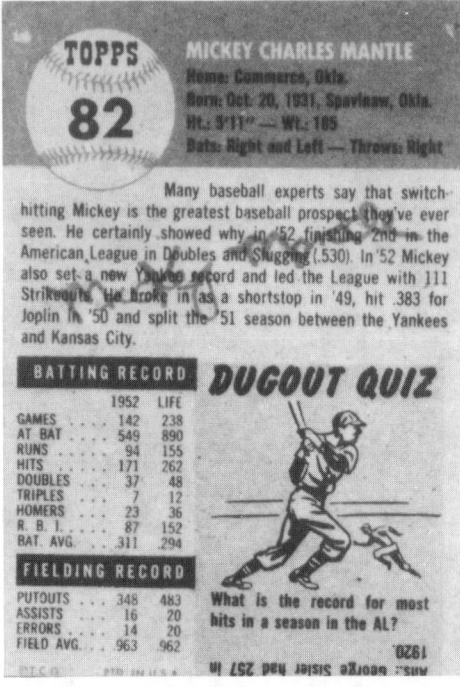

A pair of printing plate flaws, front and back, make this counterfeit easy to detect with the naked eye.

All specimens seen show a yellow "blob" in the red box at the lower-left of the card's front, above the "er" of "outfielder". On back, all of the counterfeits have a small patch of the gray cardboard stock showing through the red printing at the top-left, the left of the top seam on the baseball. This pair of marks positively identifies the card as counterfeit.

There are other indicators which can be seen under magnification, such as lettering on the front that should be solid, but is made up of tiny dots, and the clumsy retracing of the facsimile autograph in red on the counterfeit's back.

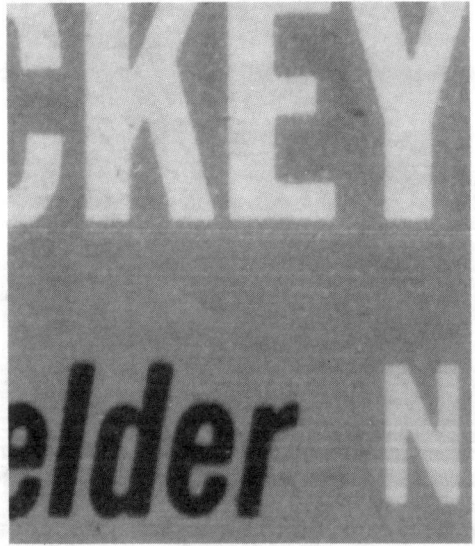

Genuine

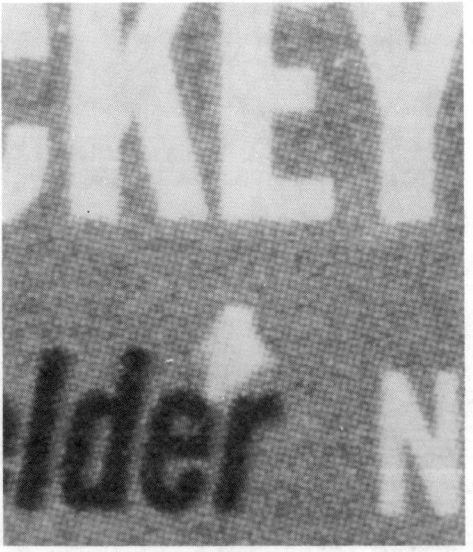

Counterfeit

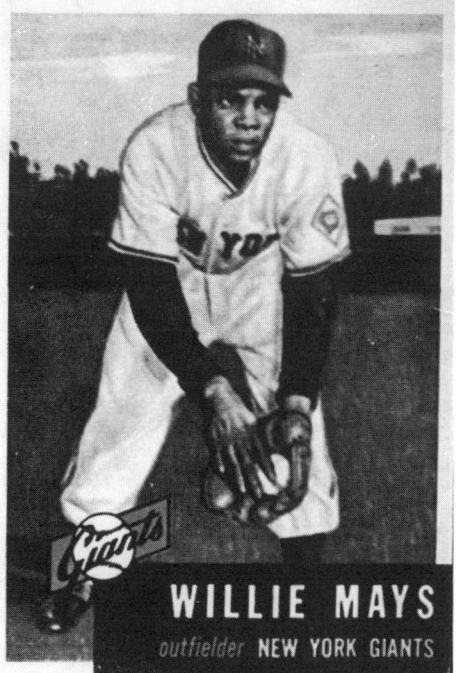

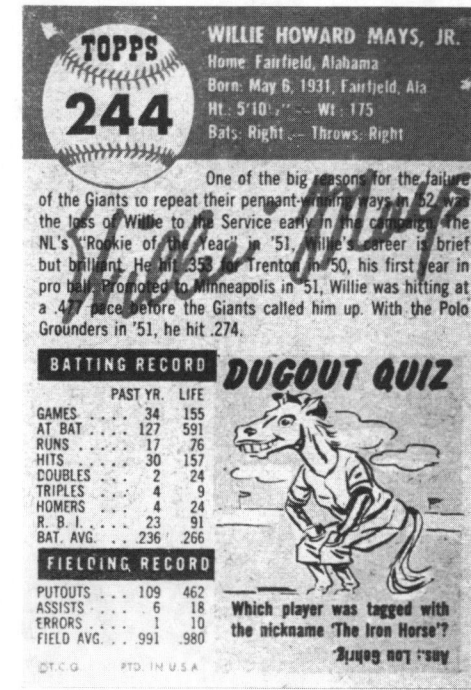

As this book went to press, no specimen of this counterfeit was available for examination. Photographs made some years back do not offer sufficient clarity of detail to allow a description of characteristics peculiar to this counterfeit.

The counterfeit lacks the clarity in the color printing on the front of a genuine card, and so is not particularly deceptive to a collector or dealer familiar with 1953 Topps.

No information about weight comparison between these counterfeits and the genuine Topps cards is currently available.

Genuine   **Counterfeit**

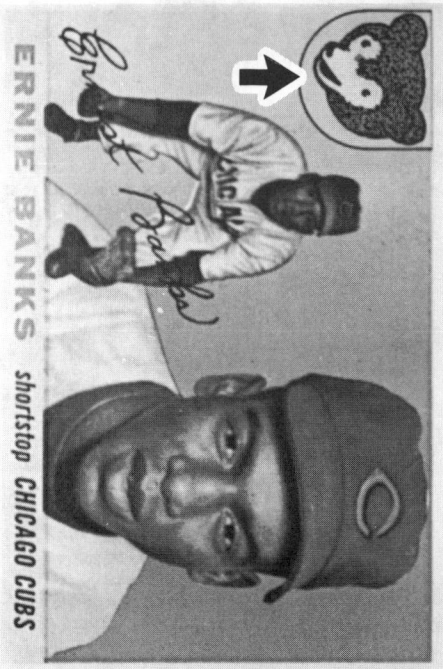

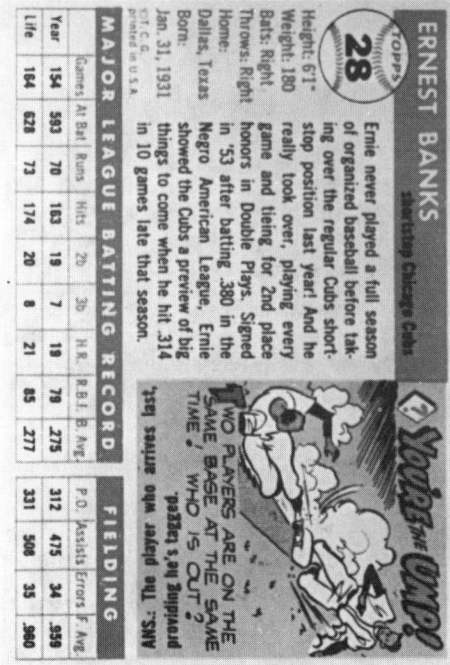

Because it is printed on thinner, whiter cardboard than the genuine 1955 Topps cards, an experienced dealer or collector should be able to spot this counterfeit with relative ease, especially when viewed outside of a plastic holder.

The presence of dot structures where they should not be provides conclusive evidence against the counterfeit, but does require a magnifying glass to verify.

The player's name, position and team at the bottom of the card and the facsimile autograph are the best places to examine a suspect card. On a genuine card, these elements will appear as clean, solid red or black lines. The counterfeit shows these elements as being made up of many tiny dots.

Likewise, the Cubs logo on the counterfeit shows dark dot patterns in the

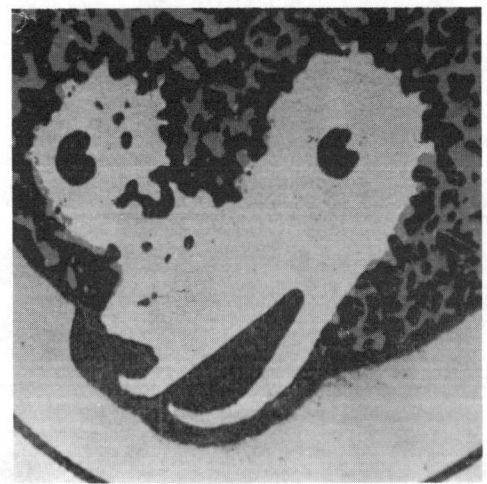

Genuine

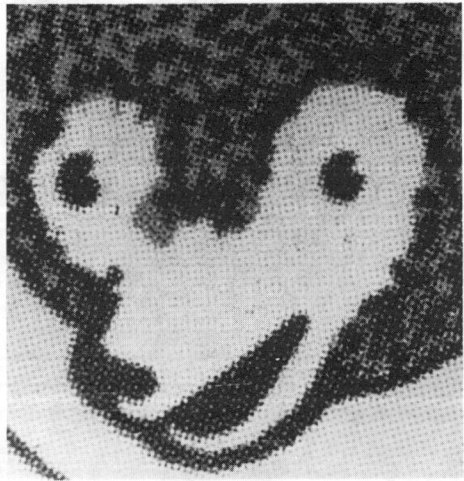

Counterfeit

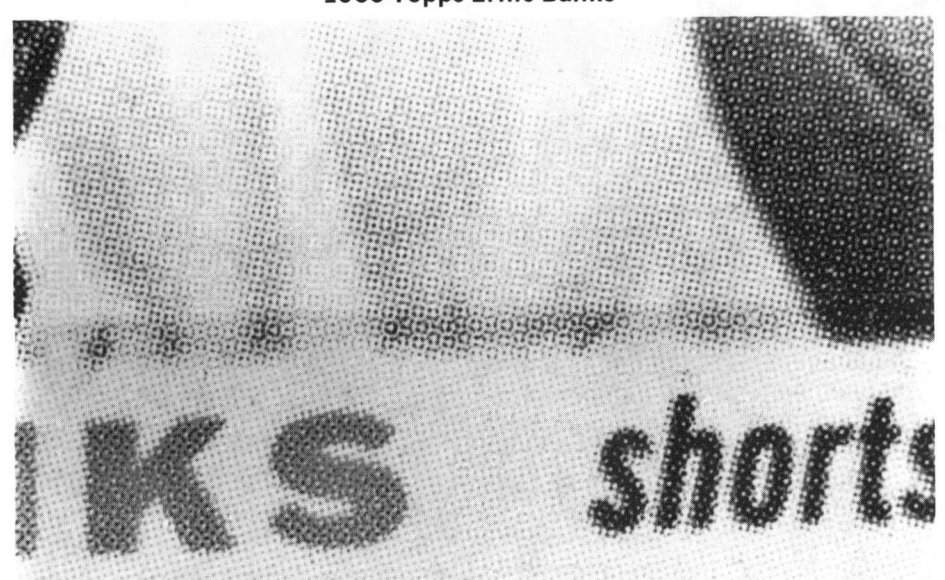

Counterfeit

white part of the bear's face and in the surrounding yellow shield. On a genuine card, these areas are free of dots.

The back of the counterfeit card is a fairly good representation of the original, except the black stats are much heavier than on a genuine card.

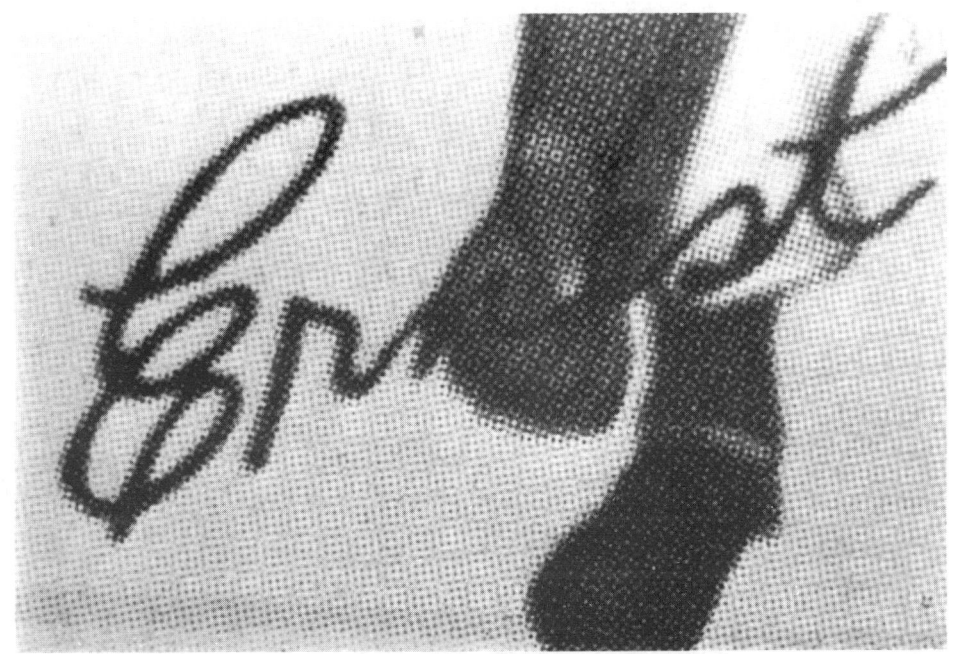

Counterfeit

No photo available

No photo available

As this book went to press, no specimen or photograph of this counterfeit was available for examination.

By hobby standards an "old" counterfeit, having been produced in the early 1970s, this card is seldom seen today.

Only a single card from the '59 Fleer set was counterfeited, card #68, "Jan. 23, 1959 — Ted Signs for '59". Hobby lore has it that this card was pulled from distribution when Topps made a stink about its depiction of Red Sox general manager, who was still under baseball card contract with Topps. While most of the rest of the cards in this set sell for $3 in top grade, card #68 is a $450 card.

According to contemporary hobby press accounts, the counterfeit is easily spotted by the darkness of the printing on front and the extreme moire pattern on the front photo which resulted from a re-screening of a genuine card to make the counterfeit.

No photo available

No photo available

Genuine   **Counterfeit**

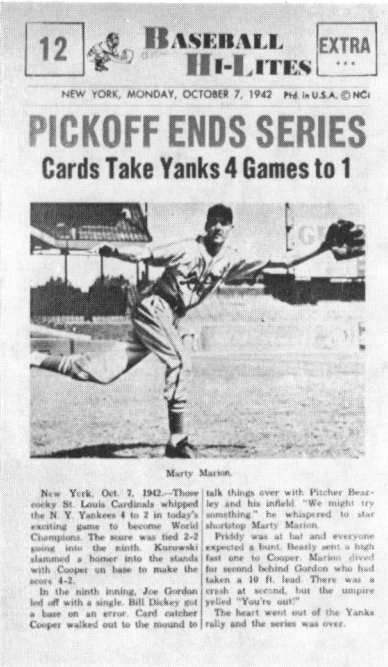

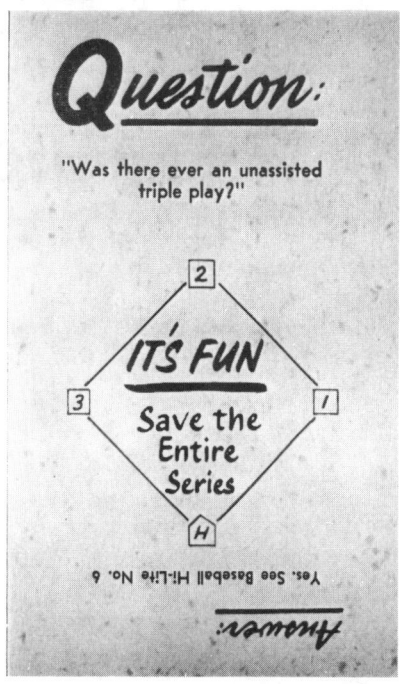

It has long been asserted in the hobby that this 72-card oversize (3¼x5⅜'') set was counterfeited in its entirety back in the 1970s.

Reproducing the set would have been fairly easy since the fronts are printed in black-white-and-red, and the backs in black-white-and-green.

The allegation of counterfeiting is apparently based on the existence of cards which are much more poorly printed and detailed than others.

With no specimens of the alleged counterfeits to examine. at this point it is probably worth mentioning only as a cautionary note in the unlikely event that anyone would ever want to buy any of these cards.

Genuine

Counterfeit

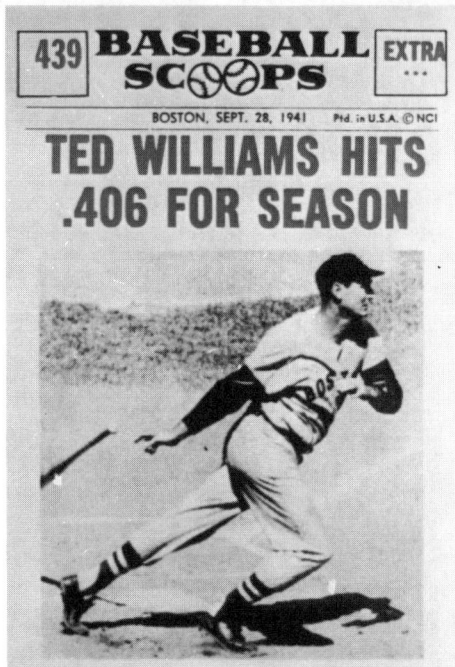

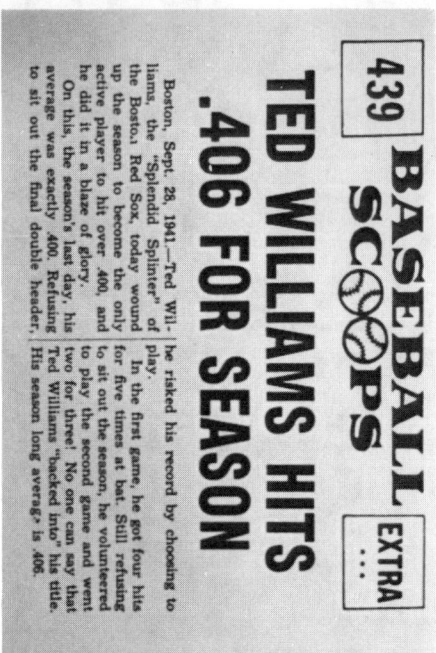

The entire run of this 80-card set is alleged to have been counterfeited in the 1970s.

Printed in black-white-and-red, it would not have been difficult to produce such counterfeits. One wonders, however, whether there could possibly have been a profit motivation since this set has never been popular with collectors. Even today, single cards in the set carry a largely optimistic book value of between 30¢ and $10 each, depending on which player is depicted in the particular great moment in baseball history.

The counterfeiting theory seems to be largely based on the appearance of cards which are much more poorly printed and detailed than others.

With inadequate specimens of the alleged counterfeits to examine, at this point it is probably worth mentioning only as a cautionary note in the unlikely event that anyone would ever want to buy any of these cards.

No photo available

No photo available

Genuine   Counterfeit

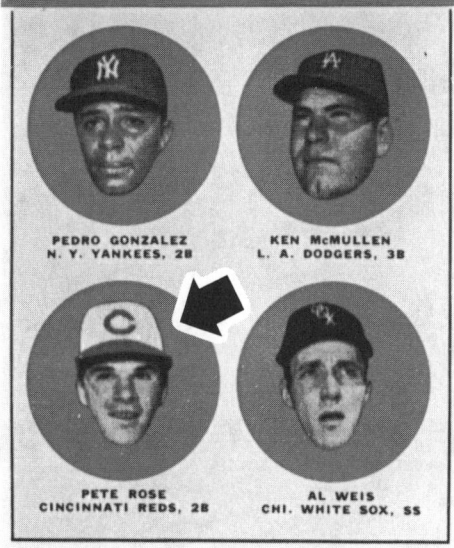

1963 ROOKIE STARS

PEDRO GONZALEZ
N. Y. YANKEES, 2B

KEN McMULLEN
L. A. DODGERS, 3B

PETE ROSE
CINCINNATI REDS, 2B

AL WEIS
CHI. WHITE SOX, SS

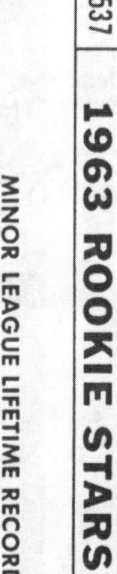

537 — 1963 ROOKIE STARS

MINOR LEAGUE LIFETIME RECORDS

	G	AB	R	H	2B	3B	HR	RBI	AVG.
PEDRO GONZALEZ N. Y. YANKEES-2B	595	2296	364	695	96	25	34	269	.304
KEN McMULLEN L. A. DODGERS-3B	281	1022			54		42	177	.285
PETE ROSE CIN. REDS-2B	354	1345	301	427	59	52	12	191	.317
AL WEIS CHI. WHITE SOX-SS	472	1870	314	497	59	18	15	159	.266

© T.C.G. PRINTED IN U.S.A.

The first known counterfeit in modern baseball card history. According to contemporary press accounts, 10,000 of the fake '63 Rose cards were printed, but fewer than 200 were sold into the hobby before they were discovered and warnings issued.

The fake is easily distinguished by the naked eye through the appearance of a black outline around the Rose's white cap. No such outline appears on a genuine card. Conversely, the ''C'' on the cap, which should have a black outline, does not on the fake.

Printed on much thinner stock than a real '63 card, the printing from the other side of the counterfeit can be seen when the card is held to strong light. No light passes through a genuine '63 Topps card.

The court-ordered rubber-stamped blue ''COUNTERFEIT'' and red ''ORIGINAL REPRINT'' is found on most — but not all — of the counterfeits seen in today's market.

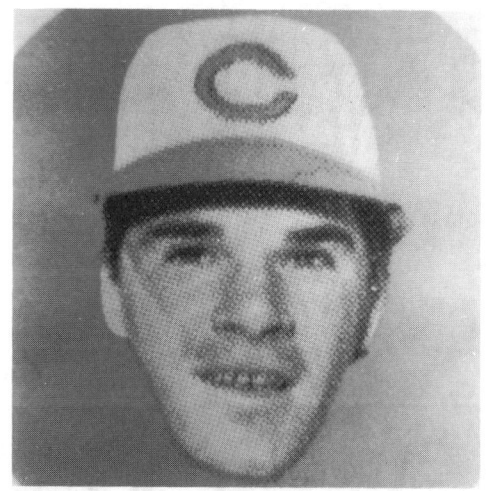

Genuine

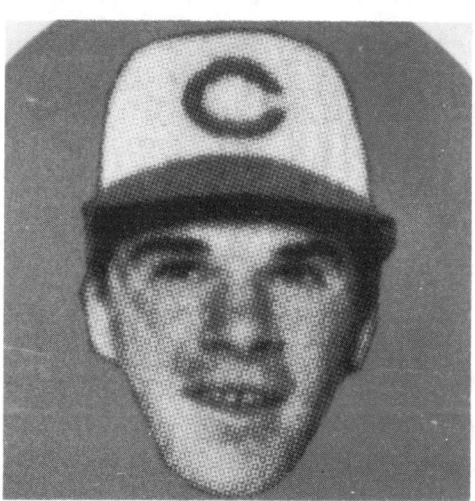

Counterfeit

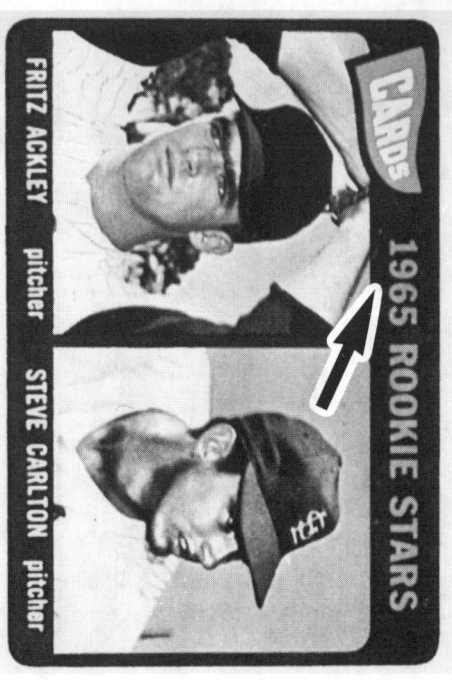

TOPPS 477

1965 CARDS' ROOKIE STARS

FRITZ ACKLEY — PITCHER

Opportunity is tapping Fritz on the shoulder after ten years in minors. Best year was with Indianapolis in '63 with an 18-5 mark. Fritz was optioned to Jacksonville (I. L.) in April of 1965. •

MINOR LEAGUE LIFETIME PITCHING RECORD

G	IP	W	L	PCT.	SO	BB	ERA
249	1167	72	61	.541	978	639	3.98

STEVE CARLTON — PITCHER

Steve was at three Cardinal way stations in his first year. He had an outstanding 10-1 mark with 1.03 ERA at Rock Hill.

MINOR LEAGUE LIFETIME PITCHING RECORD

G	IP	W	L	PCT.	SO	BB	ERA
27	178	15	6	.714	191	102	2.22

Reprint   ©T.C.G. PRINTED IN U.S.A.

An overall fuzziness of the color printing on the front of this counterfeit, and an unnatural gloss to the front surface should raise warning flags.

Examination with a magnifying glass of the color design elements on the front of the card reveals sure evidence of the counterfeit's status.

Easy differentiation between real and fake on this card can be made by checking the red "1965 ROOKIE STARS" at the top of the card.

Those letters on a genuine card will be clean, solid red. On the counterfeit, these letters are composed of a pattern of tiny dots creating a fuzzy appearance at the edges. Similar dot structures can be seen at the edges of the players' names and positions. On back, the small black type is made fuzzy by an unintended red shadow of dots behind and left of the letters.

The black "Reprint" which appears on the back of the card shown here may not be present on all cards encountered in the hobby market.

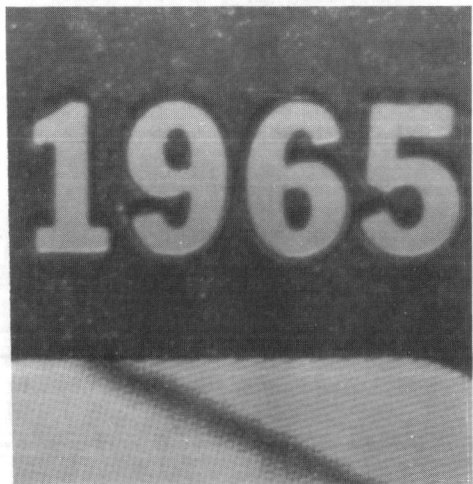

Genuine

Counterfeit

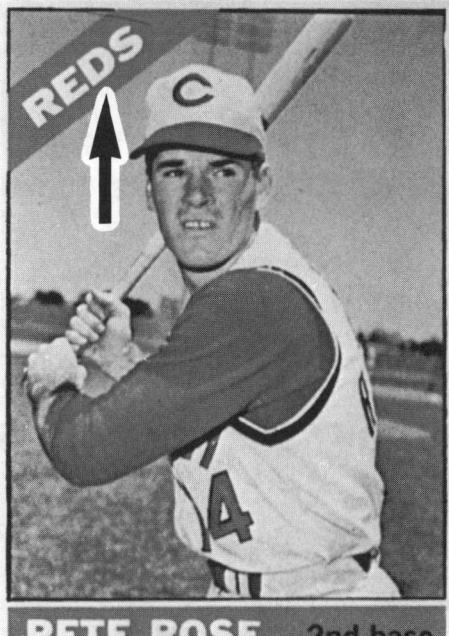

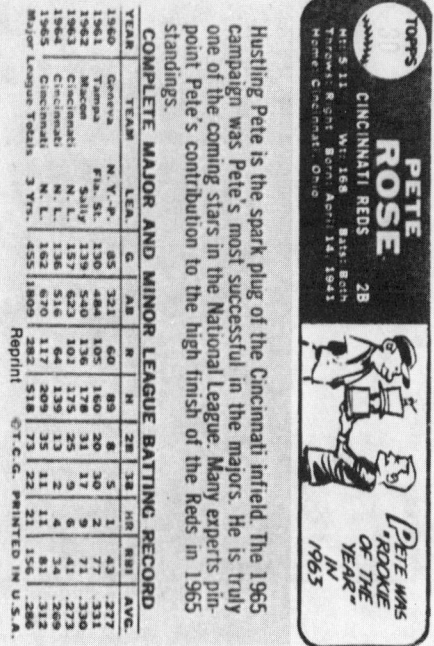

At first glance a pretty good imitation, an overall fuzziness of the color printing and an unnatural gloss to the front surface should raise suspicions.

Detailed examination of the color design elements reveals sure evidence of the counterfeit's status.

Easy differentiation between real and fake on this card can be made by checking the blue stripe and white "REDS" at the upper-left of the card.

Those letters on a genuine card will have clean edges. On the counterfeit, the edges of the letters are made fuzzy by a pattern of tiny blue dots creating a fuzzy appearance at the edges. A black hairline (literally) can be seen above and to the right of the "S" in "REDS" on the counterfeit. Likewise, the position, which should be rendered in solid black letters, is composed of tiny black dots.

The black "Reprint" which appears on the back of the card shown here may not be present on all cards encountered in the hobby market.

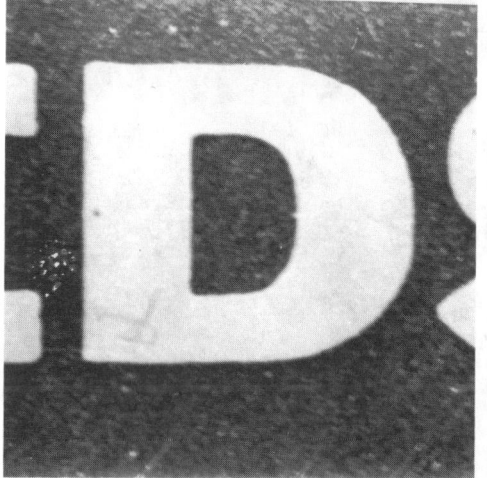

Genuine

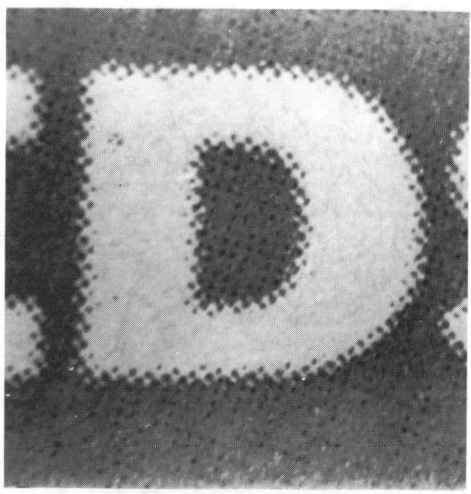

Counterfeit

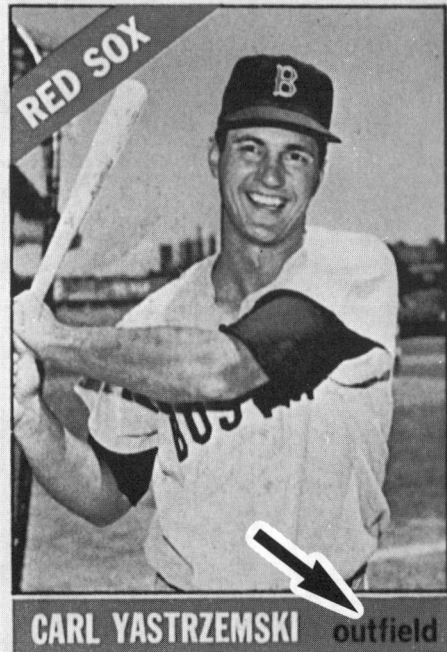

While an overall lack of crispness to the color printing and generally washed-out colors should raise warning flags when this card is viewed, such subjective indicators should not be relied upon in counterfeit card detection.

Using a magnifying glass to examine the lettering will provide definite proof that this card is a phony. On a genuine Topps card, the words "RED SOX" and the player's name and position will be printed as solid white (team and player name) or black (position) letters with edges that

end crisply and cleanly at the red background bars. On this counterfeit, the edges of the letters are made fuzzy by a pattern of tiny blue and red dots.

On the back, the small black type which is made up of solid letters on the genuine card is seen as composed of tiny dots on the counterfeit.

The black "Reprint" which appears on the back of the card shown here may not be present on all cards encountered in the hobby market.

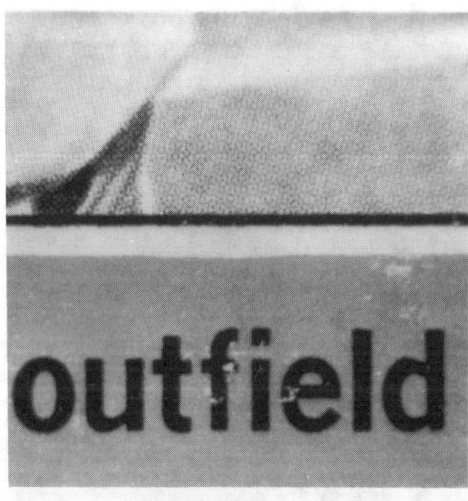

Genuine

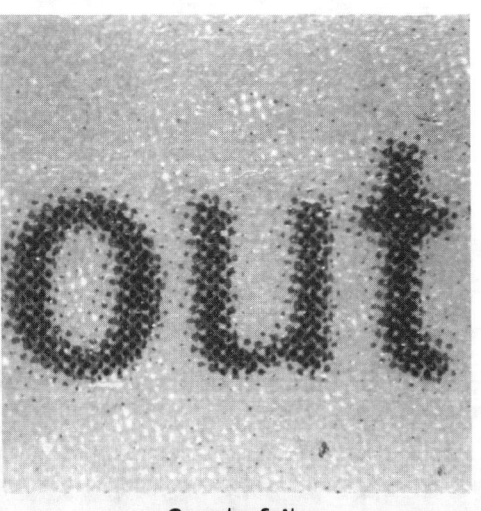

Counterfeit

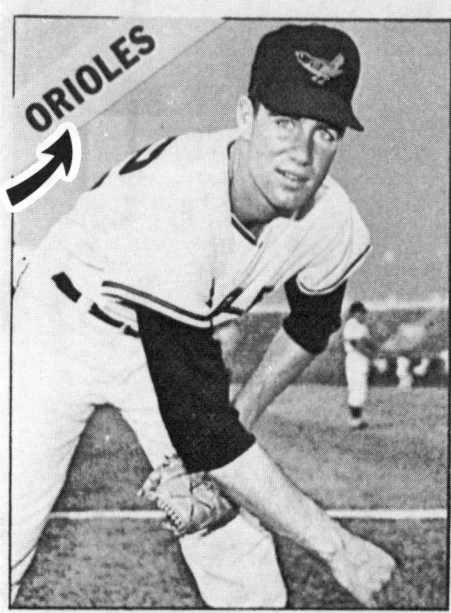

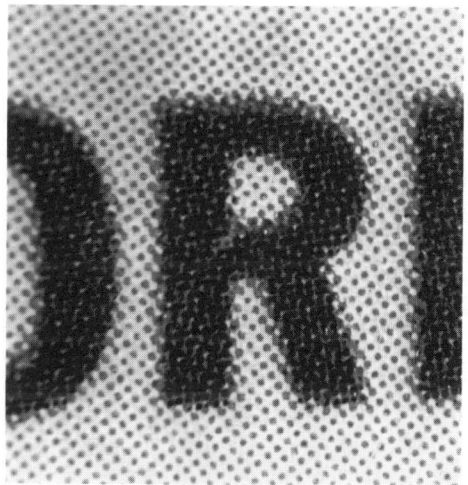

A fairly good reproduction of the photo on a genuine Palmer rookie card may be misleading at first exposure to this counterfeit. When viewed outside of a card holder, however, the card exhibits an unnatural gloss on the front and a fuzziness of the black lettering.

Using a magnifying glass to examine the lettering, it will be found to provide definite proof that this card is a phony. On a genuine Topps card, the words "ORIOLES", "JIM PALMER" and "pitcher" will be printed as solid black letters, with edges that end crisply and cleanly at the green background bars. On this counterfeit, the edges of the letters are made fuzzy by a pattern of tiny black dots which make up the letters.

It's interesting to note that all specimens of this counterfeit seen to date have no white border at the bottom of the card.

The black "Reprint" which appears on the back of the card shown here may not be present on all cards encountered.

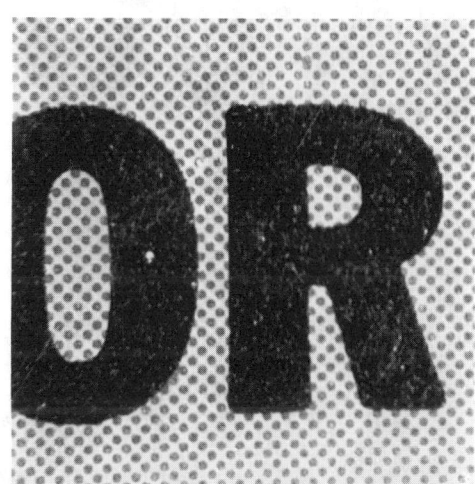

Genuine

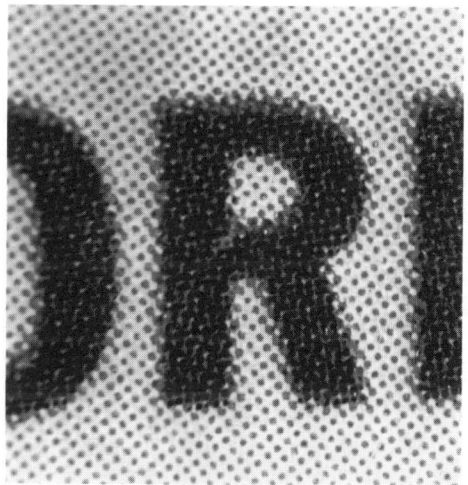

Counterfeit

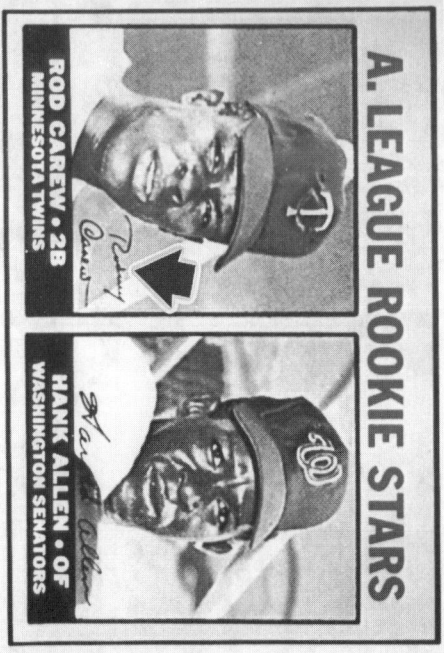

| TOPPS 569 | **1967 AMER. LEA. ROOKIE STARS** |

ROD CAREW—MINNESOTA TWINS

Into late May, this 21 year old second baseman was battling Al Kaline for the batting leadership in the American League. In 1964 with the Florida Twins, Rod batted a crisp .325. The following season he hit .303 at Orlando.

MINOR LEAGUE LIFETIME BATTING RECORD

AB	H	2B	3B	HR	RBI	AVG.
945	285	44	14	2	103	.302

HANK ALLEN—WASH. SENATORS

Hank stands 6 feet tall and weighs in at 190 pounds. The outfielder has been in organized baseball since 1960. At Magic Valley in 1962, Hank had his finest year, batting .346 while clouting 37 home runs and 140 RBIs.

MINOR LEAGUE LIFETIME BATTING RECORD

AB	H	2B	3B	HR	RBI	AVG.
3443	1001	167	48	126	604	.291

©T.C.G.   PRINTED IN U.S.A.

Visually almost perfect, this counterfeit is often presented in a heavy plastic holder, disguising its weight of nearly 30% more than a genuine '67 Topps card.

The first visual clue a prospective buyer might have is on the card's back, where most of the counterfeits seen are too white. A genuine 25-year-old Topps card has usually yellowed somewhat. Since that, too, can be faked, the degree of aging evident on the back should not be used as a definitive indicator of status.

Rather, with a good magnifying glass, examine the signatures on the front. A genuine card will show these facsimile autographs as solid black letters. On the counterfeit, the letters of these signatures can be seen to have a "shadow" of tiny color dots visible beneath the black. This requires strong magnification to see, but on a card that sells for this much money, it's important to be sure.

The "COUNTERFEIT" stamp on the back of the photographed card is unique to that specimen.

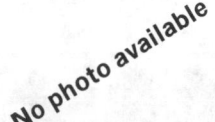

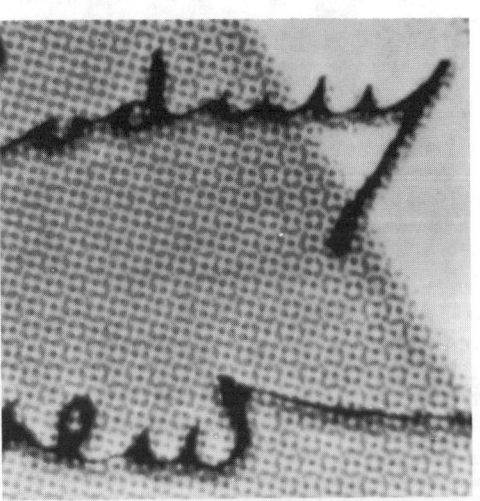

Genuine   **Counterfeit**

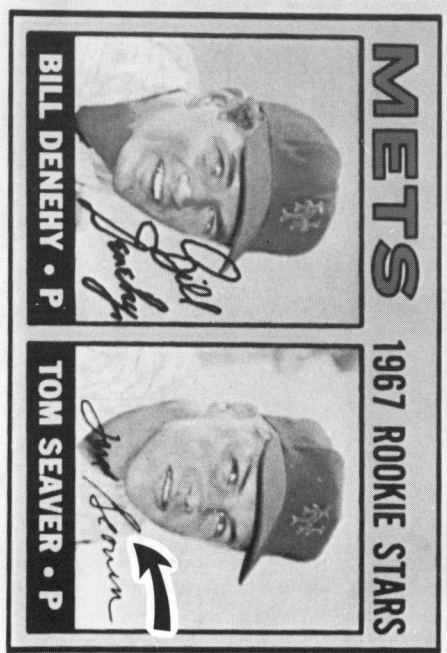

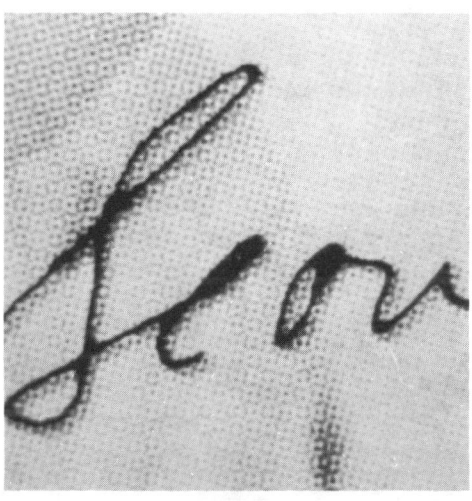

TOPPS 581	1967 METS' ROOKIE STARS

BILL DENEHY—PITCHER

In 1965, the 6'3" righthanded pitcher won 13 ballgames at Auburn. Last year at Williamsport he won nine of eleven decisions and was then brought up into Triple-A competition at Jacksonville.

MINOR LEAGUE LIFETIME PITCHING RECORD

W	L	PCT.	SO	BB	ERA
22	15	.595	262	168	2.79

TOM SEAVER—PITCHER

Tom won 3 out of his first 4 ballgames for the New York Mets this season. The rookie righthander clinched a job after performing sensationally in the spring exhibitions. He has only one year of minor league experience behind him.

MINOR LEAGUE LIFETIME PITCHING RECORD

W	L	PCT.	SO	BB	ERA
12	12	.500	188	66	3.13

©T.C.G.   PRINTED IN U.S.A.

Visually almost perfect, this counterfeit is usually presented in a heavy plastic holder to disguise the fact that it weighs nearly 22% more than a genuine '67 Topps card.

The first visual clue a prospective buyer might have is on the card's back, where most of the counterfeits seen are too white. A genuine 25-year-old Topps card has usually yellowed somewhat. Since that, too, can be faked, the degree of ageing evident on the back should not be used as a definitive indicator of genuineness status.

Rather, with a good magnifying glass, examine the areas of the signatures on the front. A genuine card will show these facsimile autographs as solid black letters. On the counterfeit, the letters of these signatures can be seen to have a "shadow" of tiny color dots visible beneath the black. This requires strong magnification to see, but on a card that sells for this much money, it's important to be sure.

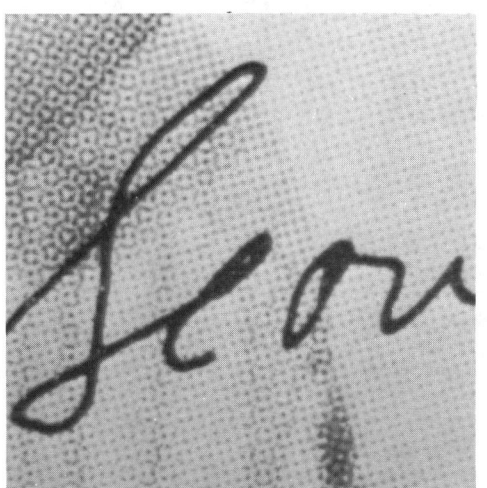

Genuine

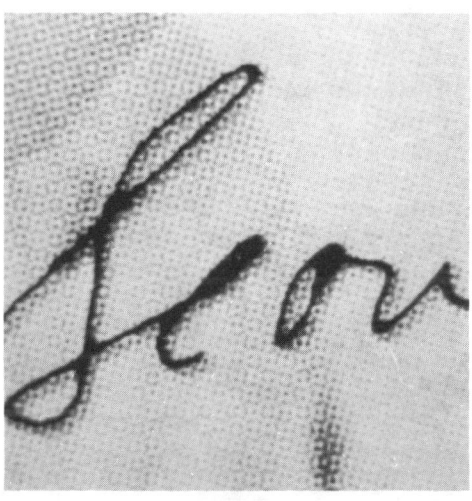

Counterfeit

No photo available

No photo available

Perhaps it would be better not to cast suspicions on all the genuine examples of this card without the "proof" of existence of a counterfeit version. However, we believe it is in the best interest of the hobby to err on the side of protection, and so will report the long-standing hobby rumor that a counterfeit '67 Brooks Robinson card exists, possibly created by the same hand as the fake Carew and Seaver rookies.

If such is the case, expect the fake Robby to be similarly deceptive and look for the same type of indicators of genuineness status as presented for the other two known counterfeit '67 Topps cards.

No photo available

No photo available

Genuine   **Counterfeit**

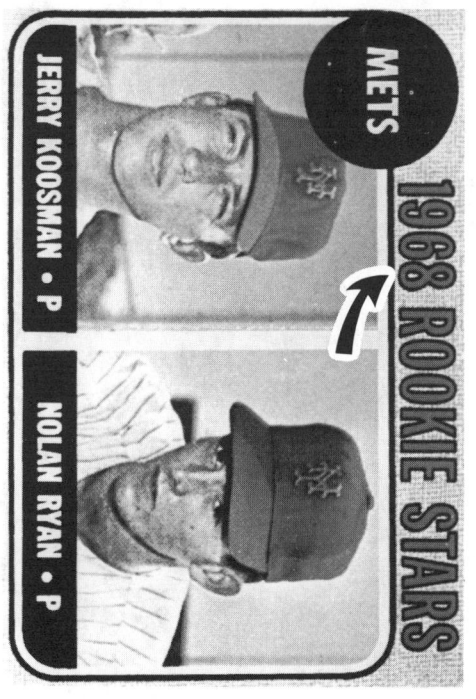

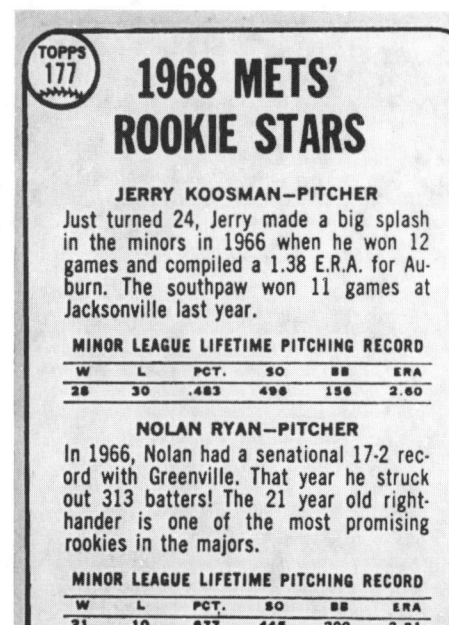

1968 METS' ROOKIE STARS

JERRY KOOSMAN—PITCHER

Just turned 24, Jerry made a big splash in the minors in 1966 when he won 12 games and compiled a 1.38 E.R.A. for Auburn. The southpaw won 11 games at Jacksonville last year.

MINOR LEAGUE LIFETIME PITCHING RECORD

W	L	PCT.	SO	BB	ERA
28	30	.483	498	156	2.60

NOLAN RYAN—PITCHER

In 1966, Nolan had a senational 17-2 record with Greenville. That year he struck out 313 batters! The 21 year old right-hander is one of the most promising rookies in the majors.

MINOR LEAGUE LIFETIME PITCHING RECORD

W	L	PCT.	SO	BB	ERA
21	10	.677	445	200	2.81

©T.C.G. PRINTED IN U.S.A.

The counterfeit Nolan Ryan rookie card is easily identified by the existence of a dot pattern in the red letters and black outlines of "1968 ROOKIE STARS" at the top of the card. The genuine card has these letters in solid red, outlined with solid black.

Most people would describe the color of the fake card's back as more orange and less bright than on a genuine card, though it must be noted that there are wide color variances on the backs of genuine 1968 Topps baseball cards.

It appears that an attempt was made to mute and "age" the white cardboard of the counterfeit's back by brushing on a weak wash, perhaps watercolor or coffee.

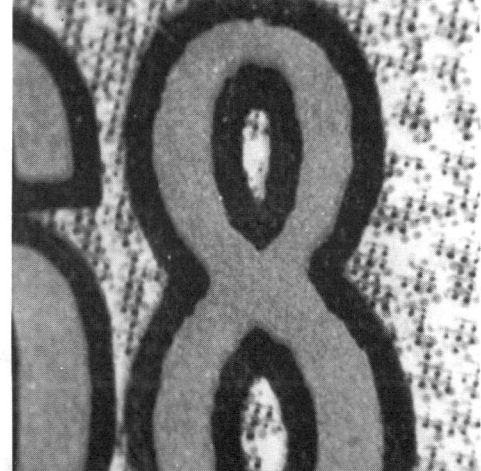

Genuine

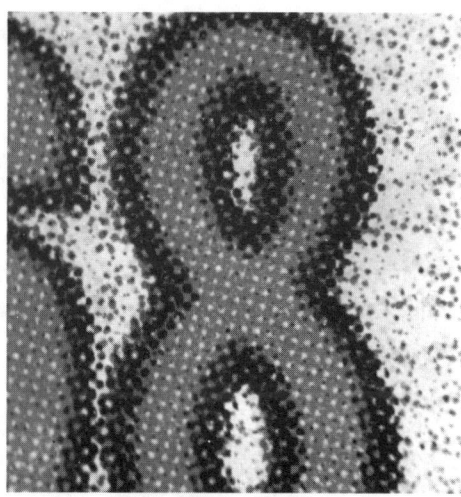

Counterfeit

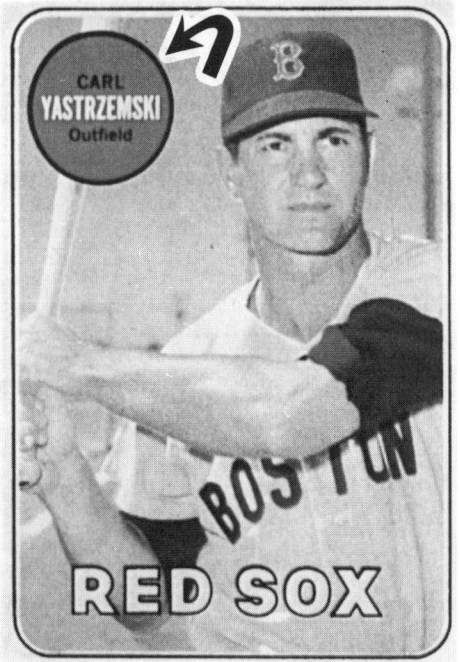

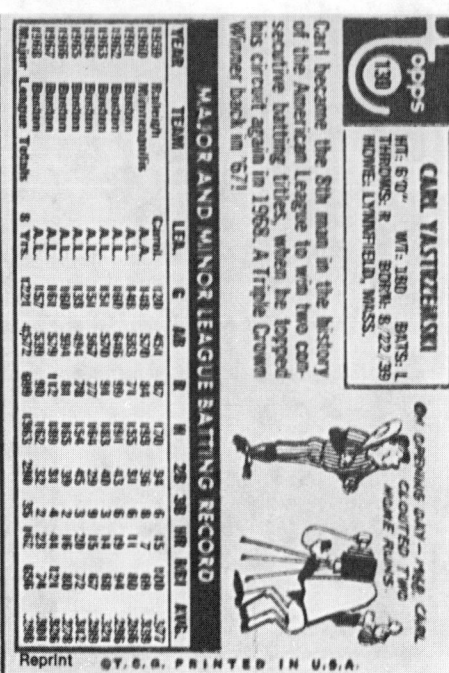

A slightly glossy finish to the card and an overall fuzziness to the photo should alert a person who has any familiarity with genuine 1969 Topps baseball cards.

The definite indicators of this card's counterfeit status will be found in the magenta circle at the upper-left. On a genuine card, each element — the black perimeter of the circle, the black and white name, the black "Outfield" and the magenta background — will be printed in solid color. The counterfeit exhibits these elements as a composition of tiny dots, totally unlike the crisp, clean elements of the genuine card. Similar fuzziness will be noted on the counterfeit in the black outlines of the team name letters at bottom.

Most viewers would describe the background color of the card's back as being more orange than the genuine '69 Topps cards, which are something of a salmon color. The word "REPRINT" which appears on the back of the card shown here may not be present on all specimens of this counterfeit.

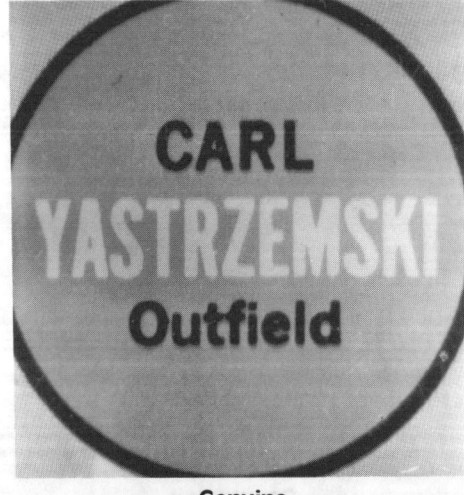

Genuine

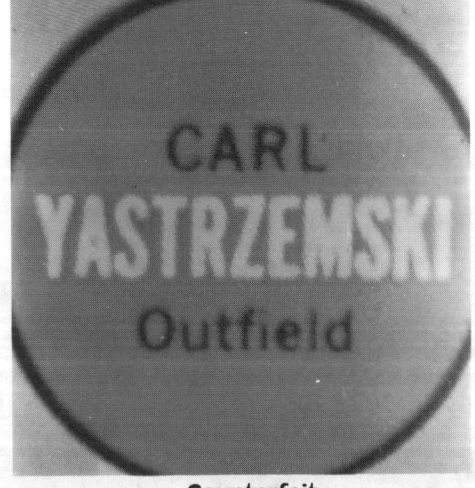

Counterfeit

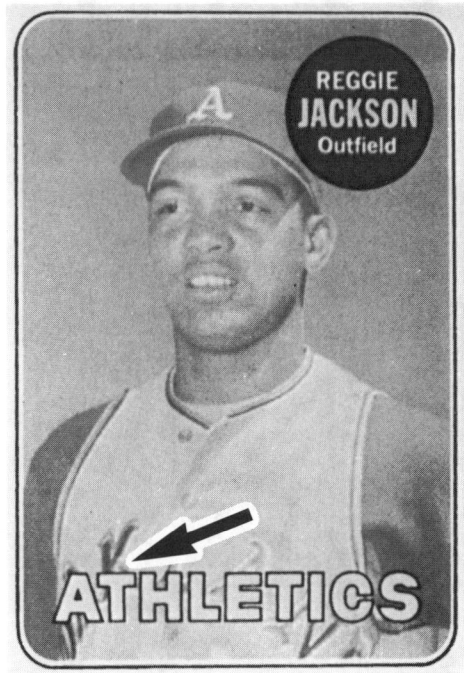

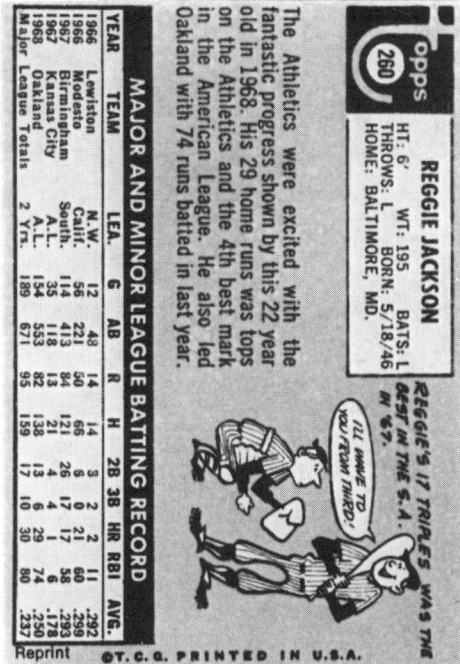

Many hobbyists, upon viewing this counterfeit for the first time may think they've lucked onto an unusually well-centered specimen of the Reggie rookie card. However, a slightly glossy finish on the front and an overall fuzziness to the photo should raise a warning flag to a person who has a passing familiarity with genuine 1969 Topps baseball cards.

While definite indicators of this card's counterfeit status can be found in the purple circle at the upper-right (a fuzziness of elements that should be printed in solid colors), it is easier to present in a black-and-white photograph the differences to be found in the letters of "ATHLETICS" at the bottom of the card.

The counterfeit exhibits the black lines around the yellow letters as a series of tiny black dots, totally unlike the solid black lines found on the genuine card.

The word "REPRINT", which appears on the back of the card shown here may not be present on all specimens of this counterfeit.

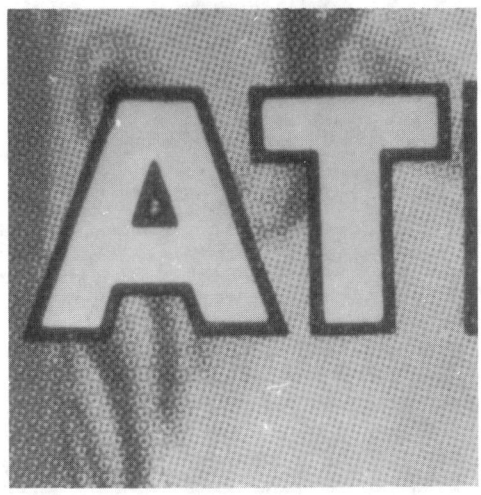

Genuine

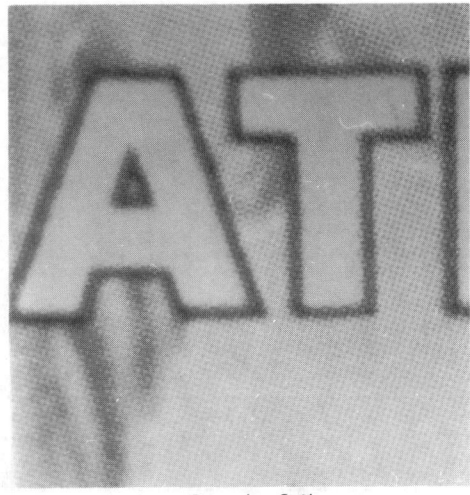

Counterfeit

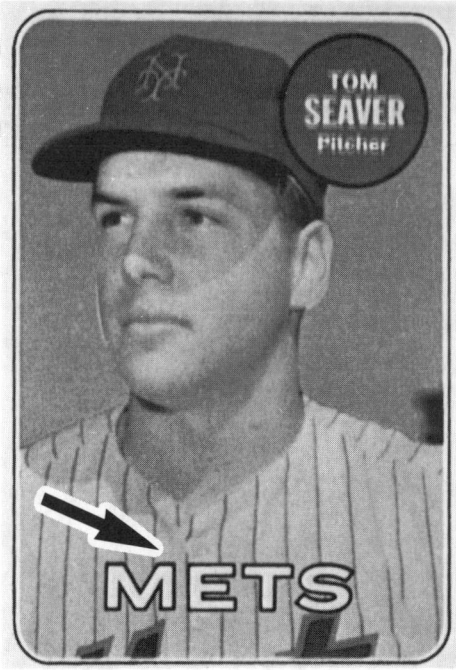

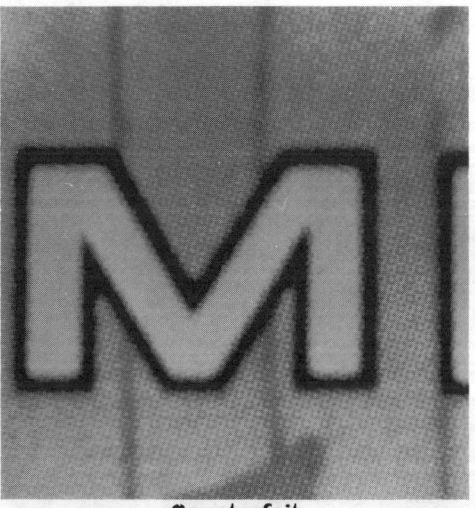

A slightly glossy finish on the front and an overall fuzziness to the photo should raise a warning flag to a person who has a passing familiarity with genuine 1969 Topps baseball cards.

While definite indicators of this card's counterfeit status can be found in the purple circle at the upper-right (a fuzziness of elements that should be printed in solid colors), it is easier to present in a black-and-white photograph the differences to be found in the letters of "METS" at the bottom of the card.

The counterfeit exhibits the black lines around the yellow letters as a series of tiny black dots, totally unlike the solid black lines found on the genuine card.

Most viewers would describe the background color of the card's back as being more orange in tone than the genuine '69 Topps cards, which are more of a salmon color. The word "REPRINT", which appears on the back of the card shown here may not be present on all specimens of this counterfeit.

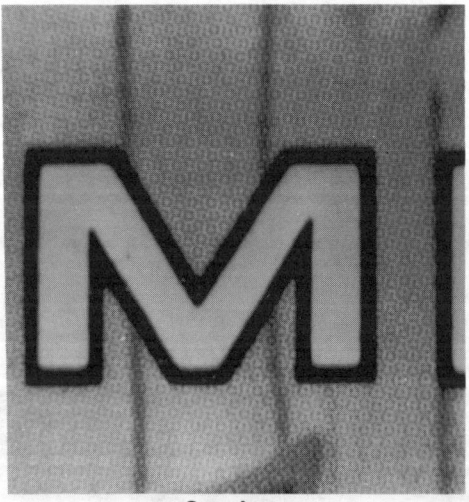

Genuine

Counterfeit

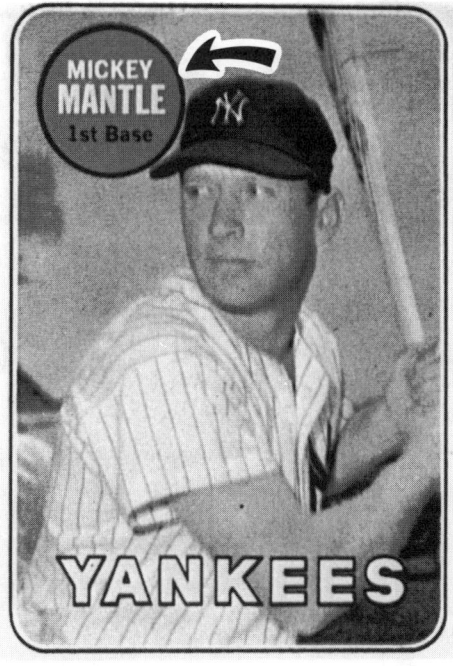

Reprint

500

MICKEY MANTLE

HEIGHT: 6' WEIGHT: 194   BATS: BOTH THROWS: RIGHT
BORN: OCTOBER 20, 1931   HOME: DALLAS, TEX.

Mickey is 3rd on the All-Time Home Run list! The All-Star announced his retirement from baseball on March 1st, 1969!

MAJOR LEAGUE BATTING RECORD

YEAR	TEAM	LEA.	G	AB	R	H	2B	3B	HR	RBI	AVG.
1951	New York	A.L.	96	341	61	91	11	5	13	65	.267
1952	New York	A.L.	142	549	94	171	37	7	23	87	.311
1953	New York	A.L.	127	461	105	136	24	3	21	92	.295
1954	New York	A.L.	146	543	129	163	17	12	27	102	.300
1955	New York	A.L.	147	517	121	158	25	11	37	99	.306
1956	New York	A.L.	150	533	132	188	22	5	52	130	.353
1957	New York	A.L.	144	474	121	173	28	6	34	94	.365
1958	New York	A.L.	150	519	127	158	21	1	42	97	.304
1959	New York	A.L.	144	541	104	154	23	4	31	75	.285
1960	New York	A.L.	153	527	119	145	17	6	40	94	.275
1961	New York	A.L.	153	514	132	163	16	6	54	128	.317
1962	New York	A.L.	123	377	96	121	15	1	30	89	.321
1963	New York	A.L.	65	172	40	54	8	0	15	35	.314
1964	New York	A.L.	143	465	92	141	25	2	35	111	.303
1965	New York	A.L.	122	361	44	92	12	1	19	46	.255
1966	New York	A.L.	108	333	40	96	12	1	23	56	.288
1967	New York	A.L.	144	440	63	108	17	0	22	55	.245
1968	New York	A.L.	144	435	57	103	14	1	18	54	.237
Major League Totals	18 Yrs.		2401	8102	1677	2415	344	72	536	1509	.298

A slightly glossy finish to the card and an overall fuzziness to the photo should raise the suspicions of a person who has some familiarity with genuine 1969 Topps baseball cards. As with most counterfeit cards, however, it will take a magnifying lens to make a final determination.

The easiest identifiers are to be found in the red circle at the front upper-left, containing the player's name and position. On a genuine card, each element — the black perimeter of the circle, the white and yellow name, the black "1st Base" and the red background — will be printed in solid color. The counterfeit exhibits these elements in a composition of tiny dots, totally unlike the crisp, clean elements of the genuine card. Similar fuzziness will be noted on the counterfeit in the black outlines of the team name letters at bottom.

The word "REPRINT", which appears on the back of the card shown here may not be present on all specimens of this counterfeit.

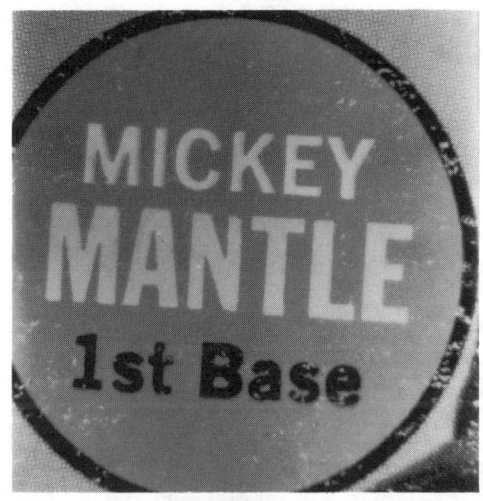

Genuine

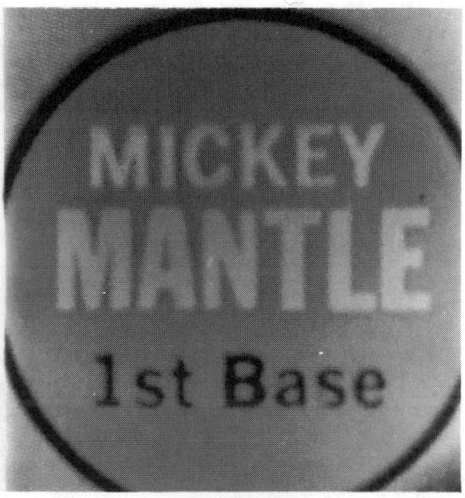

Counterfeit

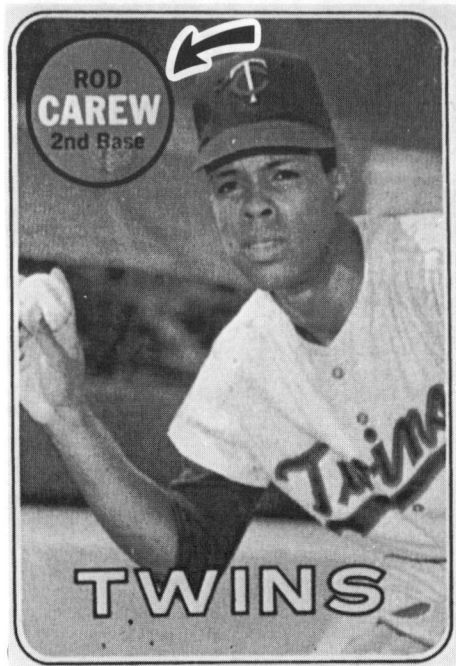

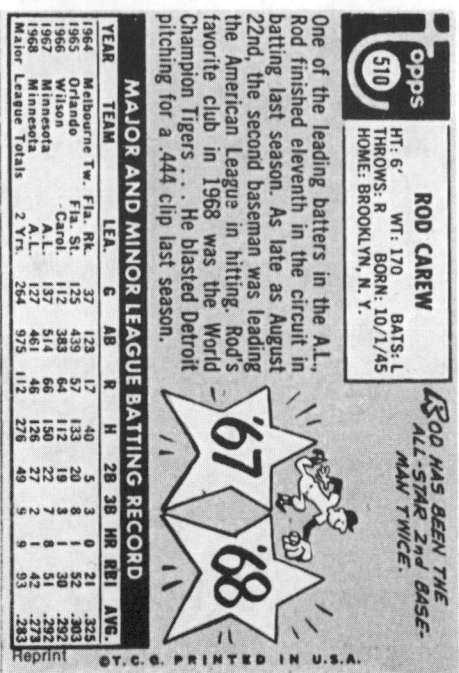

YEAR	TEAM	LEA.	G	AB	R	H	2B	3B	HR	RBI	AVG.
1964	Melbourne Tw.	Fla. Rk.	37	123	17	40	5	3	—	21	.325
1965	Orlando	Fla. St.	125	439	57	133	20	5	3	32	.303
1966	Wilson	Carol.	112	383	66	112	19	7	3	30	.292
1967	Minnesota	A.L.	137	514	66	150	22	7	8	51	.292
1968	Minnesota	A.L.	127	461	46	126	27	2	1	30	.273
Major League Totals	2 Yrs.		264	975	112	276	49	9	9	93	.283

MAJOR AND MINOR LEAGUE BATTING RECORD

Topps 510

ROD CAREW
HT: 6′   WT: 170   BATS: L
THROWS: R   BORN: 10/1/45
HOME: BROOKLYN, N.Y.

ROD HAS BEEN THE ALL-STAR 2nd BASE-MAN TWICE.

'67 '68

One of the leading batters in the A.L., Rod finished eleventh in the circuit in batting last season. As late as August 22nd, the second baseman was leading the American League in hitting. Rod's favorite club in 1968 was the World Champion Tigers . . . He blasted Detroit pitching for a .444 clip last season.

Reprint   ©T.C.G. PRINTED IN U.S.A.

A quick glance at the blue circle containing the player's name and position will identify this counterfeit. A printing flaw under the word "Base" has created a mess of black and white violations in the blue background. A slightly glossy finish to the card and an overall fuzziness to the photo should also raise the suspicions of persons familiar with genuine 1969 Topps baseball cards.

Other definite identifiers are to be found in the blue circle. On a genuine card, each element — the black perimeter of the circle, the black and white name, the black "2nd Base" and the blue background — will be printed in solid color. The counterfeit exhibits these elements in a composition of tiny dots, totally unlike the crisp, clean elements of the genuine card. Similar fuzziness will be noted on the counterfeit in the black outlines of the team name letters at bottom.

The word "REPRINT", which appears on the back of the card shown here may not be present on all specimens.

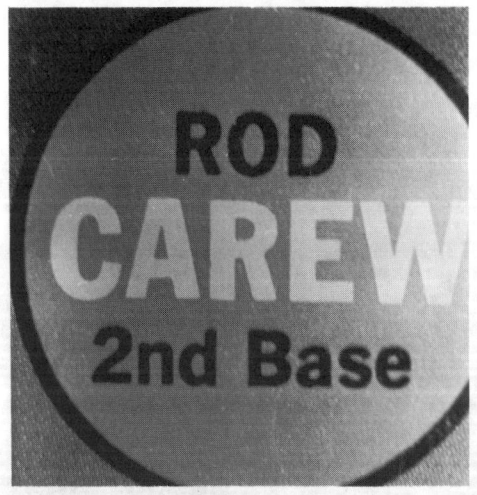

Genuine

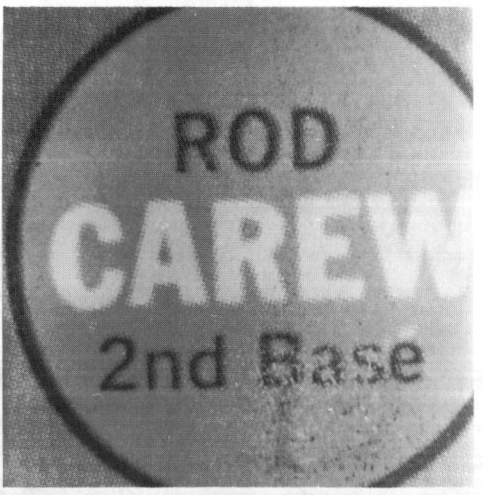

Counterfeit

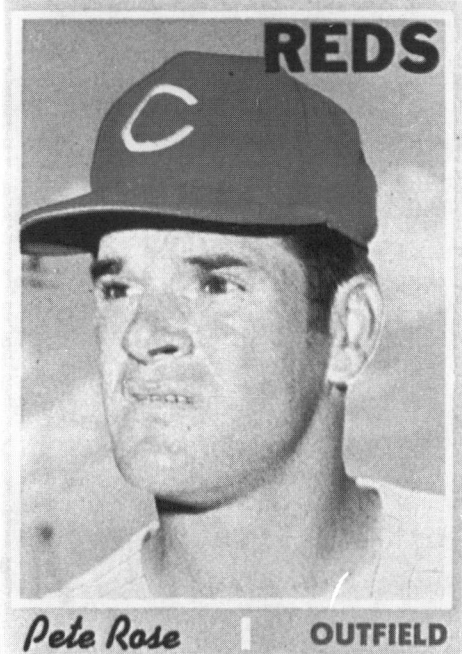

An overall fuzziness of the color printing on the front of this counterfeit should raise warning flags. Close examination of the team name and the player's name reveals even more fuzziness at the edges than will be seen on a genuine card.

However, easiest differentiation between real and fake on this card can be made by checking the area of the card number on the back of the card.

On a genuine card, the "TOPPS" and "580" will be clean, solid blue and the background circle will be pure yellow. On the counterfeit, a pattern of tiny blue dots intrudes into the yellow circle, while the blue letters will be littered with yellow dots. Likewise, the rest of the back printing, including the blue printed stats and the cartoon, are composed of dots on the counterfeit, rather than being solid as on a Topps original.

The black "Reprint" which appears on the back of the card shown here may not be present on all cards encountered in the hobby market.

Genuine   **Counterfeit**

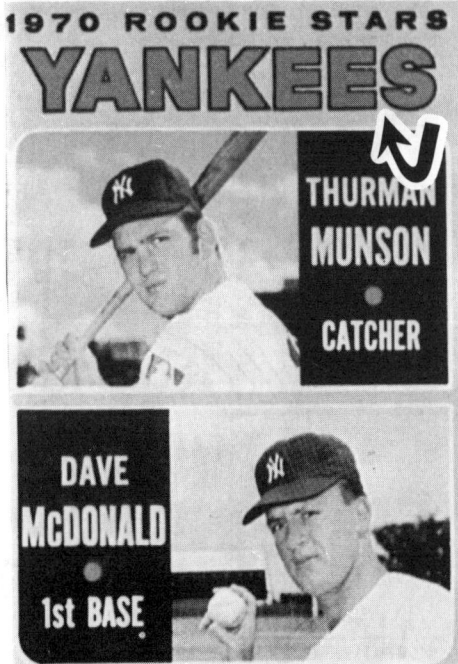

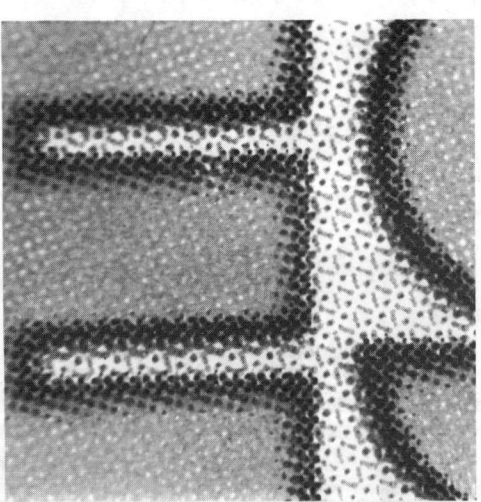

An unnatural glossiness on the front of the card and overall fuzziness of printing on both sides makes this counterfeit fairly easy to spot.

Examination of the color design details with a magnifying glass reveals sure evidence of the counterfeit's status.

Easy differentiation between real and fake on this card can be made by examining the large red "YANKEES" on the front of the card.

Those letters on a genuine card will be clean, solid red, with solid black outlines.

On the counterfeit, the letters are composed of many tiny dots, giving a fuzzy appearance. Similar evidence can be seen in the letters of "1970 ROOKIE STARS" and in the players' names and positions.

On back, the blue printed wording is likewise composed of dots, rather than being solid as on a Topps original.

The black "Reprint" which appears on the back of the card shown here may not be present on all cards encountered in the hobby market.

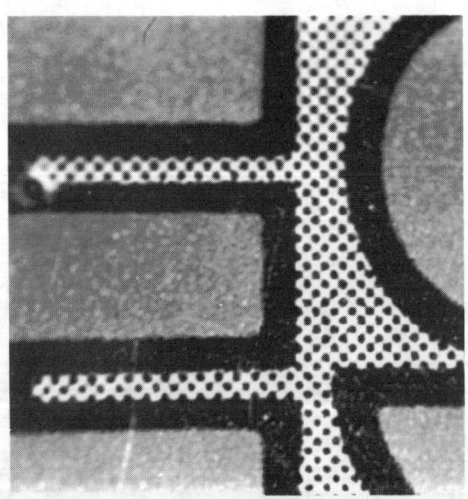

Genuine

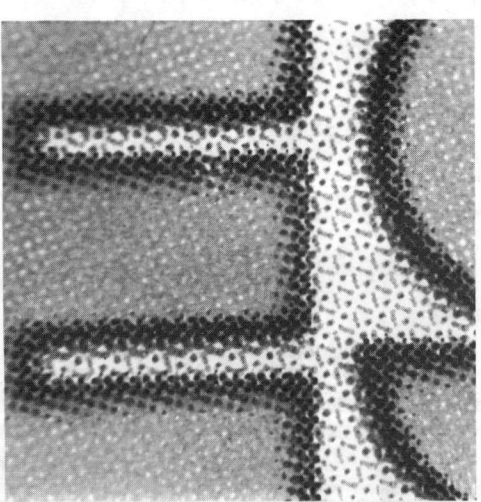

Counterfeit

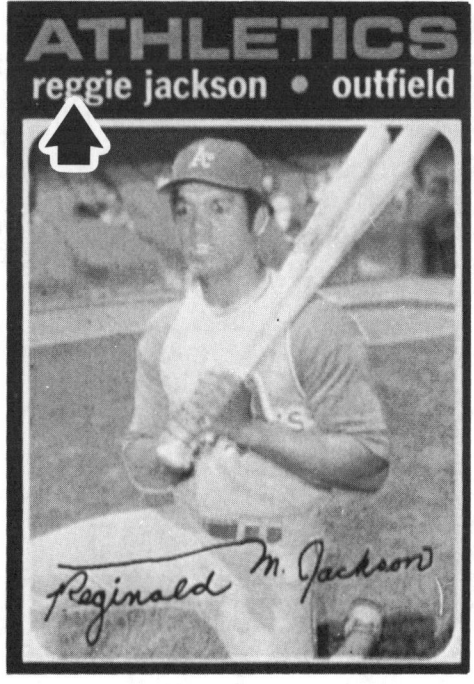
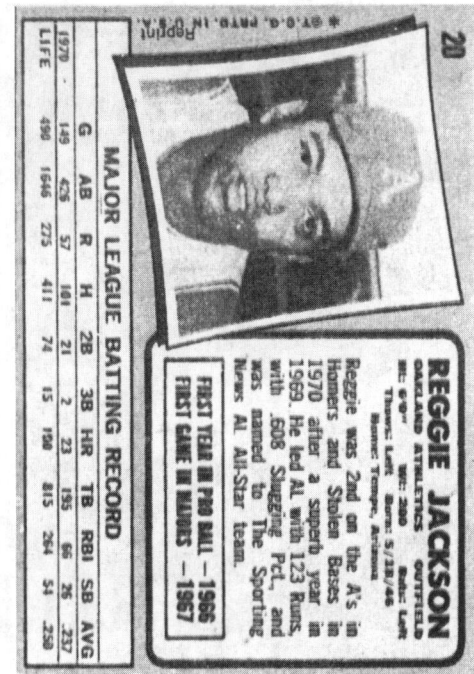

Not a particularly deceptive counterfeit, this card displays an overall lack of sharpness in the photo and front color design elements.

With the use of a magnifying glass, the cause of that fuzziness can be used to pinpoint the status of this card as counterfeit. Close examination of the red-orange ''ATHLETICS'' and the yellow player name at the top of the card will reveal on the counterfeit that the letters are comprised of many tiny color dots, rather than the sharp, clean lines of the letters on a genuine card.

Similarly, the facsimile autograph, which on a genuine card is comprised of sharp black lines, is reproduced on the counterfeit as a collection of black dots.

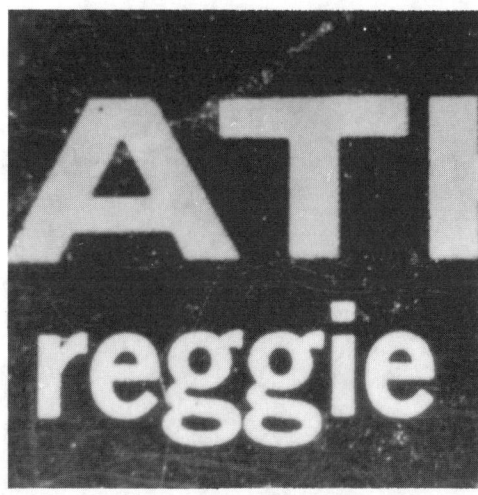

Genuine

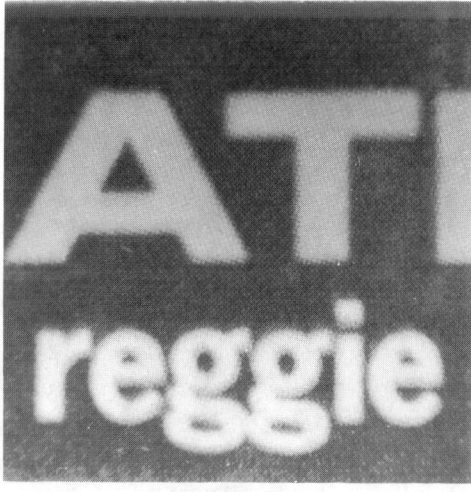

Counterfeit

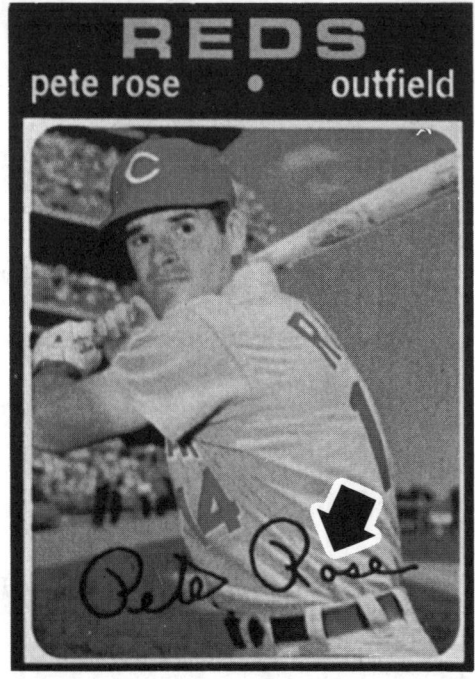

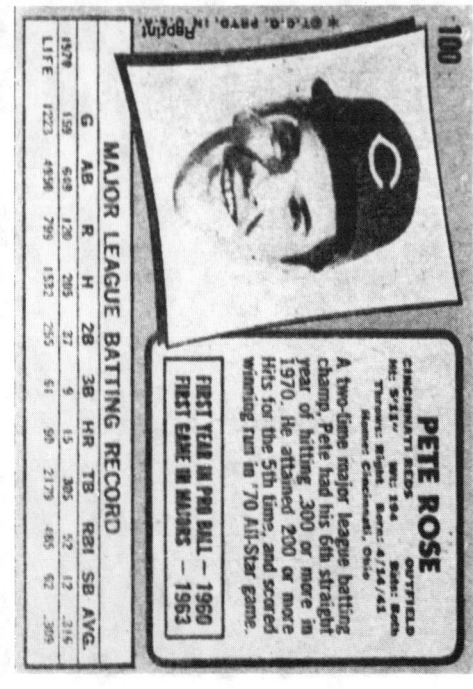

Because of the color combination of the player and team name and position at the top of the card, this counterfeit is not as easy to spot as the other known 1971 Topps counterfeits.

Still, a quick glance with a magnifying glass at the area of the facsimile signature will tell good from bad. A genuine '71 Topps Pete Rose card will have the autograph reproduced as a solid black element. On the counterfeit, the signature is composed of many tiny black dots, giving it a fuzzy appearance.

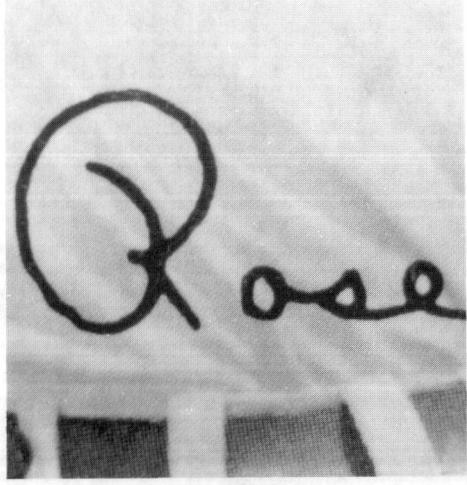

Genuine

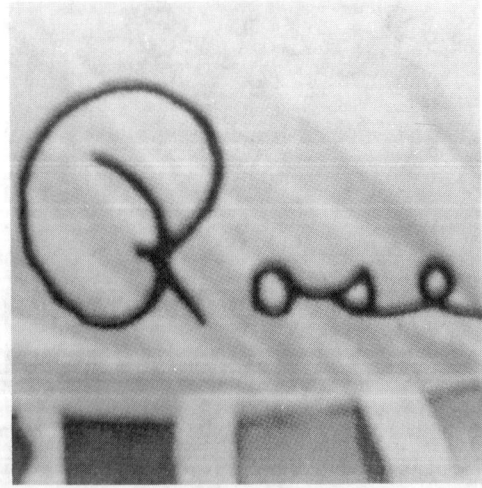

Counterfeit

No photo available

No photo available

No specimen has yet been made available for examination and photography.

According to a May 15, 1983, article in *Baseball Card News*, this card is one of a group of eight 1971-1973 Topps baseball cards that were apparently produced by the same hand. The fakes surfaced in Southern California but then, as now, were rarely seen in the hobby market.

Unlike virtually every other counterfeit, the persons responsible for production of this group did not simply photo-reproduce the existing typography on the genuine cards, but rather had most of it — front and back — reset. The noticeable differences in size and shape of type which resulted make this group of counterfeits fairly easy to spot.

An even more noticeable difference between the cards in this group and genuine Topps cards is that (with the exception of the 1973 Schmidt rookie) all of the fakes have omitted the Topps copyright symbol (©) before the copyright line on the back of the card.

No photo available

No photo available

Genuine   **Counterfeit**

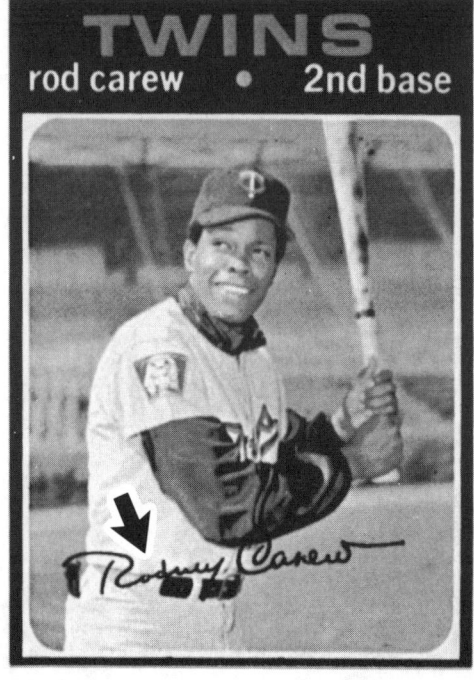

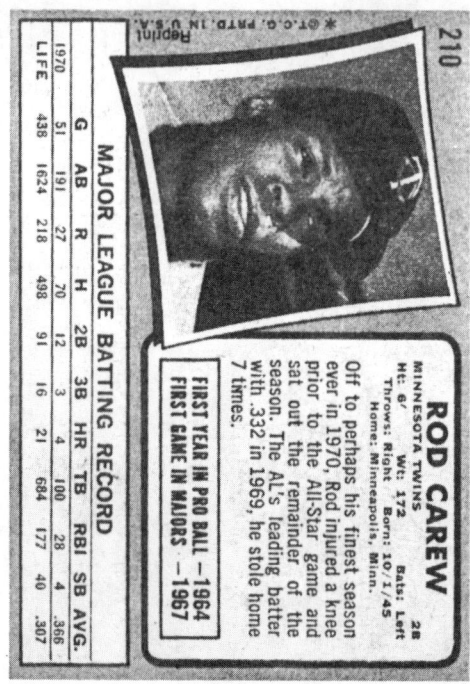

		G	AB	R	H	2B	3B	HR	TB	RBI	SB	AVG.
	1970	51	191	27	70	12	3	4	100	28	4	.366
	LIFE	438	1624	218	498	91	16	21	684	177	40	.307

MAJOR LEAGUE BATTING RECORD

ROD CAREW 2B
MINNESOTA TWINS
Ht: 6'   Wt: 172   Bats: Left
Throws: Right   Born: 10/1/45
Home: Minneapolis, Minn.

Off to perhaps his finest season ever in 1970, Rod injured a knee prior to the All-Star game and sat out the remainder of the season. The AL's leading batter with .332 in 1969, he stole home 7 times.

FIRST YEAR IN PRO BALL — 1964
FIRST GAME IN MAJORS — 1967

Not a particularly deceptive counterfeit, this card displays an overall lack of sharpness in the photo and front color design elements.

Because of the color scheme used on this particular card for the team and player names and the position, it is easier to spot this counterfeit by examination of the black facsimile autograph.

On a genuine card, the signature is comprised of sharp black lines. The counterfeit reproduces the autograph as a collection of black dots, creating a fuzzy appearance.

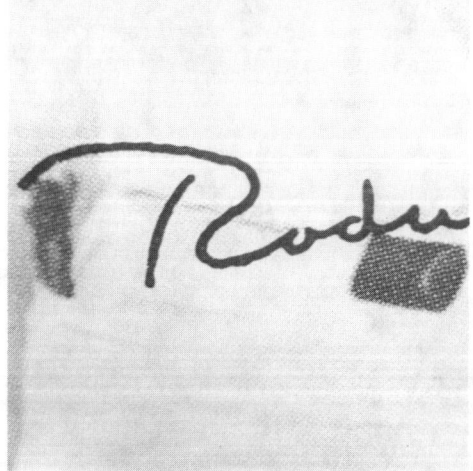

Genuine

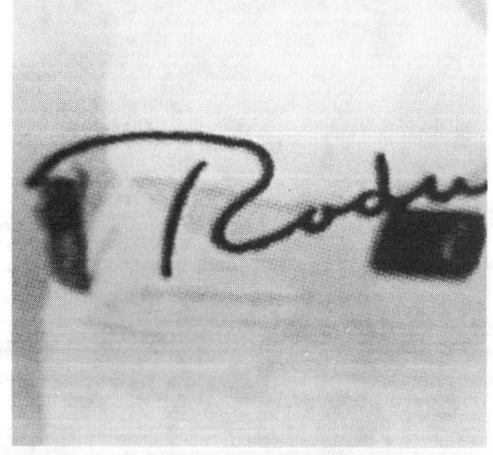

Counterfeit

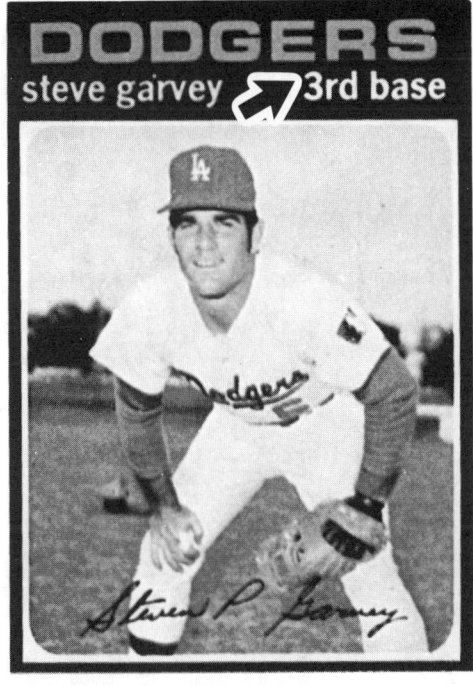
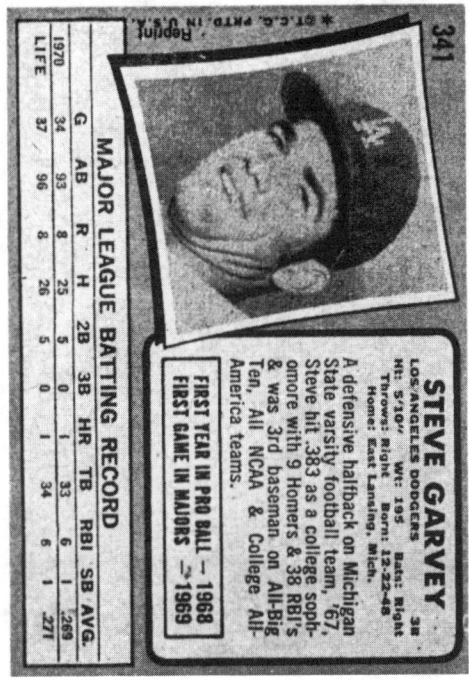

Not a particularly deceptive counterfeit, this card displays an overall lack of sharpness in the photo and front color design elements.

With the use of a magnifying glass, the cause of that fuzziness can be used to pinpoint the status of this card as counterfeit. Close examination of the red-orange "DODGERS", the orange player name and the yellow position at the top of the card will reveal on the counterfeit that the letters are comprised of many tiny color dots, rather than the sharp, clean lines of the letters on a genuine card.

Similarly, the facsimile autograph, which on a genuine card is comprised of sharp black lines, is reproduced on the counterfeit as a collection of black dots.

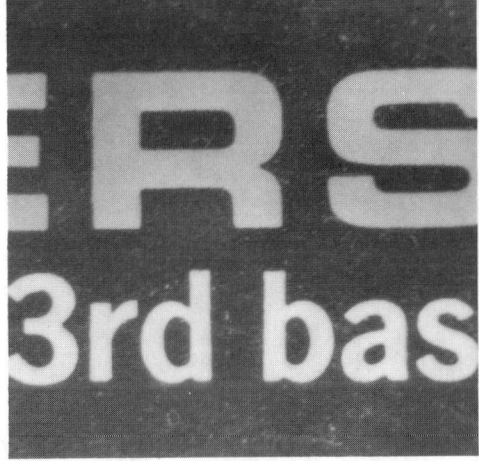

Genuine

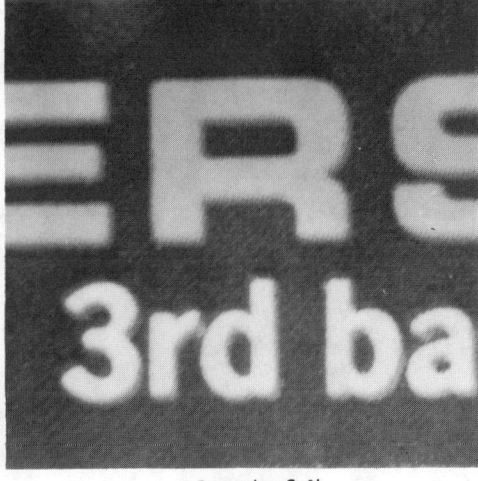

Counterfeit

No photo available

No photo available

No specimen has yet been made available for examination and photography.

According to a May 15, 1983, article in *Baseball Card News*, this card is one of a group of eight 1971-1973 Topps baseball cards that were apparently produced by the same hand. The fakes surfaced in Southern California but then, as now, were rarely seen in the hobby market.

Unlike virtually every other counterfeit, the persons responsible for production of this group did not simply photo-reproduce the existing typography on the genuine cards, but rather had most of it — front and back — reset. The noticeable differences in size and shape of type which resulted make this group of counterfeits fairly easy to spot.

An even more noticeable difference between the cards in this group and genuine Topps cards is that (with the exception of the 1973 Schmidt rookie) all of the fakes have omitted the Topps copyright line on the back of the card.

No photo available

No photo available

Genuine   **Counterfeit**

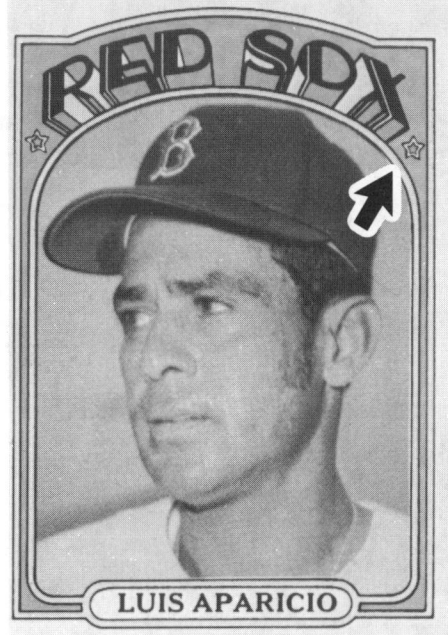

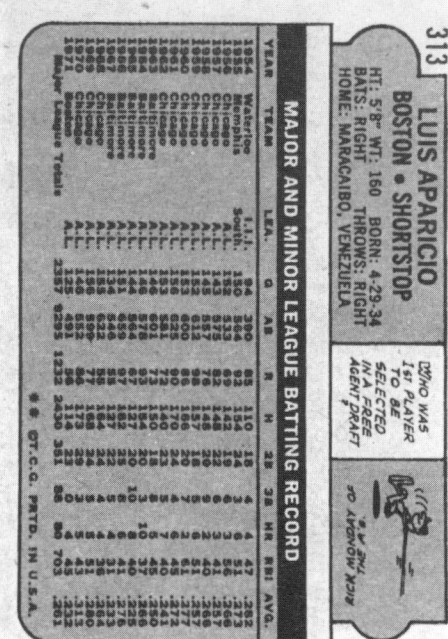

The counterfeiters were too clever in creating this fake. By cleaning up the orange-and-yellow star to the lower-right of "SOX," they created a surefire identifier. A *genuine* card will show this star with missing black outlines of its lower-right "leg." The fake is well-formed.

One of the "Quebec counterfeits" this may exhibit a number of traits common to many of the 50 fake Topps cards which were the work of the same counterfeiter.

All were made by combining rescreened photos with painstakingly reproduced graphic elements of genuine cards.

Many of the counterfeits show random black ink streaks in various areas on the front, usually horizontally oriented.

The borders of these counterfeits often show a stray overspray of color, especially near the edges.

All the fakes are within weight tolerances of genuine contemporary cards.

Some of the counterfeits, by accident or design, are cut off-center, like Topps cards of the era, though many of the fakes are not cut to exactly correct size.

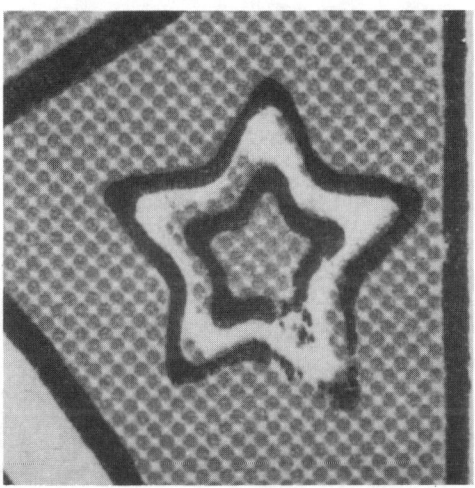

Genuine

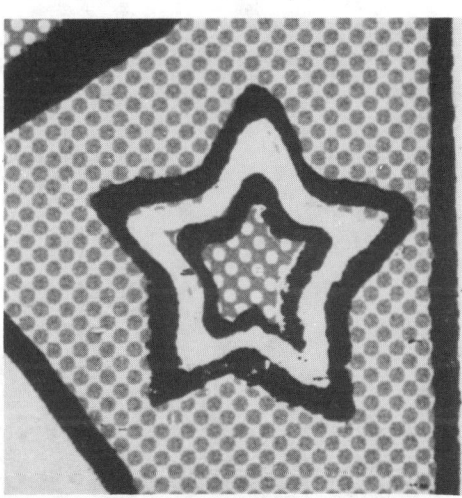

Counterfeit

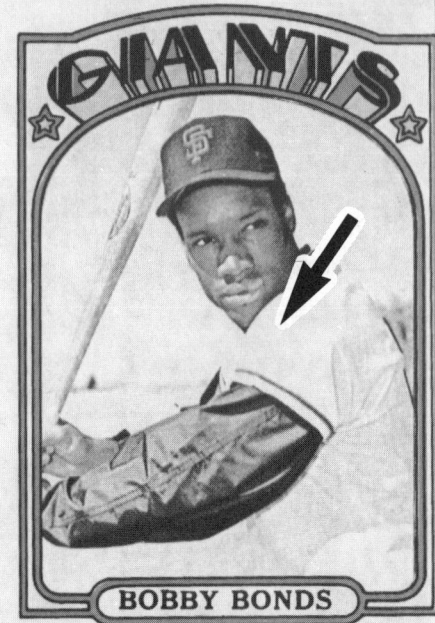

BOBBY BONDS

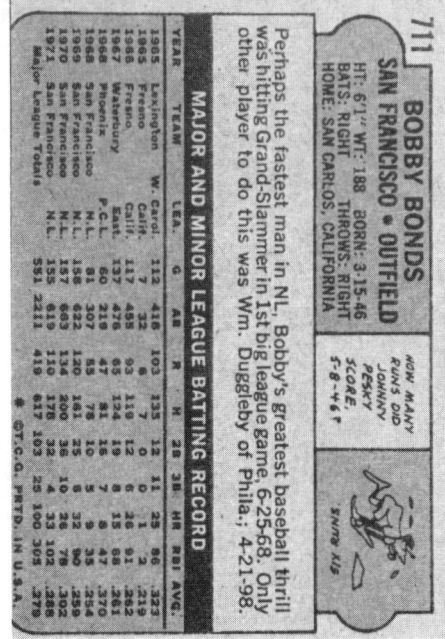

With a magnifying glass, examine the left sleeve just above the orange trim. Genuine cards show a tiny stray blue dot here. On the counterfeit, the dot was rescreened into several even tinier dots. Ditto the black speck above the right elbow.

This counterfeit may exhibit a number of other traits common to the 50 "Quebec counterfeit" Topps cards which were the work of the same counterfeiter.

All were made by combining rescreened photos with painstakingly reproduced graphic elements of genuine cards.

Many of the counterfeits show random black ink streaks in various areas on the front, usually horizontally oriented.

The borders of these counterfeits often show a stray overspray of color, especially near the edges.

All the fakes are within weight tolerances of genuine contemporary cards.

Some of the counterfeits, by accident or design, are cut off-center, like Topps cards of the era, though many of the fakes are not cut to exactly correct size.

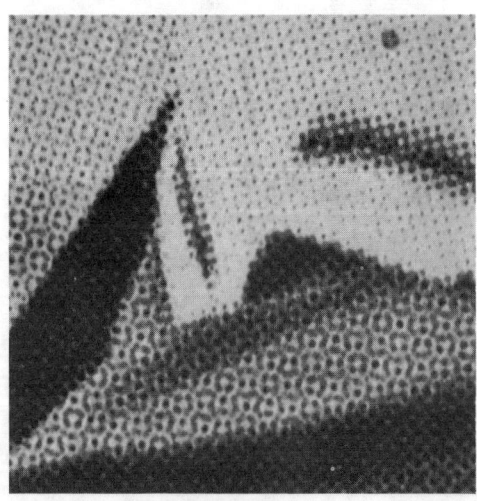

Genuine

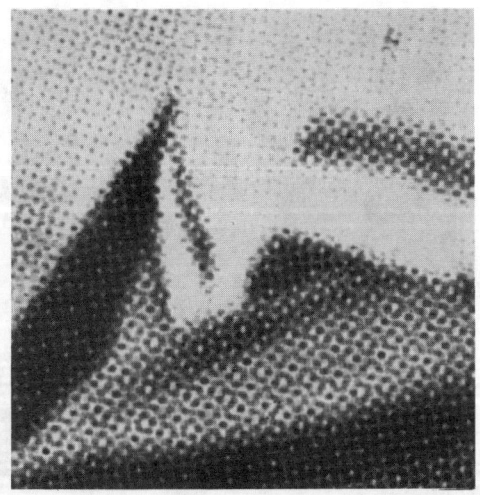

Counterfeit

No photo available

No photo available

No specimen has yet been made available for examination and photography.

According to a May 15, 1983, article in *Baseball Card News*, this card is one of a group of eight 1971-1973 Topps baseball cards that were apparently produced by the same hand. The fakes surfaced in Southern California but then, as now, were rarely seen in the hobby market.

Unlike virtually every other counterfeit, the persons responsible for production of this group did not simply photo-reproduce the existing typography on the genuine cards, but rather had most of it — front and back — reset. The noticeable differences in size and shape of type which resulted make this group of counterfeits fairly easy to spot.

An even more noticeable difference between the cards in this group and genuine Topps cards is that (with the exception of the 1973 Schmidt rookie) all of the fakes have omitted the Topps copyright symbol (©) before the copyright line on the back of the card.

No photo available

No photo available

Genuine   **Counterfeit**

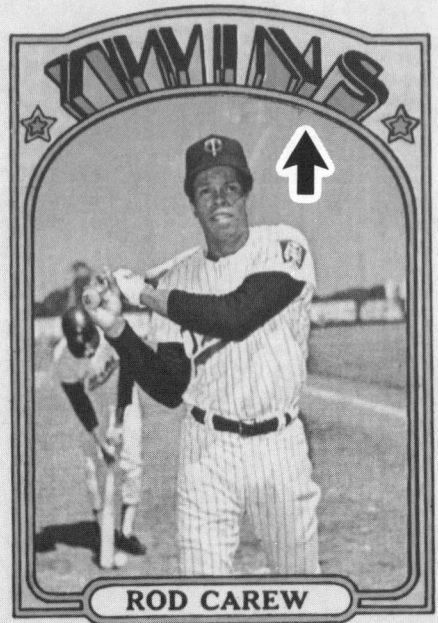

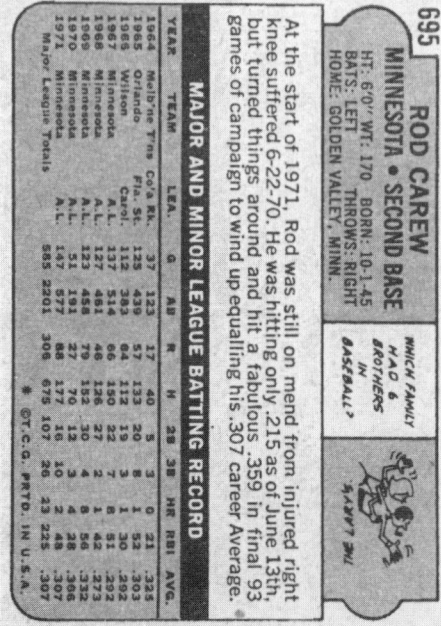

One of the most deceptive of the "Quebec counterfeits." With a magnifying glass, examine the photo just under the "N" in "TWINS". The counterfeit shows a tiny purple patch in the blue sky. Note also the poor mating of the photo and the black frame line in this area.

This counterfeit may exhibit a number of traits common to many of the 50 fake Topps cards which were the work of the same counterfeiter.

All were made by combining rescreened photos with painstakingly reproduced graphic elements of genuine cards.

Many of the counterfeits show random black ink streaks in various areas on the front, usually horizontally oriented.

The borders of these counterfeits often show a stray overspray of color, especially near the edges.

All the fakes are within weight tolerances of genuine contemporary cards.

Some of the counterfeits, by accident or design, are cut off-center, like Topps cards of the era, though many of the fakes are not cut to exactly correct size.

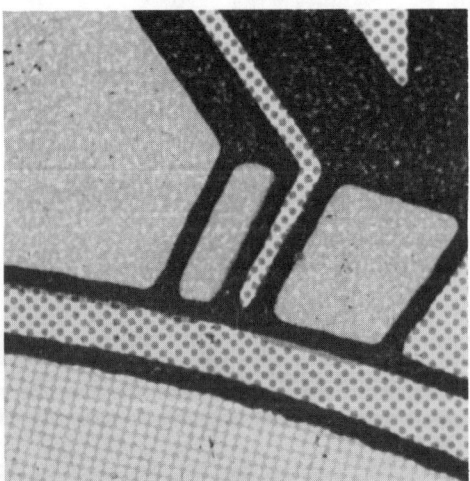

Genuine

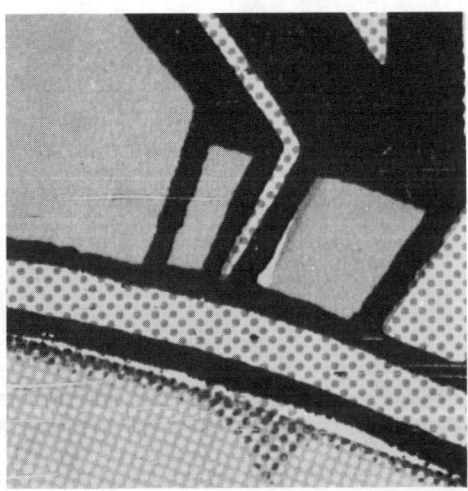

Counterfeit

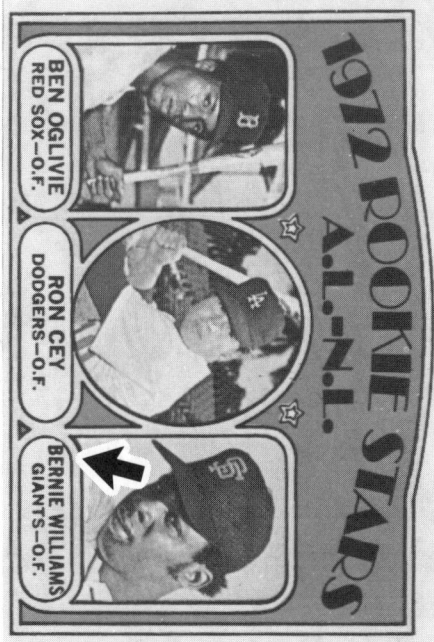

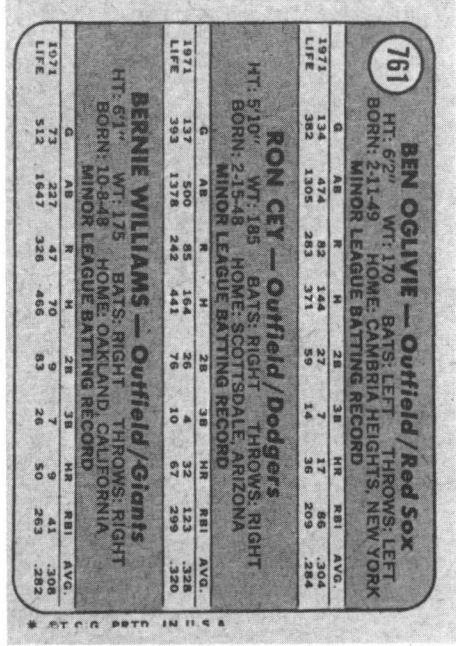

Poor positioning of the name of the least-known of these "rookie stars" gives away this "Quebec counterfeit." Note how the counterfeit displays the black frame line around Bernie Williams' name so as to obscure part of the "s" and create a disturbance near the top of the "B".

This counterfeit may exhibit a number of other traits common to many of the 50 fake 1972-1980 Topps cards which were the work of the same counterfeiter.

All were made by combining rescreened photos with painstakingly reproduced graphic elements of genuine cards.

Many of the counterfeits show random black ink streaks in various areas on the front, usually horizontally oriented.

The borders of these counterfeits often show a stray overspray of color, especially near the edges.

All the fakes are within weight tolerances of genuine contemporary cards.

Some of the counterfeits, by accident or design, are cut off-center, like Topps cards of the era, though many of the fakes are not cut to exactly correct size.

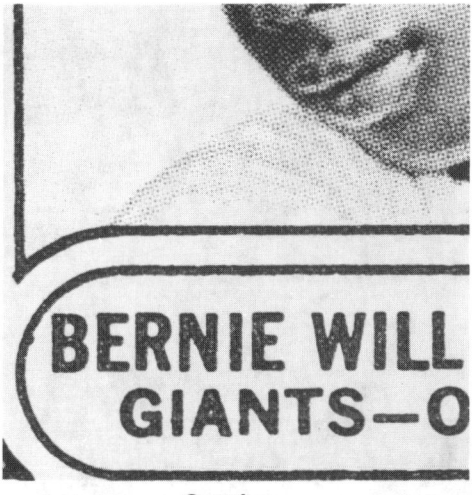

Genuine

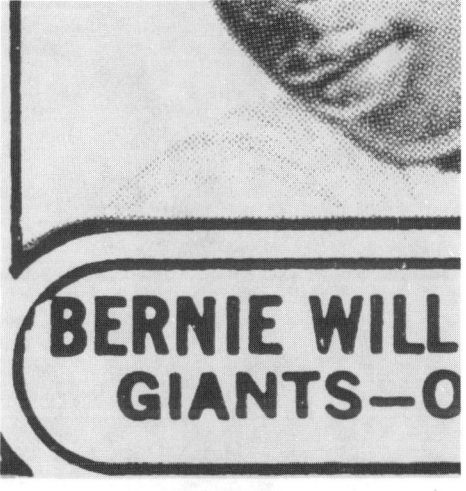

Counterfeit

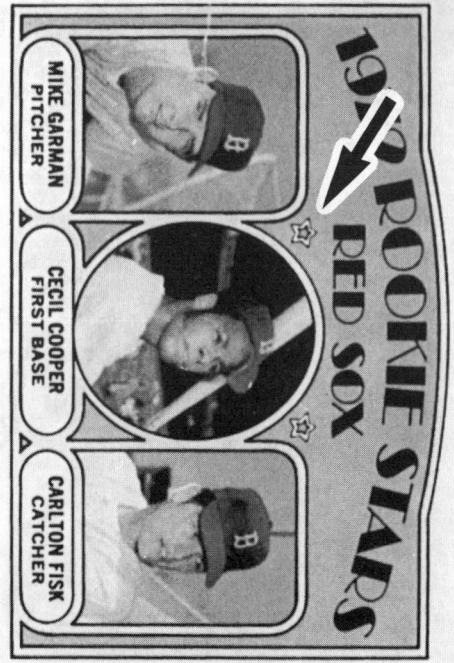

1972 ROOKIE STARS RED SOX

MIKE GARMAN
PITCHER

CECIL COOPER
FIRST BASE

CARLTON FISK
CATCHER

(79) MIKE GARMAN — Pitcher
HT: 6'3" WT: 198 BATS: RIGHT THROWS: RIGHT
BORN: 9-16-49 HOME: WILDER, IDAHO
MINOR LEAGUE PITCHING RECORD

	G	IP	W	L	PCT.	SO.	BB.	ERA.
1971	29	129	8	7	.533	128	88	4.15
LIFE	113	571	31	43	.419	519	414	4.10

CECIL COOPER — First Base
HT: 6'2" WT: 165 BATS: LEFT THROWS: LEFT
BORN: 12-20-49 HOME: BRENHAM, TEXAS
MINOR LEAGUE BATTING RECORD

	G	AB	R	H	2B	3B	HR	RBI	AVG.
1971	140	520	86	215	27	5	16	86	.354
LIFE	362	1236	215	426	61	15	20	149	.345

CARLTON FISK — Catcher
HT: 6'2" WT: 200 BATS: RIGHT THROWS: RIGHT
BORN: 12-26-47 HOME: CHARLESTOWN, NEW HAMPSHIRE
MINOR LEAGUE BATTING RECORD

	G	AB	R	H	2B	3B	HR	RBI	AVG.
1971	95	308	45	81	10	4	10	43	.263
LIFE	347	1096	157	287	57	10	44	162	.262

✸ ©T.C.G. PRTD. IN U.S.A.   Reprint

An overall fuzzy appearance on the front makes this counterfeit look suspicious to an experienced eye.

Examination of the design details with a magnifying glass reveals sure evidence of the counterfeit's status.

Easy differentiation between real and fake on this card can be made by examining the stars above the photo of Cecil Cooper. On a genuine card, the stars will be outlined in clean, solid black. On the counterfeit, the black lines are composed of tiny dots, giving a fuzzy appearance. Similar evidence can be seen in the other black framelines and all of the lettering on the front of the counterfeit.

On the back, a black printed screen has been used to simulate the gray cardboard of a Topps original and hide the white cardboard on which the fake was printed.

The black "Reprint" which appears on the back of the card shown here may not be present on all cards encountered in the hobby market.

No photo available

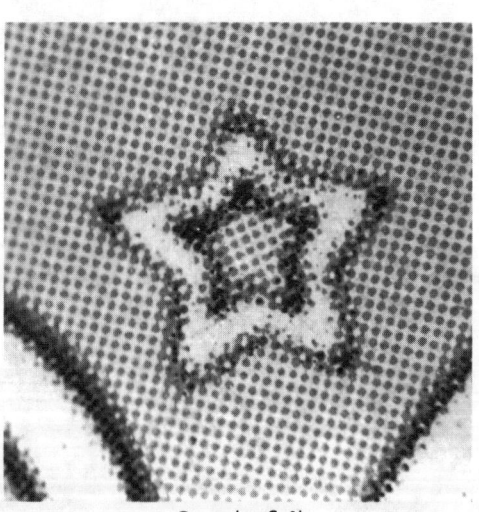

Genuine   Counterfeit

No photo available

No photo available

No specimen has yet been made available for examination and photography.

According to a May 15, 1983, article in *Baseball Card News*, this card is one of a group of eight 1971-1973 Topps baseball cards that were apparently produced by the same hand. The fakes surfaced in Southern California but then, as now, were rarely seen in the hobby market.

Unlike virtually every other counterfeit, the persons responsible for production of this group did not simply photo-reproduce the existing typography on the gen-uine cards, but rather had most of it — front and back — reset. The noticeable differences in size and shape of type which resulted make this group of counterfeits fairly easy to spot.

An even more noticeable difference between the cards in this group and genuine Topps cards is that (with the exception of the 1973 Schmidt rookie) all of the fakes have omitted the Topps copyright symbol (©) before the copyright line on the back of the card.

No photo available

No photo available

Genuine

Counterfeit

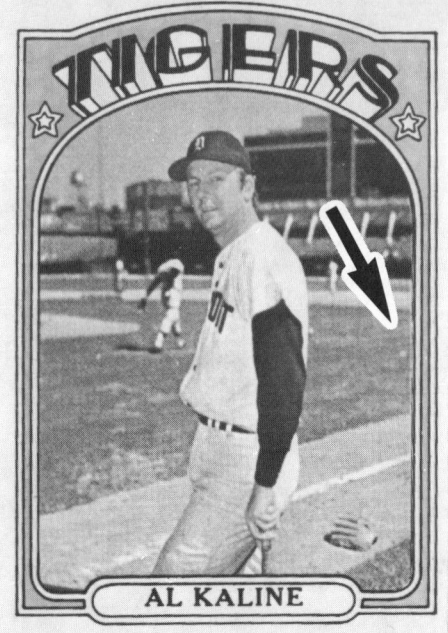

A stray orange dot in the infield just above the first base line marks this counterfeit. Note also the right end of the photo does not end cleanly at the first black frame line. Naturally, a good magnifying glass is required to pick up these flaws.

One of the "Quebec counterfeits," this may exhibit a number of traits common to many of the 50 fake Topps cards which were the work of the same counterfeiter.

All were made by combining rescreened photos with painstakingly reproduced graphic elements of genuine cards.

Many of the counterfeits show random black ink streaks in various areas on the front, usually horizontally oriented.

The borders of these counterfeits often show a stray overspray of color, especially near the edges.

All the fakes are within weight tolerances of genuine contemporary cards.

Some of the counterfeits, by accident or design, are cut off-center, like Topps cards of the era, though many of the fakes are not cut to exactly correct size.

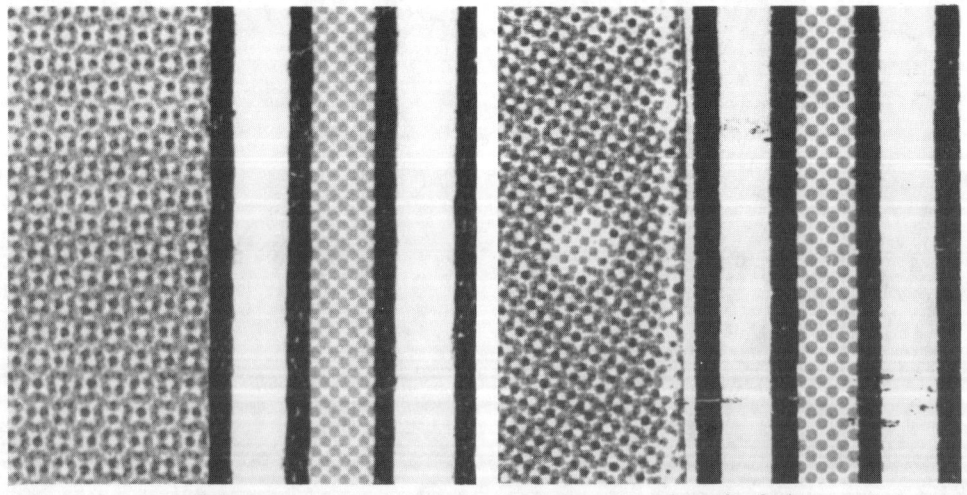

Genuine   Counterfeit

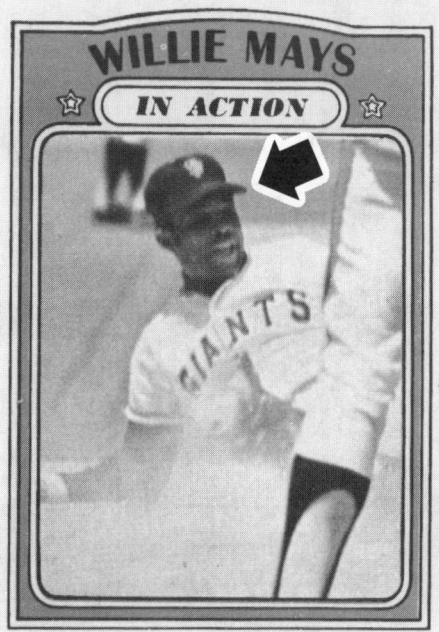

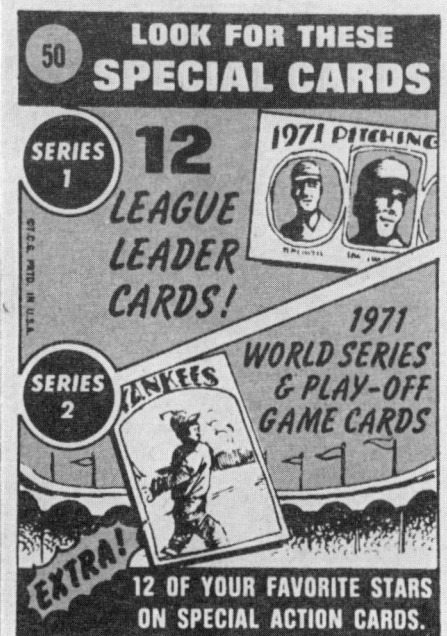

One of the more deceptive "Quebec counterfeits." With a glass, examine the intertwined "SF" logo on the cap. On the counterfeit these letters are blurred to virtual indistinguishability. A stray yellow circle between the two "L"s of "WILLIE" may or may not be diagnostic.

This counterfeit may exhibit a number of traits common to many of the 50 fake Topps cards which were the work of the same counterfeiter.

All were made by combining rescreened photos with painstakingly reproduced graphic elements of genuine cards.

Many of the counterfeits show random black ink streaks in various areas on the front, usually horizontally oriented.

The borders of these counterfeits often show a stray overspray of color, especially near the edges.

All the fakes are within weight tolerances of genuine contemporary cards.

Some of the counterfeits, by accident or design, are cut off-center, like Topps cards of the era, though many of the fakes are not cut to exactly correct size.

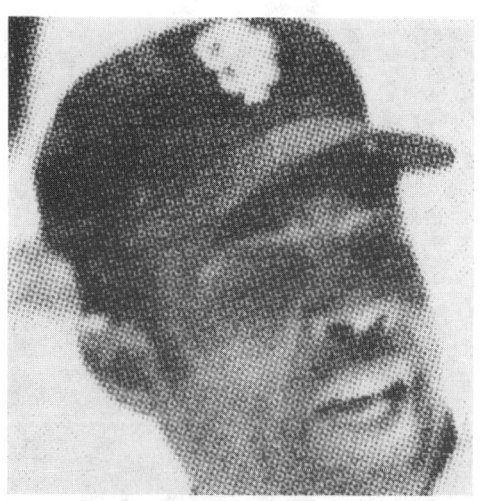

Genuine

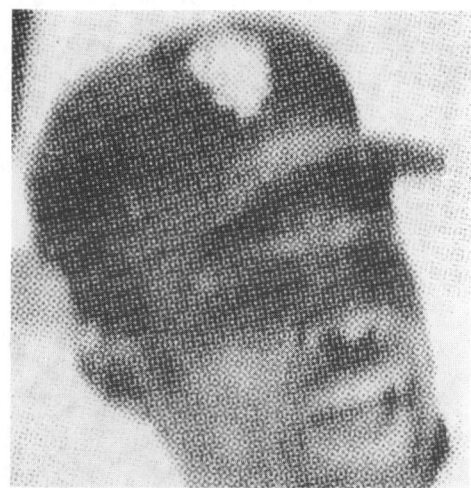

Counterfeit

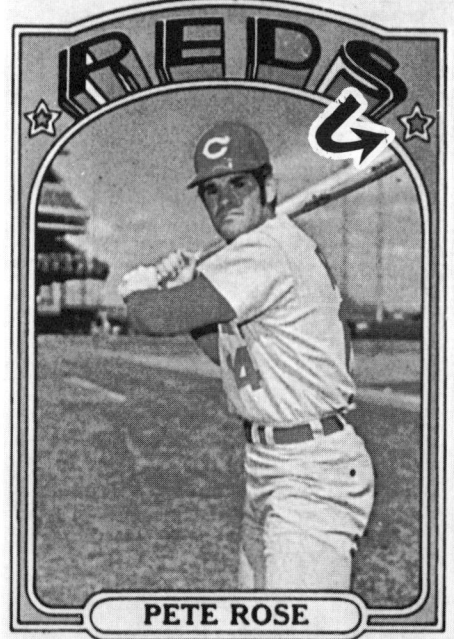

PETE ROSE

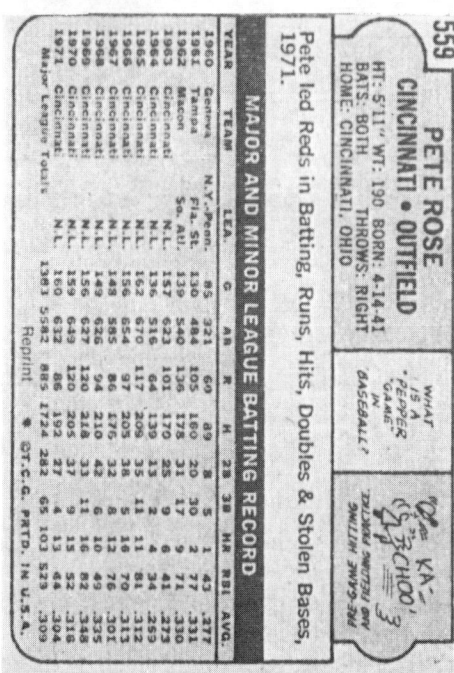

559

PETE ROSE
CINCINNATI • OUTFIELD
HT: 5'11" WT: 190 BORN: 4-14-41
BATS: BOTH THROWS: RIGHT
HOME: CINCINNATI, OHIO

Pete led Reds in Batting, Runs, Hits, Doubles & Stolen Bases, 1971.

MAJOR AND MINOR LEAGUE BATTING RECORD

YEAR	TEAM	LEA.	G	AB	R	H	2B	3B	HR	RBI	AVG.
1960	Geneva	N.Y.-Penn.	85	221	60	89	8	5	1	45	.277
1961	Tampa	Fla.-St.	130	484	105	160	20	30	2	77	.331
1962	Macon	So. Atl.	139	540	136	178	31	17	9	71	.330
1963	Cincinnati	N.L.	157	623	101	170	25	9	6	41	.273
1964	Cincinnati	N.L.	136	516	64	139	13	2	4	34	.269
1965	Cincinnati	N.L.	162	670	117	209	35	11	11	81	.312
1966	Cincinnati	N.L.	156	654	97	205	38	5	16	70	.313
1967	Cincinnati	N.L.	148	585	86	176	32	8	12	76	.301
1968	Cincinnati	N.L.	149	626	94	210	42	6	10	49	.335
1969	Cincinnati	N.L.	156	627	120	218	33	11	16	82	.348
1970	Cincinnati	N.L.	159	649	120	205	37	9	15	52	.316
1971	Cincinnati	N.L.	160	632	86	192	27	4	13	44	.304
Major League Totals			1383	5582	885	1724	282	65	103	529	.309

Reprint ❋ ©T.C.G. PRTD. IN U.S.A.

WHAT IS A "PEPPER GAME" IN BASEBALL?

Ka-choo!! "Pepper is a baseball game"

Because it is printed on thinner, whiter cardboard than the genuine 1972 Topps cards, and because the gloss of the card's front differs from that on a genuine card, an experienced dealer or collector should be able to spot this counterfeit with relative ease.

The presence of dot structures where they should not be provides evidence against the counterfeit, but does require a magnifying glass to verify.

The player's name, the black pinstripes and the stars to either side of "REDS" are the best places to examine a suspect card. On a genuine card, these elements will appear as clean, solid black lines. The counterfeit shows these elements as being made up of many tiny dots.

Similarly, the black letters on the counterfeit's back are of fuzzy composition.

The black "Reprint" which appears on the back of the card photographed here may not be present on all cards encountered in the hobby market.

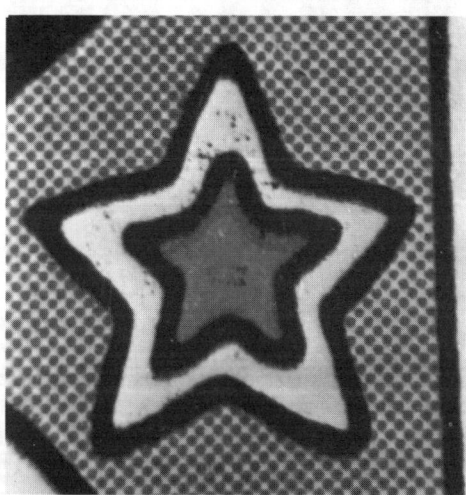

Genuine

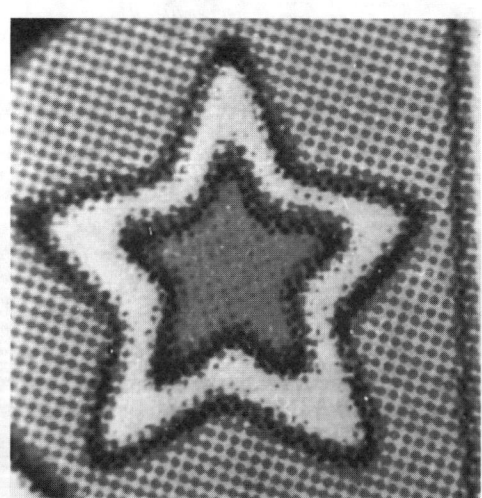

Counterfeit

No photo available

No photo available

No specimen has yet been made available for examination and photography.

According to a May 15, 1983, article in *Baseball Card News*, this card is one of a group of eight 1971-1973 Topps baseball cards that were apparently produced by the same hand. The fakes surfaced in Southern California but then, as now, were rarely seen in the hobby market.

Unlike virtually every other counterfeit, the persons responsible for production of this group did not simply photo-reproduce the existing typography on the genuine cards, but rather had most of it — front and back — reset. The noticeable differences in size and shape of type which resulted make this group of counterfeits fairly easy to spot.

An even more noticeable difference between the cards in this group and genuine Topps cards is that (with the exception of the 1973 Schmidt rookie) all of the fakes have omitted the Topps copyright symbol (©) before the copyright line on the back of the card.

No photo available

No photo available

Genuine   **Counterfeit**

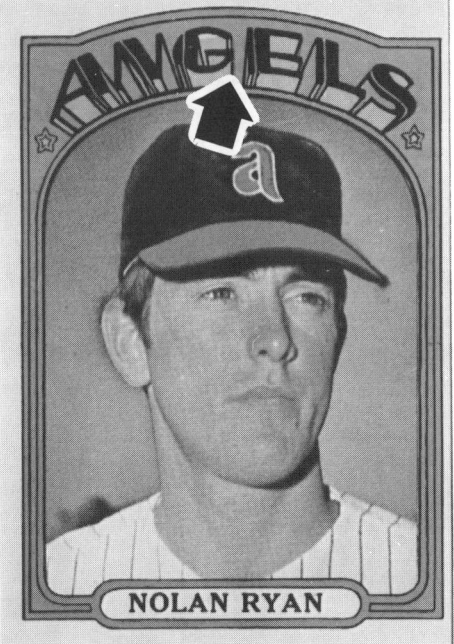

The generally deceptive work of the "Quebec counterfeiter" fell apart on this card. Some sloppy color-stripping left a yellow area beneath the top of the "G" in "ANGELS". Also, the bottom of the thin vertical line to the right of the "E" should be solid green, not white with blue dots.

This counterfeit may exhibit a number of other traits common to many of the 50 fake 1972-1980 Topps cards which were the work of the same counterfeiter.

All were made by combining rescreened photos with painstakingly reproduced graphic elements of genuine cards.

Many of the counterfeits show random black ink streaks in various areas on the front, usually horizontally oriented.

The borders of these counterfeits often show a stray overspray of color, especially near the edges.

All the fakes are within weight tolerances of genuine contemporary cards.

Some of the counterfeits, by accident or design, are cut off-center, like Topps cards of the era, though many of the fakes are not cut to exactly correct size.

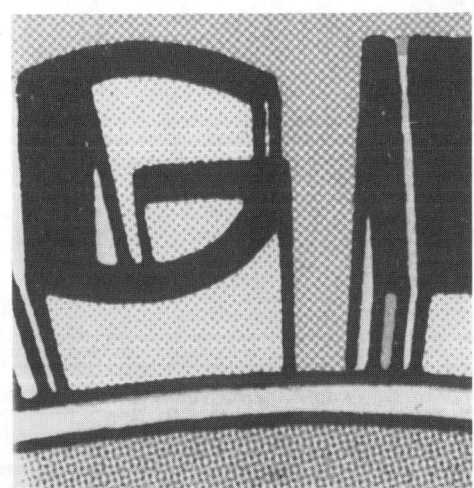

Genuine   **Counterfeit**

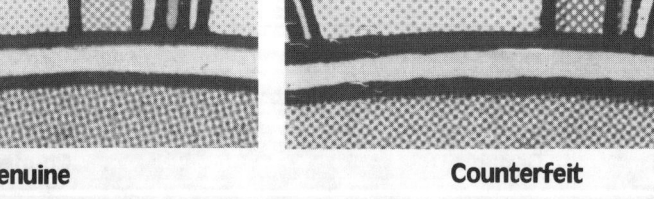

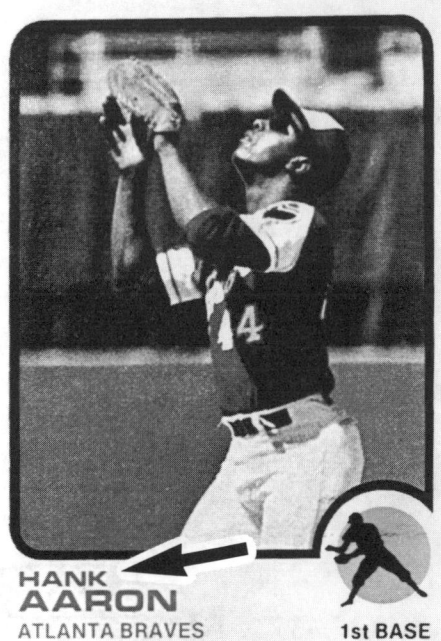

differences in size and shape of type which resulted make this group of counterfeits fairly easy to spot. The stats on back of the counterfeit, for example, are much smaller than on a genuine card.

According to a May 15, 1983, article in *Baseball Card News*, this card is one of a group of eight 1971-1973 Topps baseball card) that were apparently produced by the same hand. The fakes surfaced in Southern California but then, as now, were rarely seen in the hobby market.

Unlike virtually every other counterfeit, the persons responsible for production of this group did not simply photo-reproduce the existing typography on the genuine cards, but rather had most of it — front and back — reset. The noticeable

An even more noticeable difference between the cards in this group and genuine Topps cards is that (with the exception of the 1973 Schmidt rookie) all of the fakes have omitted the Topps copyright symbol (©) before the copyright line on the back of the card.

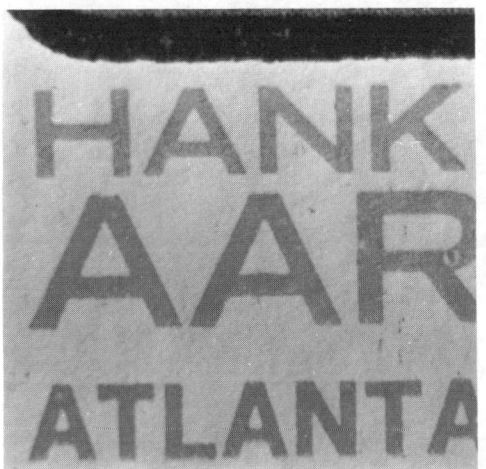

Genuine

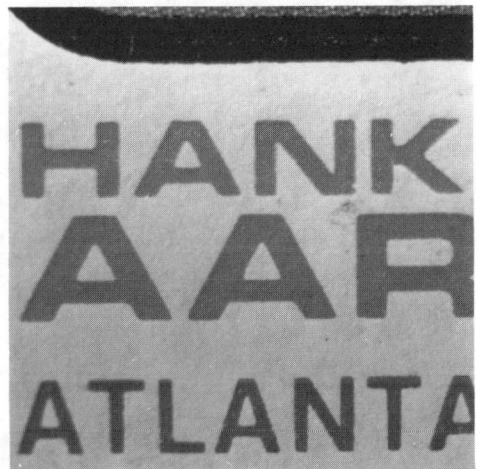

Counterfeit

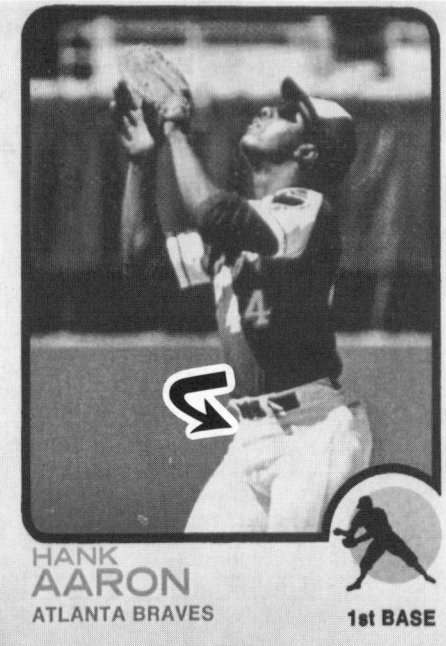

HANK
AARON
ATLANTA BRAVES
1st BASE

ANK NEEDS ONLY 41 HOMERS TO TIE BABE RUTH'S ALL-TIME RECORD.

100

HENRY LOUIS
AARON

Hgt. 6'0''　　Wgt. 180　　Bats: Right　　Throws: Right
Born: 2-5-34, Mobile, Alabama　　Home: Atlanta, Georgia

	MAJOR LEAGUE BATTING RECORD							
YEAR	TEAM	AB	H	2B	3B	HR	RBI	AVG
1954	Braves	468	131	27	6	13	69	.280
1955	Braves	602	189	37	9	27	106	.314
1956	Braves	609	200	34	14	26	92	.328
1957	Braves	615	198	27	6	44	132	.322
1958	Braves	601	196	34	4	30	95	.326
1959	Braves	629	223	46	7	39	123	.355
1960	Braves	590	172	20	11	40	126	.292
1961	Braves	603	197	39	10	34	120	.327
1962	Braves	592	191	28	6	45	128	.323
1963	Braves	631	201	29	4	44	130	.319
1964	Braves	570	187	30	2	24	95	.328
1965	Braves	570	181	40	1	32	89	.318
1966	Braves	603	168	23	1	44	127	.279
1967	Braves	600	184	37	3	39	109	.307
1968	Braves	606	174	33	4	29	86	.287
1969	Braves	547	164	30	3	44	97	.300
1970	Braves	516	154	26	1	38	118	.298
1971	Braves	495	162	22	3	47	118	.327
1972	Braves	449	119	10	0	34	77	.265
Maj. Lg. Tot.		10,926	3391	572	95	673	2037	.310

★ ©T.C.G., PRTD. IN U.S.A.

In polite society we don't do this, but counterfeiting isn't polite so search for this fake in Hank's crotch. A pair of stray blue ink marks just below his belt buckle on a genuine card were rendered very indistinct by rescreening the fake. Also note a stray patch of red and yellow dots just in front of his right thigh on the fake.

One of the "Quebec counterfeits" this card may show other traits found among the 50 fake 1972-1980 Topps cards.

All were made by combining rescreened photos with painstakingly reproduced graphic elements of genuine cards.

Many of the counterfeits show random black ink streaks in various areas on the front, usually horizontally oriented.

The borders of these counterfeits often show a stray overspray of color, especially near the edges.

All the fakes are within weight tolerances of genuine contemporary cards.

Some of the counterfeits, by accident or design, are cut off-center, like Topps cards of the era, though many of the fakes are not cut to exactly correct size.

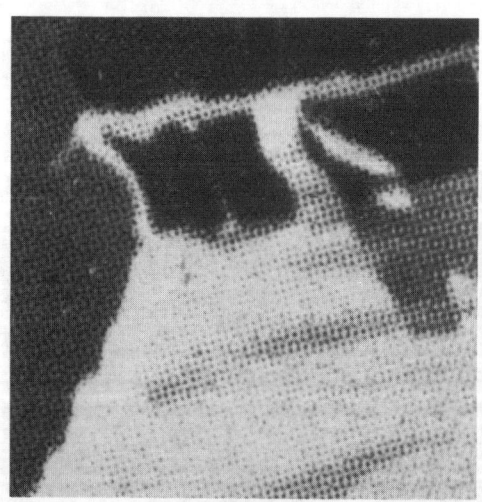

Genuine

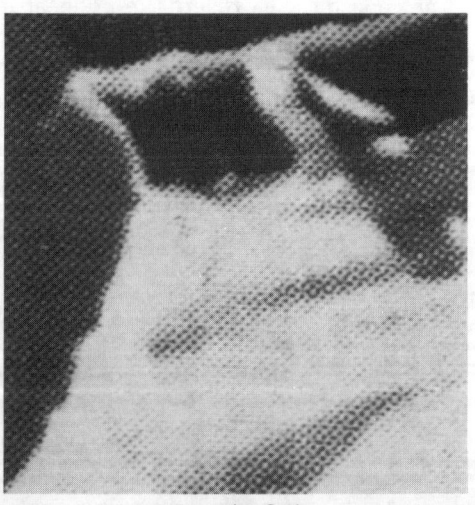

Counterfeit

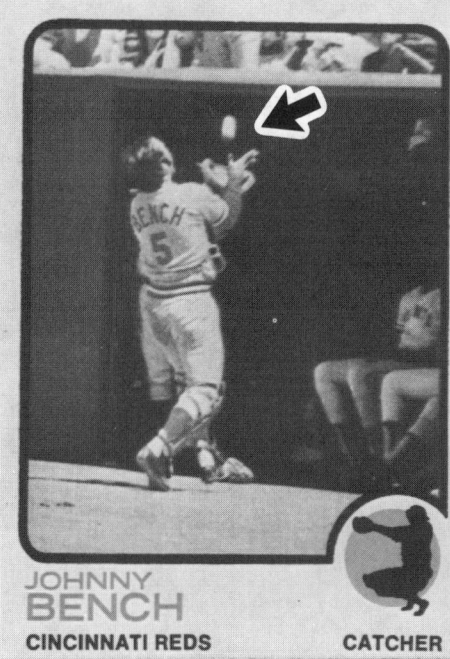

JOHNNY
BENCH
CINCINNATI REDS   **CATCHER**

JOHNNY IS ONE OF BASEBALLS' MOST ELIGIBLE BACHELORS.

380

JOHNNY LEE
BENCH

Hgt: 6'0''   Wgt: 200   Bats: Right   Throws: Right
Born: 12-7-47, Okla. City, Okla.   Home: Cincinnati, Ohio

Voted NL's MVP for the 2nd time in 3 years, 1972, Johnny's most crucial hit of the season came in 5th & final game of NL Playoffs vs. Pirates. With Reds trailing, 3-2, in 9th inning, Johnny led off with Homer to tie score. Reds added run later in inning to clinch flag & send them to Series.

MAJOR & MINOR LEAGUE BATTING RECORD								
YEAR	TEAM	AB	H	2B	3B	HR	RBI	AVG
1965	Tampa	214	53	13	1	2	35	.248
1966	Peninsula	350	103	16	0	22	68	.294
1966	Buffalo	0	0	0	0	0	0	.000
1967	Buffalo	344	89	17	2	23	68	.259
1967	Reds	86	14	3	1	1	6	.163
1968	Reds	564	155	40	2	15	82	.275
1969	Reds	532	156	23	1	26	90	.293
1970	Reds	605	177	35	4	45	148	.293
1971	Reds	562	134	19	2	27	61	.238
1972	Reds	538	145	22	2	40	125	.270
Maj. Lg. Tot.		2887	781	142	12	154	512	.271

★©T.C.G., PRTD. IN U.S.A.

"Keep your eye on the ball" is good advice for any ballplayer. It's also the best way to spot this counterfeit. In rescreening the photo of a genuine card to make the counterfeit, virtually all of the printer's dots were burned out in the area of the falling baseball, leaving it too white. You'll need a magnifier to verify this.

One of the "Quebec counterfeits" this may show some of the traits found on others among the 50 fake Topps cards.

All were made by combining rescreened photos with painstakingly reproduced graphic elements of genuine cards.

Many of the counterfeits show random black ink streaks in various areas on the front, usually horizontally oriented.

The borders of these counterfeits often show a stray overspray of color, especially near the edges.

All the fakes are within weight tolerances of genuine contemporary cards.

Some of the counterfeits, by accident or design, are cut off-center, like Topps cards of the era, though many of the fakes are not cut to exactly correct size.

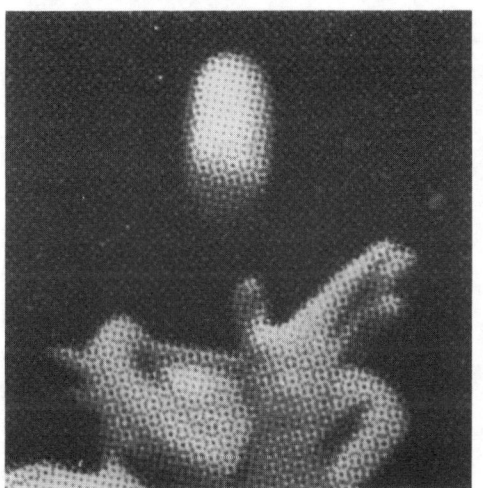

Genuine

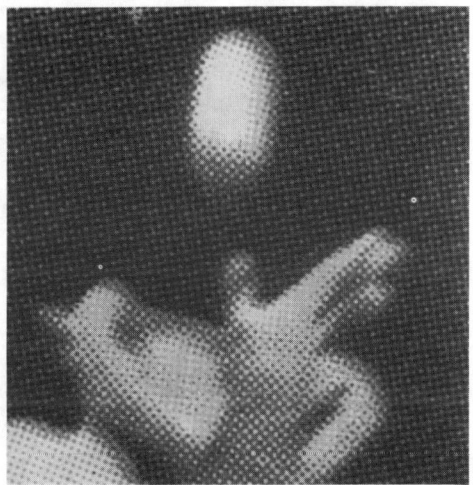

Counterfeit

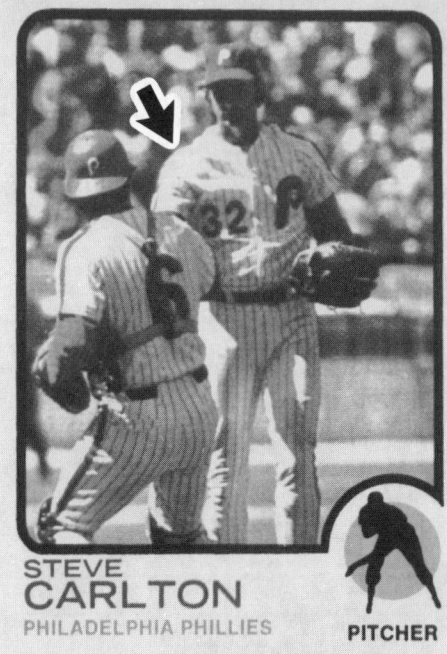

STEVE
CARLTON
PHILADELPHIA PHILLIES   **PITCHER**

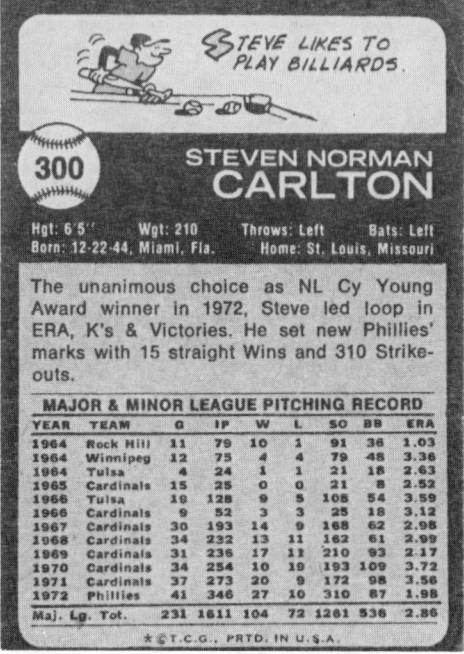

STEVE LIKES TO PLAY BILLIARDS.

300

STEVEN NORMAN
CARLTON

Hgt: 6'5"   Wgt: 210   Throws: Left   Bats: Left
Born: 12-22-44, Miami, Fla.   Home: St. Louis, Missouri

The unanimous choice as NL Cy Young Award winner in 1972, Steve led loop in ERA, K's & Victories. He set new Phillies' marks with 15 straight Wins and 310 Strike-outs.

MAJOR & MINOR LEAGUE PITCHING RECORD

YEAR	TEAM	G	IP	W	L	SO	BB	ERA
1964	Rock Hill	11	79	10	1	91	36	1.03
1964	Winnipeg	12	75	4	4	79	48	3.36
1964	Tulsa	4	24	1	1	21	18	2.63
1965	Cardinals	15	25	0	0	21	8	2.52
1966	Tulsa	19	128	9	5	108	54	3.59
1966	Cardinals	9	52	3	3	25	18	3.12
1967	Cardinals	30	193	14	9	168	62	2.98
1968	Cardinals	34	232	13	11	162	61	2.99
1969	Cardinals	31	236	17	11	210	93	2.17
1970	Cardinals	34	254	10	19	193	109	3.72
1971	Cardinals	37	273	20	9	172	98	3.56
1972	Phillies	41	346	27	10	310	87	1.98
Maj. Lg. Tot.		231	1611	104	72	1261	536	2.86

★ⒸT.C.G., PRTD. IN U.S.A.

John Denver sang, "Sunshine on My Shoulder." That's the clue to discovering this counterfeit. In rescreening the photo, the vertical stripes of Carlton's uniform were burned out in the right shoulder area and above the number "32" on the counterfeit. Under magnification, those lines are visible on a genuine card.

One of the "Quebec counterfeits" this may show some of the traits found on others among the 50 fake Topps cards.

All were made by combining rescreened photos with painstakingly reproduced graphic elements of genuine cards.

Many of the counterfeits show random black ink streaks in various areas on the front, usually horizontally oriented.

The borders of these counterfeits often show a stray overspray of color, especially near the edges.

All the fakes are within weight tolerances of genuine contemporary cards.

Some of the counterfeits, by accident or design, are cut off-center, like Topps cards of the era, though many of the fakes are not cut to exactly correct size.

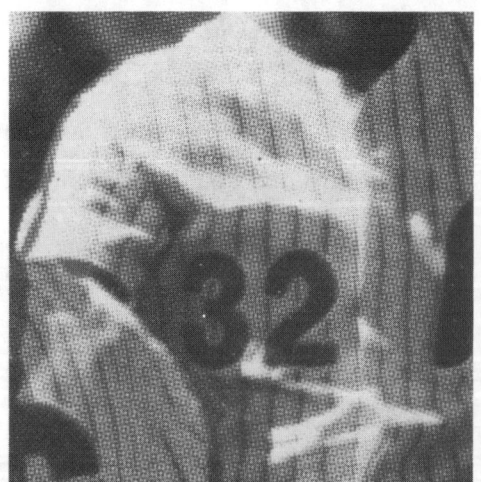

Genuine

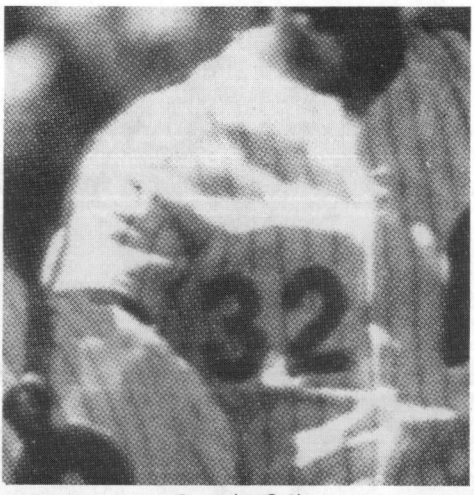

Counterfeit

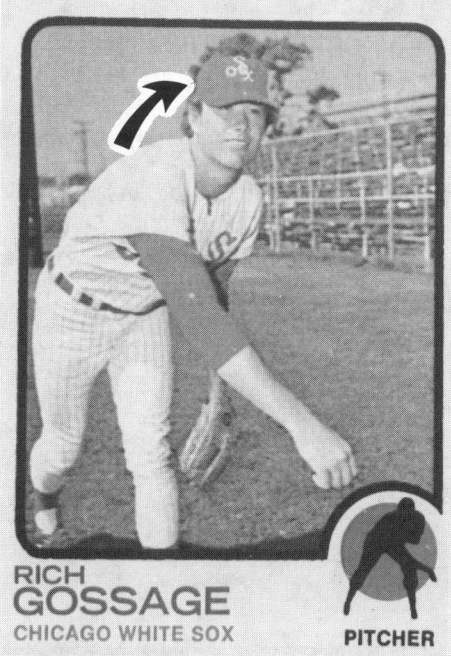

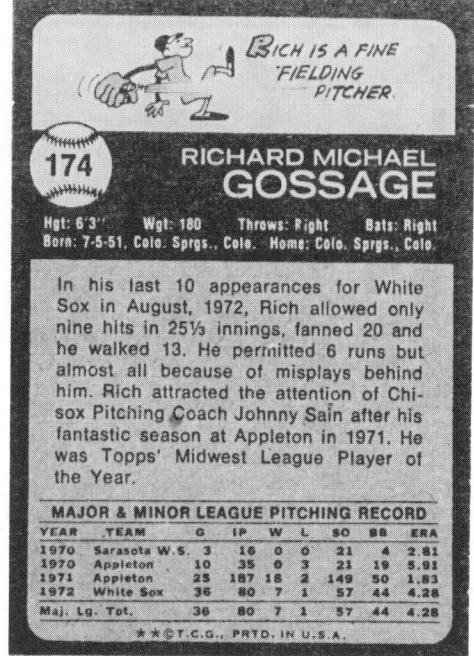

RICHARD MICHAEL
GOSSAGE

Hgt: 6'3''   Wgt: 180   Throws: Right   Bats: Right
Born: 7-5-51, Colo. Sprgs., Colo.   Home: Colo. Sprgs., Colo.

In his last 10 appearances for White Sox in August, 1972, Rich allowed only nine hits in 25⅓ innings, fanned 20 and he walked 13. He permitted 6 runs but almost all because of misplays behind him. Rich attracted the attention of Chi-sox Pitching Coach Johnny Sain after his fantastic season at Appleton in 1971. He was Topps' Midwest League Player of the Year.

MAJOR & MINOR LEAGUE PITCHING RECORD

YEAR	TEAM	G	IP	W	L	SO	BB	ERA
1970	Sarasota W.S.	3	16	0	0	21	4	2.81
1970	Appleton	10	35	0	3	21	19	5.91
1971	Appleton	25	187	18	2	149	50	1.83
1972	White Sox	36	80	7	1	57	44	4.28
Maj. Lg. Tot.		36	80	7	1	57	44	4.28

★★©T.C.G., PRTD. IN U.S.A.

A printing flaw on the genuine card from which the photo was rescreened for this counterfeit gives it away. The fake exhibits a rather large yellow "donut" on the player's cap, just to the left of the "O" in "SOX".

One of the "Quebec counterfeits" this card may exhibit some of the other common traits found among the 50 fake 1972-1980 Topps cards.

All were made by combining rescreened photos with painstakingly reproduced graphic elements of genuine cards.

Many of the counterfeits show random black ink streaks in various areas on the front, usually horizontally oriented.

The borders of these counterfeits often show a stray overspray of color, especially near the edges.

All the fakes are within weight tolerances of genuine contemporary cards.

Some of the counterfeits, by accident or design, are cut off-center, like Topps cards of the era, though many of the fakes are not cut to exactly correct size.

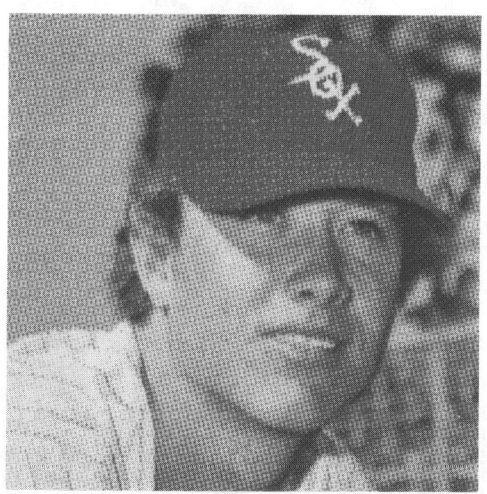

Genuine

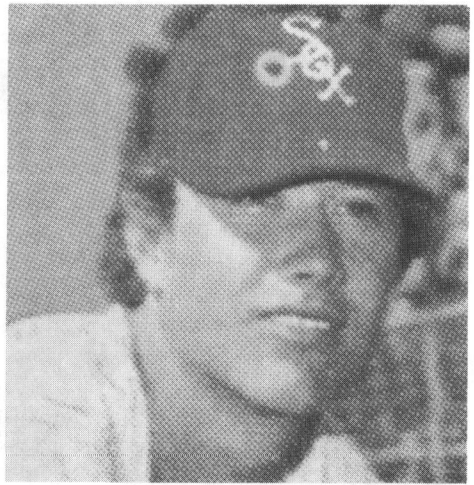

Counterfeit

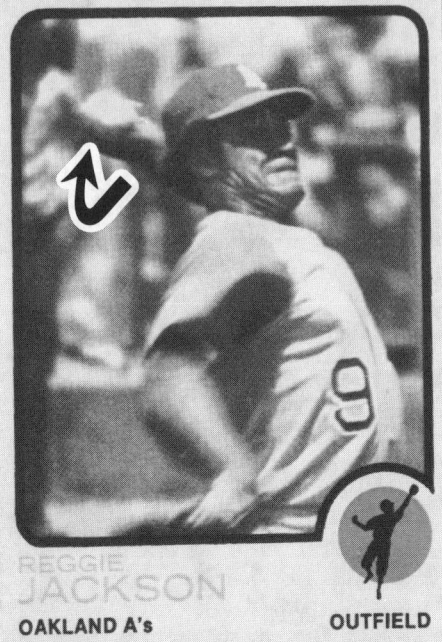

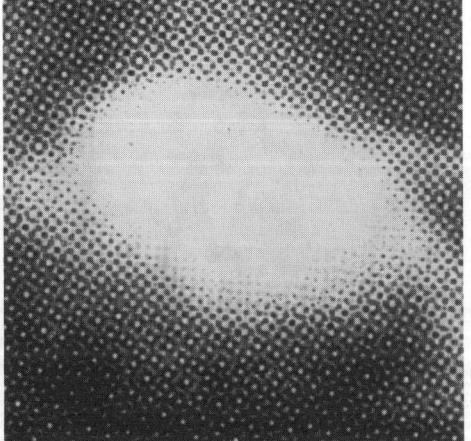

A lack of printer's dots in the areas of the baseball and the "A" of the cap, giving them a too-white appearance can be used to distinguish this counterfeit.

One of the "Quebec counterfeits" — a group of 50 Topps baseball cards first discovered in that Canadian city in late summer 1992, this counterfeit will likely exhibit a number of common traits.

All the counterfeits were made by a process combining rescreened photos with painstakingly reproduced graphic elements of genuine cards.

Many of the counterfeits show random black ink streaks in various areas on the front, usually horizontally oriented.

The borders of these counterfeits often show a stray overspray of color, especially near the edges.

All of the counterfeits are within normal weight tolerances of genuine contemporary Topps cards.

Some of the counterfeits, by accident or design, are cut off-center, like Topps cards of the era, though many of the fakes are not cut to the correct size.

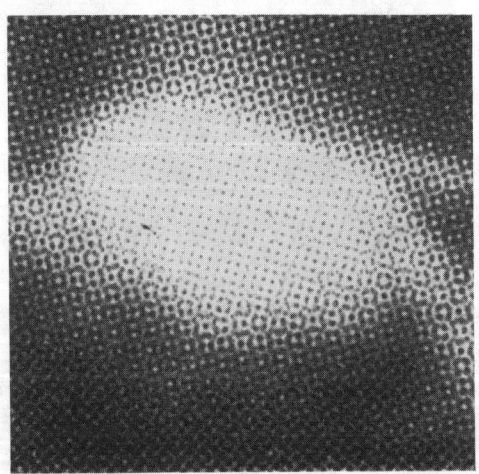

Genuine

Counterfeit

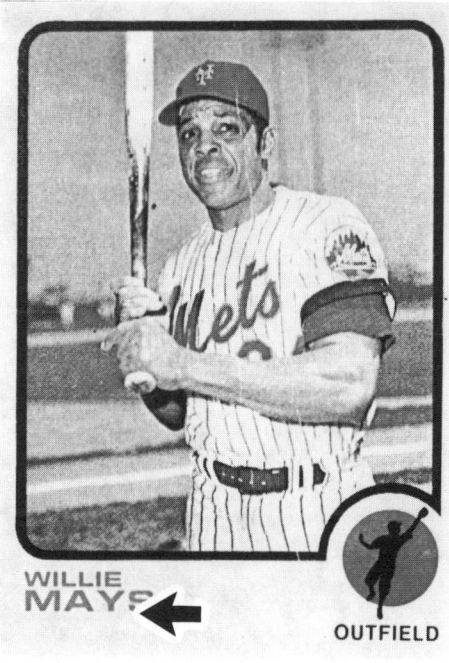

WILLIE
MAYS

OUTFIELD

This card is one of a group of eight 1971-1973 Topps baseball cards that surfaced in Southern California around 1982.

Unlike virtually every other counterfeit, the persons responsible for production of this group did not simply photo-reproduce the existing typography on the genuine cards, but rather had most of it — front and back — reset. The noticeable differences in size and shape of type which resulted make this group of counterfeits fairly easy to spot.

This counterfeit Mays card is the easiest of the group to identify because the counterfeits forgot to include the team name at the lower left corner of the card's front.

On the back, the counterfeit exhibits much smaller type in the statistics than on a genuine card. The copyright symbol (©) is also missing from the fake. On a genuine card, it will appear before the copyright line at the bottom of the card's back.

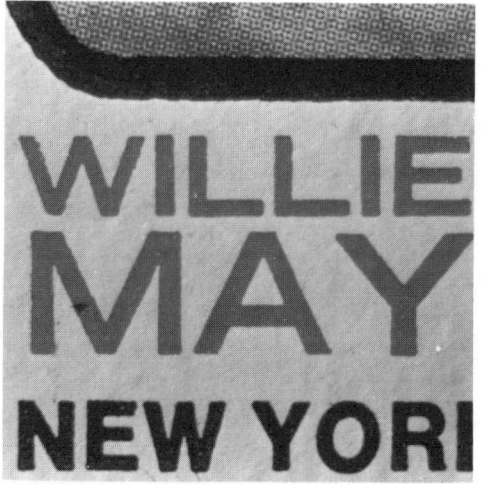

Genuine

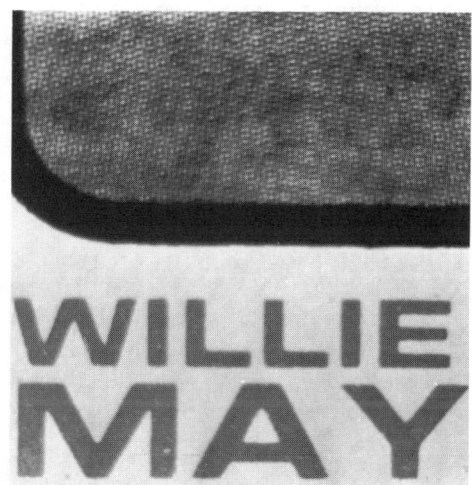

Counterfeit

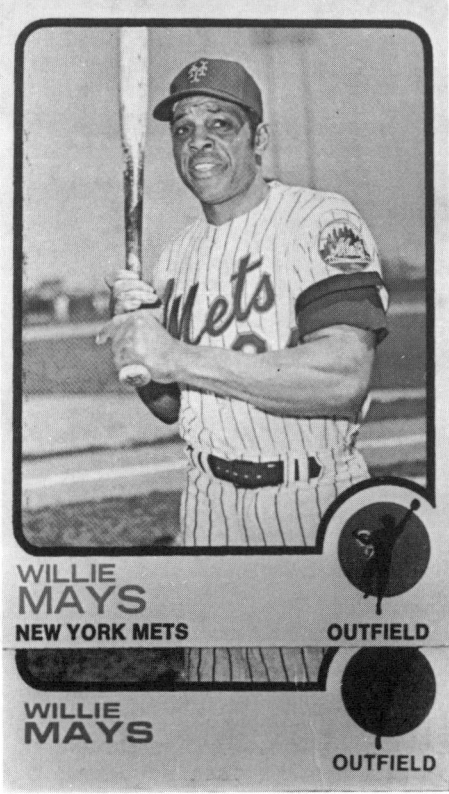
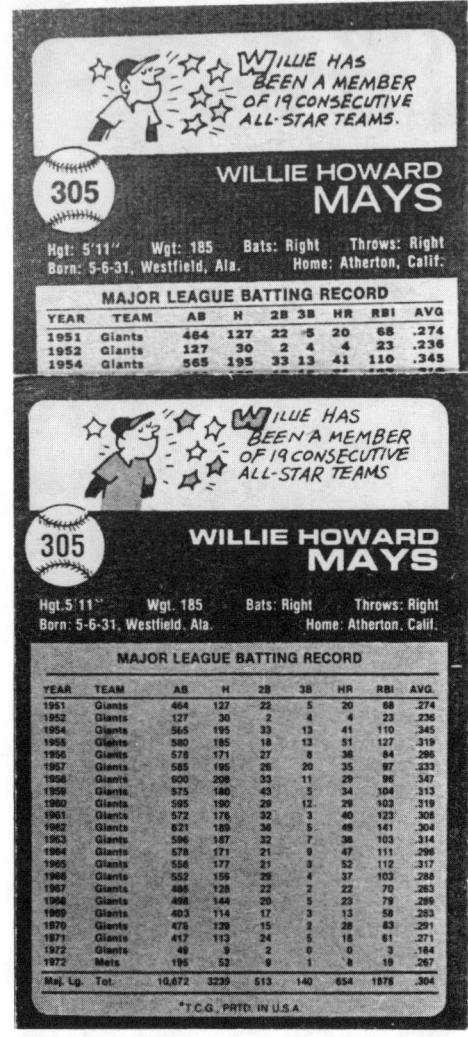

The counterfeiter of a group of early 1970s Topps star cards took the unusual step of resetting the type on the front and back of the cards, in styles and sizes slightly different from the genuine cards. Note on the front of the Willie Mays counterfeit (bottom left), the team name was omitted. The stats on the back of the counterfeit (bottom right) are much smaller than on the original.

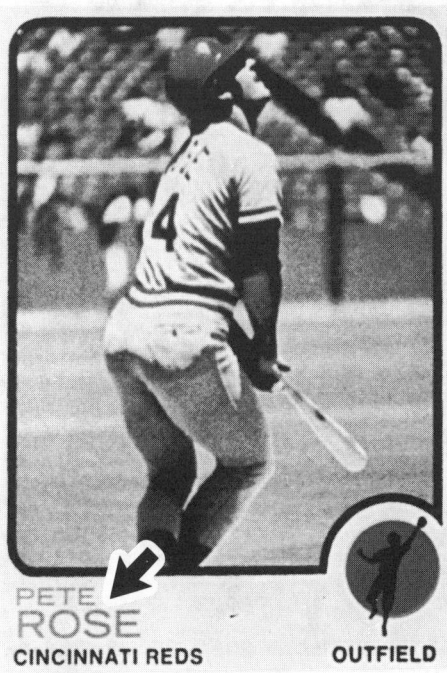

PETE
ROSE
CINCINNATI REDS   **OUTFIELD**

PETE ATTENDED THE
SAME HIGH SCHOOL
AS TIGERS'
ED BRINKMAN!

130

PETER EDWARD
ROSE

Hgt: 5'11"   Wgt: 195   Bats: Both   Throws: Right
Born: 4-14-41, Cincinnati, Ohio   Home: Cincinnati, Ohio

Pete narrowly missed reaching the 200
hit plateau for 6th time in career last season. Still he led both leagues in Hits and
continued to be one of the finest leadoff
men.

MAJOR & MINOR LEAGUE BATTING RECORD								
YEAR	TEAM	AB	H	2B	3B	HR	RBI	AVG
1960	Geneva	321	89	8	5	1	43	.277
1961	Tampa	484	160	20	30	2	77	.331
1962	Macon	540	178	21	17	9	71	.330
1963	Reds	623	170	25	9	6	41	.273
1964	Reds	516	139	13	2	4	34	.269
1965	Reds	670	209	35	11	11	81	.312
1966	Reds	654	205	38	5	16	70	.313
1967	Reds	585	176	32	8	12	76	.301
1968	Reds	626	210	42	6	10	49	.335
1969	Reds	627	218	33	11	16	82	.348
1970	Reds	649	205	37	9	15	52	.316
1971	Reds	632	192	27	4	13	44	.304
1972	Reds	645	198	31	11	6	57	.307
Maj. Lg. Tot.		6227	1922	313	76	109	586	.309

Reprint *©T.C.G., PRTD. IN U.S.A.

The fuzzy photo and lettering on the
front of this counterfeit should put most
hobbyists on notice that more detailed
examination is needed.

Using a magnifying glass to examine the
lettering will provide definite proof that
this card is a phony. On a genuine card,
such details as the player and team
names and position should appear as solid
letters with edges that end crisply and
cleanly at the white background. On this
counterfeit, the letters are composed of
many tiny color dots, giving them a ragged look at the edges. The back is likewise
not very deceptive. The black lettering is
fuzzy and close examination will show a
pattern of black and yellow dots has been
printed on the white cardboard to simulate the genuine Topps card stock.

The black "Reprint" which appears on
the back of the card shown here may not
be present on all cards offered for prospective purchase.

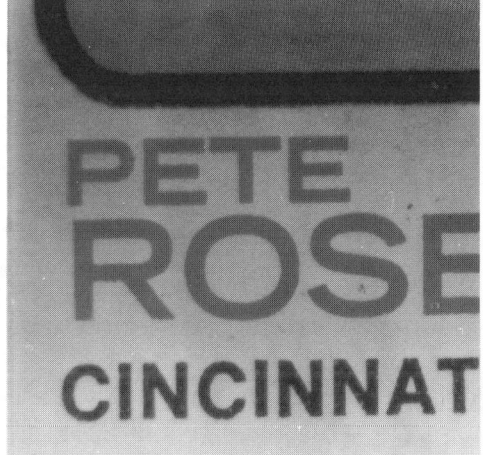

Genuine

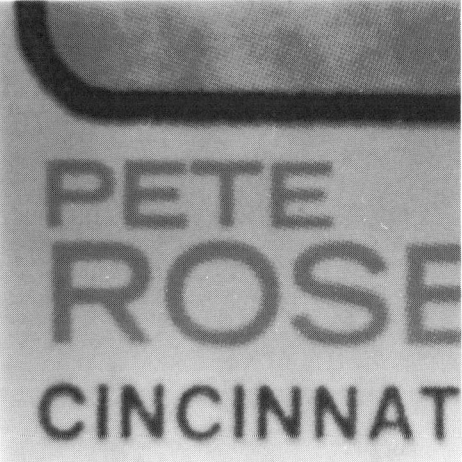

Counterfeit

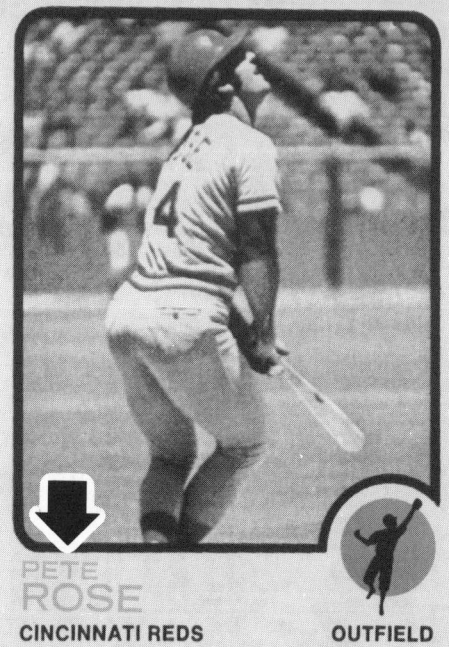

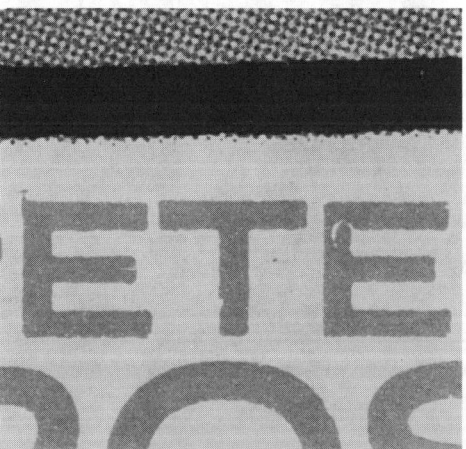

Detailed examination of the blue "E"s in "PETE" will reveal this counterfeit. The first has a "cowlick" streak of ink rising from the vertical bar, while the second shows a tiny white crescent in the vertical bar, midway between the top and middle horizontal bars.

One of the "Quebec counterfeits" this may exhibit a number of traits common to many of the 50 fake Topps cards which were the work of the same counterfeiter.

All were made by combining rescreened photos with painstakingly reproduced graphic elements of genuine cards.

Many of the counterfeits show random black ink streaks in various areas on the front, usually horizontally oriented.

The borders of these counterfeits often show a stray overspray of color, especially near the edges.

All the fakes are within weight tolerances of genuine contemporary cards.

Some of the counterfeits, by accident or design, are cut off-center, like Topps cards of the era, though many of the fakes are not cut to exactly correct size.

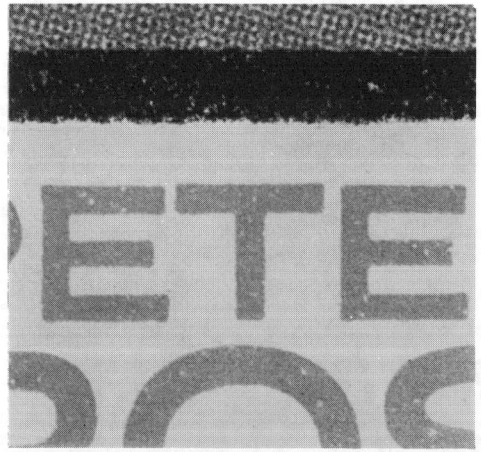

Genuine

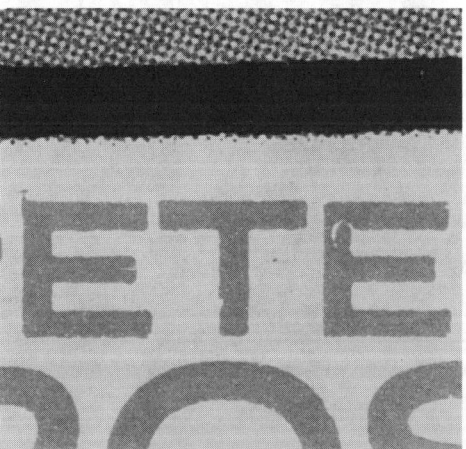

Counterfeit

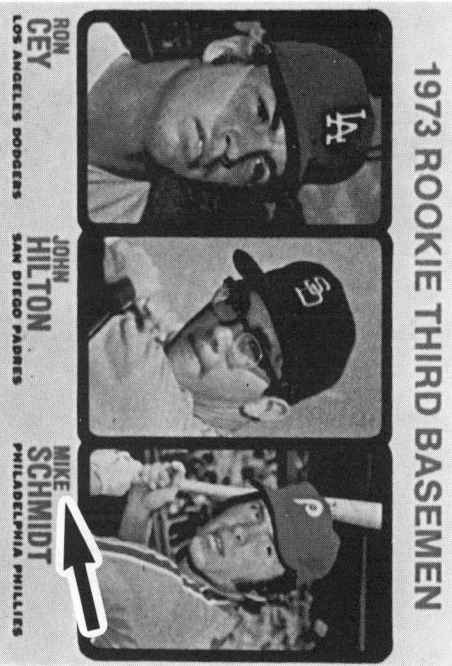

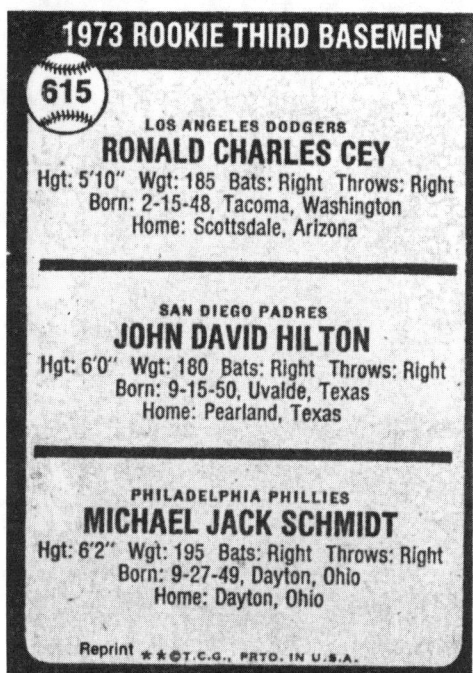

An overall fuzzy appearance of the player photos and front lettering makes this counterfeit look suspicious at first glance. Examination of the design details with a magnifying glass reveals sure evidence of the counterfeit's status.

Easy differentiation between real and fake on this card can be made by examining the player and team names. Those letters on a genuine card will be clean, solid blue (name) or black (team) letters. On the counterfeit, they are composed of many dots, giving a fuzzy appearance.

Similar evidence can be seen in the black frames around the player's photos and in "1973 ROOKIE THIRD BASEMEN" at top.

On back, a black and yellow dot pattern has been printed to simulate the cardboard of a Topps original and hide the white cardboard on which the fake was printed.

The black "Reprint" which appears on the back of the card shown here may not be present on all cards encountered in the hobby market.

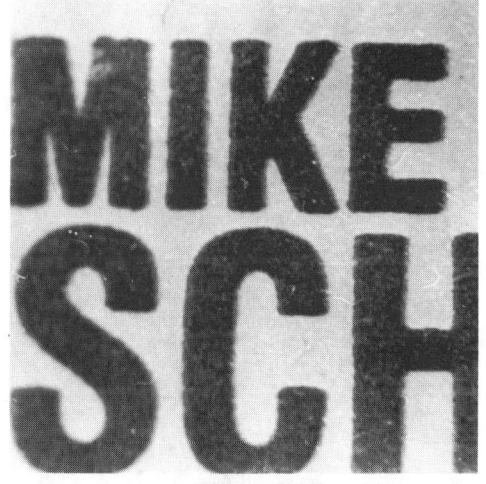

Genuine

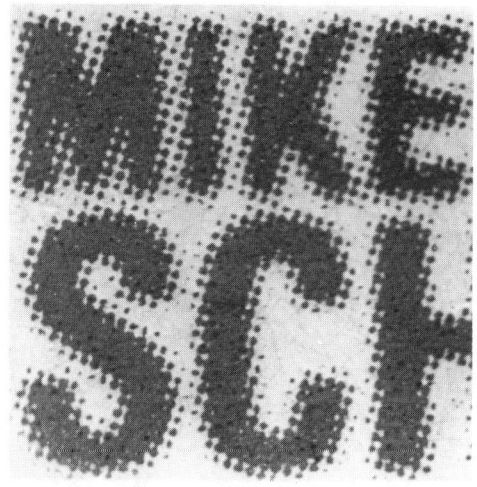

Counterfeit

No photo available

No photo available

No specimen has yet been made available for examination and photography.

According to a May 15, 1983, article in *Baseball Card News*, this card is one of a group of eight 1971-1973 Topps baseball cards that were apparently produced by the same hand. The fakes surfaced in Southern California but then, as now, were rarely seen in the hobby market.

Unlike virtually every other counterfeit, the persons responsible for production of this group did not ·simply photo-reproduce the existing typography on the genuine cards, but rather had most of it — front and back — reset. The noticeable differences in size and shape of type which resulted make this group of counterfeits fairly easy to spot.

An even more noticeable difference between the cards in this group and genuine Topps cards is that (with the exception of this 1973 Schmidt rookie) all of the fakes have omitted the Topps copyright symbol (©) before the copyright line on the back of the card.

No photo available

No photo available

Genuine

Counterfeit

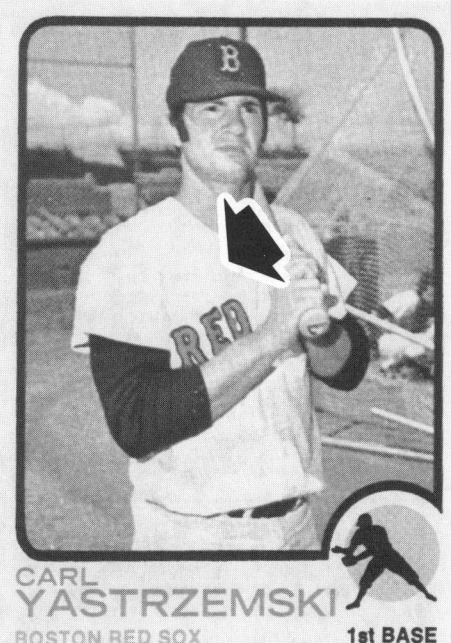

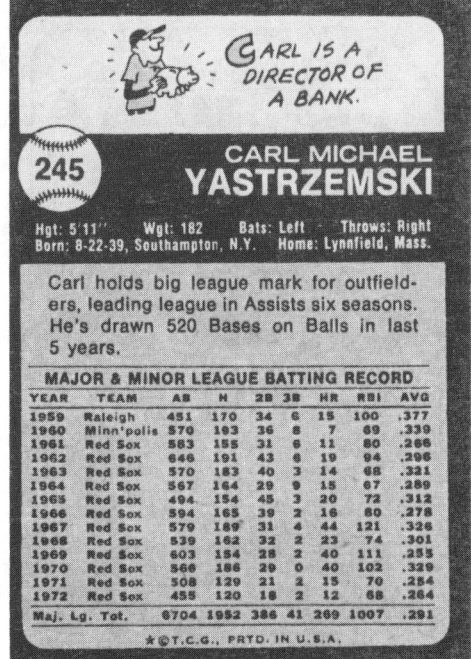

This counterfeit exhibits an area of yellowish-brown "dirt" from the top uniform button to the right shoulder. Possibly a gum stain on the genuine card from which the fake's photo was rescreened, this patch of dirty uniform is not found on genuine cards.

One of the "Quebec counterfeits" this card may exhibit some of the other common traits found among the 50 fake 1972-1980 Topps cards.

All were made by combining rescreened photos with painstakingly reproduced graphic elements of genuine cards.

Many of the counterfeits show random black ink streaks in various areas on the front, usually horizontally oriented.

The borders of these counterfeits often show a stray overspray of color, especially near the edges.

All the fakes are within weight tolerances of genuine contemporary cards.

Some of the counterfeits, by accident or design, are cut off-center, like Topps cards of the era, though many of the fakes are not cut to exactly correct size.

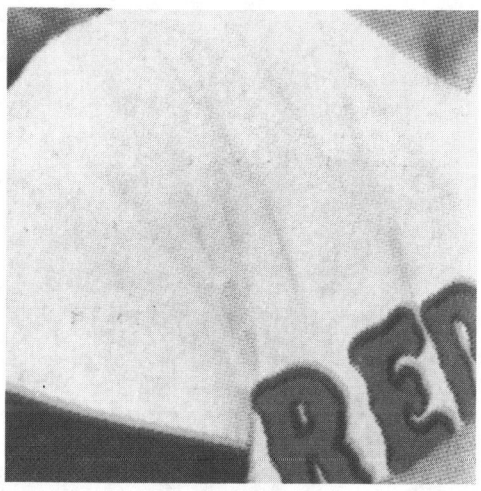

Genuine

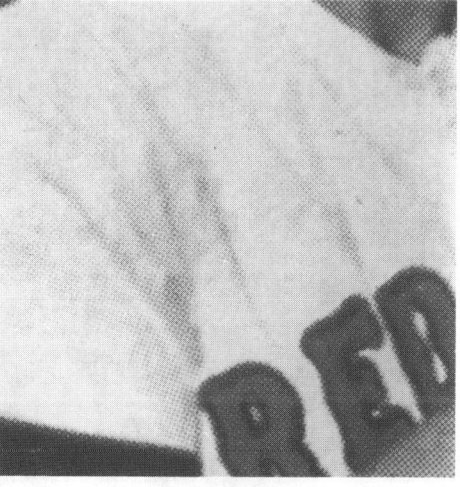

Counterfeit

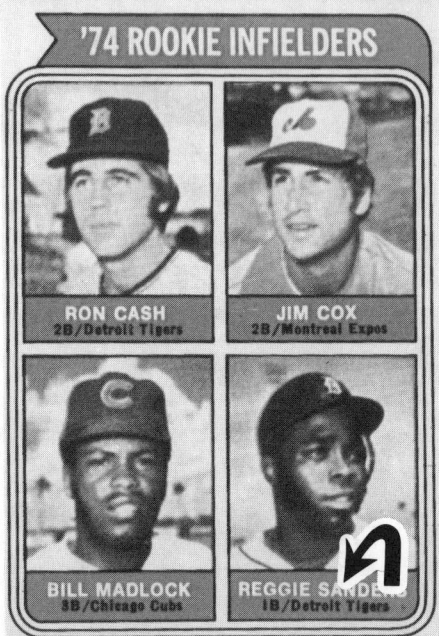

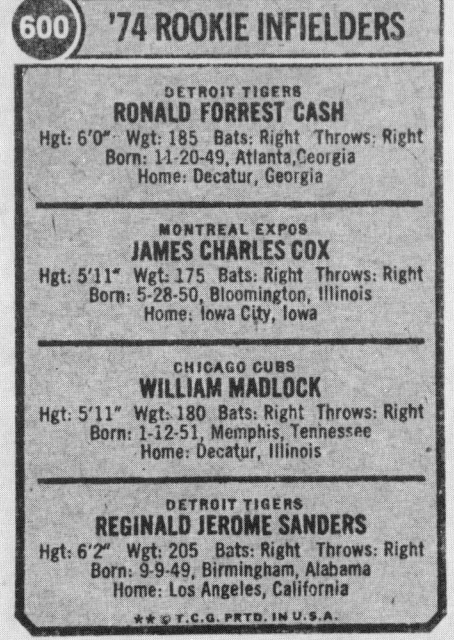

Reproduction of the smallest type on the front — the team names — is not good on this counterfeit. This is especially true on the "g"'s, where, under magnification, there is little or no definition of the lower loop, and "i"'s, where the dot is often joined to the base. This is one of the "Quebec counterfeits" and may exhibit some of the other common traits found among the 50 fake 1972-1980 Topps cards.

All were made by combining rescreened photos with painstakingly reproduced graphic elements of genuine cards.

Many of the counterfeits show random black ink streaks in various areas on the front, usually horizontally oriented.

The borders of these counterfeits often show a stray overspray of color, especially near the edges.

All the fakes are within weight tolerances of genuine contemporary cards.

Some of the counterfeits, by accident or design, are cut off-center, like Topps cards of the era, though many of the fakes are not cut to exactly correct size.

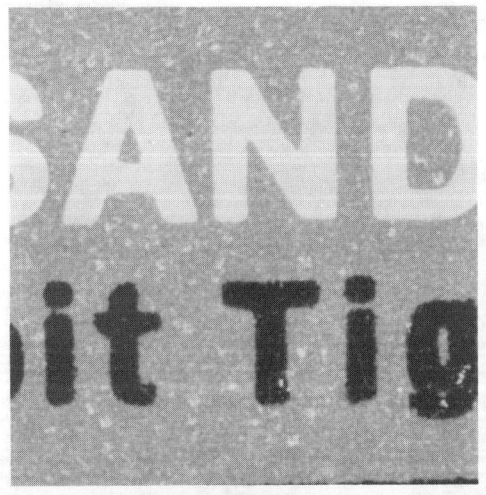

Genuine

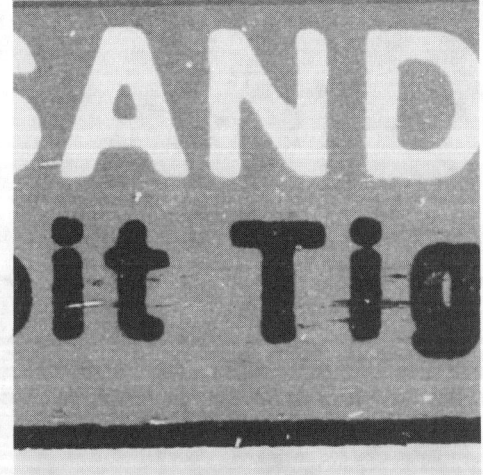

Counterfeit

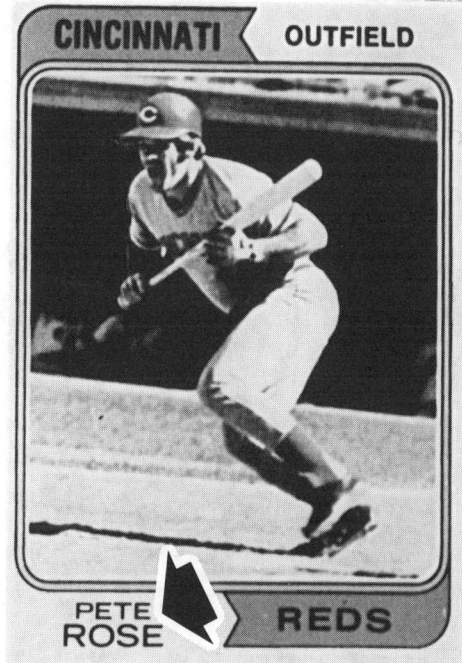

The fuzzy photo and lettering on the front of this counterfeit should put most hobbyists on notice that more detailed examination is needed.

Using a magnifying glass to examine the lettering will provide definite proof that this card is a phony. On a genuine card, such details as the black borders of the orange frame line, the player's name, team and position and the red banners should appear as solid colors with edges that end crisply and cleanly at the respective backgrounds. On this counterfeit, the letters and other color design elements are composed of many tiny color dots, giving them a ragged look at the edges. The back is likewise not very deceptive. The black lettering is fuzzy and close examination shows a pattern of black dots printed on the white cardboard to simulate the genuine Topps card stock.

The black "Reprint" which appears on the back of the card shown here may not be present on all cards offered for prospective purchase.

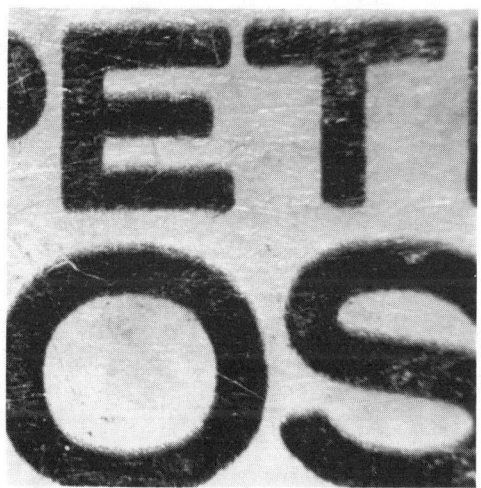

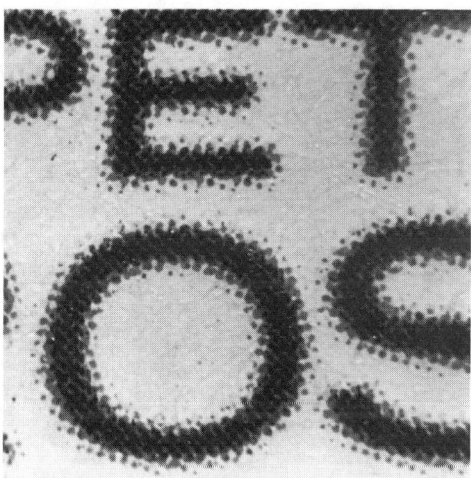

Genuine   **Counterfeit**

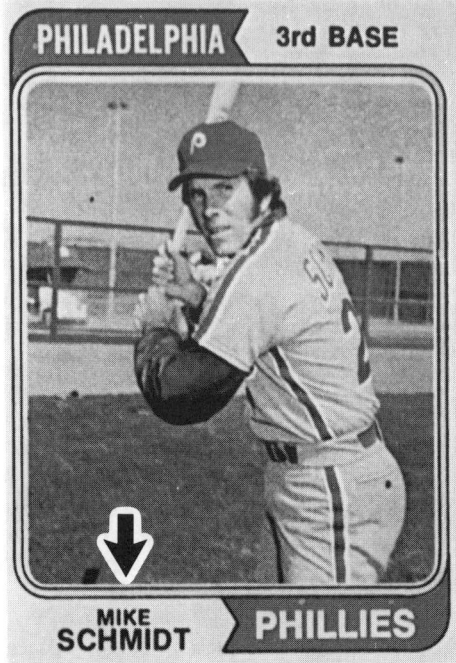
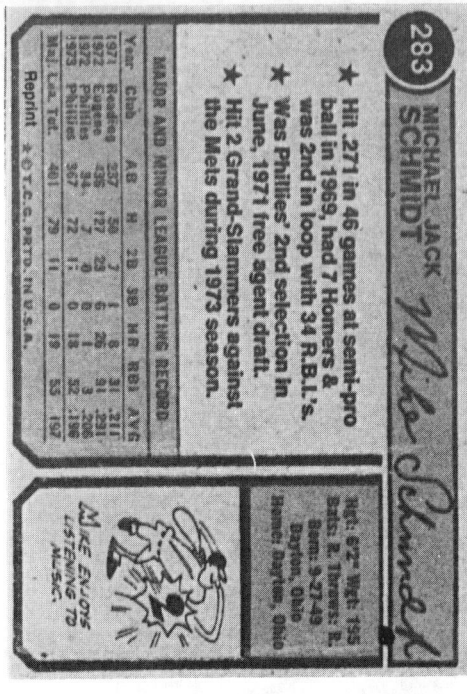

An overall fuzziness of appearance on the front of this counterfeit was created by the re-screening of design elements to create printing materials for the counterfeit.

The result is that elements that should be composed of solid black letters and lines have been reproduced on the counterfeit as a composite of tiny color dots. This is especially noticeable in the black frame lines around the photo and team name flags, and in the player's name and position.

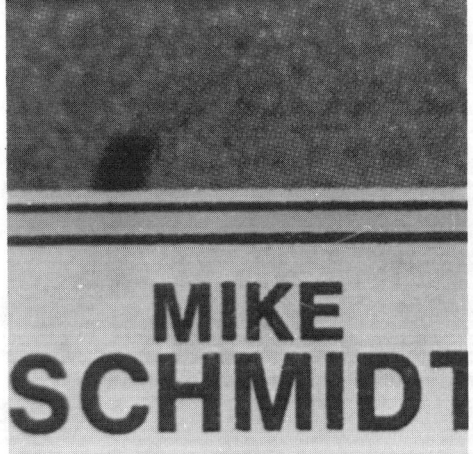

Genuine

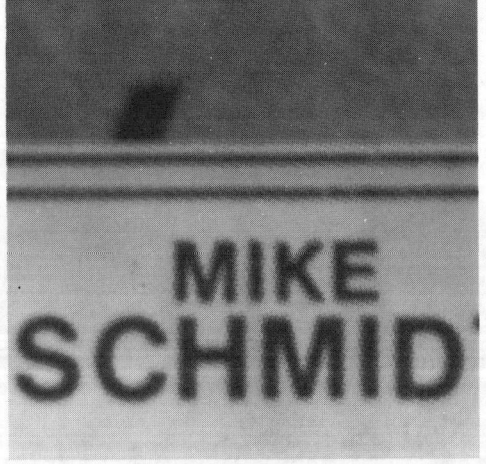

Counterfeit

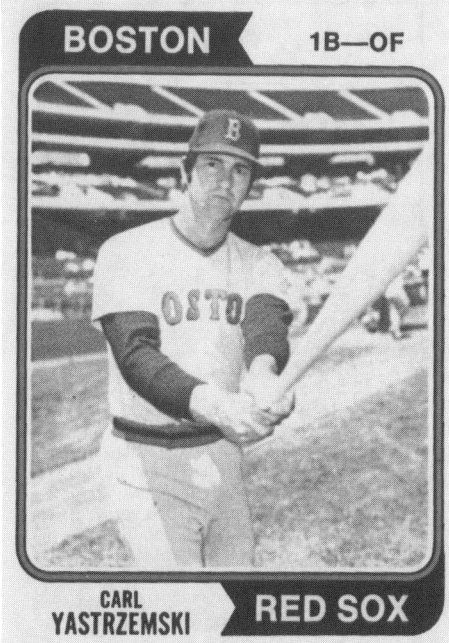

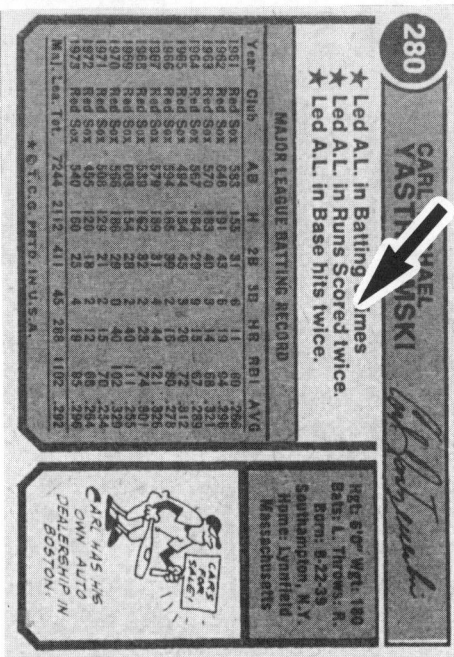

One of the most deceptive of the "Quebec counterfeits," this card is best exposed by a flaw on the back printing. The counterfeit exhibits a broken top loop of the "d" in "Scored" in the middle line of career highlights printed above the stats box. The tiny stats are also noticeably muddier on the counterfeit. This card may exhibit some of the other common traits found among the 50 fake 1972-1980 Topps cards.

All were made by combining rescreened photos with painstakingly reproduced graphic elements of genuine cards.

Many of the counterfeits show random black ink streaks in various areas on the front, usually horizontally oriented.

The borders of these counterfeits often show a stray overspray of color, especially near the edges.

All the fakes are within weight tolerances of genuine contemporary cards.

Some of the counterfeits, by accident or design, are cut off-center, like Topps cards of the era, though many of the fakes are not cut to exactly correct size.

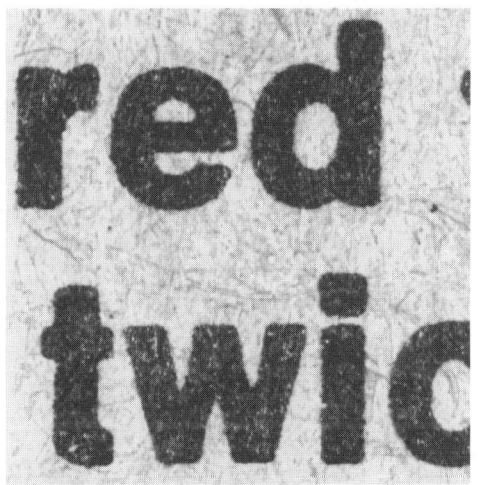

Genuine

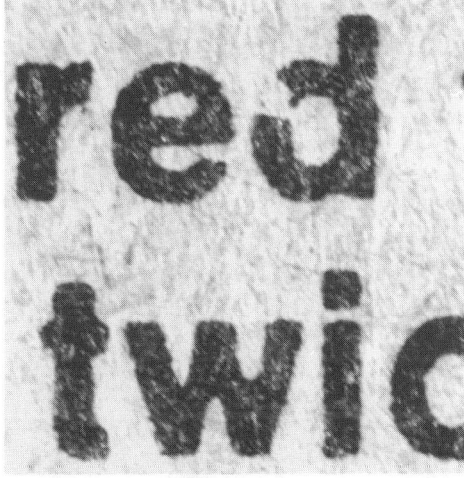

Counterfeit

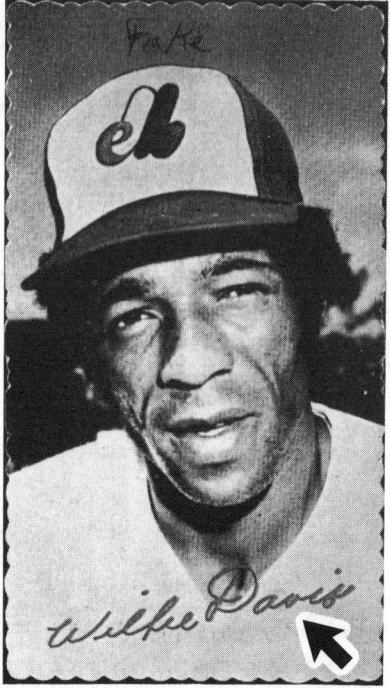

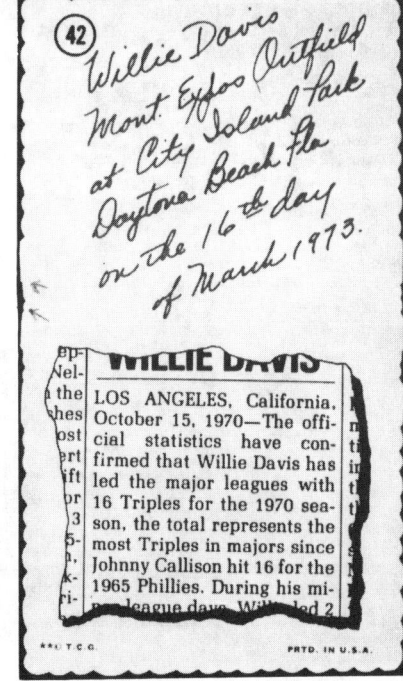

Original cards of this test issue are so scarce that most hobbyists have never seen one. It should be assumed that each of the 72 large-format (2⅞x5″) cards in the issue was counterfeited, though not all have been seen to date.

Generally, the counterfeits can be seen to have a much grayer appearance than the genuine black-and-white cards, lacking much of the contrast. This is caused by the counterfeit having a black dot structure to the photo that is much heavier than the genuine.

The easiest method of distinguishing the counterfeit '74 deckles from the genuine cards is to examine the area of the blue facsimile signature on the front of the card. The counterfeits have a black "shadow" of dots visible under magnification beneath the signature. This is not present on genuine cards.

The word "Fake" which was penned on the front of the card shown here will not be present on cards encountered in the hobby market.

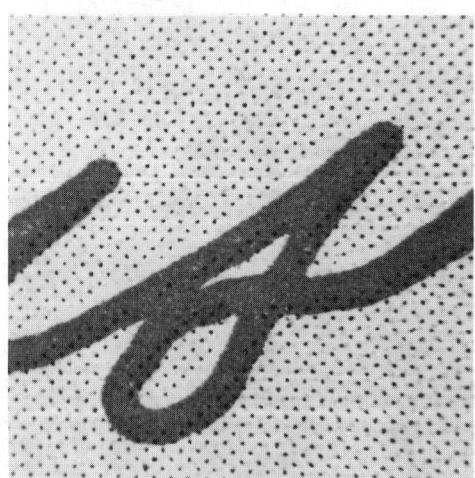

Genuine

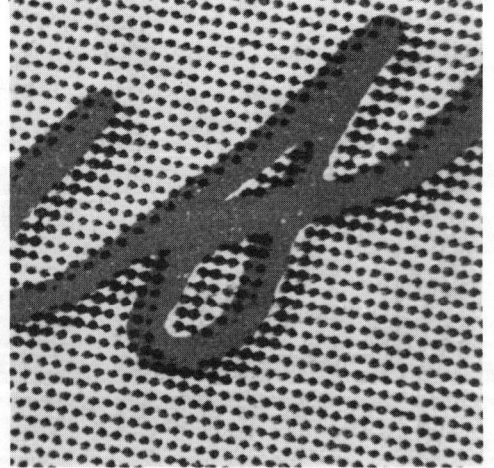

Counterfeit

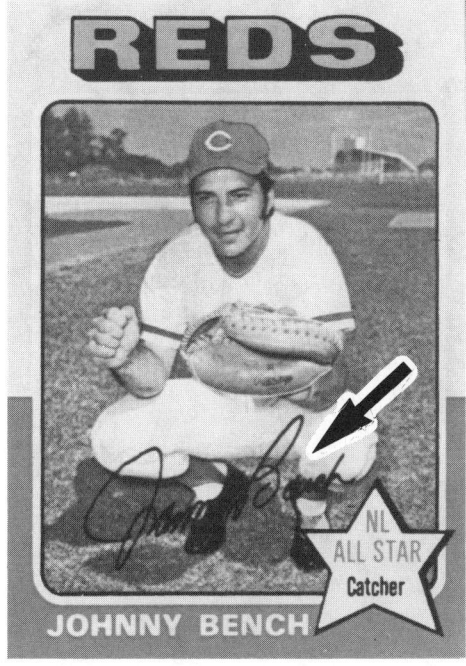

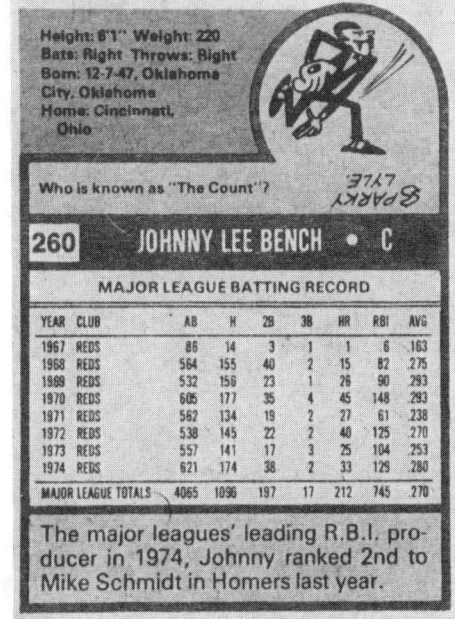

Height: 6'1" Weight: 220
Bats: Right Throws: Right
Born: 12-7-47, Oklahoma
City, Oklahoma
Home: Cincinnati,
Ohio

Who is known as "The Count"? SPARKY LYLE

260	JOHNNY LEE BENCH • C						
MAJOR LEAGUE BATTING RECORD							
YEAR CLUB	AB	H	2B	3B	HR	RBI	AVG
1967 REDS	86	14	3	1	1	6	.163
1968 REDS	564	155	40	2	15	82	.275
1969 REDS	532	156	23	1	26	90	.293
1970 REDS	605	177	35	4	45	148	.293
1971 REDS	562	134	19	2	27	61	.238
1972 REDS	538	145	22	2	40	125	.270
1973 REDS	557	141	17	3	25	104	.253
1974 REDS	621	174	38	2	33	129	.280
MAJOR LEAGUE TOTALS	4065	1096	197	17	212	745	.270

The major leagues' leading R.B.I. producer in 1974, Johnny ranked 2nd to Mike Schmidt in Homers last year.

★ © 1975 TOPPS CHEWING GUM, INC. PRTD IN U.S.A.

Examination of the facsimile autograph with a magnifying glass will identify this counterfeit. The rescreened counterfeit card will show the autograph composed of many tiny dots, giving it a fuzzy appearance. On a genuine card, the autograph will be made up of clean solid black lines.

One of the "Quebec counterfeits" this card may exhibit some of the other common traits found among the 50 fake 1972-1980 Topps cards.

All were made by combining rescreened photos with painstakingly reproduced graphic elements of genuine cards.

Many of the counterfeits show random black ink streaks in various areas on the front, usually horizontally oriented.

The borders of these counterfeits often show a stray overspray of color, especially near the edges.

All the fakes are within weight tolerances of genuine contemporary cards.

Some of the counterfeits, by accident or design, are cut off-center, like Topps cards of the era, though many of the fakes are not cut to exactly correct size.

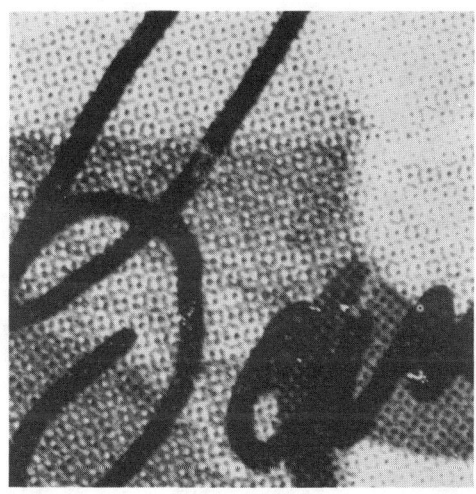

Genuine

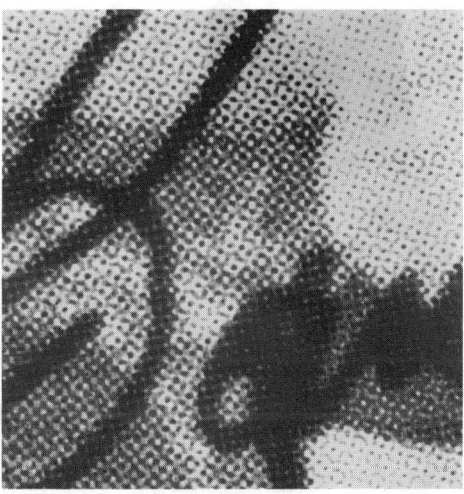

Counterfeit

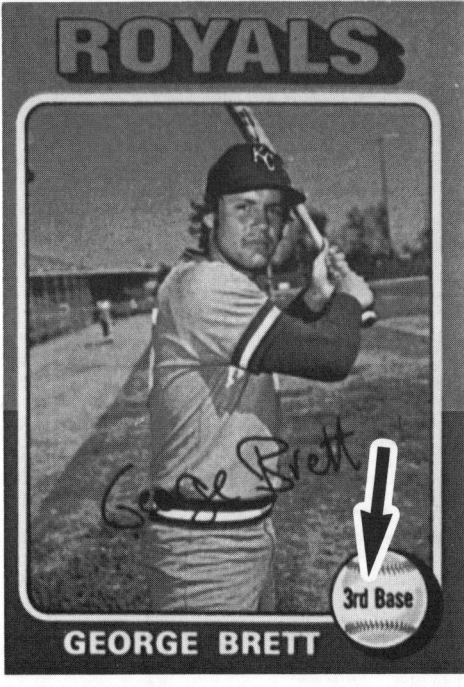

GEORGE BRETT

Height: 6'0" Weight: 190
Bats: Left Throws: Right
Born: 5-15-53, Wheeling, West Virginia
Home: Hermosa Beach, California

What is it called when a batter bunts to score runner?

228　　GEORGE HOWARD BRETT • 3B

MAJOR AND MINOR LEAGUE BATTING RECORD

YEAR	CLUB	AB	H	2B	3B	HR	RBI	AVG
1971	BILLINGS	258	75	8	5	5	44	.291
1972	SAN JOSE	431	118	13	5	10	68	.274
1973	OMAHA	405	115	16	4	8	64	.284
1973	ROYALS	40	5	2	0	0	0	.125
1974	OMAHA	64	17	2	0	2	14	.266
1974	ROYALS	457	129	20	5	2	47	.282
MAJOR LEAGUE TOTALS		497	134	22	5	2	47	.270

One of A.L.'s fine rookies of 1974, George was named A.A.'s All-Star 3rd baseman for 1973. He led California League with 8 Sacrifice Hits in 1972.

* © 1975 TOPPS CHEWING GUM, INC. PRTD IN U.S.A.
Reprint

Hobbyists who are familiar with the genuine Brett rookie card might be immediately suspicious of this counterfeit based on a generally poor ability to mimic the colors of the genuine card, especially in the area of the team name. Overall, the colors on front of the fake are not as bold as on the real thing. However, as the perception of color is subjective among individuals, and because even genuine cards can vary widely in the intensity or shade of color, it is never recommended to base an authenticity judgement on color alone.

Easy differentiation between real and fake on this card can be made by examining the ''3rd Base'' inside the ball at lower right. Those letters on a genuine card will be clean, solid black; on the counterfeit, they are composed of many dots, giving a fuzzy appearance.

The black ''Reprint'' which appears on the back of the card shown here may not be present on all cards encountered in the hobby market.

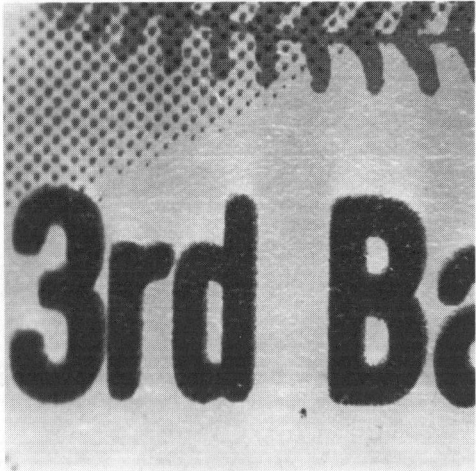

Genuine

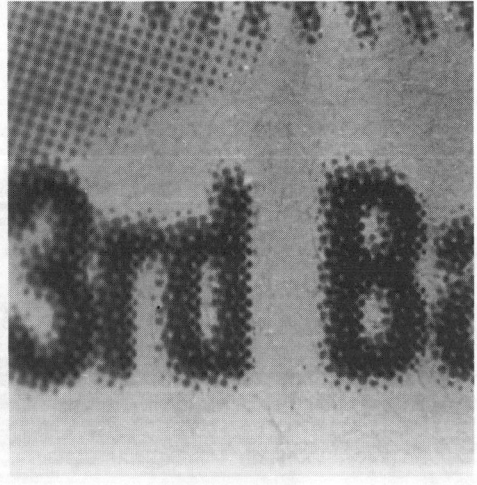

Counterfeit

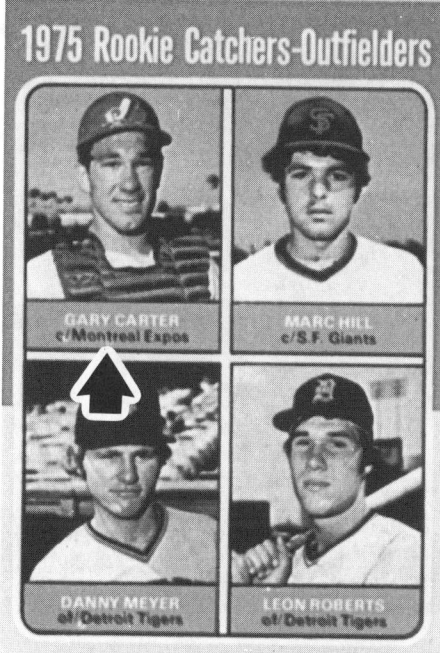

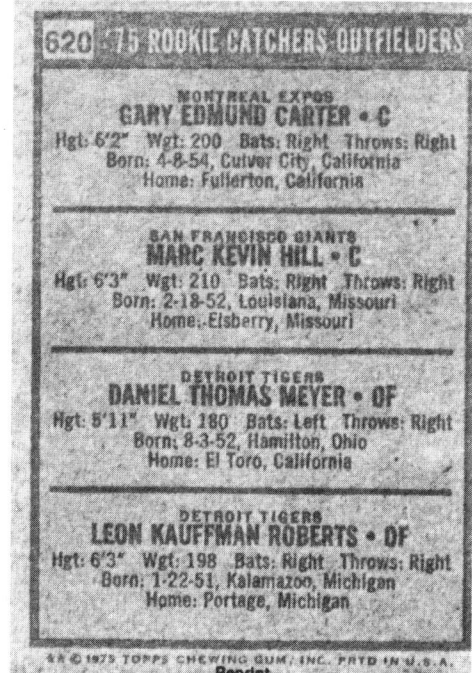

Because it is printed on thinner, whiter cardboard than the genuine 1975 Topps cards, and because the gloss on the front differs from that on a genuine card, an experienced hobbyist should be able to spot this counterfeit with relative ease.

The presence of dot structures where they should not be provides evidence against the counterfeit, but does require a magnifying glass to verify.

The players' names and teams are the best places to examine a suspect card. On a genuine card, these words will appear as clean, solid white (names) or black (teams) letters. The counterfeit shows these elements as being made up of many tiny dots.

Red and green ink used on the back to simulate gray cardboard gives the counterfeit's reverse a muddy appearance.

The black "Reprint" which appears on the back of the card photographed here may not be present on all cards encountered in the hobby market.

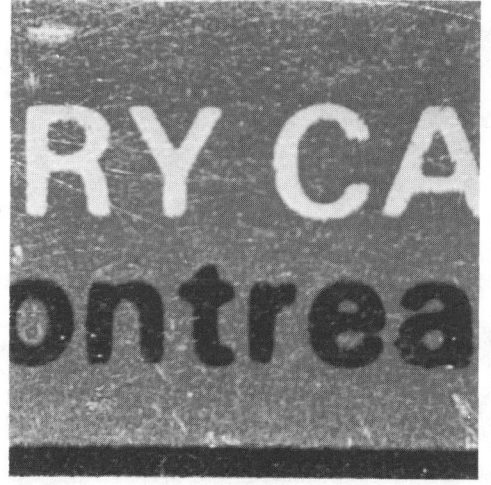

Genuine

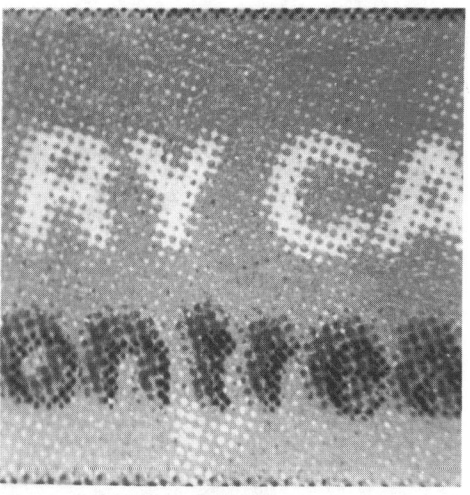

Counterfeit

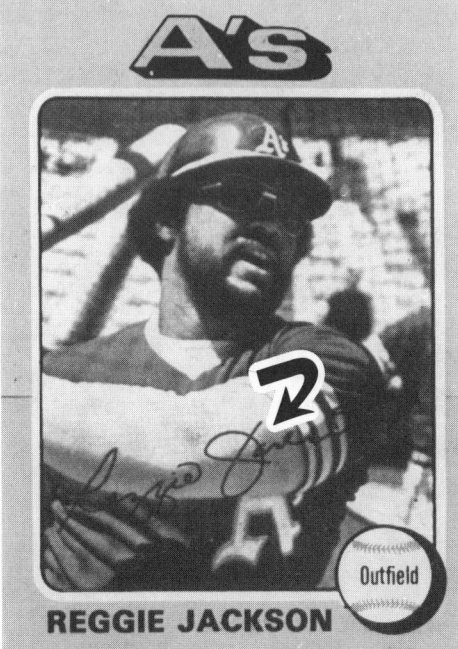

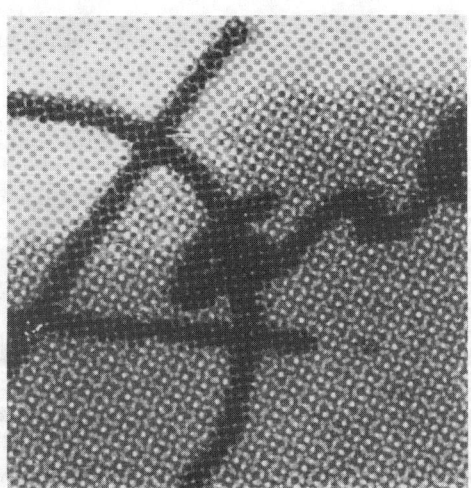

REGGIE JACKSON

Height: 6'0" Weight: 200
Bats: Left Throws: Left
Born: 5-18-46, Wyncote,
Pennsylvania
Home: Tempe,
Arizona

Who ran a squeeze play, in 1st
game of 1974 World Series?

BEAT CAMPANERIS

| 300 | REGINALD MARTINEZ JACKSON • OF |

MAJOR LEAGUE BATTING RECORD

YEAR	CLUB	AB	H	2B	3B	HR	RBI	AVG
1967	A's	118	21	4	4	1	6	.178
1968	A's	553	138	13	6	29	74	.250
1969	A's	549	151	36	3	47	118	.275
1970	A's	426	101	21	2	23	66	.237
1971	A's	567	157	29	3	32	80	.277
1972	A's	499	132	25	2	25	75	.265
1973	A's	539	158	28	2	32	117	.293
1974	A's	506	146	25	1	29	93	.289
MAJOR LEAGUE TOTALS		3757	1004	181	23	218	629	.267

The A.L.'s 2nd leading Homer hitter in
1974, Reggie's .514 Slugging Percentage was also 2nd best in loop.

** © 1975 TOPPS CHEWING GUM, INC. PRTD IN U.S.A.

Examination of the facsimile autograph with a magnifying glass will identify this counterfeit. The rescreened counterfeit card will show the autograph composed of many tiny dots, giving it a fuzzy appearance. On a genuine card, the autograph will be made up of clean solid black lines.

One of the "Quebec counterfeits" this card may exhibit some of the other common traits found among the 50 fake 1972-1980 Topps cards.

All were made by combining rescreened photos with painstakingly reproduced graphic elements of genuine cards.

Many of the counterfeits show random black ink streaks in various areas on the front, usually horizontally oriented.

The borders of these counterfeits often show a stray overspray of color, especially near the edges.

All the fakes are within weight tolerances of genuine contemporary cards.

Some of the counterfeits, by accident or design, are cut off-center, like Topps cards of the era, though many of the fakes are not cut to exactly correct size.

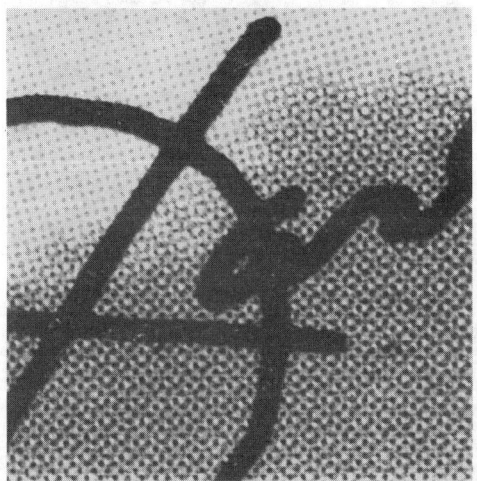

Genuine

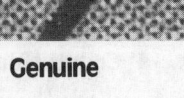

Counterfeit

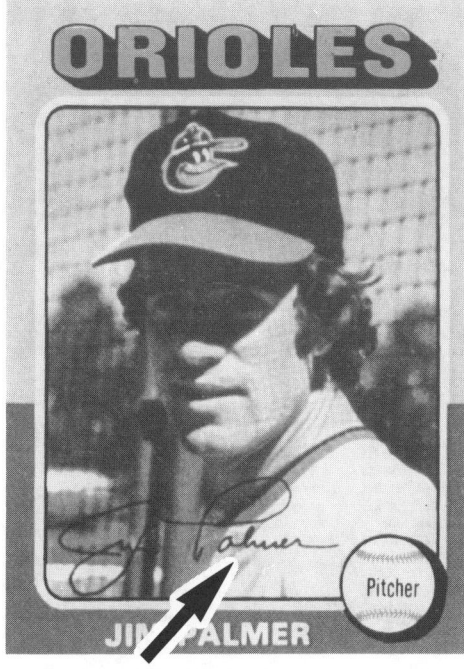

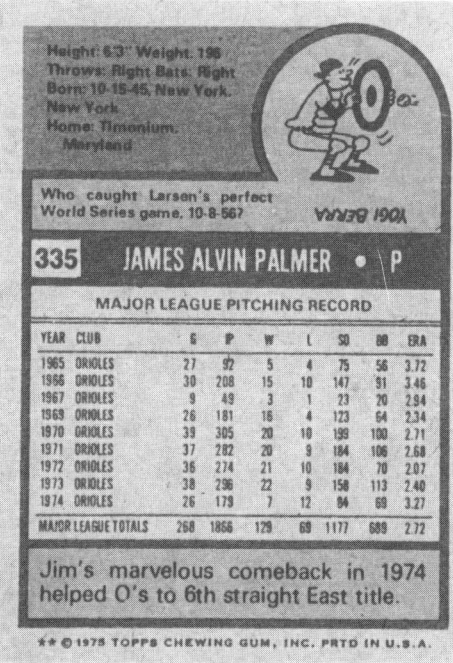

Height: 6'3" Weight: 196
Throws: Right Bats: Right
Born: 10-15-45, New York,
New York
Home: Timonium,
Maryland

Who caught Larsen's perfect
World Series game, 10-8-56?   YOGI BERRA 1951

335   JAMES ALVIN PALMER • P

MAJOR LEAGUE PITCHING RECORD

YEAR	CLUB	G	IP	W	L	SO	BB	ERA
1965	ORIOLES	27	92	5	4	75	56	3.72
1966	ORIOLES	30	208	15	10	147	91	3.46
1967	ORIOLES	9	49	3	1	23	20	2.94
1969	ORIOLES	26	181	16	4	123	64	2.34
1970	ORIOLES	39	305	20	10	199	100	2.71
1971	ORIOLES	37	282	20	9	184	106	2.68
1972	ORIOLES	36	274	21	10	184	70	2.07
1973	ORIOLES	38	296	22	9	158	113	2.40
1974	ORIOLES	26	179	7	12	84	69	3.27
MAJOR LEAGUE TOTALS		268	1866	129	69	1177	689	2.72

Jim's marvelous comeback in 1974
helped O's to 6th straight East title.

** © 1975 TOPPS CHEWING GUM, INC. PRTD IN U.S.A.

Examination of the facsimile autograph with a magnifying glass will identify this counterfeit. The rescreened counterfeit card will show the autograph composed of many tiny dots, giving it a fuzzy appearance. On a genuine card, the autograph will be made up of clean solid black lines.

One of the "Quebec counterfeits" this card may exhibit some of the other common traits found among the 50 fake 1972-1980 Topps cards.

All were made by combining rescreened photos with painstakingly reproduced graphic elements of genuine cards.

Many of the counterfeits show random black ink streaks in various areas on the front, usually horizontally oriented.

The borders of these counterfeits often show a stray overspray of color, especially near the edges.

All the fakes are within weight tolerances of genuine contemporary cards.

Some of the counterfeits, by accident or design, are cut off-center, like Topps cards of the era, though many of the fakes are not cut to exactly correct size.

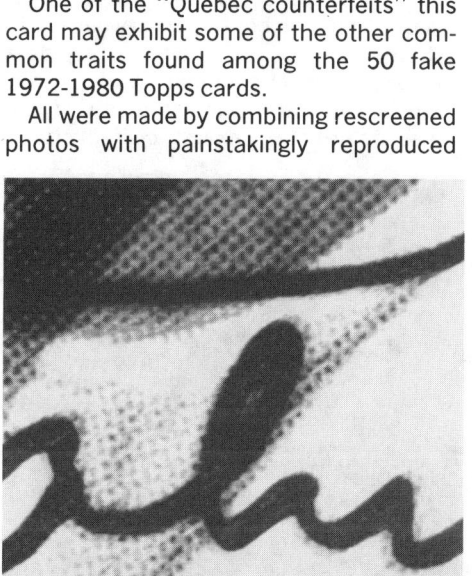

Genuine

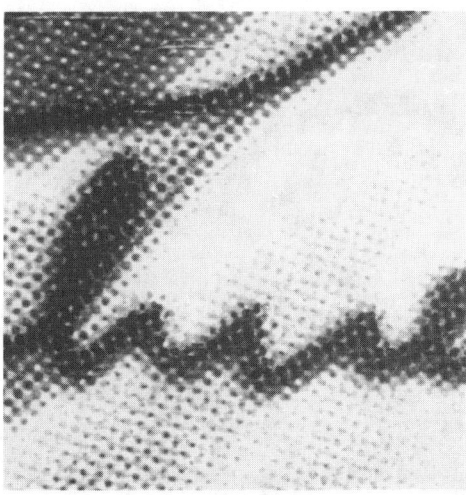

Counterfeit

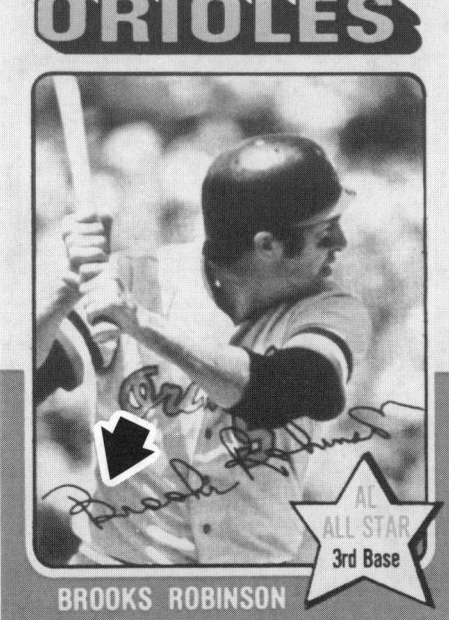

ORIOLES

BROOKS ROBINSON

AL ALL STAR
3rd Base

Height: 6'1" Weight: 190
Bats: Right Throws: Right
Born: 5-18-37, Little
Rock, Arkansas
Home: Lutherville, Md.

What is a "high can of corn"?

A LAZY FLY TO THE OUTFIELD.

| 50 | BROOKS CALBERT ROBINSON • 3B |

YEAR	CLUB	AB	H	2B	3B	HR	RBI	AVG
1955	ORIOLES	22	2	0	0	0	1	.091
1956	ORIOLES	44	10	4	0	1	1	.227
1957	ORIOLES	117	28	6	1	2	14	.239
1958	ORIOLES	463	110	16	3	3	32	.238
1959	ORIOLES	313	89	15	2	4	24	.284
1960	ORIOLES	595	175	27	9	14	88	.294
1961	ORIOLES	668	192	38	7	7	61	.287
1962	ORIOLES	634	192	29	9	23	86	.303
1963	ORIOLES	589	148	26	4	11	67	.251
1964	ORIOLES	612	194	35	3	28	118	.317
1965	ORIOLES	559	166	25	2	18	80	.297
1966	ORIOLES	620	167	35	2	23	100	.269
1967	ORIOLES	610	164	25	5	22	77	.269
1968	ORIOLES	608	154	36	6	17	75	.253
1969	ORIOLES	598	140	21	3	23	84	.234
1970	ORIOLES	608	168	31	4	18	94	.276
1971	ORIOLES	589	160	21	1	20	92	.272
1972	ORIOLES	556	139	23	2	8	64	.250
1973	ORIOLES	549	141	17	2	9	72	.257
1974	ORIOLES	553	159	27	0	7	59	.288
MAJOR LEAGUE TOTALS		9907	2698	457	65	258	1289	.272

★ © 1975 TOPPS CHEWING GUM, INC. PRTD IN U.S.A.

Examination of the facsimile autograph with a magnifying glass will identify this counterfeit. The rescreened counterfeit card will show the autograph composed of many tiny dots, giving it a fuzzy appearance. On a genuine card, the autograph will be made up of clean solid black lines.

One of the "Quebec counterfeits" this card may exhibit some of the other common traits found among the 50 fake 1972-1980 Topps cards.

All were made by combining rescreened photos with painstakingly reproduced graphic elements of genuine cards.

Many of the counterfeits show random black ink streaks in various areas on the front, usually horizontally oriented.

The borders of these counterfeits often show a stray overspray of color, especially near the edges.

All the fakes are within weight tolerances of genuine contemporary cards.

Some of the counterfeits, by accident or design, are cut off-center, like Topps cards of the era, though many of the fakes are not cut to exactly correct size.

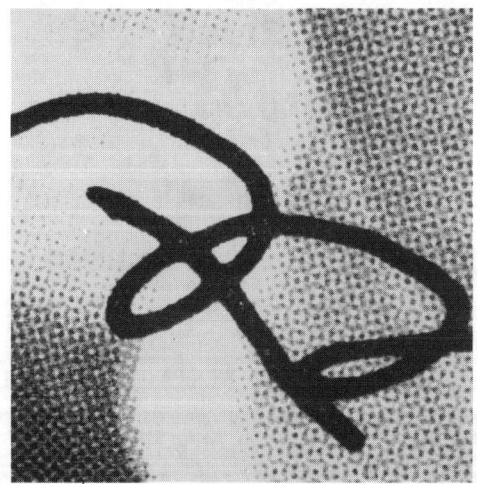

Genuine

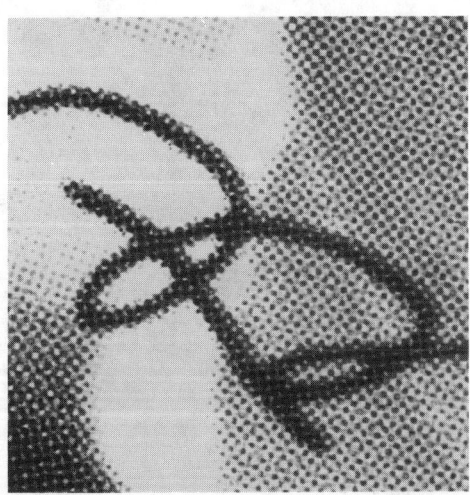

Counterfeit

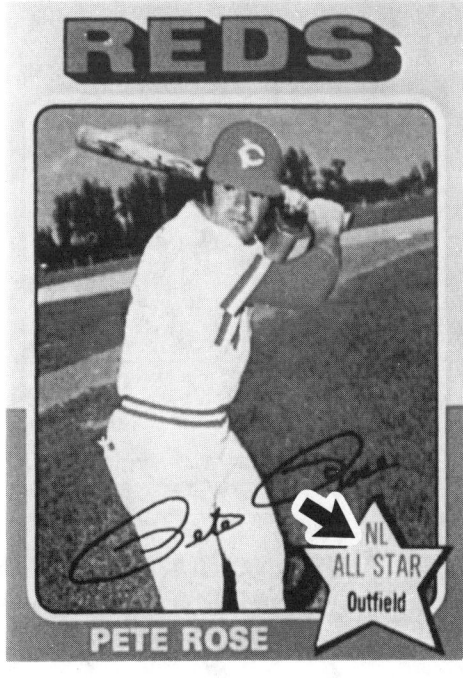

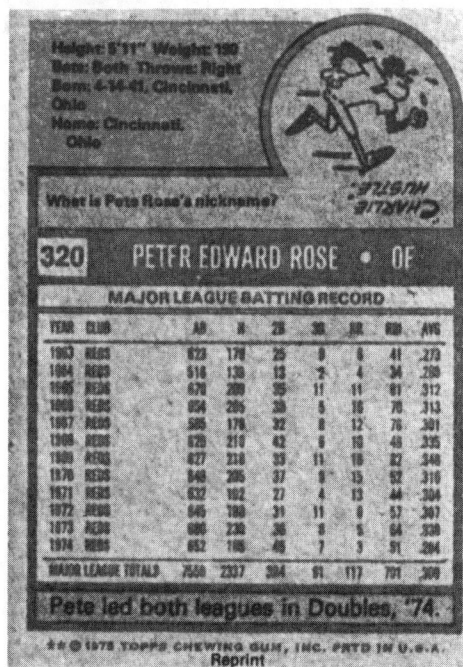

Because it is printed on thinner, whiter cardboard than genuine 1975 Topps cards, and the gloss of the card's front differs from that on a genuine card, an experienced hobbyist should be able to easily spot this counterfeit.

The presence of dot structures where they should not be is evidence of the counterfeit, but requires a magnifying glass to verify. The "NL ALL STAR" designation and position in the star at lower right are the best places to examine a suspect card. On a genuine card, these words will appear as clean, solid magenta ("NL ALL STAR") or black ("Outfield") letters. The counterfeit shows these elements as being made up of many tiny dots.

The counterfeit's back lacks contrast because red and green ink was used to simulate the gray background.

The black "Reprint" which appears on the back of the card photographed here may not be present on all cards encountered in the hobby market.

Genuine

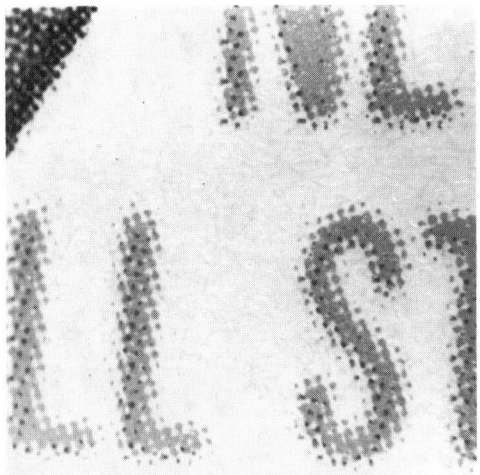

Counterfeit

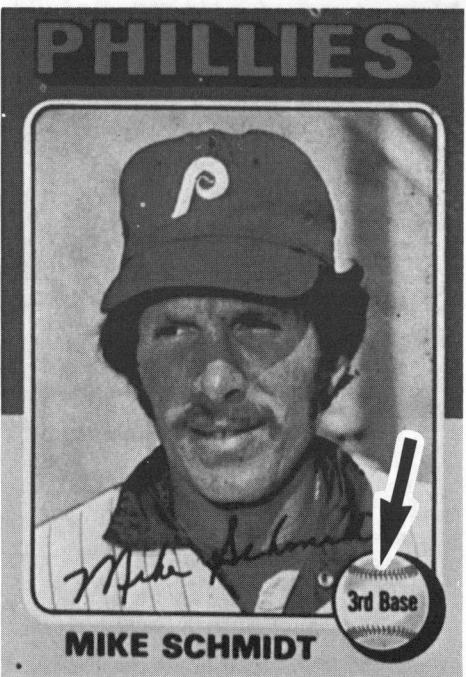

While the player photo on this counterfeit is fairly deceptive, many hobbyists would be immediately suspicious of the card based on a general fuzziness of the other color elements on the front, especially in the areas of black printing.

Such things as the frame around the photo, the player's name, facsimile autograph and position should be represented as clean, solid lines. On the counterfeit, these elements are composed of many tiny black dots.

Easy differentiation between real and fake card can be made by examining the "3rd Base" inside the ball at lower right.

The card back also lacks any contrast, the result of red and green ink being used to simulate the gray cardboard of a genuine Topps card and hide the white cardboard on which the counterfeit was produced.

The black "Reprint" which appears on the back of the card shown here may not be present on all cards encountered in the hobby market.

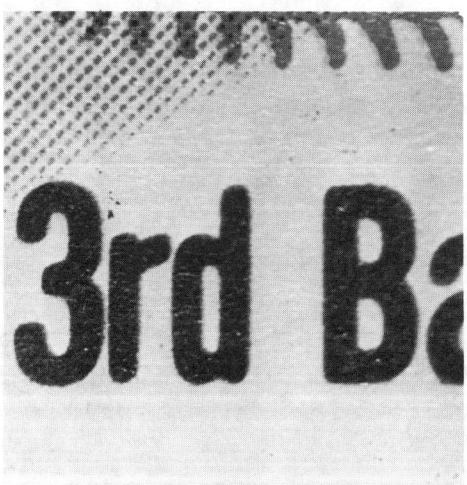

Genuine

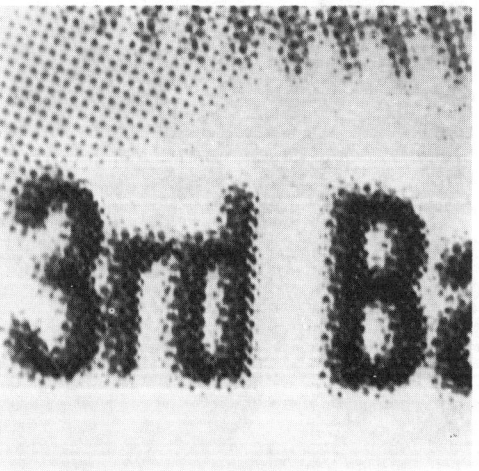

Counterfeit

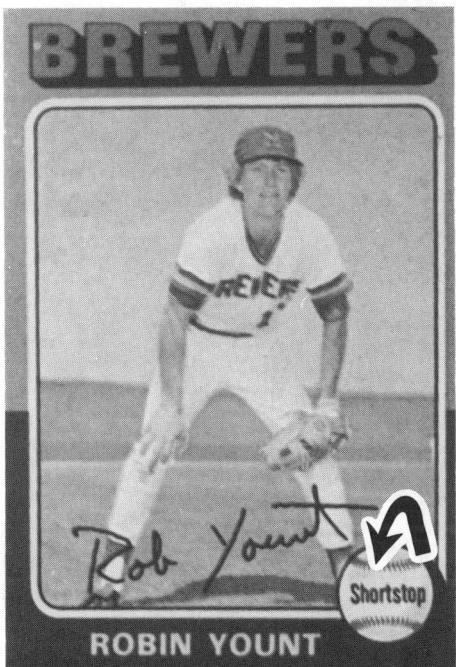

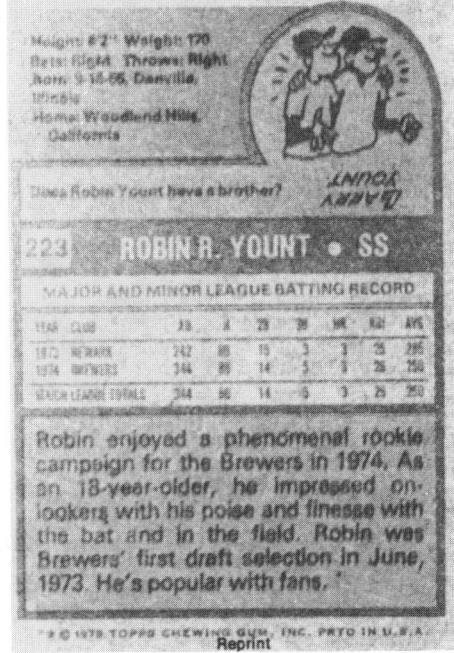

Another of the three dozen so-called "Cleveland reprints," this is not a particularly dangerous counterfeit due to the generally washed-out appearance of the colors on the front of the card and the overall darkness of the card back. However, as the perception of color is subjective among individuals, and because even genuine cards can vary widely in the intensity or shade of color, it is never recommended to base an authenticity judgement on color alone.

Easy differentiation between real and fake on this card can be made by using a magnifying glass to examine the "Shortstop" inside the ball at lower right. Those letters on a genuine card will be clean, solid black. On the counterfeit, they are composed of many colored dots, creating an overall fuzzy appearance. Similar evidence of rescreening is seen on other typographic elements on the counterfeit.

The black "Reprint" which appears at the bottom on the back of the card shown here may not be present on all cards encountered in the hobby market.

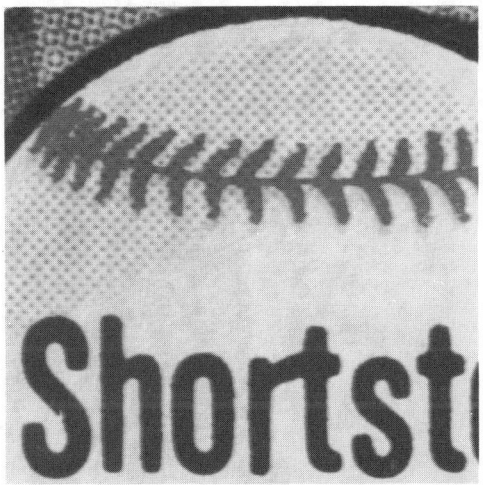

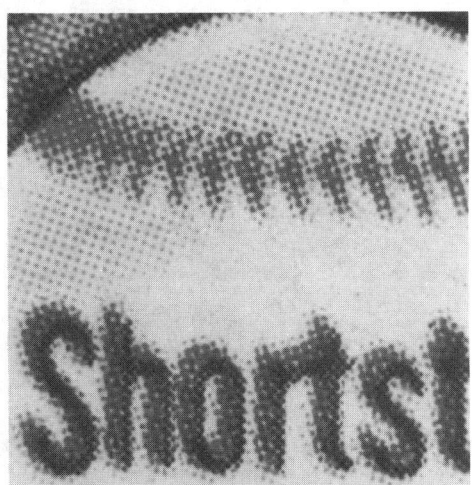

Genuine   **Counterfeit**

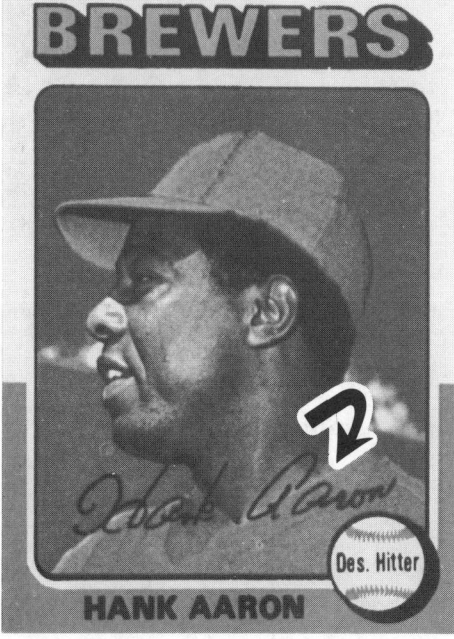

Height: 6 0" Weight: 180
Bats: Right Throws: Right
Born: 2-5-34, Mobile, Alabama
Home: Atlanta, Georgia

Name Ernie Bank's cousin?

660   **HENRY LOUIS AARON** • **DH**

		MAJOR LEAGUE BATTING RECORD						
YEAR	CLUB	AB	H	2B	3B	HR	RBI	AVG
1954	BRAVES	468	131	27	6	13	69	.280
1955	BRAVES	602	189	37	9	27	106	.314
1956	BRAVES	609	200	34	14	26	92	.328
1957	BRAVES	615	198	27	6	44	132	.322
1958	BRAVES	601	196	34	4	30	95	.326
1959	BRAVES	629	223	46	7	39	123	.355
1960	BRAVES	590	172	20	11	40	126	.292
1961	BRAVES	603	197	39	10	34	120	.327
1962	BRAVES	592	191	28	6	45	128	.323
1963	BRAVES	631	201	29	4	44	130	.319
1964	BRAVES	570	187	30	2	24	95	.328
1965	BRAVES	570	181	40	1	32	89	.318
1966	BRAVES	603	168	23	1	44	127	.279
1967	BRAVES	600	184	37	3	39	109	.307
1968	BRAVES	606	174	33	4	29	86	.287
1969	BRAVES	547	164	30	3	44	97	.300
1970	BRAVES	516	154	26	1	38	118	.298
1971	BRAVES	495	162	22	3	47	118	.327
1972	BRAVES	449	119	10	0	34	77	.265
1973	BRAVES	392	118	12	1	40	96	.301
1974	BRAVES	340	91	16	0	20	69	.268
MAJOR LEAGUE TOTALS		11,628	3600	600	96	733	2202	.310

** © 1975 TOPPS CHEWING GUM, INC. PRTD IN U.S.A.

Examination of the facsimile autograph with a magnifying glass will identify this counterfeit. The rescreened counterfeit card will show the autograph composed of many tiny dots, giving it a fuzzy appearance. On a genuine card, the autograph will be made up of clean solid black lines.

One of the "Quebec counterfeits" this card may exhibit some of the other common traits found among the 50 fake 1972-1980 Topps cards.

All were made by combining rescreened photos with painstakingly reproduced graphic elements of genuine cards.

Many of the counterfeits show random black ink streaks in various areas on the front, usually horizontally oriented.

The borders of these counterfeits often show a stray overspray of color, especially near the edges.

All the fakes are within weight tolerances of genuine contemporary cards.

Some of the counterfeits, by accident or design, are cut off-center, like Topps cards of the era, though many of the fakes are not cut to exactly correct size.

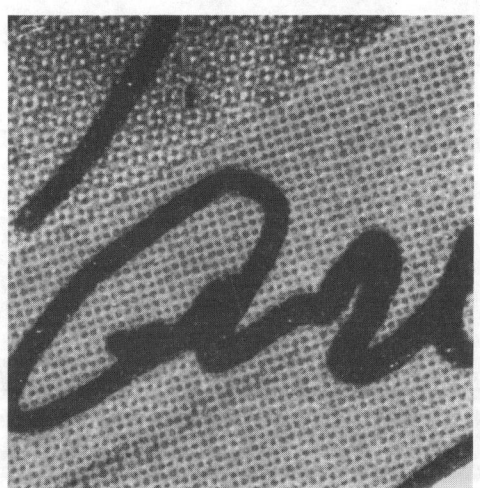

Genuine

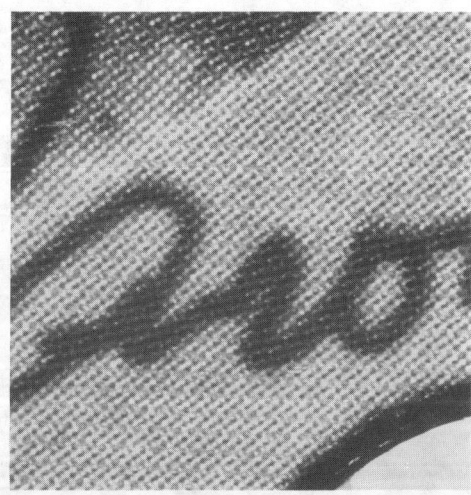

Counterfeit

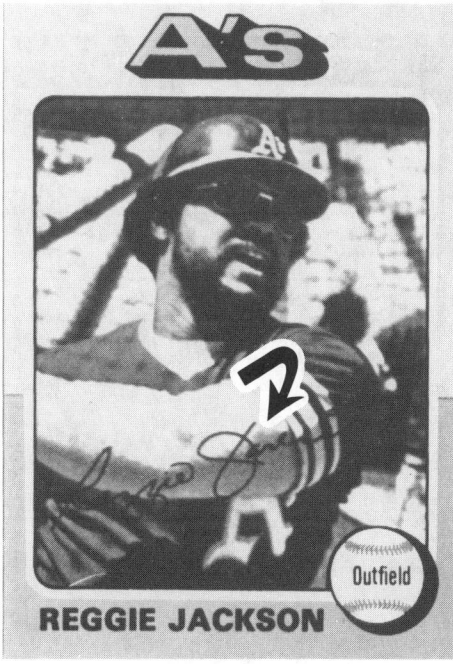

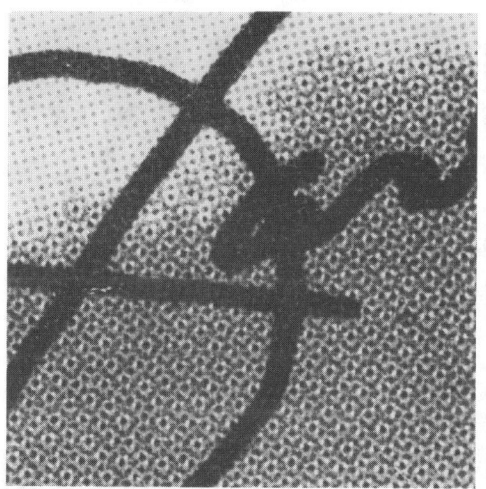

Examination of the facsimile autograph with a magnifying glass will identify this counterfeit. The rescreened counterfeit card will show the autograph composed of many tiny dots, giving it a fuzzy appearance. On a genuine card, the autograph will be made up of clean solid black lines.

One of the "Quebec counterfeits" this card may exhibit some of the other common traits found among the 50 fake 1972-1980 Topps cards.

All were made by combining rescreened photos with painstakingly reproduced graphic elements of genuine cards.

Many of the counterfeits show random black ink streaks in various areas on the front, usually horizontally oriented.

The borders of these counterfeits often show a stray overspray of color, especially near the edges.

All the fakes are within weight tolerances of genuine contemporary cards.

Some of the counterfeits, by accident or design, are cut off-center, like Topps cards of the era, though many of the fakes are not cut to exactly correct size.

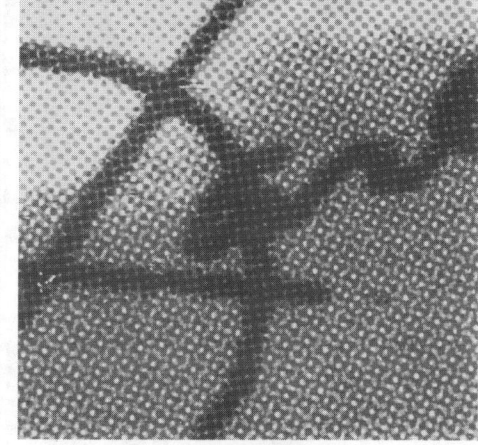

Genuine   **Counterfeit**

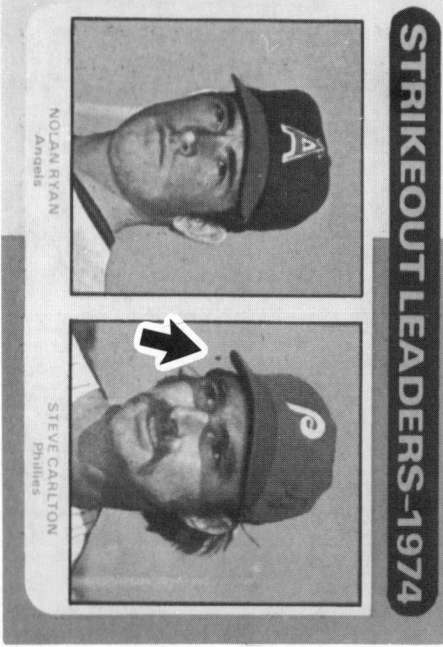

STRIKEOUT LEADERS-1974

312	'74 STRIKEOUT LDRS		
	AMERICAN LEAGUE		
	Pitcher	Team	No
1.	Nolan Ryan	Angels	367
2.	Bert Blyleven	Twins	249
3.	Fergie Jenkins	Rangers	225
4.	Gaylord Perry	Indians	216
5.	Mickey Lolich	Tigers	202
6.	Steve Busby	Royals	198
7.	Frank Tanana	Angels	180
8.	Joe Coleman	Tigers	177
9.	Luis Tiant	Red Sox	176
10.	Vida Blue	A's	174
	NATIONAL LEAGUE		
	Pitcher	Team	No
1.	Steve Carlton	Phillies	240
2.	Andy Messersmith	Dodgers	221
3.	Tom Seaver	Mets	201
4.	Jon Matlack	Mets	195
4.	Phil Niekro	Braves	195
6.	Bill Bonham	Cubs	191
7.	Jerry Koosman	Mets	188
8.	Don Gullett	Reds	183
9.	Don Sutton	Dodgers	179
10.	John D'Acquisto	Giants	167

✶★ © 1975 TOPPS CHEWING GUM, INC. PRTD IN U.S.A.

One of the easier of the "Quebec counterfeits" to spot. Look for a stray blob of dark dots falling off the visor of·Carlton's cap, parallel to his right eyebrow. If you see the blob, you've got the counterfeit.

This counterfeit may exhibit a number of other traits common to the 50 1972-1980 Topps cards which were the work of the same counterfeiter.

All were made by combining rescreened photos with painstakingly reproduced graphic elements of genuine cards.

Many of the counterfeits show random black ink streaks in various areas on the front, usually horizontally oriented.

The borders of these counterfeits often show a stray overspray of color, especially near the edges.

All the fakes are within weight tolerances of genuine contemporary cards.

Some of the counterfeits, by accident or design, are cut off-center, like Topps cards of the era, though many of the fakes are not cut to exactly correct size.

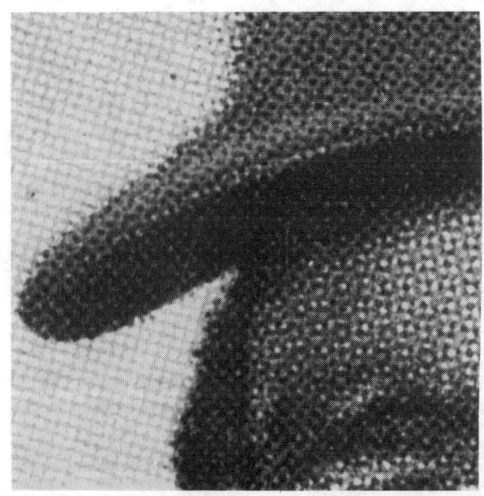

Genuine

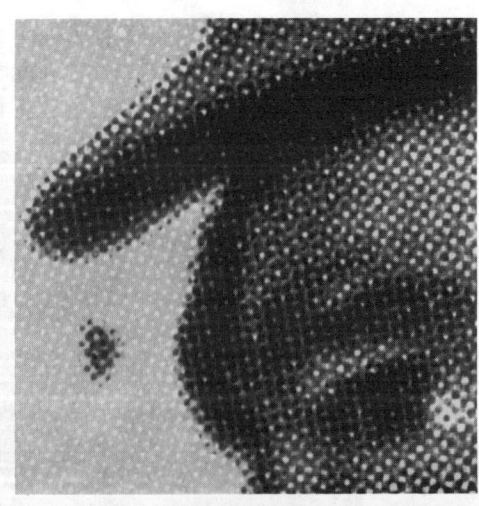

Counterfeit

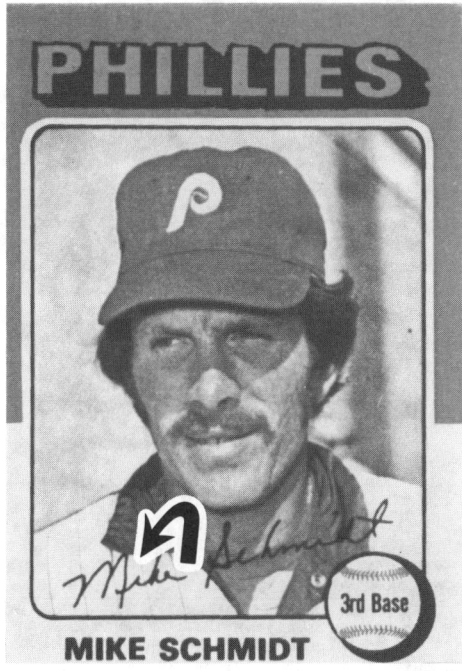

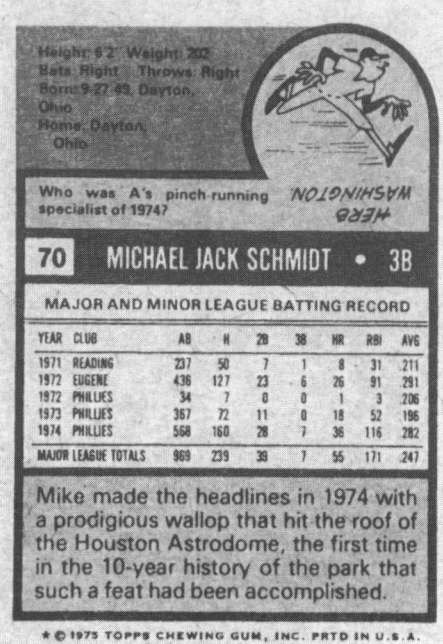

Examination of the facsimile autograph with a magnifying glass will identify this counterfeit. The rescreened counterfeit card will show the autograph composed of many tiny dots, giving it a fuzzy appearance. On a genuine card, the autograph will be made up of clean solid black lines.

One of the "Quebec counterfeits" this card may exhibit some of the other common traits found among the 50 fake 1972-1980 Topps cards.

All were made by combining rescreened photos with painstakingly reproduced graphic elements of genuine cards.

Many of the counterfeits show random black ink streaks in various areas on the front, usually horizontally oriented.

The borders of these counterfeits often show a stray overspray of color, especially near the edges.

All the fakes are within weight tolerances of genuine contemporary cards.

Some of the counterfeits, by accident or design, are cut off-center, like Topps cards of the era, though many of the fakes are not cut to exactly correct size.

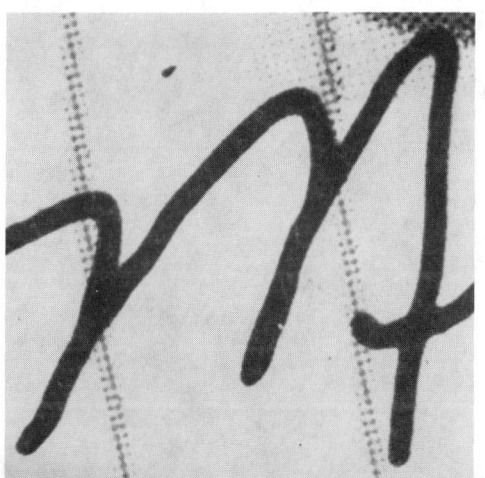

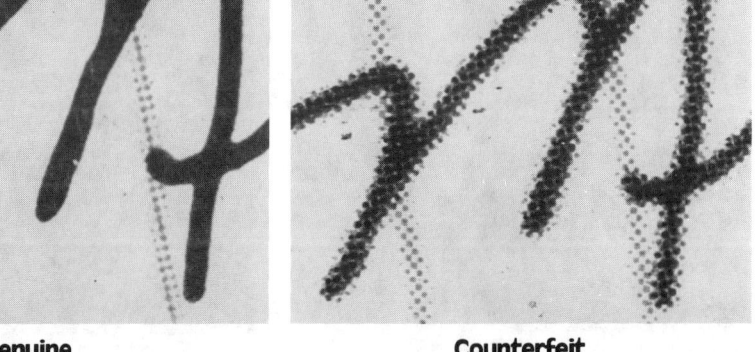

Genuine   **Counterfeit**

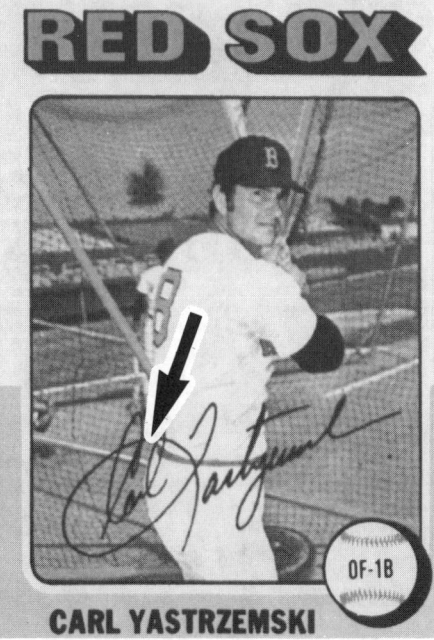

CARL YASTRZEMSKI

Height: 5'11" Weight: 198
Bats: Left Throws: Right
Born: 8-22-39, Southhampton,
New York
Home: Lynnfield,
Massachusetts

BALTIMORE

What team traded Frank
Robinson to Baltimore?

CINCINNATI, 12-6-65.

| 280 | CARL MICHAEL YASTRZEMSKI • OF-1B |

MAJOR LEAGUE BATTING RECORD

YEAR	CLUB	AB	H	2B	3B	HR	RBI	AVG
1961	RED SOX	583	155	31	6	11	80	.266
1962	RED SOX	646	191	43	6	19	94	
1963	RED SOX	570	183	40	3	14	68	
1964	RED SOX	567	164	29	9	15	67	.289
1965	RED SOX	494	154	45	3	20	72	.312
1966	RED SOX	594	165	39	2	16	80	.278
1967	RED SOX	579	189	31	4	44	121	.326
1968	RED SOX	539	162	32	2	23	74	.301
1969	RED SOX	603	154	28	2	40	111	.255
1970	RED SOX	566	186	29	0	40	102	.329
1971	RED SOX	508	129	21	2	15	70	.254
1972	RED SOX	455	120	18	2	12	68	.264
1973	RED SOX	540	160	25	4	19	95	.296
1974	RED SOX	515	155	25	2	15	79	.301
MAJOR LEAGUE TOTALS		7759	2267	436	47	303	1181	.292

★ © 1975 TOPPS CHEWING GUM, INC. PRTD IN U.S.A.

Examination of the facsimile autograph with a magnifying glass will identify this counterfeit. The rescreened counterfeit card will show the autograph composed of many tiny dots, giving it a fuzzy appearance. On a genuine card, the autograph will be made up of clean solid black lines.

One of the "Quebec counterfeits" this card may exhibit some of the other common traits found among the 50 fake 1972-1980 Topps cards.

All were made by combining rescreened photos with painstakingly reproduced graphic elements of genuine cards.

Many of the counterfeits show random black ink streaks in various areas on the front, usually horizontally oriented.

The borders of these counterfeits often show a stray overspray of color, especially near the edges.

All the fakes are within weight tolerances of genuine contemporary cards.

Some of the counterfeits, by accident or design, are cut off-center, like Topps cards of the era, though many of the fakes are not cut to exactly correct size.

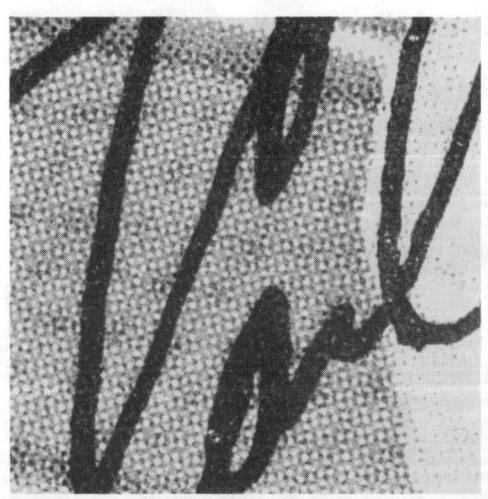

Genuine

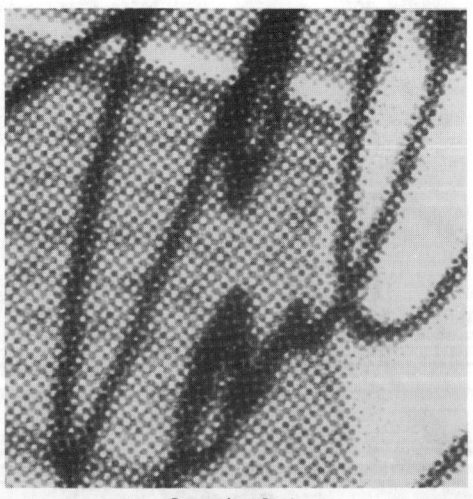

Counterfeit

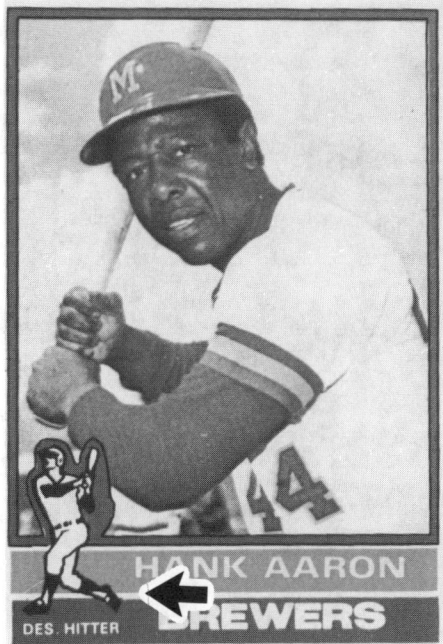

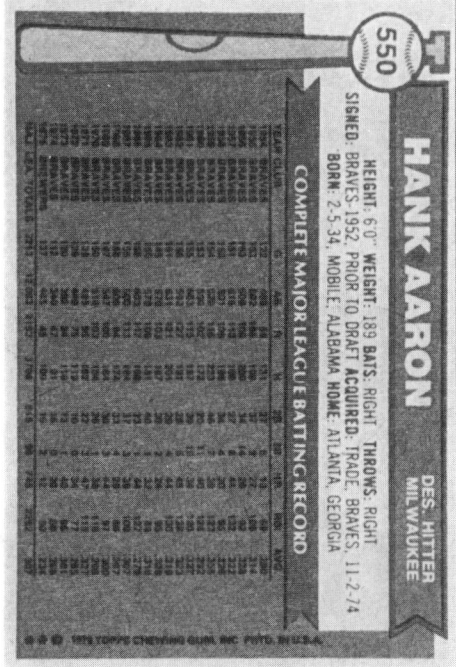

The small batting figure at lower left is the key to identifying this counterfeit. Note on the counterfeit how the purple-blue area behind the left arm and bat is much larger than on a genuine card. With a magnifying glass, the counterfeit also exhibits a "stair step" effect in the purple band behind the figure's right foot.

One of the "Quebec counterfeits" this card may show other traits found among the 50 fake 1972-1980 Topps cards.

All were made by combining rescreened photos with painstakingly reproduced graphic elements of genuine cards.

Many of the counterfeits show random black ink streaks in various areas on the front, usually horizontally oriented.

The borders of these counterfeits often show a stray overspray of color, especially near the edges.

All the fakes are within weight tolerances of genuine contemporary cards.

Some of the counterfeits, by accident or design, are cut off-center, like Topps cards of the era, though many of the fakes are not cut to exactly correct size.

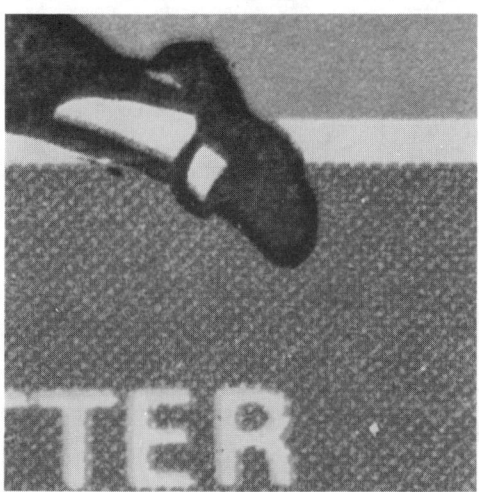

Genuine

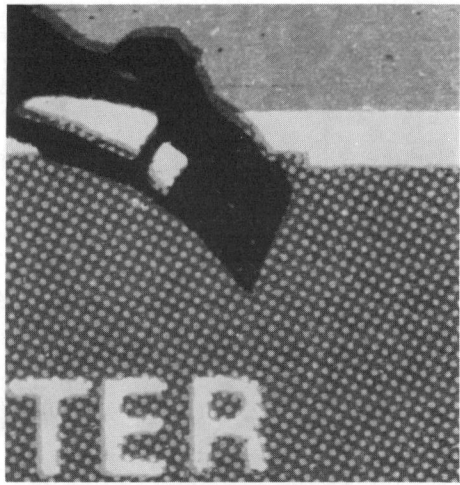

Counterfeit

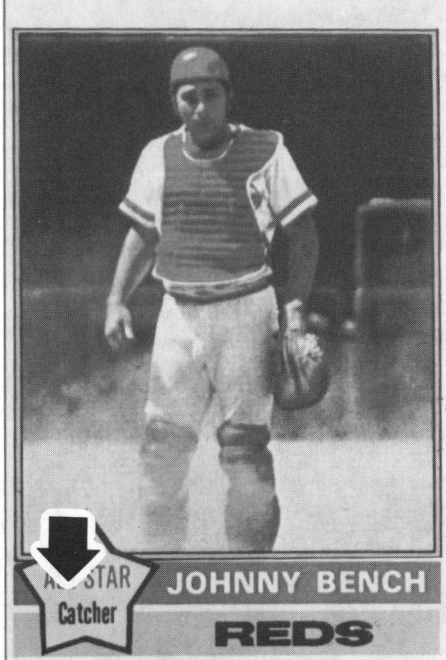
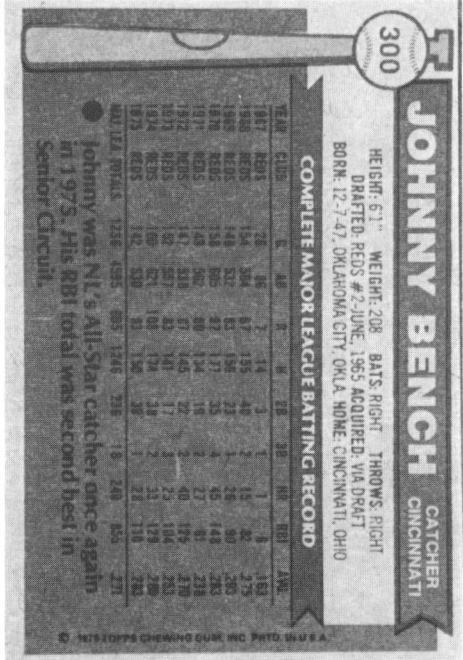

The "Quebec counterfeiters" generally did a good job of reproducing graphic elements, but a magnifier will reveal this counterfeit in the word "Catcher" at lower-left. On the counterfeit, the "C" and "a" are joined at their bottom loops. A narrow strip of yellow background separates those letters on the real card.

This counterfeit may also show some of the other traits commonly found among the 50 fake 1972-1980 Topps cards.

All were made by combining rescreened photos with painstakingly reproduced graphic elements of genuine cards.

Many of the counterfeits show random black ink streaks in various areas on the front, usually horizontally oriented.

The borders of these counterfeits often show a stray overspray of color, especially near the edges.

All the fakes are within weight tolerances of genuine contemporary cards.

Some of the counterfeits, by accident or design, are cut off-center, like Topps cards of the era, though many of the fakes are not cut to exactly correct size.

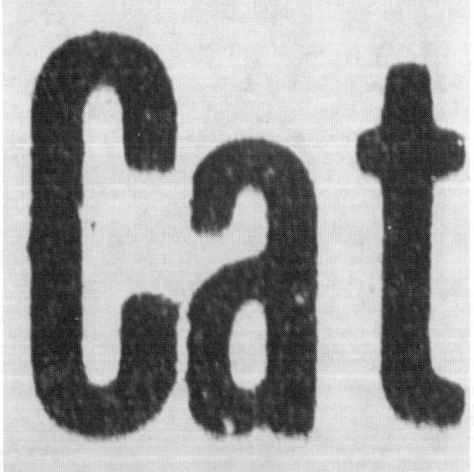

Genuine

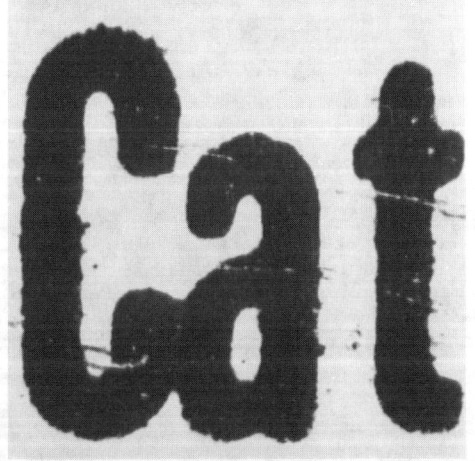

Counterfeit

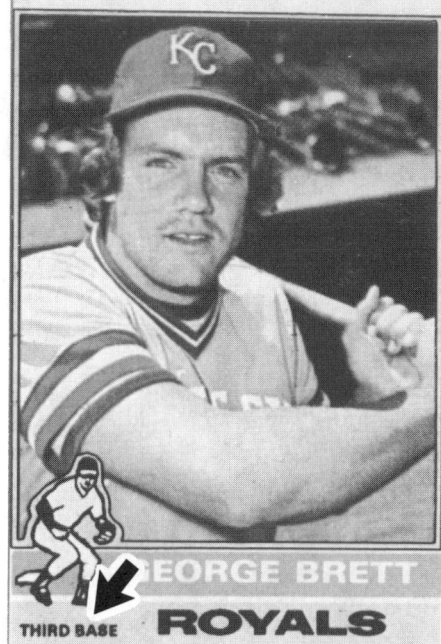

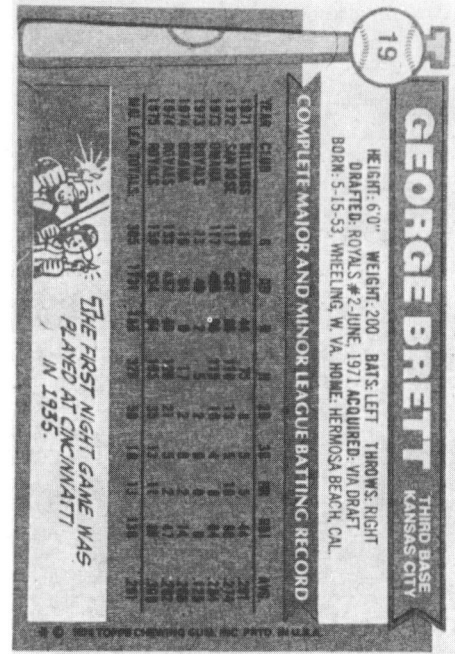

This counterfeit is identified by using a magnifying glass to examine the "B" of "BASE". On a genuine card, this letter is solid black. On this counterfeit, the lower-left corner of the vertical bar is broken, and the blue-and-white dots of the background stripe show through the break.

One of the "Quebec counterfeits," this card may exhibit some of the other common traits found among the 50 fake 1972-1980 Topps cards.

All were made by combining rescreened photos with painstakingly reproduced graphic elements of genuine cards.

Many of the counterfeits show random black ink streaks in various areas on the front, usually horizontally oriented.

The borders of these counterfeits often show a stray overspray of color, especially near the edges.

All the fakes are within weight tolerances of genuine contemporary cards.

Some of the counterfeits, by accident or design, are cut off-center, like Topps cards of the era, though many of the fakes are not cut to exactly correct size.

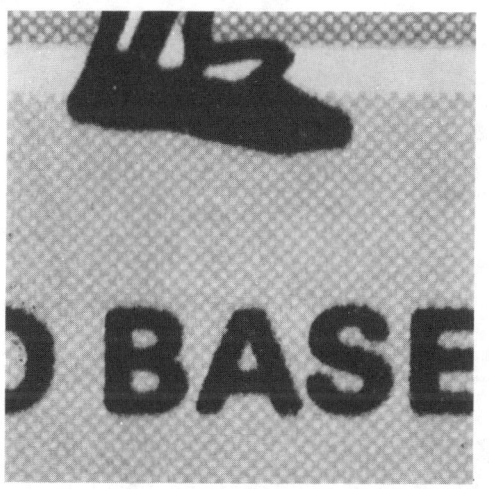

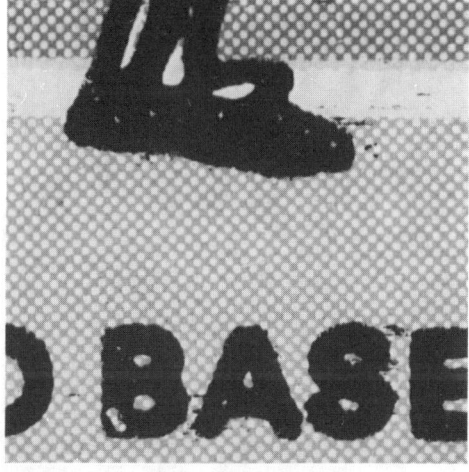

| Genuine | Counterfeit |

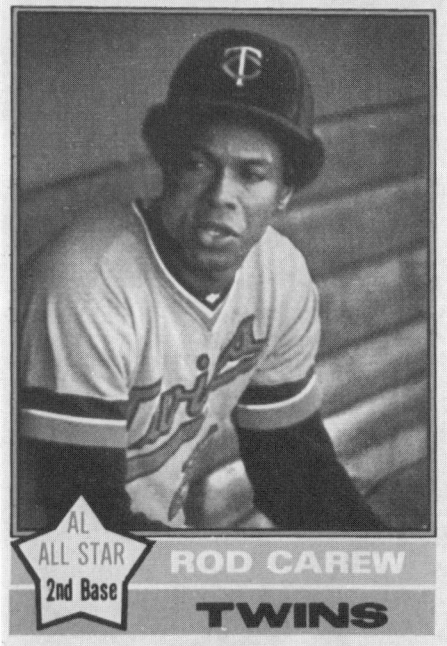

One of the more difficult of the "Quebec counterfeits" to identify. With a magnifying glass, examine the dates in the stats box on back. On a genuine card, each of the numerals will be clear and distinct. On this counterfeit, many of the numerals have run together and lost their distinctiveness.

This card may exhibit some of the other common traits found among the 50 fake 1972-1980 Topps cards.

All were made by combining rescreened photos with painstakingly reproduced graphic elements of genuine cards.

Many of the counterfeits show random black ink streaks in various areas on the front, usually horizontally oriented.

The borders of these counterfeits often show a stray overspray of color, especially near the edges.

All the fakes are within weight tolerances of genuine contemporary cards.

Some of the counterfeits, by accident or design, are cut off-center, like Topps cards of the era, though many of the fakes are not cut to exactly correct size.

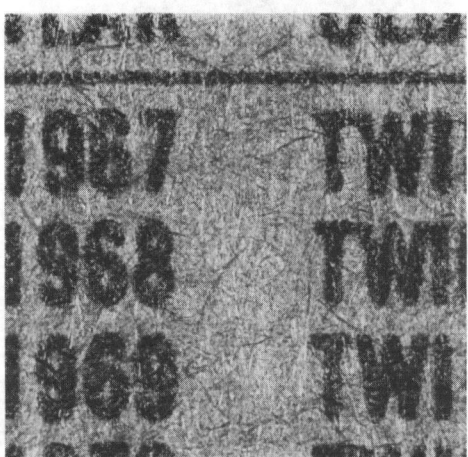

Genuine

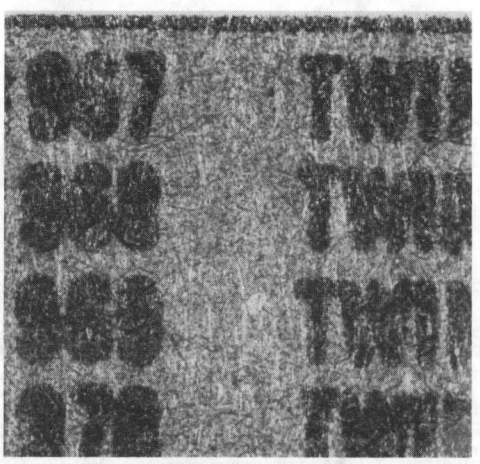

Counterfeit

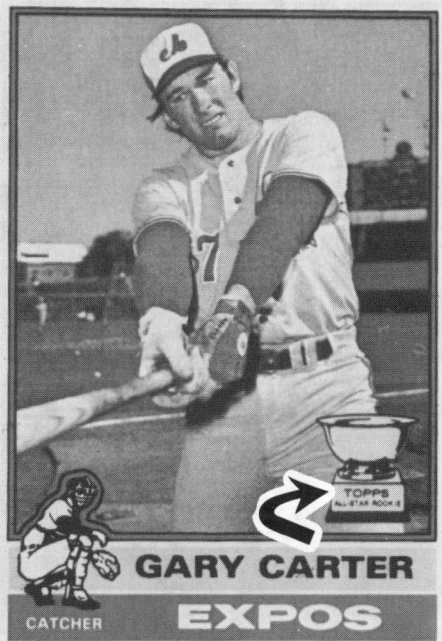

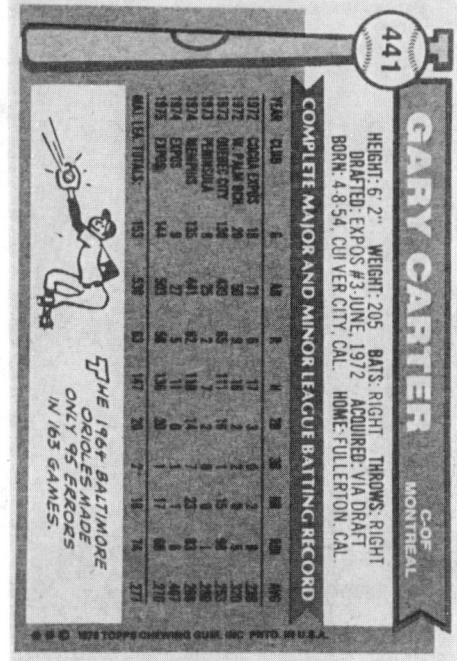

One of the easiest of the "Quebec counterfeits" to identify. With a magnifying glass, examine the typography at the base of the Topps All-Star Rookie trophy. On a genuine card, each letter is made up of solid black lines. On this counterfeit the letters have been screened, rendering them as dot composites.

This card may exhibit some of the other common traits found among the 50 fake 1972-1980 Topps cards.

All were made by combining rescreened photos with painstakingly reproduced graphic elements of genuine cards.

Many of the counterfeits show random black ink streaks in various areas on the front, usually horizontally oriented.

The borders of these counterfeits often show a stray overspray of color, especially near the edges.

All the fakes are within weight tolerances of genuine contemporary cards.

Some of the counterfeits, by accident or design, are cut off-center, like Topps cards of the era, though many of the fakes are not cut to exactly correct size.

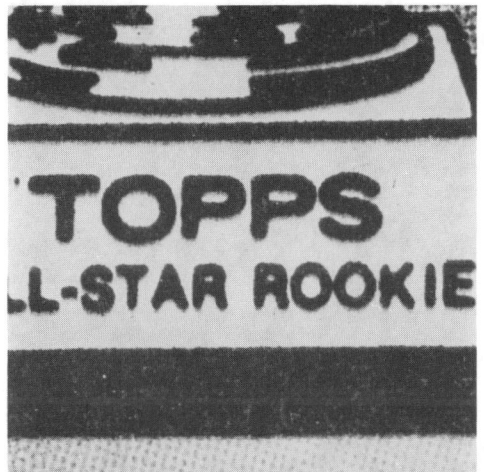

Genuine

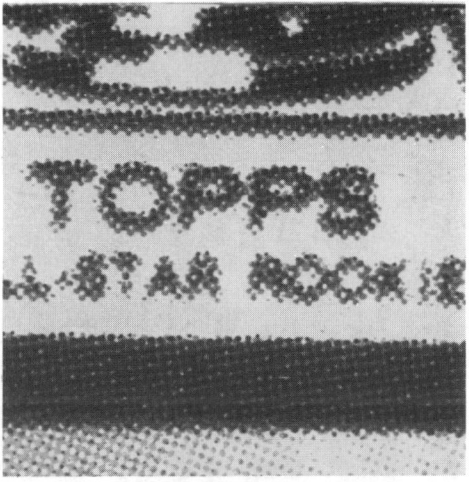

Counterfeit

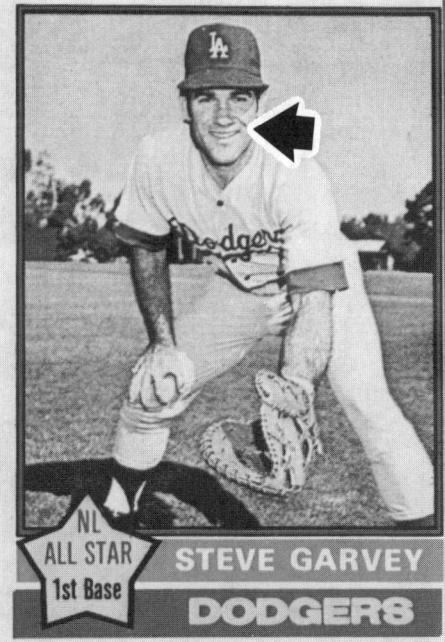

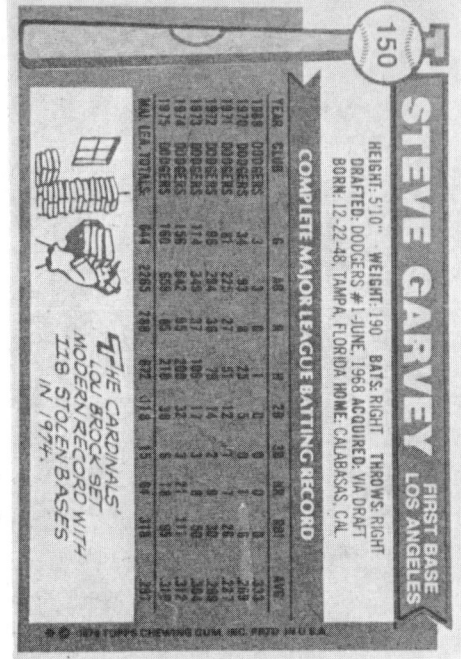

A quick dental examination will reveal this counterfeit. A genuine card will show six distinct teeth in Garvey's upper jaw. The counterfeit, when viewed with a magnifying glass, shows most of the lines separating the teeth have been burned out.

One of the "Quebec counterfeits" this card may exhibit some of the other common traits found among the 50 fake 1972-1980 Topps cards.

All were made by combining rescreened photos with painstakingly reproduced graphic elements of genuine cards.

Many of the counterfeits show random black ink streaks in various areas on the front, usually horizontally oriented.

The borders of these counterfeits often show a stray overspray of color, especially near the edges.

All the fakes are within weight tolerances of genuine contemporary cards.

Some of the counterfeits, by accident or design, are cut off-center, like Topps cards of the era, though many of the fakes are not cut to exactly correct size.

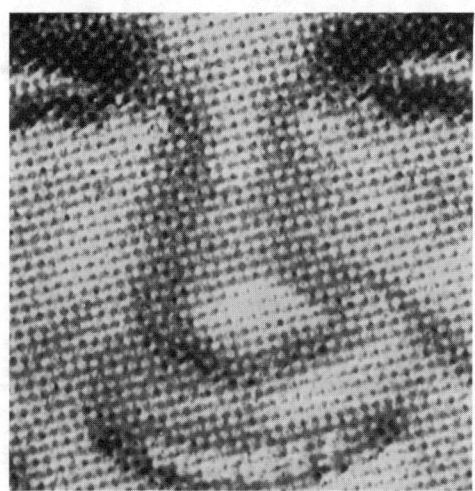

Genuine

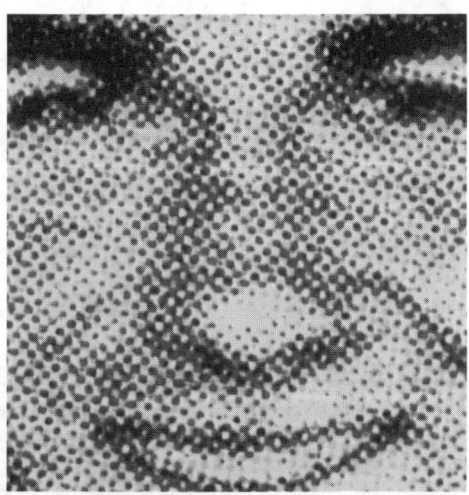

Counterfeit

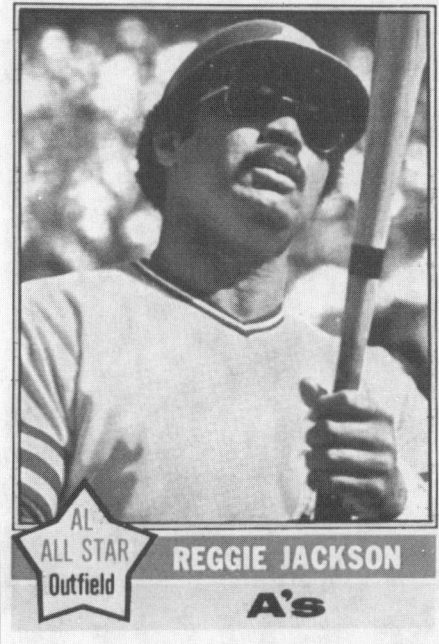

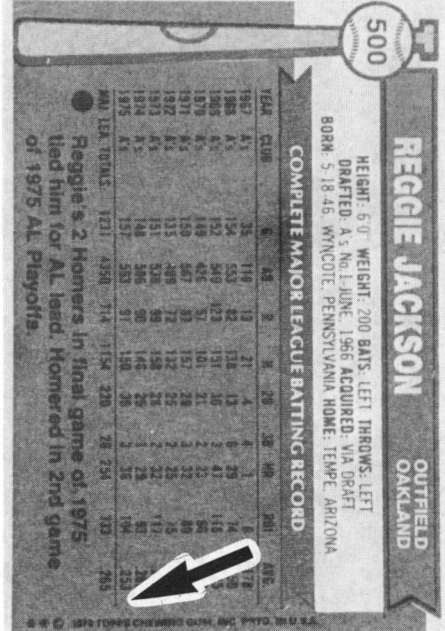

The toughest of the "Quebec counterfeits" to spot. Check the copyright line on back, where the counterfeit shows little or no definition in the copyright symbol, "1976" or "TOPPS". The stats are also too muddy; much less distinct than the letters and numbers on a genuine card.

Like other "Quebec" fakes, this will often exhibit a number of common traits.

All the counterfeits were made by a process combining rescreened photos with painstakingly reproduced graphic elements of genuine cards.

Many of the counterfeits show random black ink streaks in various areas on the front, usually horizontally oriented.

The borders of these counterfeits often show a stray overspray of color, especially near the edges.

All of the counterfeits are within normal weight tolerances of genuine contemporary Topps cards.

Some of the counterfeits, by accident or design, are cut off-center, like Topps cards of the era, though many of the fakes are not cut to the correct size.

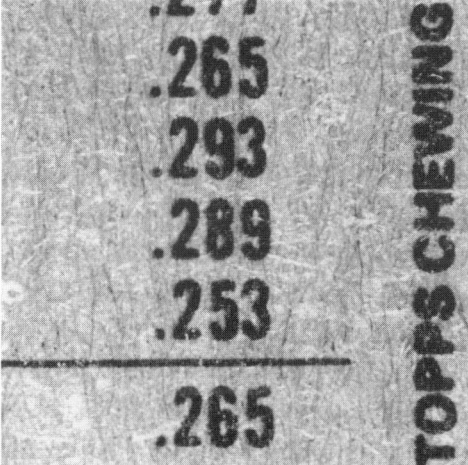

Genuine

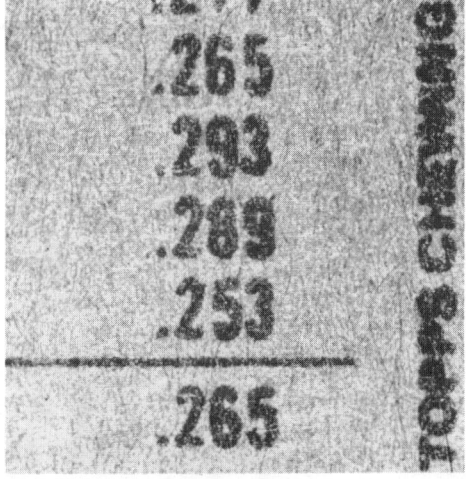

Counterfeit

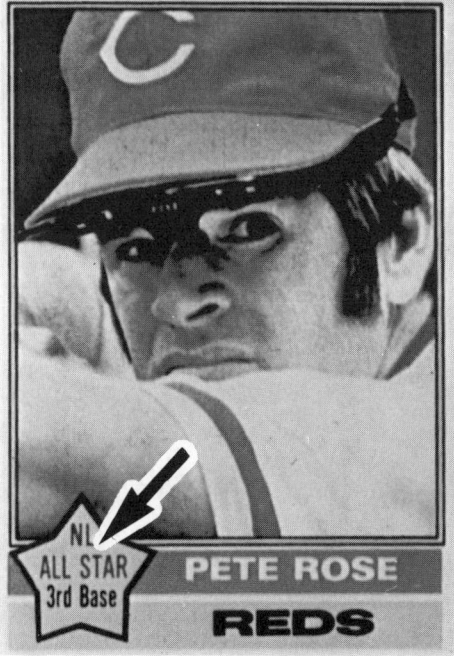

While the player's photo on this counterfeit is quite deceptive, the fact that all of the other front design elements were re-screened from an original card makes this counterfeit fairly easy to identify — as long as a magnifying glass is at hand.

A quick check of the star at lower-left provides the proof of status. A genuine card will have the "NL ALL STAR" in crisp, clean green letters, and the position in solid black letters. The counterfeit shows these elements as being made up of many tiny dots.

The green printing on the back has little of the original card's contrast, as a result of being printed over a screened black pattern designed to make the thin white cardboard stock of the fake look like the traditional gray Topps cardstock.

The black "Reprint" which appears on the back of the card shown here may not be present on all cards encountered in buy and sell transactions.

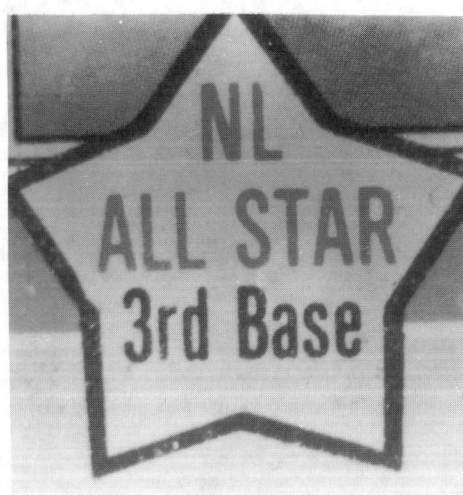

Genuine

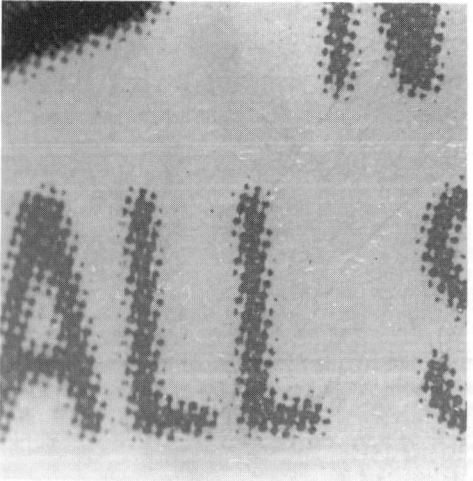

Counterfeit

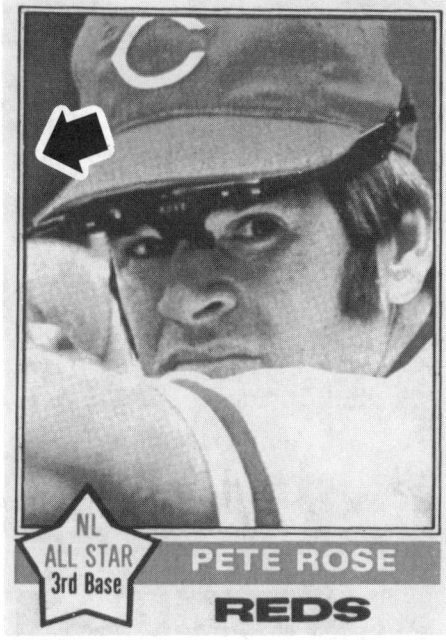

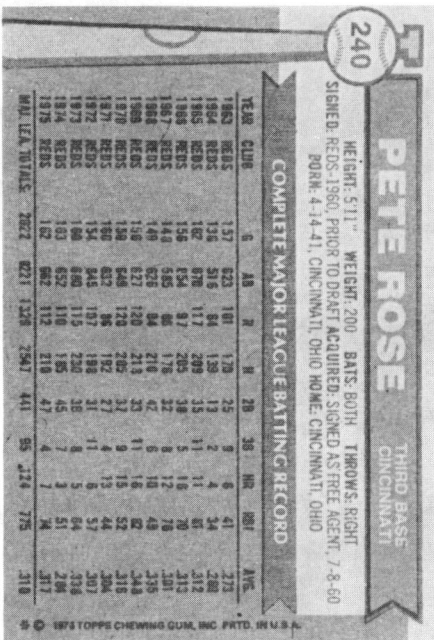

A difficult "Quebec counterfeit" to identify. With a magnifying glass, examine the inside black frame line to the left of Rose's cap visor. The counterfeit shows two tiny "bites" taken out of black, resulting in patches of the red dots on yellow background showing through. On a genuine card this line will be solid black.

This card may exhibit some of the other common traits found among the 50 fake 1972-1980 Topps cards.

All were made by combining rescreened photos with painstakingly reproduced graphic elements of genuine cards.

Many of the counterfeits show random black ink streaks in various areas on the front, usually horizontally oriented.

The borders of these counterfeits often show a stray overspray of color, especially near the edges.

All the fakes are within weight tolerances of genuine contemporary cards.

Some of the counterfeits, by accident or design, are cut off-center, like Topps cards of the era, though many of the fakes are not cut to exactly correct size.

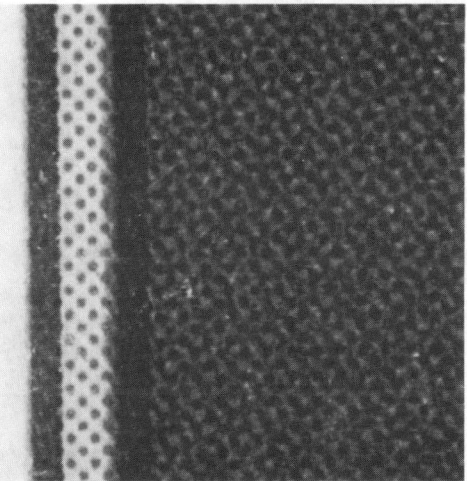

Genuine

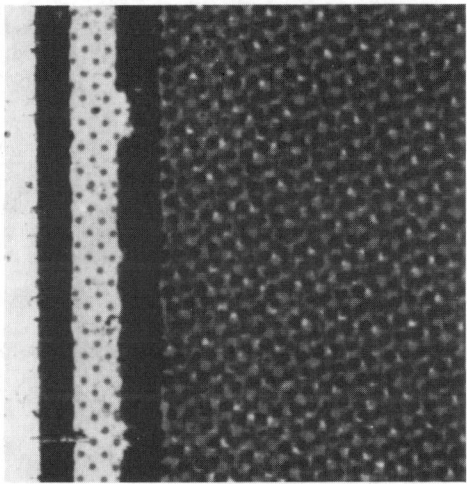

Counterfeit

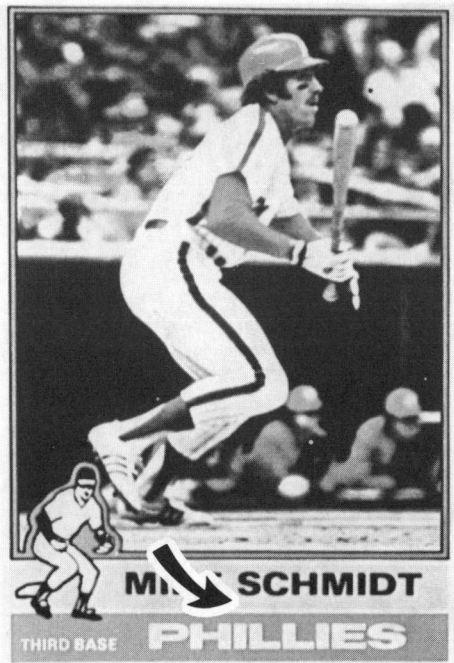

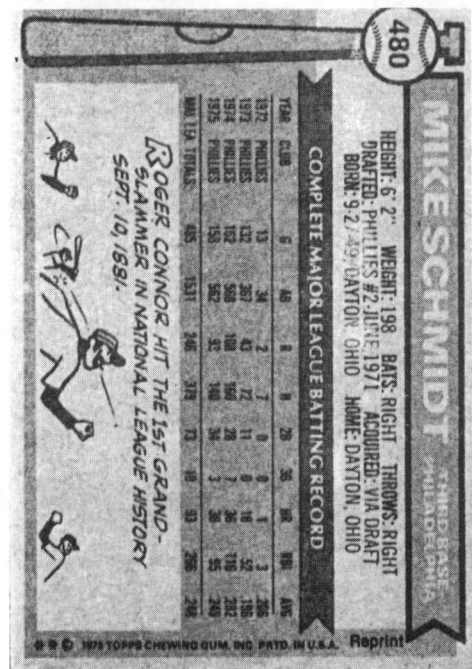

Because it is printed on thinner, whiter cardboard than the genuine 1976 Topps cards, and because the gloss of the card's front differs from that on a genuine card, an experienced dealer or collector should be able to spot this counterfeit with relative ease.

A fuzzy-appearing player photo and the fact that all of the other front design elements were re-screened from an original card make this counterfeit easy to identify — as long as a magnifying glass is at hand.

A quick check of the color bars at the bottom of the card provides the proof of status. A genuine card will have the yellow and magenta stripes printed in solid colors. The player's name on a genuine card will be printed in solid black letters. The counterfeit shows these elements as being made up of many tiny dots.

The black "Reprint" which appears on the back of the card shown here may not be present on all cards encountered in buy and sell transactions.

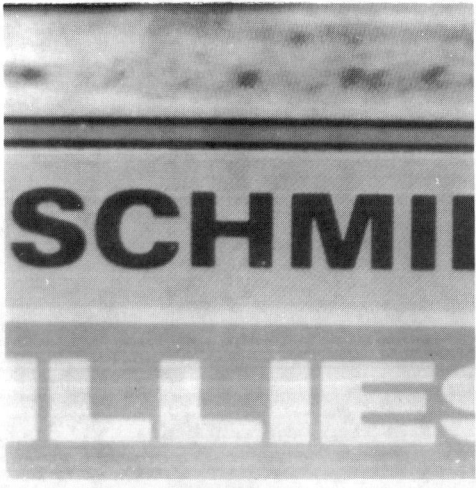

Genuine

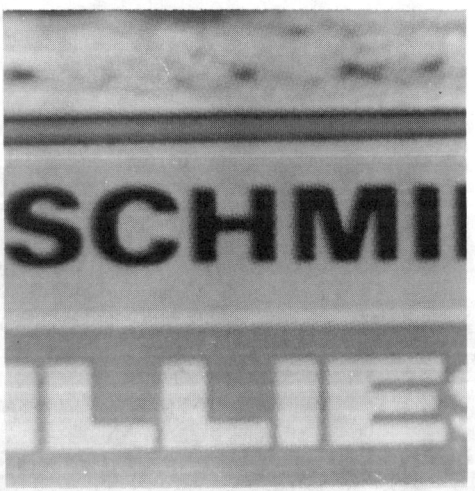

Counterfeit

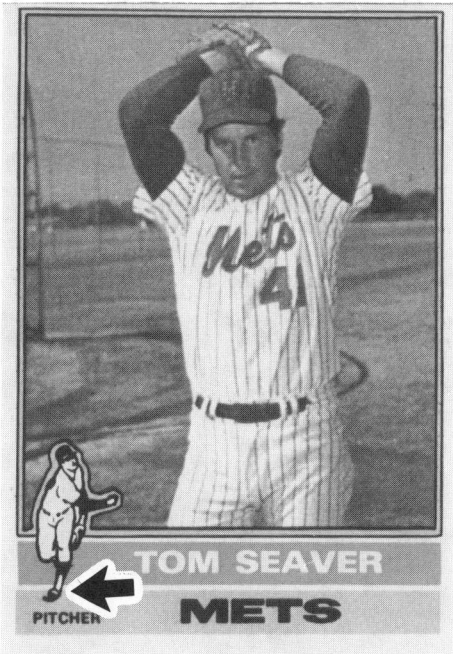

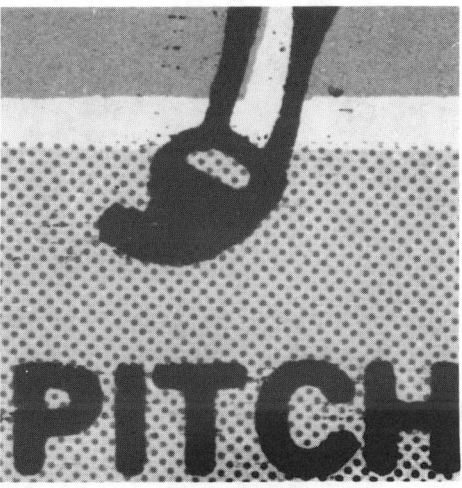

The left shoe of the pitching figure in the lower-left corner is the key to spotting this counterfeit. On a genuine card, the top flap of the shoe will be white. On this counterfeit, the flap exhibits the pattern of red dots on yellow background that makes up the orange bar at bottom.

One of the "Quebec counterfeits" this may exhibit a number of traits common to many of the 50 fake Topps cards which were the work of the same counterfeiter.

All were made by combining rescreened photos with painstakingly reproduced graphic elements of genuine cards.

Many of the counterfeits show random black ink streaks in various areas on the front, usually horizontally oriented.

The borders of these counterfeits often show a stray overspray of color, especially near the edges.

All the fakes are within weight tolerances of genuine contemporary cards.

Some of the counterfeits, by accident or design, are cut off-center, like Topps cards of the era, though many of the fakes are not cut to exactly correct size.

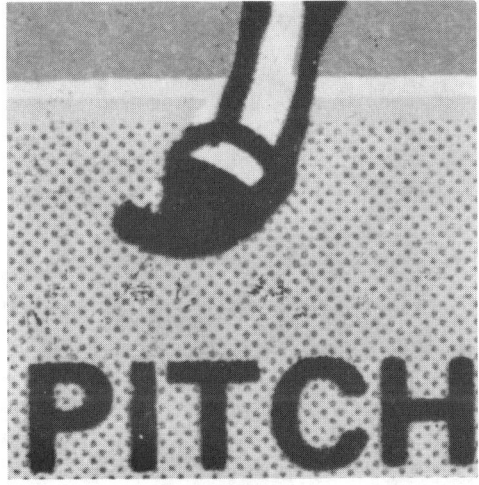

Genuine

Counterfeit

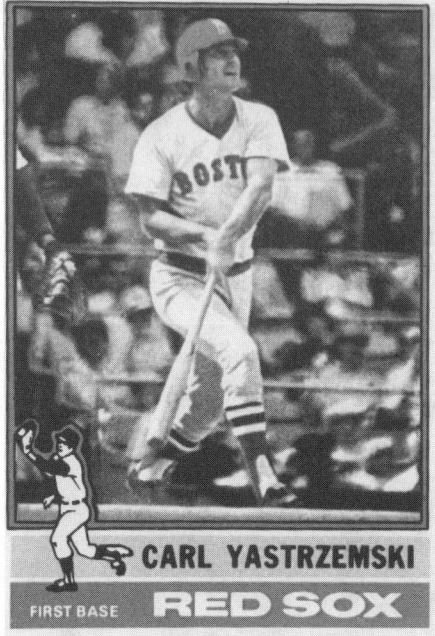

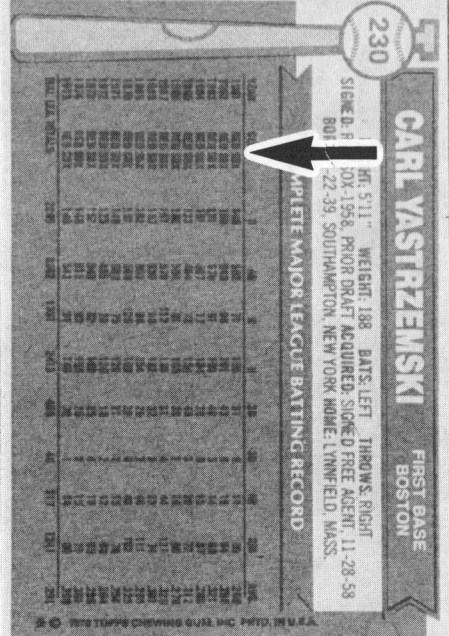

One of the more difficult of the "Quebec counterfeits" to identify. The best place to look is on the back, where the tiny print in the stats box has been plugged up and rendered often indecipherable on the counterfeit. This is especially noticeable in the dates and in the "RED SOX" team name.

This counterfeit may exhibit some of the other common traits found among the 50 fake 1972-1980 Topps cards.

All were made by combining rescreened photos with painstakingly reproduced graphic elements of genuine cards.

Many of the counterfeits show random black ink streaks in various areas on the front, usually horizontally oriented.

The borders of these counterfeits often show a stray overspray of color, especially near the edges.

All the fakes are within weight tolerances of genuine contemporary cards.

Some of the counterfeits, by accident or design, are cut off-center, like Topps cards of the era, though many of the fakes are not cut to exactly correct size.

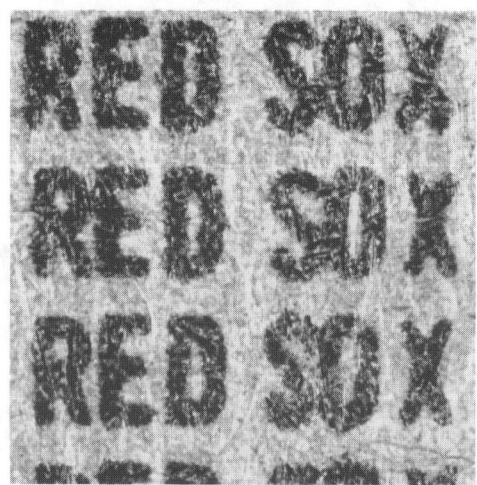

Genuine

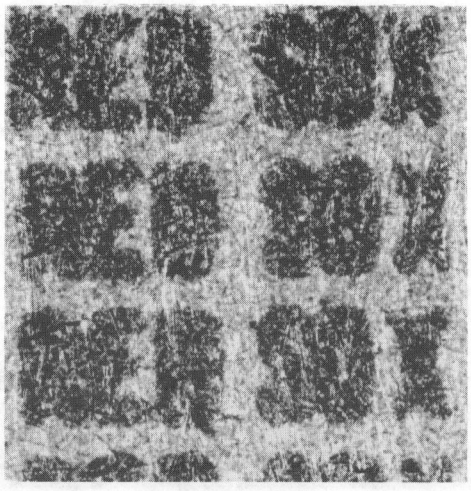

Counterfeit

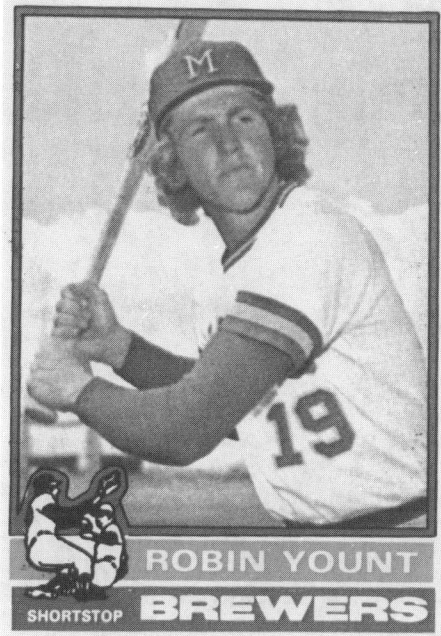
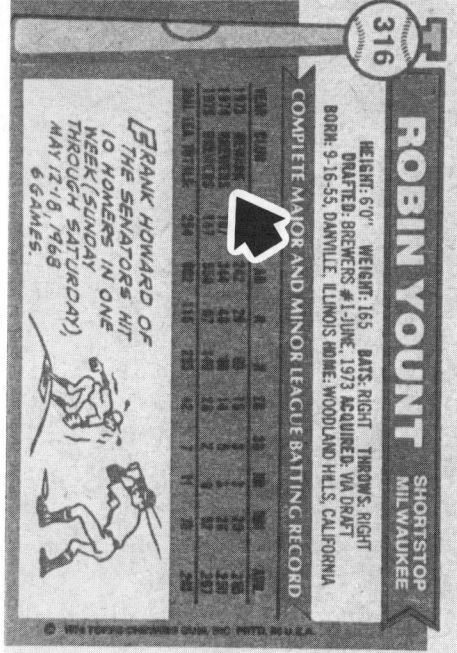

One of the more difficult of the "Quebec counterfeits" to identify. With a magnifying glass, examine the team names in the stats box on back. On a genuine card, each of the letters will be clear and distinct. On this counterfeit, many of the letters have run together and lost their distinctiveness.

This card may exhibit some of the other common traits found among the 50 fake 1972-1980 Topps cards.

All were made by combining rescreened photos with painstakingly reproduced graphic elements of genuine cards.

Many of the counterfeits show random black ink streaks in various areas on the front, usually horizontally oriented.

The borders of these counterfeits often show a stray overspray of color, especially near the edges.

All the fakes are within weight tolerances of genuine contemporary cards.

Some of the counterfeits, by accident or design, are cut off-center, like Topps cards of the era, though many of the fakes are not cut to exactly correct size.

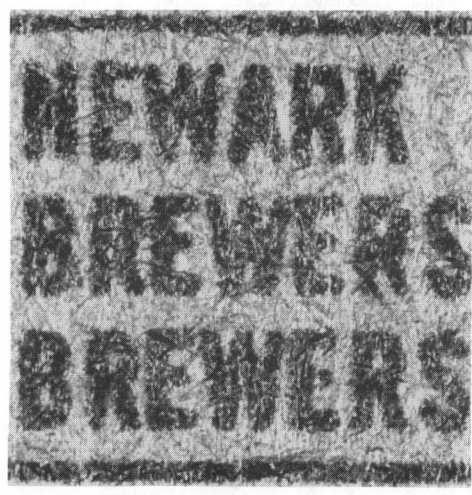

Genuine

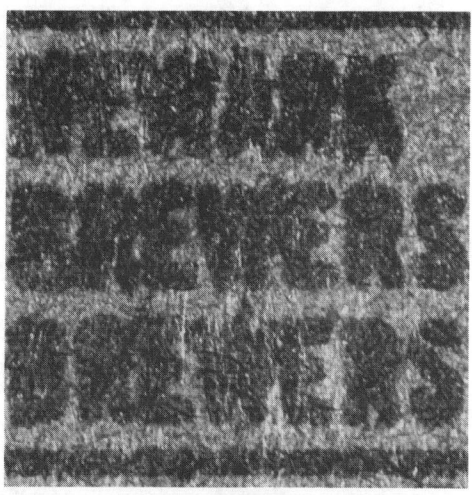

Counterfeit

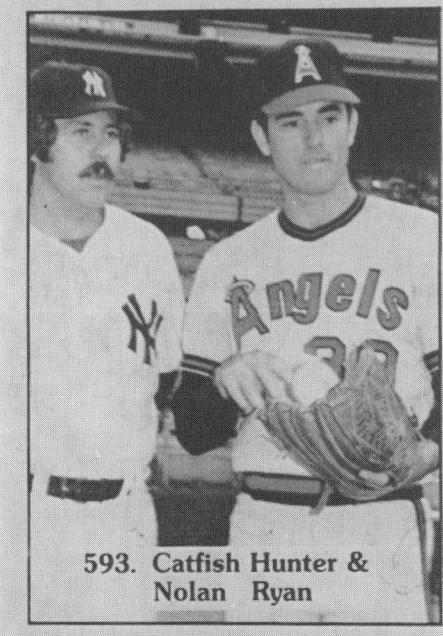
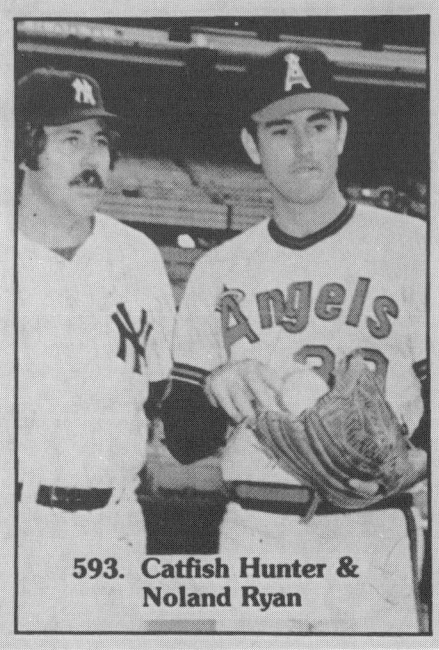

Until 1992, the SSPC "Noland" Ryan error checklist card was a rarity.

These cards would more appropriately be found in the reprint section of this book, but because of current hobby perceptions, the greatest number of suspicious collectors will be looking for them in the body of the counterfeit listings.

Originally produced in 1976, but representing players in the 1975 season, this 630-card set was halted in mid-distribution by a lawsuit from Topps to uphold its contemporary virtual monopoly on the production of baseball cards.

Because of its scarcity, player selection and creative, if not always well-focused, photo selection, over the ensuing 15 years, the issue gained a significant price tag (the 3rd edition *Standard Catalog of Baseball Cards* says $200) in the face of rising collector demand.

In 1992, however, large numbers of the set began to appear in the hobby market. Quantities were so large that they were offered on home shopping television programs, in the wholesale catalogs of comic book distributors and in a multitude of ads in the trade papers. Amazingly, virtually all of the newly emergent sets included the "Noland" Ryan error on checklist card £593, listed in the catalog as a $45 variation. At wholesale levels, price of the sets was around $60.

Quickly, hobbyists began to speculate that the set had been counterfeited. Detailed examination, however, indicates the "new" cards were printed from the same plates as the "old" cards. Since hobby lore had it that the original plates and negatives were destroyed to settle the Topps' litigation, the question of origin was put to one of the original principals in the creation of the set.

According to that source, the current hoard is, indeed, an original 1976 printing which had lain in uncut sheet form at the printers until recently. Because the sheets were cut using modern technology, it is easy to differentiate a 1976-cut set from a 1990s version. The original sets were cut by a guillotine cutter, putting a crimp to the edges. The newly cut cards were slit-cut on modern equipment, eliminating the crimping. Also, SSPC sets compiled in 1976 show a discernible disparity in card length and width as the result of cutting. The 1990s version is precision cut to a uniform size.

The cardboard of the newly available sets is much whiter than older sets, which may be due to the use of different stock during printing or differences in paper aging because of storage.

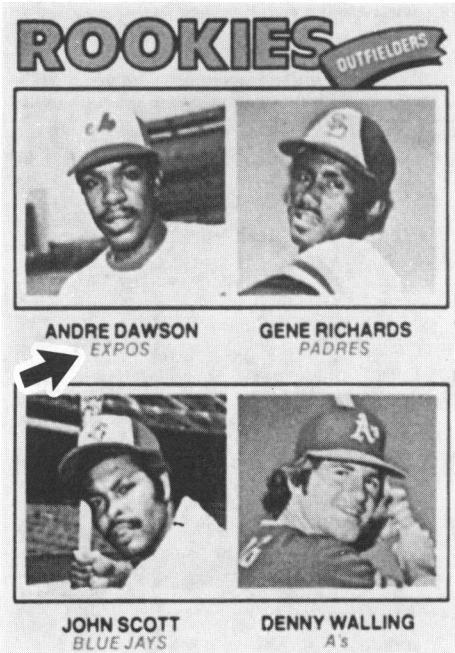

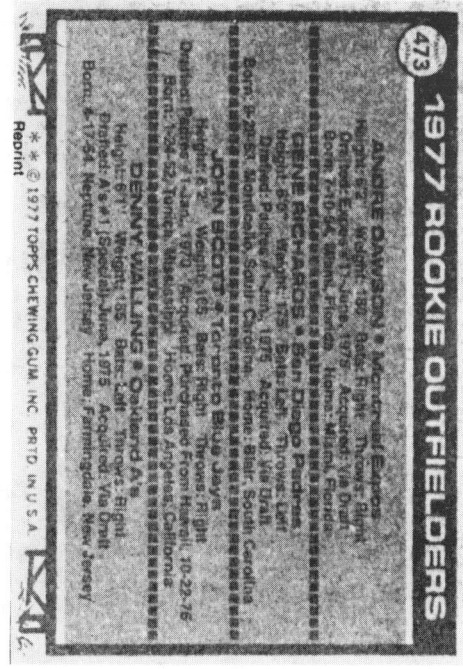

A definite fuzziness of the color printing on the front, along with an unnatural gloss, combine with back printing almost totally lacking contrast to produce this rather easy-to-spot counterfeit.

As always, however, get out the magnifying glass to be sure. An examination of Andre Dawson's name and team are all that is necessary to brand this card a fake. On a genuine Dawson rookie, his name should appear in solid black letters, and his team name in solid magenta let-ters. The counterfeit renders these words as a composite of tiny color dots.

The counterfeit's back lacks the contrast of an original as a result of the green ink being printed over a screened black pattern designed to make the thin white cardboard stock of the fake look like the traditional gray Topps cardstock.

The black "Reprint" which appears on the back of the specimen photographed here may not be present on all cards encountered in buy and sell transactions.

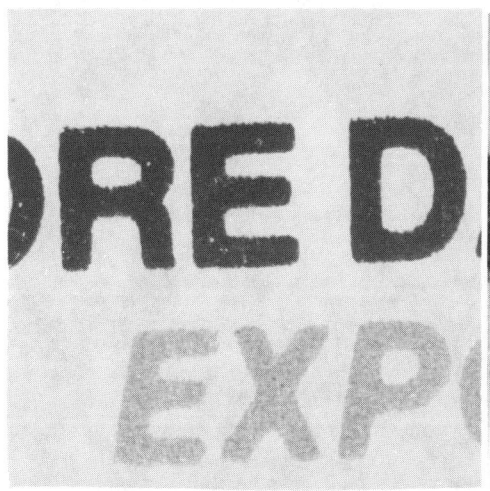

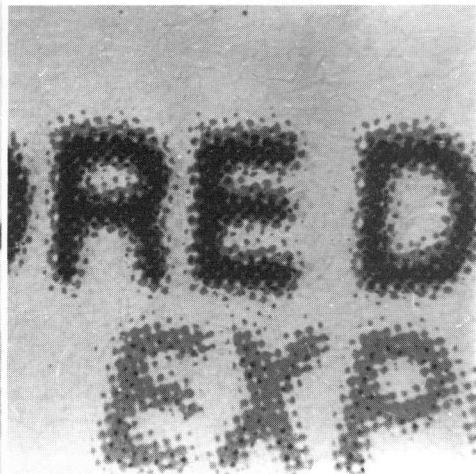

Genuine   **Counterfeit**

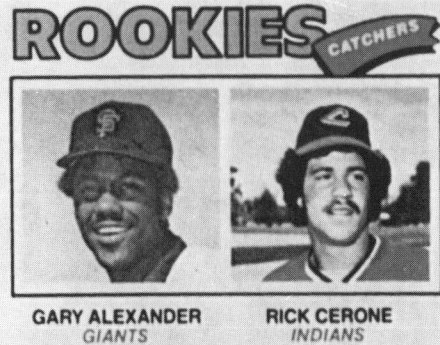

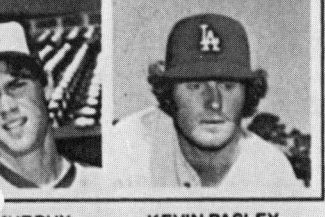

A definite fuzziness of the color printing on the front, along with an unnatural gloss, combine with back printing almost totally lacking contrast to produce this rather easy-to-spot counterfeit.

As always, however, get out the magnifying glass to be sure. An examination of Dale Murphy's name and team are all that is necessary to brand this card a fake. On a genuine Murphy rookie, his name should appear in solid black letters, and his team name in solid magenta letters. The counterfeit renders these words as a composite of tiny color dots.

The counterfeit's back lacks the contrast of an original as a result of the green ink being printed over a screened black pattern designed to make the thin white cardboard stock of the fake look like the traditional gray Topps cardstock.

The black "Reprint" which appears on the back of the specimen photographed here may not be present on all cards encountered in buy and sell transactions.

No photo available

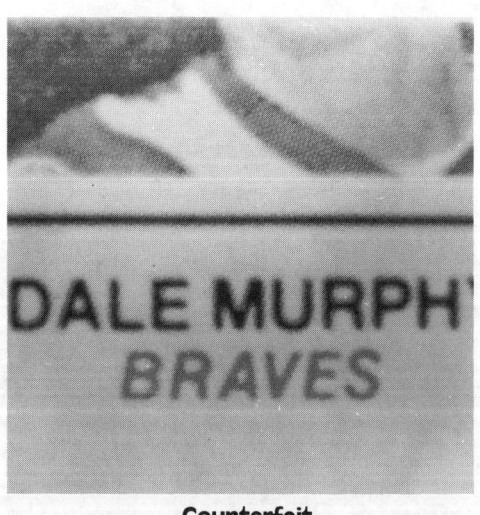

Genuine   **Counterfeit**

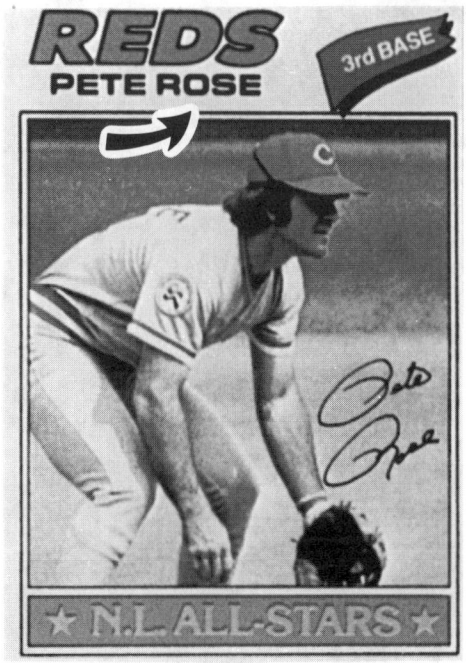

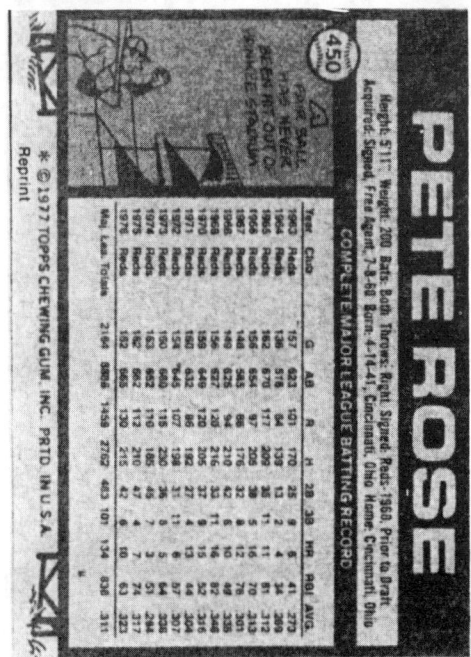

The use of a magnifying glass to check virtually any of the non-photo color elements on the front of this counterfeit will immediately and irrefutably brand the fake. The black printing, such as the frame lines around the photo and team name, the player's name and the shadow under the flag are seen as composed of many tiny dots, rather than as clean black lines and letters as found on an original card.

The counterfeit's back lacks the contrast of an original as a result of the green ink being printed over a screened black pattern designed to make the thin white cardboard stock of the fake look like the traditional gray Topps cardstock.

The black "Reprint" which appears on the back of the specimen photographed here may not be present on all cards encountered in buy and sell transactions.

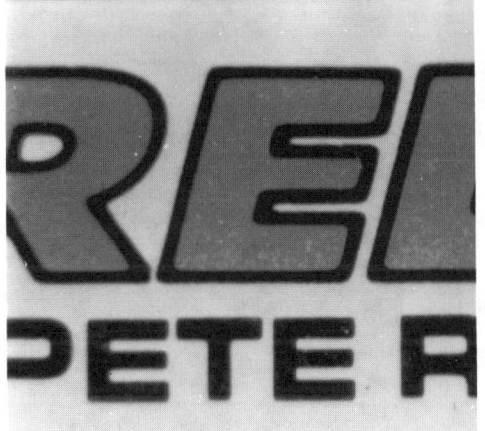

Genuine

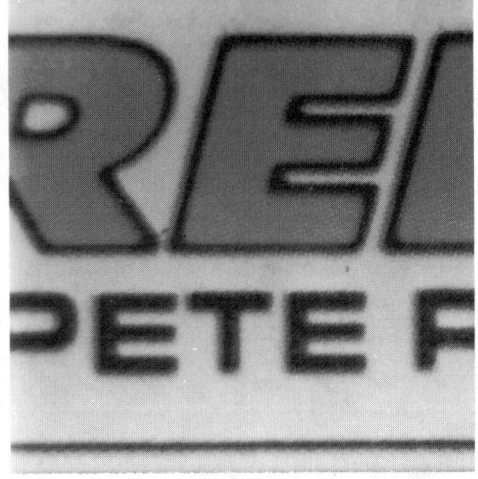

Counterfeit

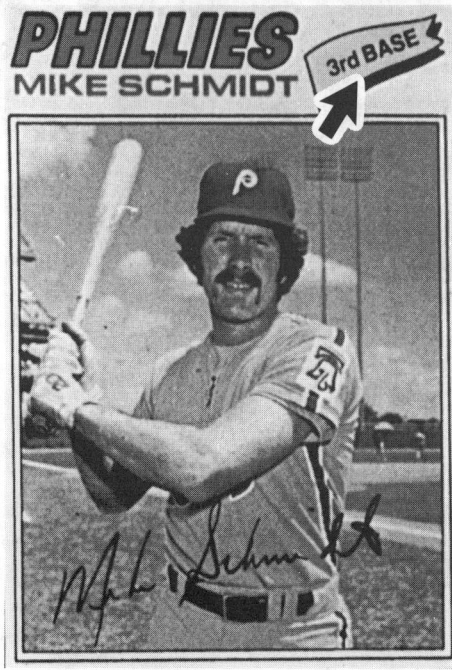

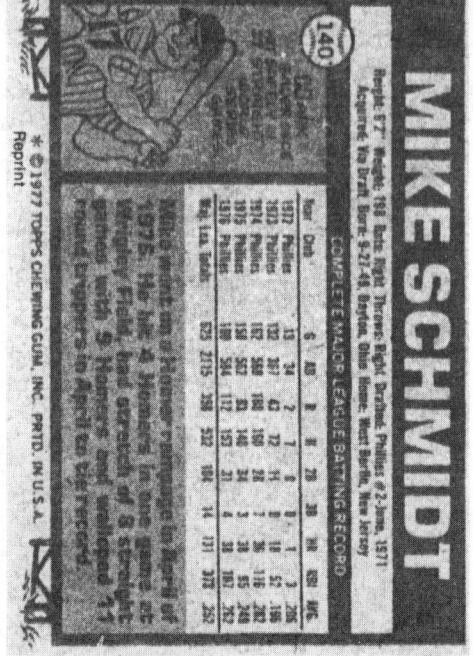

Not particularly deceptive because of an unusual gloss on the front and an over-all fuzziness of the color printing, this counterfeit is easily identifiable using a magnifying glass. The proof of this counterfeit's status can be easily seen at the top-front of the card. There, the black outlines of the team name, the green rendering of the player's name, and the black printing in and around the yellow flag can be seen on the counterfeit to be made up of many small color dots. On a genuine card, these elements will be solid color,

with no discernible dot pattern.

While you have your glass out, check the gray background on the back of the card. Note that it has been produced by printing a screened black pattern onto otherwise white cardboard. The thinner-than-genuine white cardboard stock can be seen on the edges of the card.

The black "Reprint" which appears on the back of the specimen photographed here may not be present on all cards encountered in the market.

No photo available

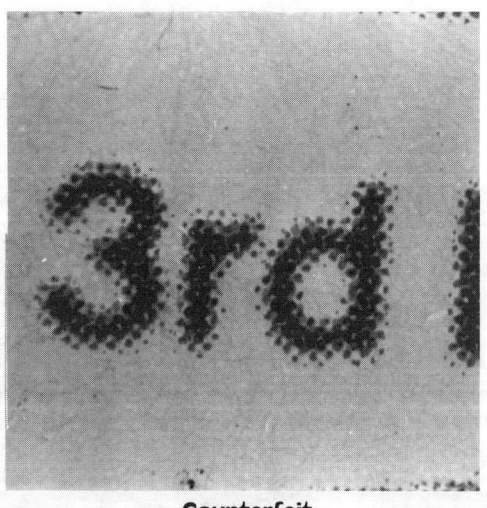

Genuine   **Counterfeit**

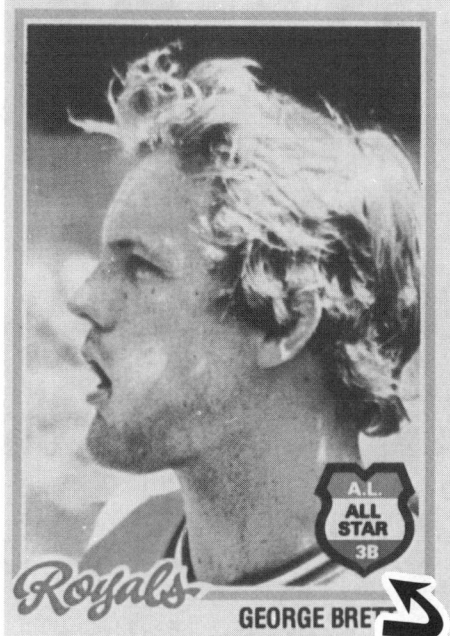

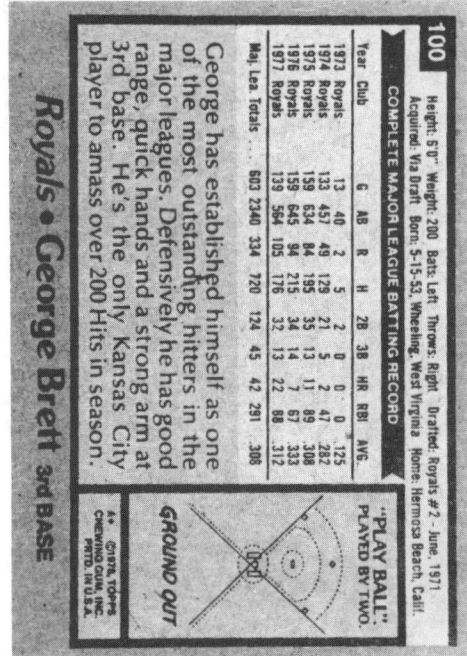

One of the easier "Quebec counterfeits" to identify. With a magnifying glass, examine the outer edge of the All-Star shield's heavy black border. If there is a "shadow" of dots at the left and bottom, the card is a counterfeit. A genuine card shows this edge as clean and sharp against the background.

This counterfeit may exhibit some of the other common traits found among the 50 fake 1972-1980 Topps cards.

All were made by combining rescreened photos with painstakingly reproduced graphic elements of genuine cards.

Many of the counterfeits show random black ink streaks in various areas on the front, usually horizontally oriented.

The borders of these counterfeits often show a stray overspray of color, especially near the edges.

All the fakes are within weight tolerances of genuine contemporary cards.

Some of the counterfeits, by accident or design, are cut off-center, like Topps cards of the era, though many of the fakes are not cut to exactly correct size.

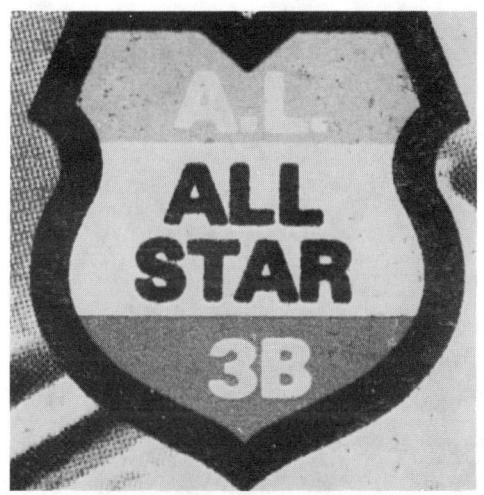

Genuine

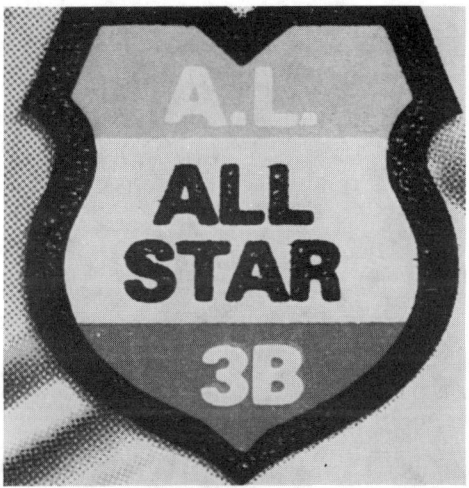

Counterfeit

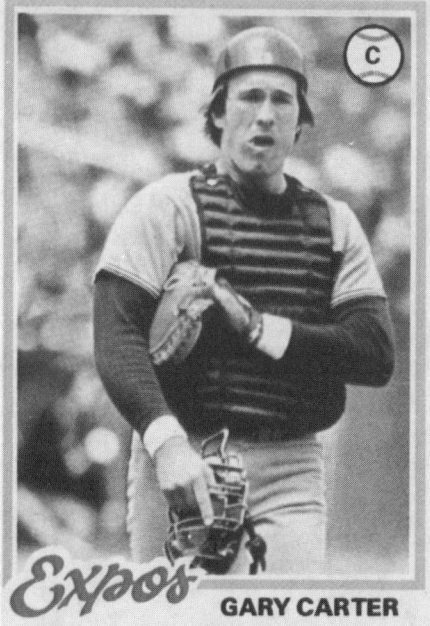

GARY CARTER

Because the type for the biography on back was reset by the fakers, this counterfeit can be identified by examining the fourth and fifth lines. On a genuine card, the descender of the "g" in "game" connects with ascender of the "d" in "led". On the counterfeit, those two letters do not connect.

One of the "Quebec counterfeits" this card may share other common traits with the 50 fake 1972-1980 Topps cards.

All were made by combining rescreened photos with painstakingly reproduced graphic elements of genuine cards.

Many of the counterfeits show random black ink streaks in various areas on the front, usually horizontally oriented.

The borders of these counterfeits often show a stray overspray of color, especially near the edges.

All the fakes are within weight tolerances of genuine contemporary cards.

Some of the counterfeits, by accident or design, are cut off-center, like Topps cards of the era, though many of the fakes are not cut to exactly correct size.

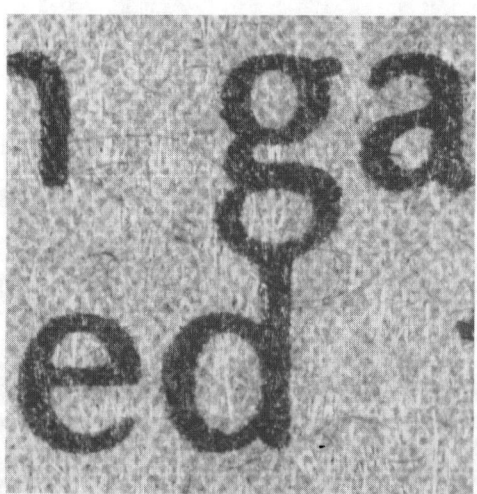

Genuine

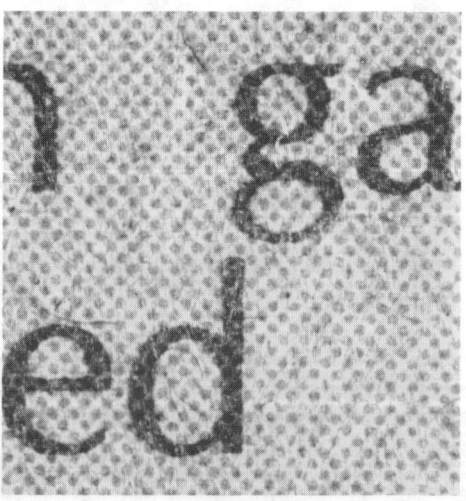

Counterfeit

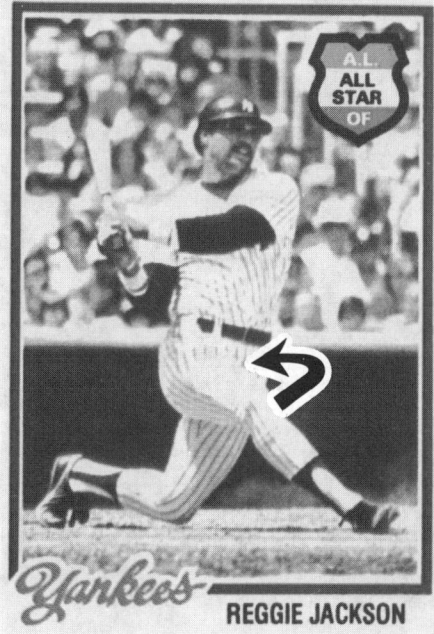

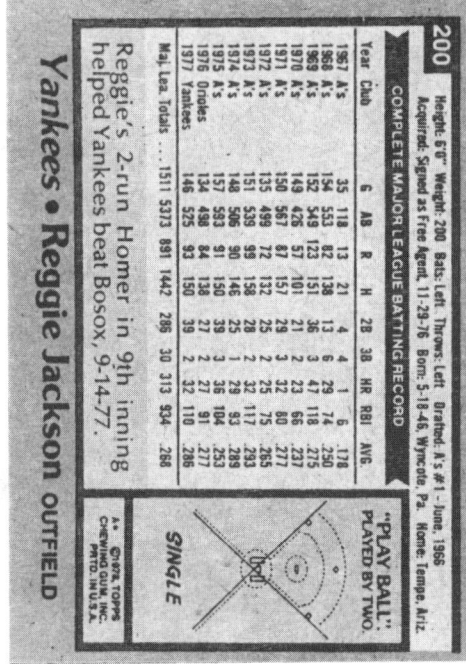

One of the easier "Quebec counterfeits" to identify. With a magnifying glass, examine the outstretched right thigh. When rescreening the photo to make the counterfeit, many of the tiny dots which make up the pinstripes on the original card were burned out, leaving this area too white.

This counterfeit may exhibit some of the other common traits found among the 50 fake 1972-1980 Topps cards.

All were made by combining rescreened photos with painstakingly reproduced graphic elements of genuine cards.

Many of the counterfeits show random black ink streaks in various areas on the front, usually horizontally oriented.

The borders of these counterfeits often show a stray overspray of color, especially near the edges.

All the fakes are within weight tolerances of genuine contemporary cards.

Some of the counterfeits, by accident or design, are cut off-center, like Topps cards of the era, though many of the fakes are not cut to exactly correct size.

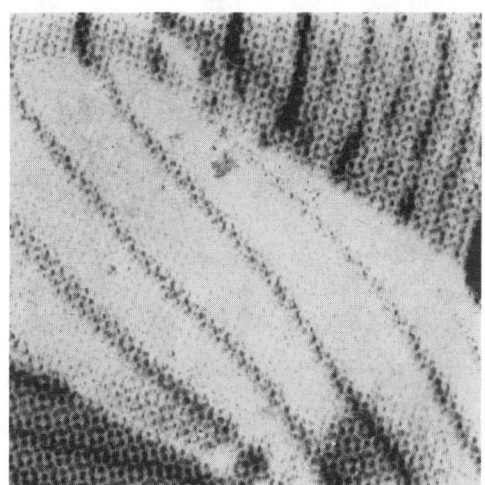

Genuine

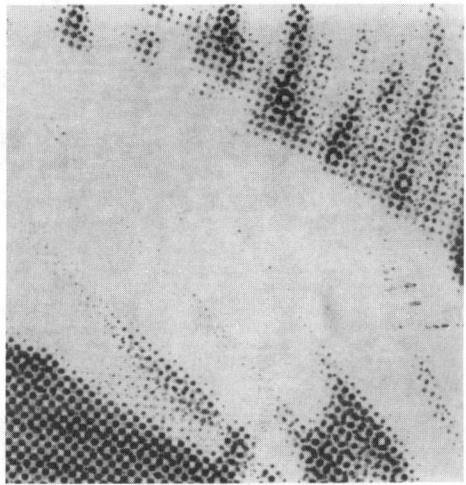

Counterfeit

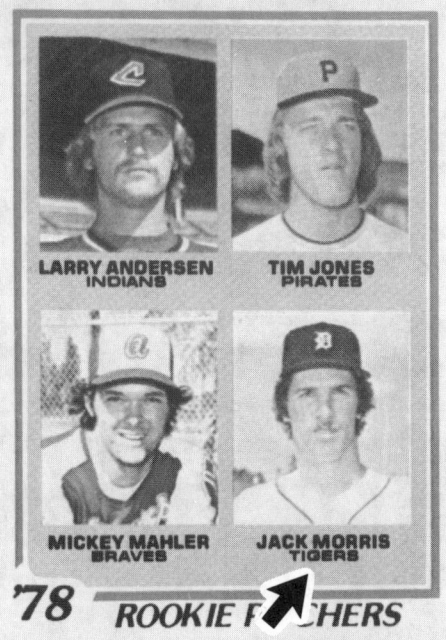

One of the more difficult of the "Quebec counterfeits" to identify. The best place to look is the "TIGERS" team name. On the genuine card, there is a space between the top and bottom loops of the "G", and between the end's of "S" and the center bar. On the counterfeit, these elements are connected with black ink.

This counterfeit may exhibit some of the other common traits found among the 50 fake 1972-1980 Topps cards.

All were made by combining rescreened photos with painstakingly reproduced graphic elements of genuine cards.

Many of the counterfeits show random black ink streaks in various areas on the front, usually horizontally oriented.

The borders of these counterfeits often show a stray overspray of color, especially near the edges.

All the fakes are within weight tolerances of genuine contemporary cards.

Some of the counterfeits, by accident or design, are cut off-center, like Topps cards of the era, though many of the fakes are not cut to exactly correct size.

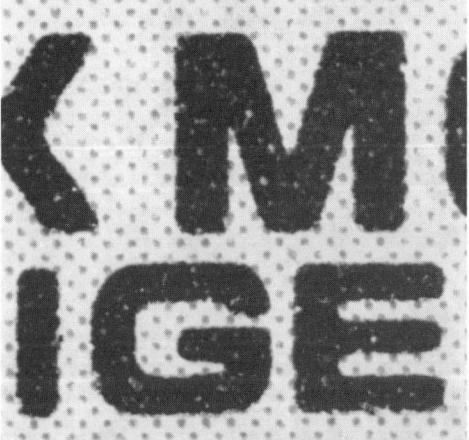

Genuine

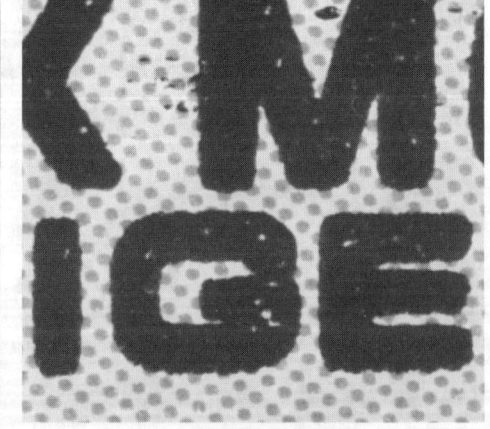

Counterfeit

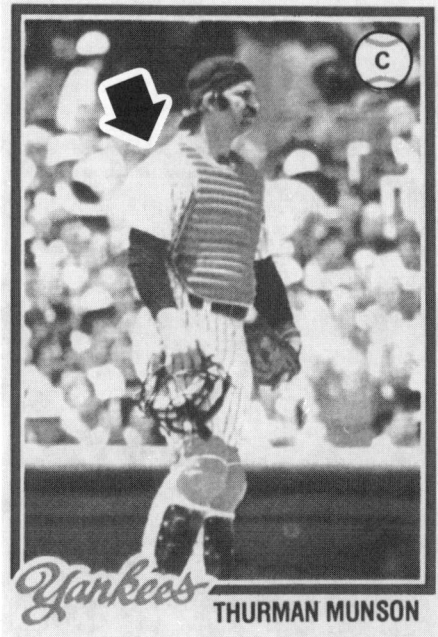

THURMAN MUNSON

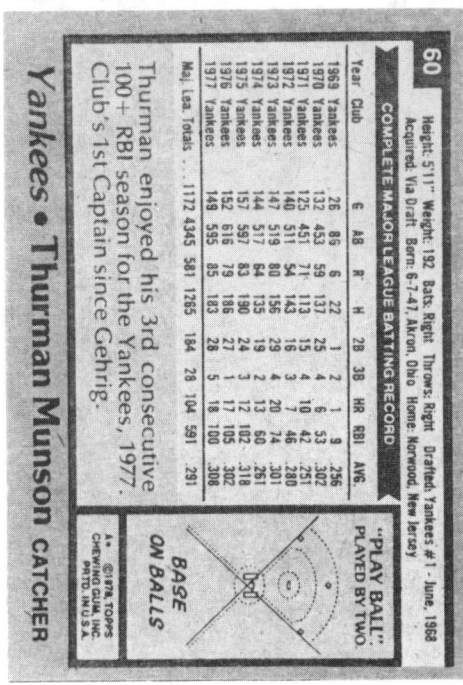

One of the more difficult "Quebec counterfeits" to identify. With a magnifying glass, examine the right shoulder area. When rescreening the photo to make the counterfeit, many of the tiny dots which make up the pinstripes on the original card were burned out, leaving this area too white.

This counterfeit may exhibit some of the other common traits found among the 50 fake 1972-1980 Topps cards.

All were made by combining rescreened photos with painstakingly reproduced graphic elements of genuine cards.

Many of the counterfeits show random black ink streaks in various areas on the front, usually horizontally oriented.

The borders of these counterfeits often show a stray overspray of color, especially near the edges.

All the fakes are within weight tolerances of genuine contemporary cards.

Some of the counterfeits, by accident or design, are cut off-center, like Topps cards of the era, though many of the fakes are not cut to exactly correct size.

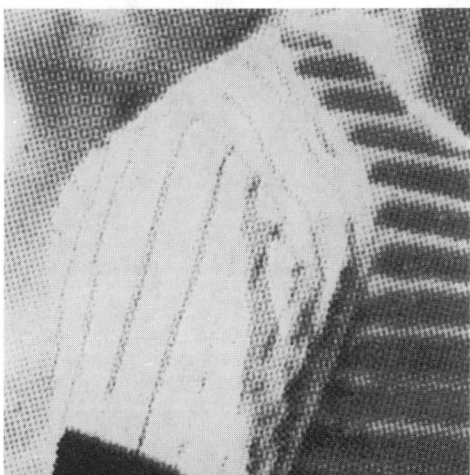

Genuine

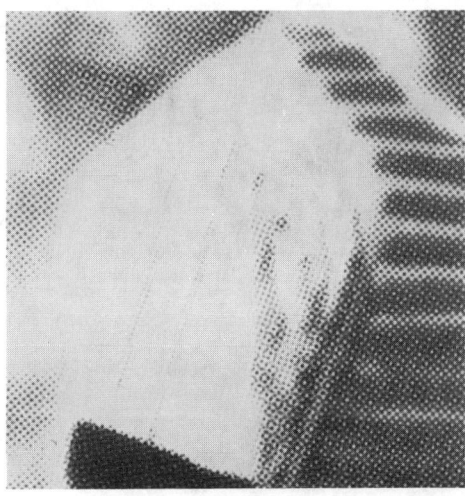

Counterfeit

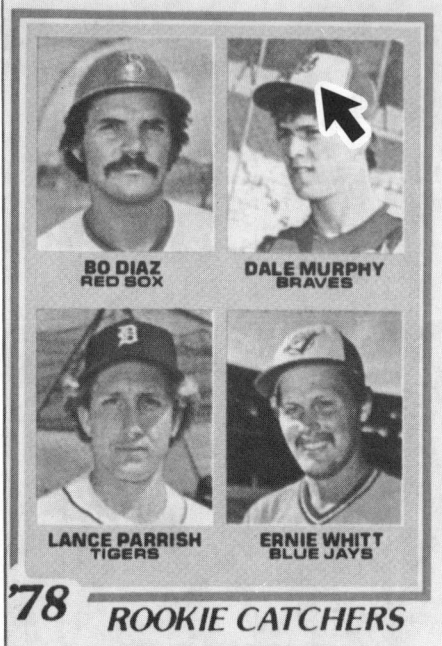

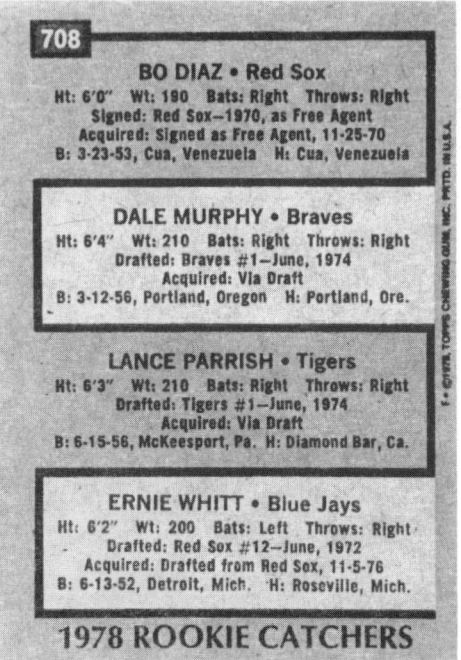

One of the more difficult of the "Quebec counterfeits" to identify. The best place to look for overall fuzziness of the rescreened photos on the counterfeit is on Murphy's cap. On the genuine card, the red "a" and its white and blue outlines are each distinct. On the counterfeit, they are very fuzzy, creating a blob.

This counterfeit may exhibit some of the other common traits found among the 50 fake 1972-1980 Topps cards.

All were made by combining rescreened photos with painstakingly reproduced graphic elements of genuine cards.

Many of the counterfeits show random black ink streaks in various areas on the front, usually horizontally oriented.

The borders of these counterfeits often show a stray overspray of color, especially near the edges.

All the fakes are within weight tolerances of genuine contemporary cards.

Some of the counterfeits, by accident or design, are cut off-center, like Topps cards of the era, though many of the fakes are not cut to exactly correct size.

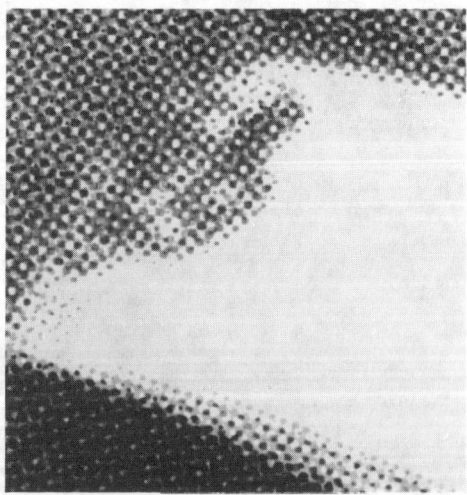

Genuine   **Counterfeit**

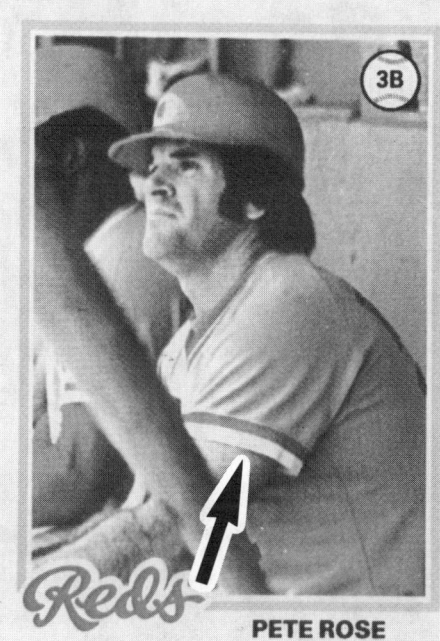

PETE ROSE

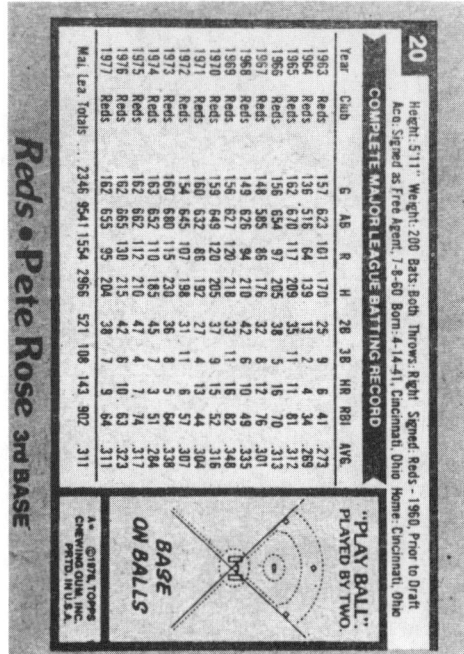

One of the most difficult "Quebec counterfeits" to identify. With a magnifying glass, examine the left end of the white band on Rose's left sleeve. When rescreening the photo to make the counterfeit, many of the tiny blue dots on the original card were burned out, leaving this area too white.

This counterfeit may exhibit some of the other common traits found among the 50 fake 1972-1980 Topps cards.

All were made by combining rescreened photos with painstakingly reproduced graphic elements of genuine cards.

Many of the counterfeits show random black ink streaks in various areas on the front, usually horizontally oriented.

The borders of these counterfeits often show a stray overspray of color, especially near the edges.

All the fakes are within weight tolerances of genuine contemporary cards.

Some of the counterfeits, by accident or design, are cut off-center, like Topps cards of the era, though many of the fakes are not cut to exactly correct size.

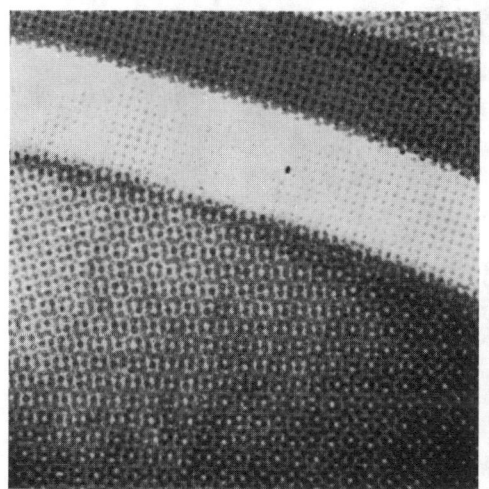

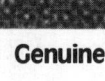

Genuine

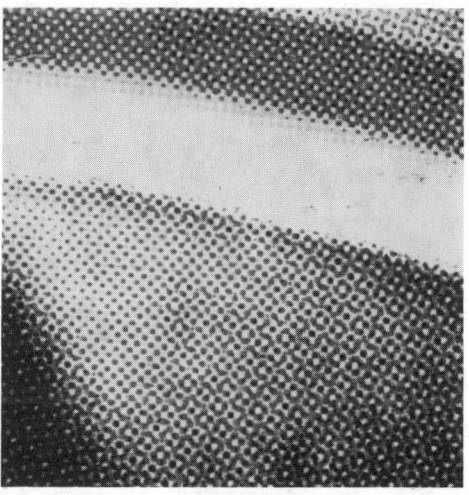

Counterfeit

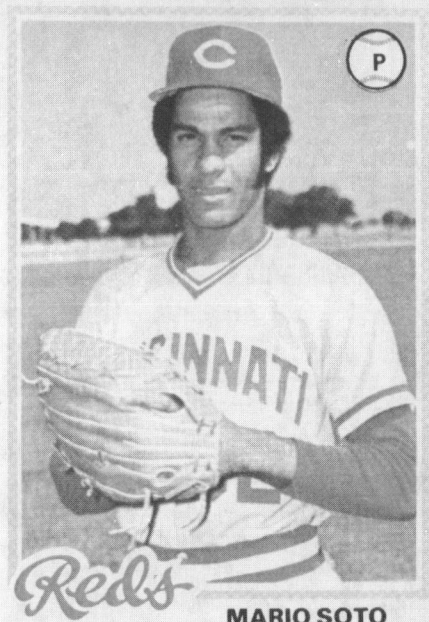

MARIO SOTO

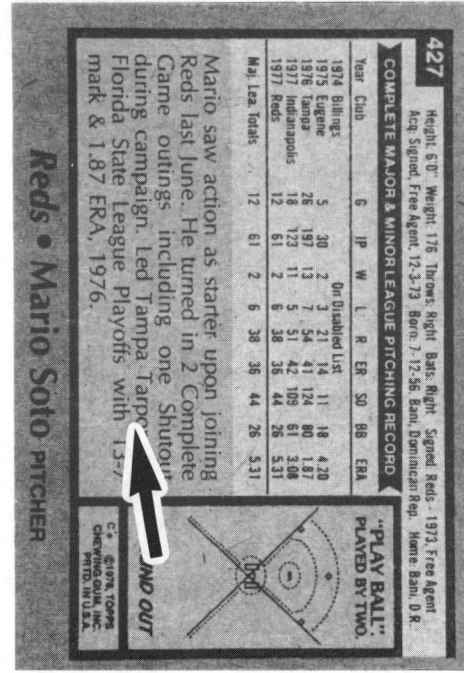

Because the type for the biography on back was reset by the fakers, this counterfeit can be identified by examining the fourth and fifth lines. On a genuine card, the descender of the "p" in "Tarpons" connects with the dot of the "i" in "with". On the counterfeit, that "p" is over the "t" and does not connect.

One of the "Quebec counterfeits" this card may share other common traits with the 50 fake 1972-1980 Topps cards.

All were made by combining rescreened photos with painstakingly reproduced graphic elements of genuine cards.

Many of the counterfeits show random black ink streaks in various areas on the front, usually horizontally oriented.

The borders of these counterfeits often show a stray overspray of color, especially near the edges.

All the fakes are within weight tolerances of genuine contemporary cards.

Some of the counterfeits, by accident or design, are cut off-center, like Topps cards of the era, though many of the fakes are not cut to exactly correct size.

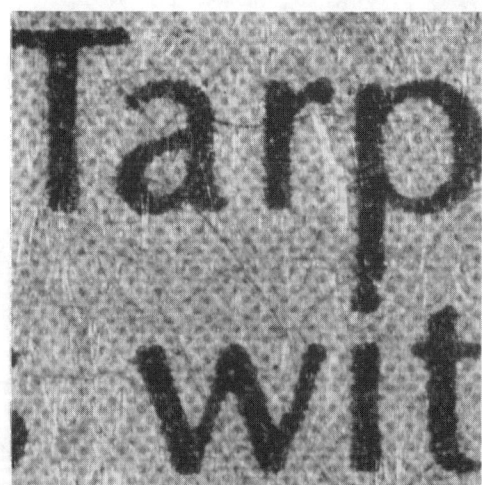

Genuine

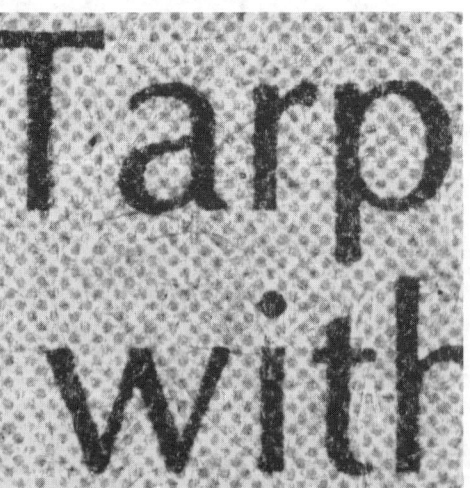

Counterfeit

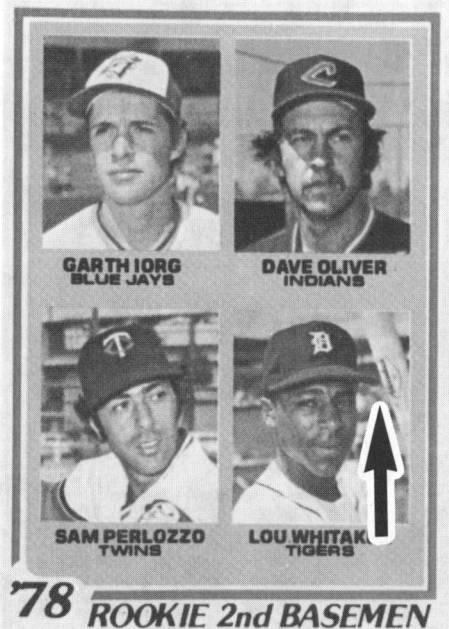

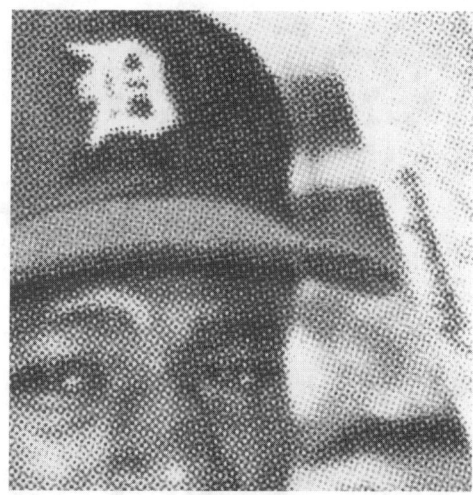

One of the most difficult of the "Quebec counterfeits" to identify. The best place to look for overall fuzziness of the rescreened photos on the counterfeits is on Whitaker's portrait. On the genuine card, most of "Adirondack" on the bat's label will be distinguishable. On the counterfeit, they are very fuzzy and indistinct.

This counterfeit may exhibit some of the other common traits found among the 50 fake 1972-1980 Topps cards.

All were made by combining rescreened photos with painstakingly reproduced graphic elements of genuine cards.

Many of the counterfeits show random black ink streaks in various areas on the front, usually horizontally oriented.

The borders of these counterfeits often show a stray overspray of color, especially near the edges.

All the fakes are within weight tolerances of genuine contemporary cards.

Some of the counterfeits, by accident or design, are cut off-center, like Topps cards of the era, though many of the fakes are not cut to exactly correct size.

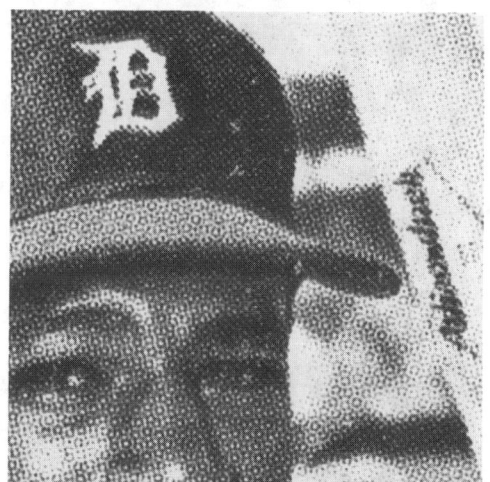

Genuine

Counterfeit

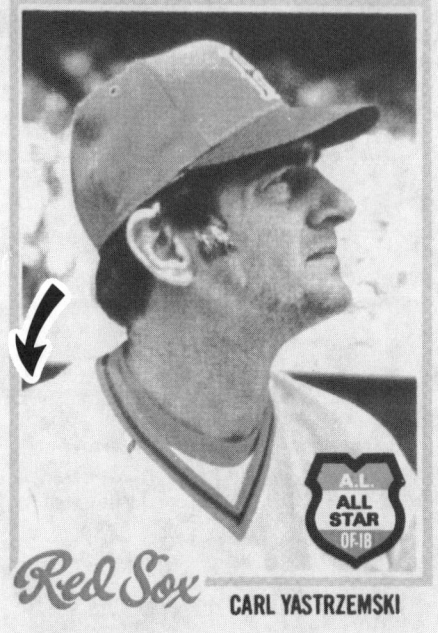

One of the most difficult of the "Quebec counterfeits" to identify. The best place to look is on Yaz's right shoulder, near the left orange border. On the fake, a magnifying glass will reveal a speck comprised of six tiny red dots. On a genuine card, this speck is seen as a single, larger, red dot.

This counterfeit may exhibit some of the other common traits found among the 50 fake 1972-1980 Topps cards.

All were made by combining rescreened photos with painstakingly reproduced graphic elements of genuine cards.

Many of the counterfeits show random black ink streaks in various areas on the front, usually horizontally oriented.

The borders of these counterfeits often show a stray overspray of color, especially near the edges.

All the fakes are within weight tolerances of genuine contemporary cards.

Some of the counterfeits, by accident or design, are cut off-center, like Topps cards of the era, though many of the fakes are not cut to exactly correct size.

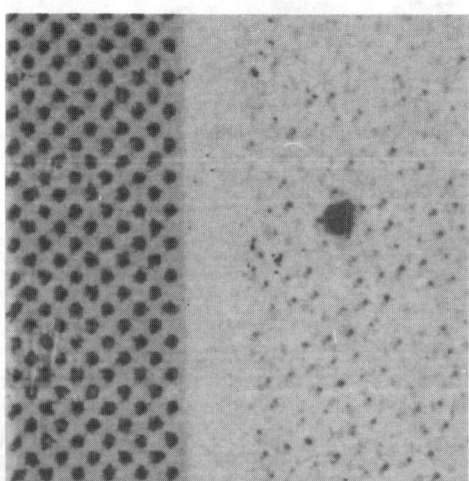

Genuine

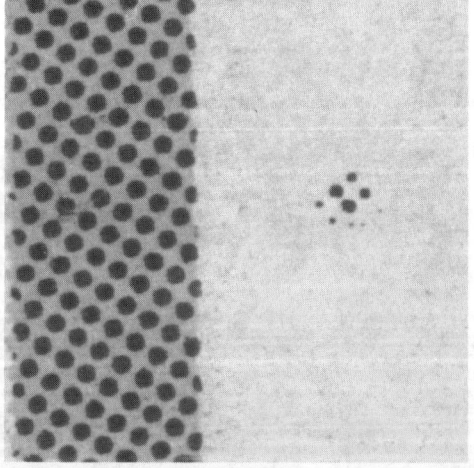

Counterfeit

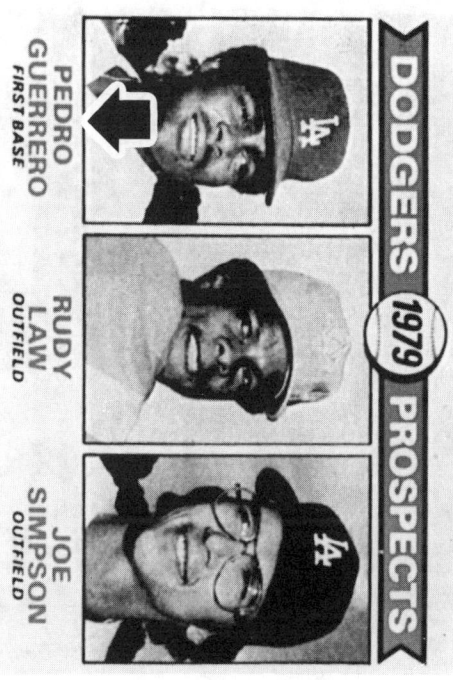

Despite the fact the player photos are black-and-white, this counterfeit is no more deceptive than the others in this "series."

Examination of the color design details with a magnifying glass reveals sure evidence of the counterfeit's status.

Easy differentiation between real and fake on this card can be made by examining the players' names and positions on the front of the card.

Those letters on a genuine card will be clean, solid blue (names) and black (position); on the counterfeit, they are composed of many dots, giving a fuzzy appearance. Similar evidence can be seen in the letters of "DODGERS 1979 PROSPECTS".

On back, a black printed screen has been used to simulate the gray cardboard of a Topps original and hide the white cardboard on which the fake was printed.

The black "Reprint" which appears on the back of the card shown here may not be present on all cards encountered.

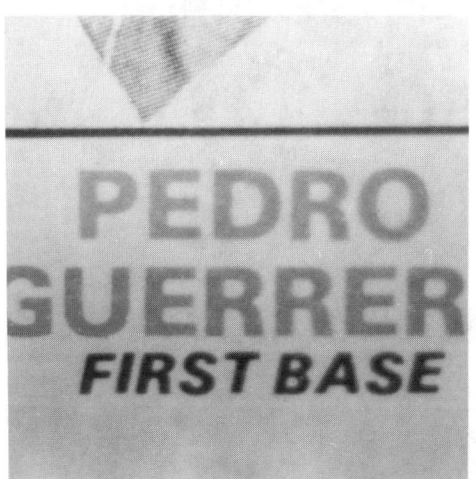

Genuine

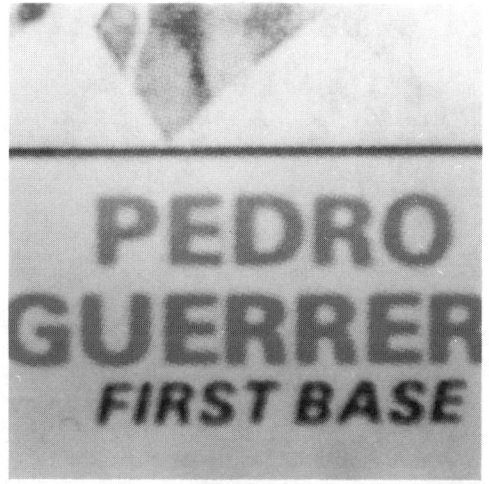

Counterfeit

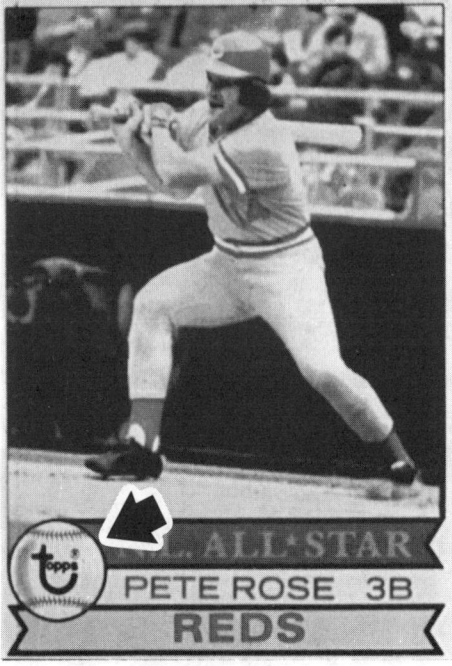

An overall fuzzy appearance — front and back — makes this counterfeit look suspicious to an experienced eye.

Examination of the design details with a magnifying glass reveals sure evidence of the counterfeit's status.

Easy differentiation between real and fake on this card can be made by examining the Topps logo inside the baseball at lower left. Those letters on a genuine card will be clean, solid black; on the counterfeit, they are composed of many dots,

giving a fuzzy appearance. Similar evidence can be seen in the letters of the All Star designation, the player's name and position and the team name.

On back, a black printed screen has been used to simulate the gray cardboard of a Topps original and hide the white cardboard on which the fake was printed.

The black "Reprint" which appears on the back of the card shown here may not be present on all cards encountered in the hobby market.

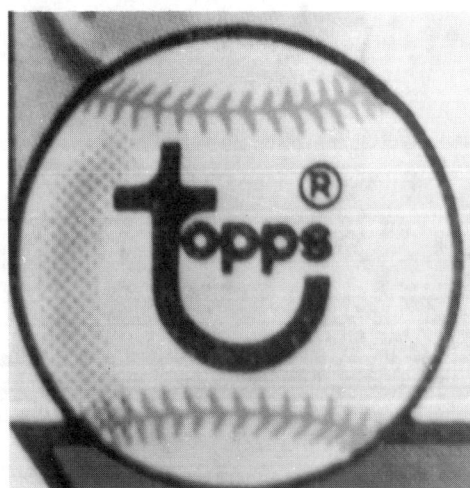

Genuine

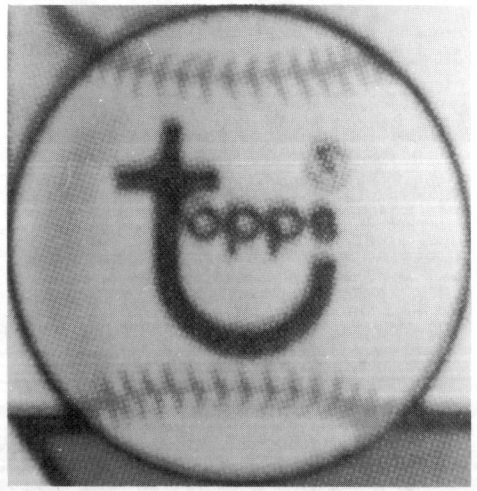

Counterfeit

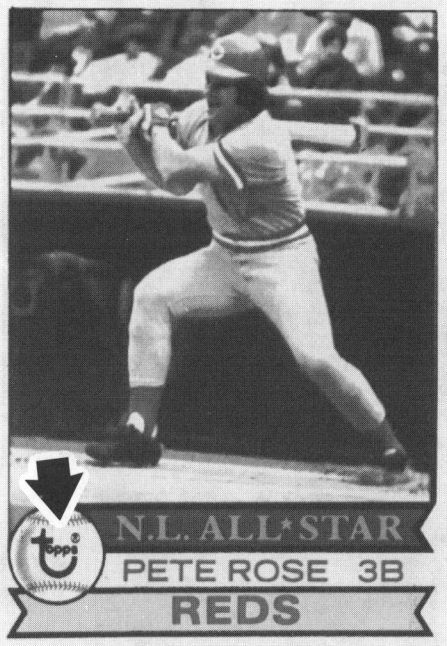

N.L. ALL★STAR
PETE ROSE 3B
REDS

Use of a magnifying glass to examine the Topps logo at lower left will reveal this counterfeit. The registration mark (®) on a genuine card will be clear and distinct. On the counterfeit, the "R" is badly blurred, having no top loop and connecting with the circle above it.

One of the "Quebec counterfeits" this may exhibit a number of traits common to many of the 50 fake Topps cards which were the work of the same counterfeiter.

All were made by combining rescreened photos with painstakingly reproduced graphic elements of genuine cards.

Many of the counterfeits show random black ink streaks in various areas on the front, usually horizontally oriented.

The borders of these counterfeits often show a stray overspray of color, especially near the edges.

All the fakes are within weight tolerances of genuine contemporary cards.

Some of the counterfeits, by accident or design, are cut off-center, like Topps cards of the era, though many of the fakes are not cut to exactly correct size.

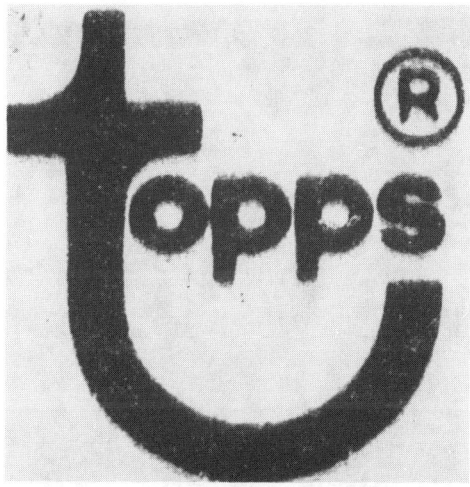

Genuine

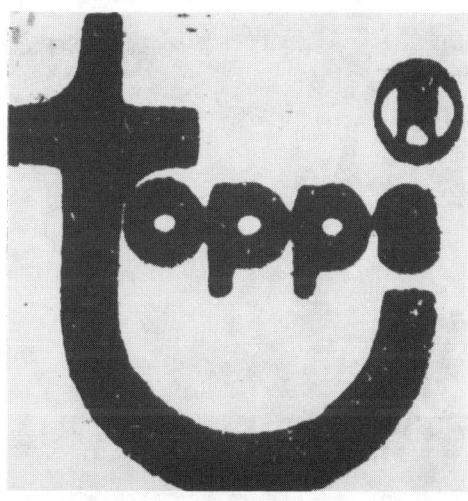

Counterfeit

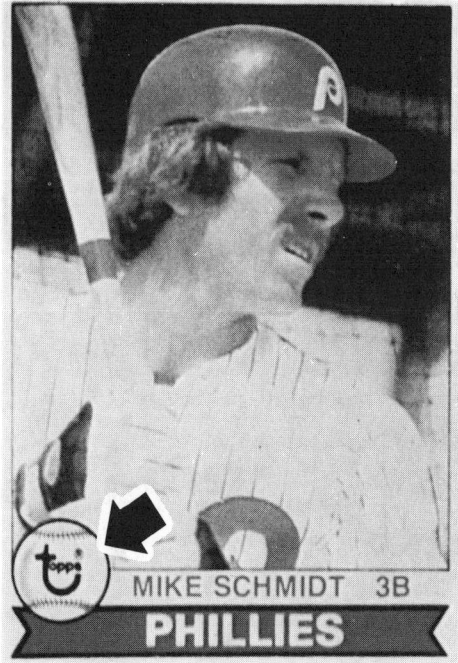

Reprint

Year	Club	G	AB	R	H	2B	3B	HR	RBI	AVG.
1972	Phillies	13	34	2	7	0	0	1	3	.206
1973	Phillies	132	367	43	72	11	0	18	52	.196
1974	Phillies	162	568	108	160	28	7	36	116	.282
1975	Phillies	158	562	93	140	34	3	38	95	.249
1976	Phillies	160	584	112	153	31	4	38	107	.262
1977	Phillies	154	544	114	149	27	11	38	101	.274
1978	Phillies	145	513	93	129	27	2	21	78	.251
Maj. Lea. Totals		924	3772	565	810	158	27	190	552	.255

COMPLETE MAJOR LEAGUE BATTING RECORD

610

Phillies • Mike Schmidt 3rd BASE

Height: 6'2" Weight: 198 Bats: Right Throws: Right Drafted: Phillies #2 - June, 1971
Acquired: Via Draft Born: 9-27-49, Dayton, Ohio Home: West Berlin, New Jersey

Set record with 17 Total Bases in an extra-inning game, April 17, 1976. Tied National League record with two Grand-Slammers during month of June, 1973. Hit .308 in 1976 N.L. Playoffs.

BASEBALL DATES

What Happened MAY 9, 1888. Homers & Single in Game. Giants' Roger Connor hit 3

© Dr. 6978, TOPPS CHEWING GUM, INC. PRTD. IN U.S.A.

An overall fuzzy appearance — front and back — makes this counterfeit look suspicious to an experienced eye.

Examination of the design details with a magnifying glass reveals sure evidence of the counterfeit's status.

Easy differentiation between real and fake on this card can be made by examining the Topps logo inside the baseball at lower left. Those letters on a genuine card will be clean, solid black; on the counterfeit, they are composed of many dots, giving a fuzzy appearance. Similar evidence can be seen in the magenta color of the player's name and the seams of the ball, and the purple color bar at bottom.

On back, a black printed screen has been used to simulate the gray cardboard of a Topps original and hide the white cardboard on which the fake was printed.

The black "Reprint" which appears on the back of the card shown here may not be present on all cards encountered in the hobby market.

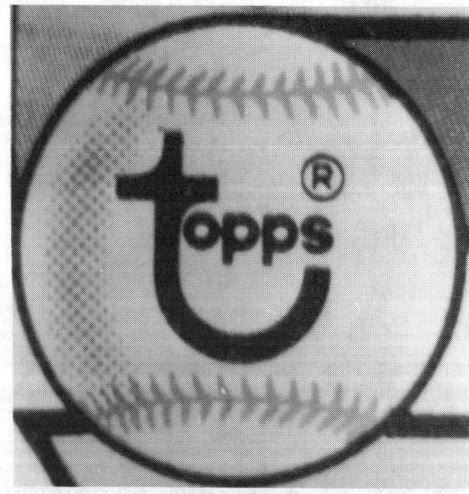

Genuine

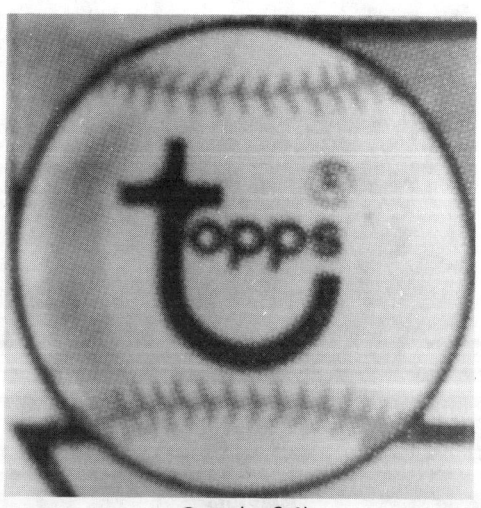

Counterfeit

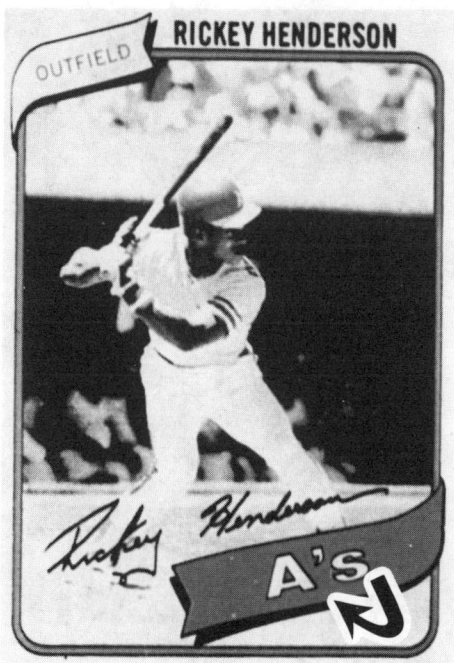

The fuzzy photo and lettering on the front of this counterfeit should put most hobbyists on warning that more detailed examination is needed.

Using a magnifying glass to examine the lettering will provide definite proof that this card is a phony. On a genuine card, such details as the black borders of the frame line, the player's name, position and facsimile autograph, the green position designation and the yellow ''A's'' should show up as solid colors with edges that end crisply and cleanly at the respective backgrounds. On this counterfeit, the letters and other color design elements are composed of many tiny color dots, giving them a ragged look at the edges. The back is fairly deceptive, although close examination will show a pattern of gray dots has been printed on the white cardboard to simulate the genuine Topps card stock.

The black ''Reprint'' which appears on the back of the card shown here may not be present on all cards encountered.

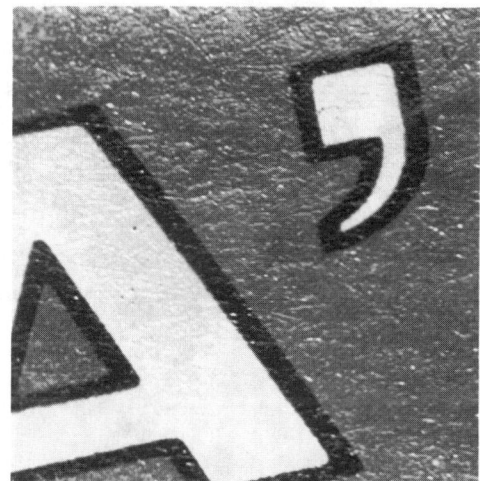

Genuine

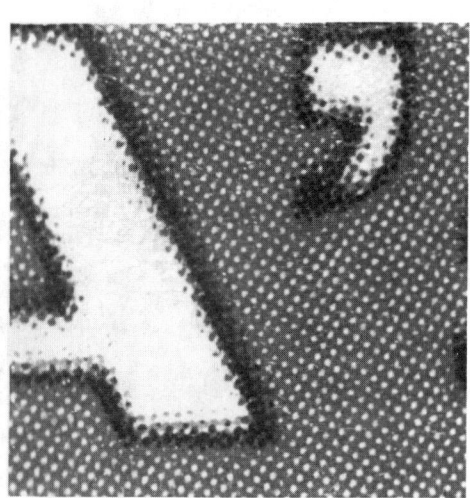

Counterfeit

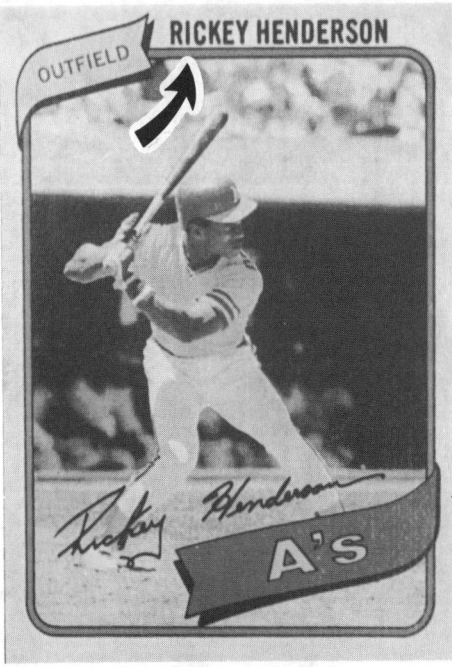

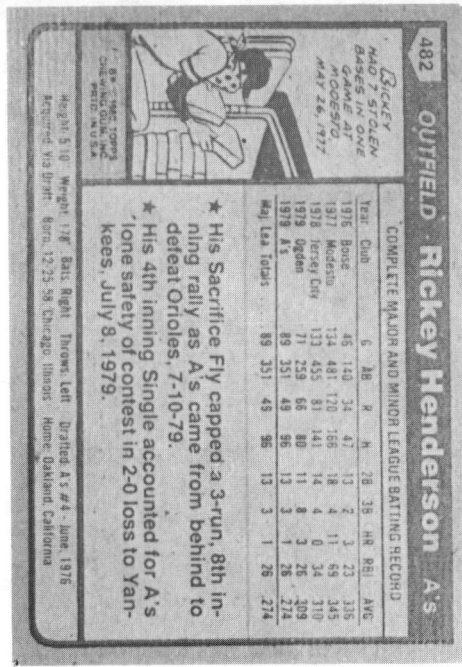

Without close inspection, this counterfeit is visually quite deceptive — much more so than the "Cleveland reprint" of the Henderson rookie card.

Using a magnifying glass to examine the lettering on the front will provide definite proof that this card is bogus. On a genuine card, such details as the lines around the blue frame and the yellow pennant, the player's name and facsimile autograph are printed in solid black, with clean edges. On the counterfeit, these elements are printed as composites of many tiny colored dots, resulting in a fuzzy appearance. The same can be seen in the green "OUTFIELD" designation which shows up as solid letters on an original, but dot composites on the counterfeit.

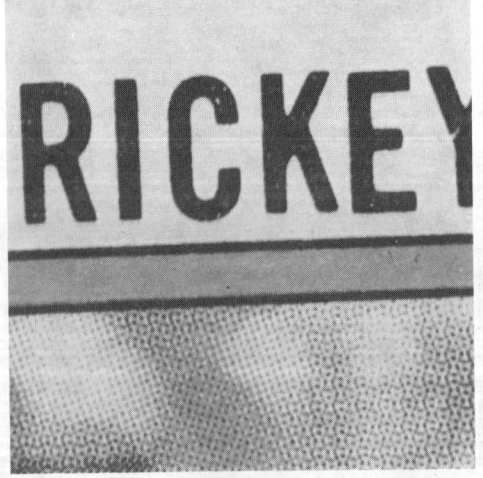

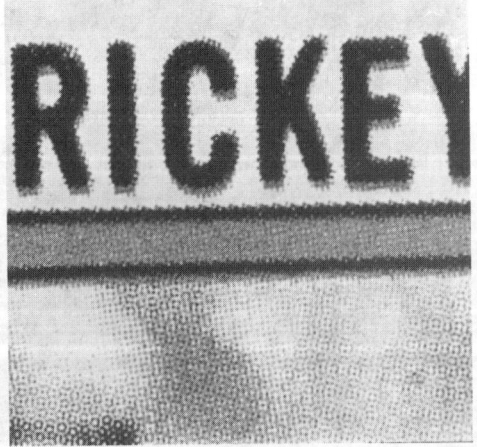

Genuine   **Counterfeit**

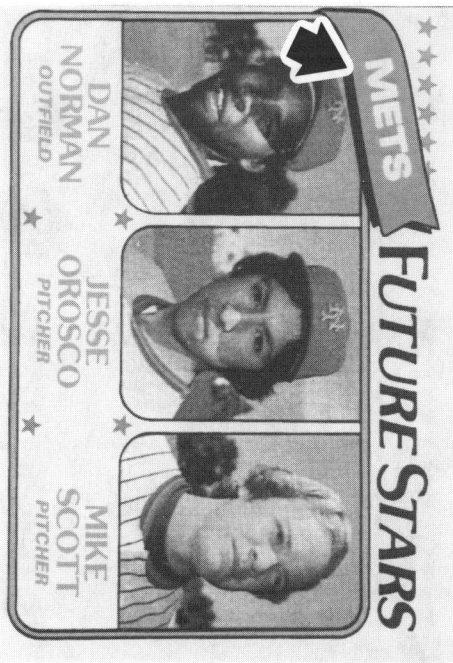

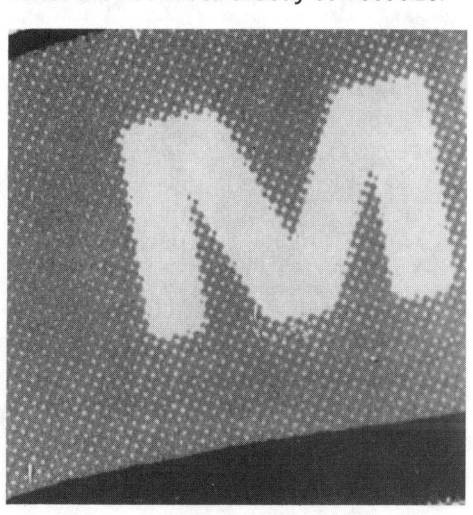

This counterfeit can be identified by using a magnifier to examine the green banner and yellow "METS". On a genuine card, the green is a solid color and the letters' edges end crisply at the background. On the counterfeit, there are tiny yellow dots throughout the green banner and the yellow letters have fuzzy edges.

One of the "Quebec counterfeits" this card may share other common traits with the 50 fake 1972-1980 Topps cards.

All were made by combining rescreened photos with painstakingly reproduced graphic elements of genuine cards.

Many of the counterfeits show random black ink streaks in various areas on the front, usually horizontally oriented.

The borders of these counterfeits often show a stray overspray of color, especially near the edges.

All the fakes are within weight tolerances of genuine contemporary cards.

Some of the counterfeits, by accident or design, are cut off-center, like Topps cards of the era, though many of the fakes are not cut to exactly correct size.

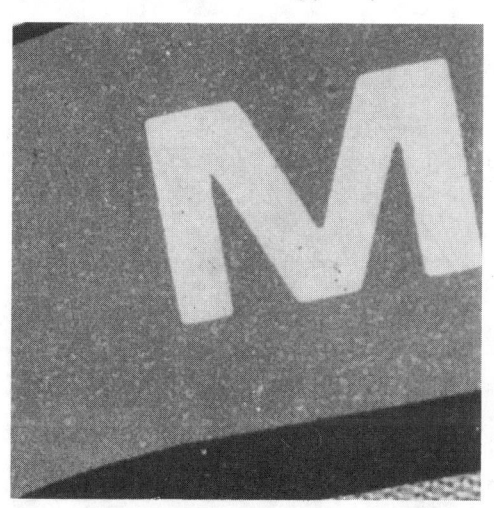

Genuine

Counterfeit

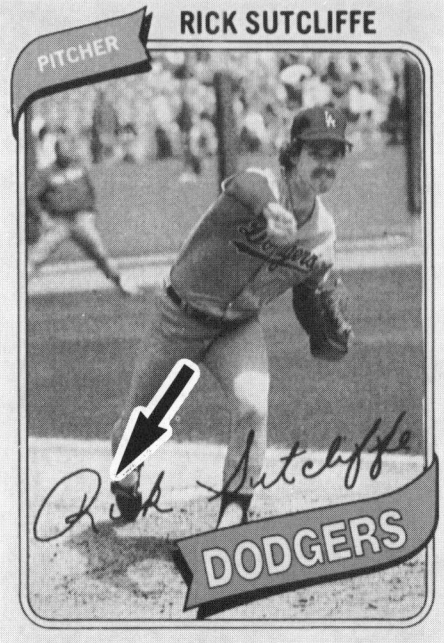

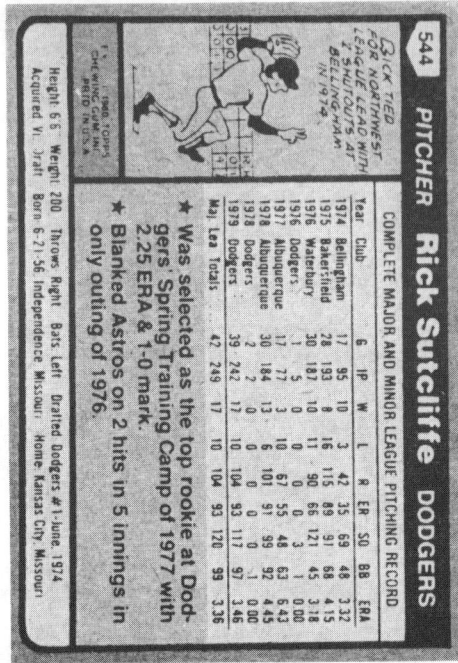

Examination of the facsimile autograph with a magnifying glass will identify this counterfeit. The rescreened counterfeit card will show the autograph composed of many tiny dots, giving it a fuzzy appearance. On a genuine card, the autograph will be made up of clean solid black lines.

One of the "Quebec counterfeits" this card may exhibit some of the other common traits found among the 50 fake 1972-1980 Topps cards.

All were made by combining rescreened photos with painstakingly reproduced graphic elements of genuine cards.

Many of the counterfeits show random black ink streaks in various areas on the front, usually horizontally oriented.

The borders of these counterfeits often show a stray overspray of color, especially near the edges.

All the fakes are within weight tolerances of genuine contemporary cards.

Some of the counterfeits, by accident or design, are cut off-center, like Topps cards of the era, though many of the fakes are not cut to exactly correct size.

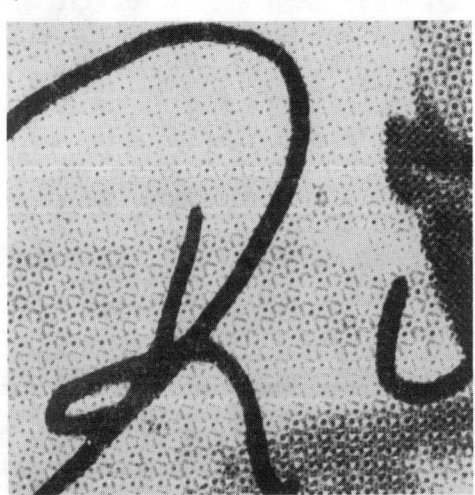

Genuine

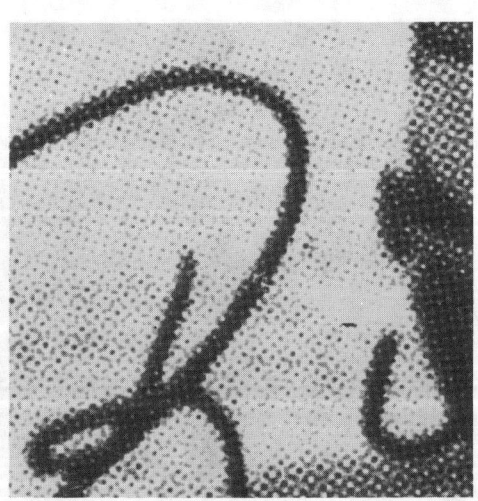

Counterfeit

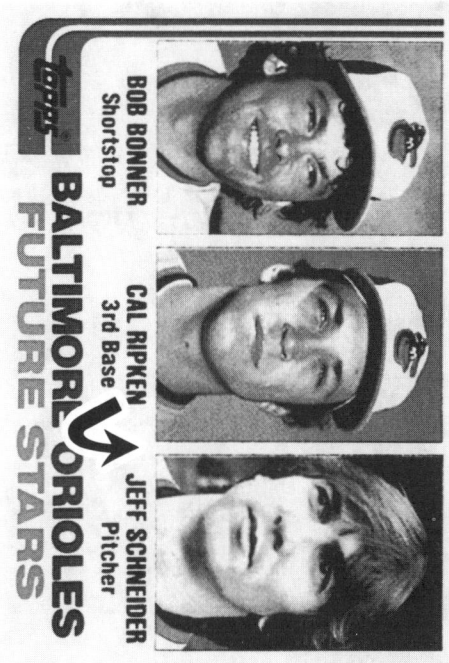
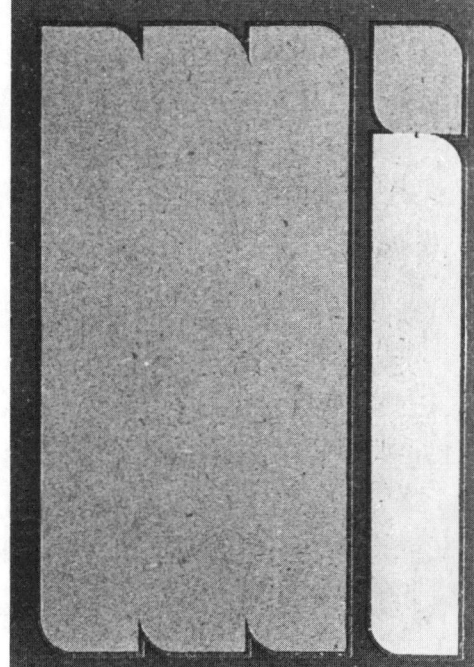

One of the more frequently encountered counterfeits, this phony Ripken rookie is too often thought to be an error card, missing the typography on the back. The absence of the printed wording on the card's back is irrefutable proof of its bogus nature.

A later version of this counterfeit has been seen with complete back printing, but the type style is not a close match for that used on the genuine card.

As a double-check, study the front of the card with a magnifying glass.

The color printing is excellent on this counterfeit. An easy means of detection, however, is found in the black borders which surround the players' portraits.

On a genuine card, those black boxes will be made up of clean, solid lines. On the counterfeit, the lines are rendered as fuzzy black structures made up of numerous tiny dots.

This counterfeit is often seen as an eight-card sheet, usually offered as some sort of test issue.

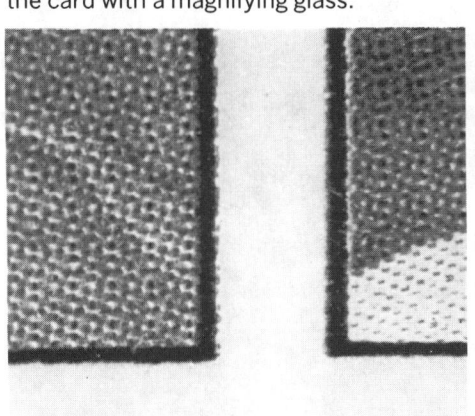
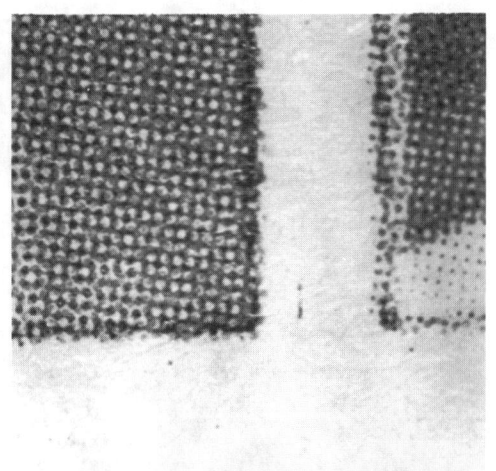

Genuine   **Counterfeit**

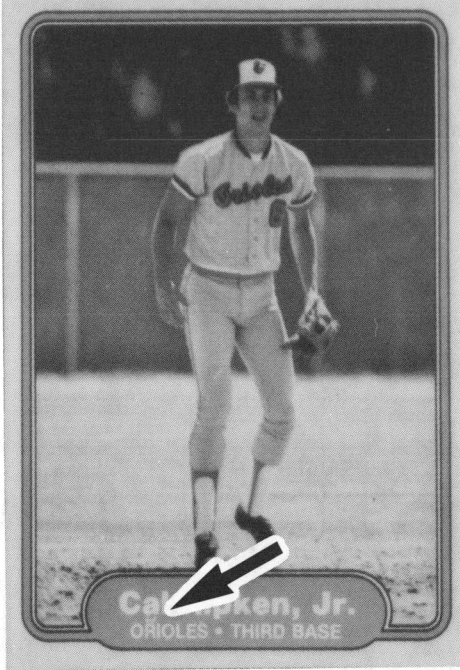
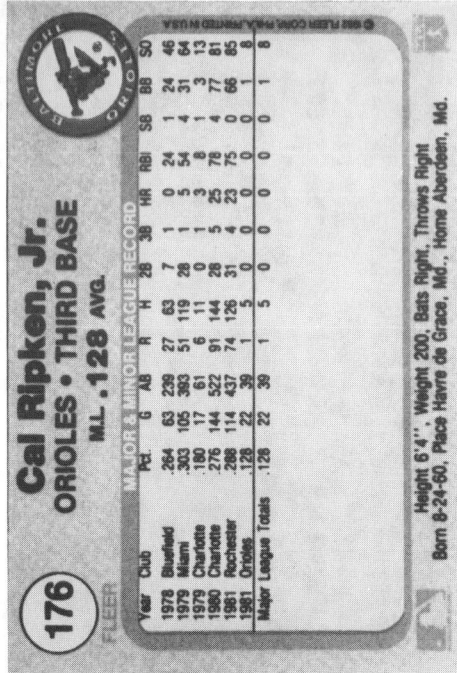

A quick check for this counterfeit involves flipping the card over from front to back. When a genuine '82 Fleer card is thus turned, the Orioles logo on back appears at the lower-right. When the fake is flipped, the logo is at upper-left. As with all counterfeits, a study of graphic details with a magnifying glass is recommended to confirm the status.

The best place to detect this counterfeit is the name on the card front. A genuine card will show these letters as solid white type. On the counterfeit, the letters show a pattern of many tiny red and yellow colored dots within.

Similarly, the black frame lines around the photo can be studied. On a genuine card, these lines will be solid black with clean edges. On the counterfeit, these lines are composed of many tiny colored dots, creating a ragged appearance.

A checkpoint on all specimens seen to date, though possibly corrected later in the counterfeit's press run, shows a yellow "blob" between the "a" of "Cal" and the "R" of "ORIOLES".

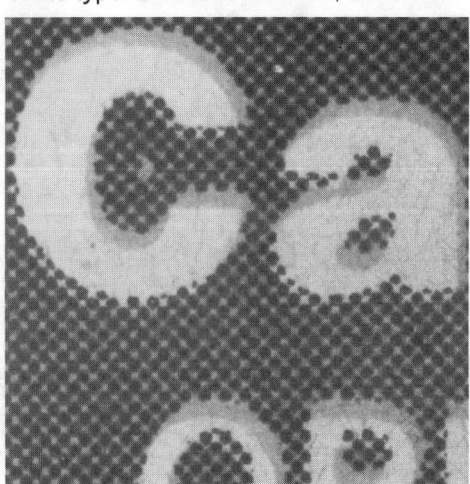

Genuine

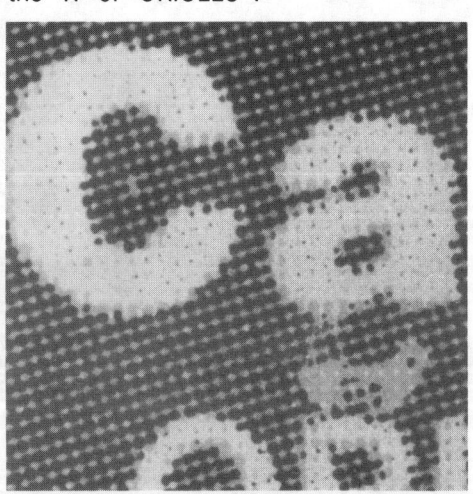

Counterfeit

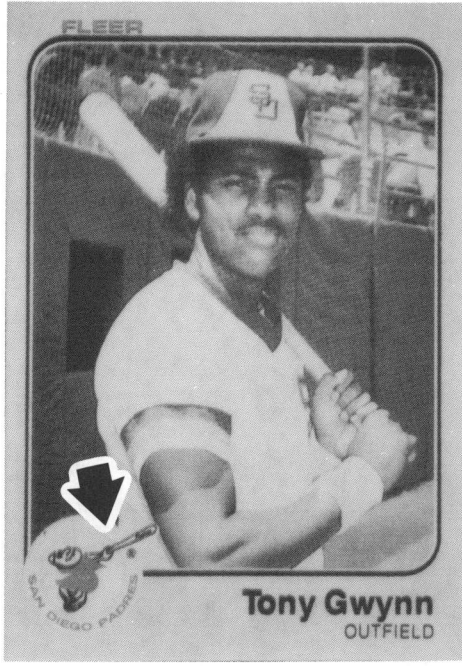

Tony Gwynn
OUTFIELD

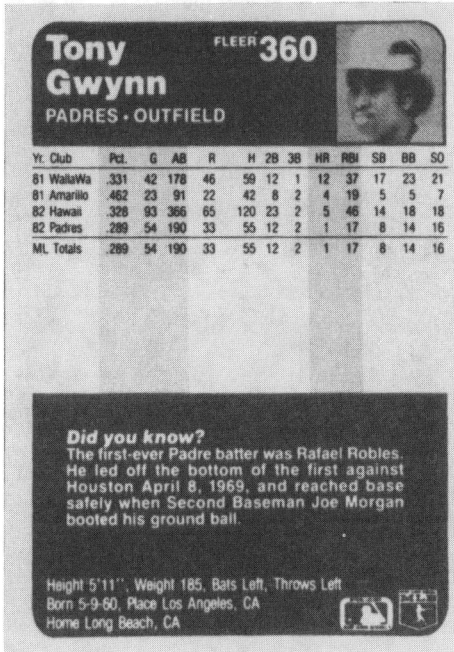

Tony Gwynn
FLEER 360
PADRES · OUTFIELD

Yr. Club	Pct.	G	AB	R	H	2B	3B	HR	RBI	SB	BB	SO
81 WallaWa	.331	42	178	46	59	12	1	12	37	17	23	21
81 Amarillo	.462	23	91	22	42	8	2	4	19	5	5	7
82 Hawaii	.328	93	366	65	120	23	2	5	46	14	18	18
82 Padres	.289	54	190	33	55	12	2	1	17	8	14	16
ML Totals	.289	54	190	33	55	12	2	1	17	8	14	16

Did you know?
The first-ever Padre batter was Rafael Robles. He led off the bottom of the first against Houston April 8, 1969, and reached base safely when Second Baseman Joe Morgan booted his ground ball.

Height 5'11", Weight 185, Bats Left, Throws Left
Born 5-9-60, Place Los Angeles, CA
Home Long Beach, CA

Use of a magnifying glass to examine the graphic details on the front of the card will easily reveal this counterfeit. The black elements (name, position, photo border and details of the team logo), on a genuine card will all be solid black, with clean edges. On this counterfeit, those elements have been created by a combination of blue, red, yellow and black dots, creating ragged edges and problems with color registration.

Another checkpoint on the front is the red "FLEER" logo. On a genuine card, there will be no extraneous print dots within the red letters. On the counterfeit, the letters are littered with extra color dots.

On the back, check the MLB and MLBPA logos. A real card will show the words on these logos clearly under magnification. On this counterfeit, the words are a jumble of indecipherable letter-like elements. Also, a genuine card will have Gwynn's photo on back printed in brown-and-white, while the counterfeit has this picture in black-and-white.

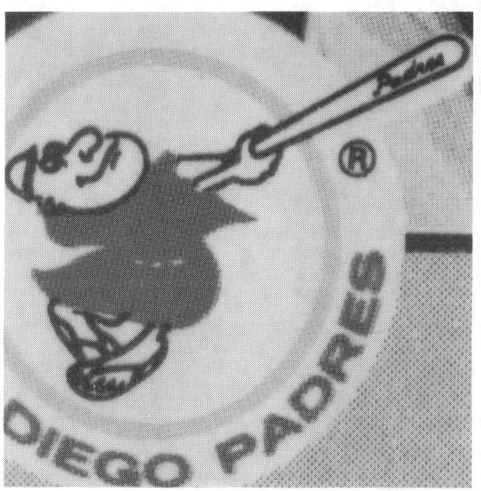

Genuine

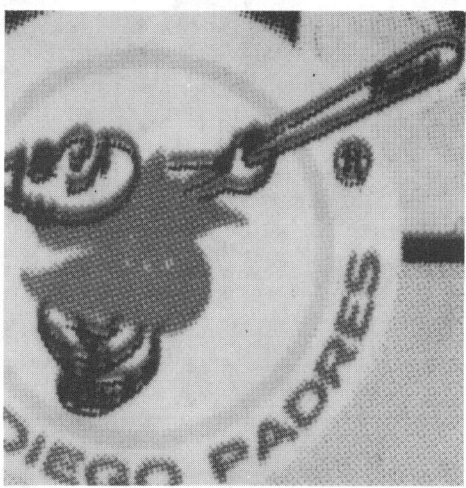

Counterfeit

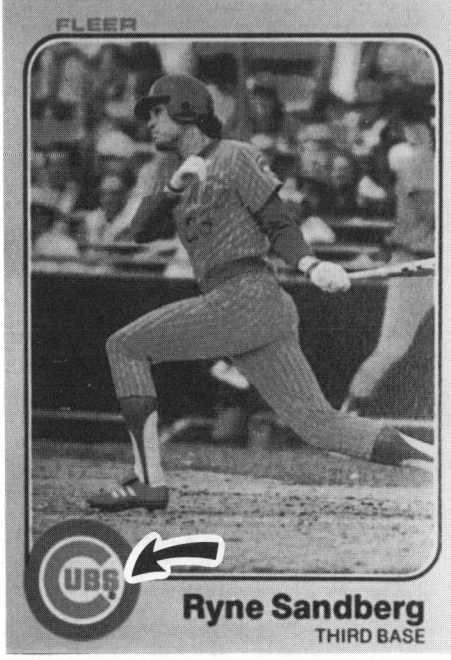

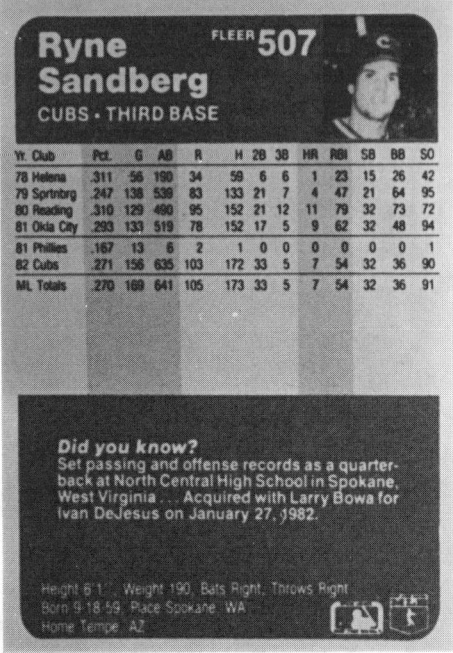

Yr. Club	Pct.	G	AB	R	H	2B	3B	HR	RBI	SB	BB	SO
78 Helena	.311	56	190	34	59	6	6	1	23	15	26	42
79 Sprtnbrg	.247	138	539	83	133	21	7	4	47	21	64	95
80 Reading	.310	129	490	95	152	21	12	11	79	32	73	72
81 Okla City	.293	133	519	78	152	17	5	9	62	32	48	94
81 Phillies	.167	13	6	2	1	0	0	0	0	0	0	1
82 Cubs	.271	156	635	103	172	33	5	7	54	32	36	90
ML Totals	.270	169	641	105	173	33	5	7	54	32	36	91

Did you know?
Set passing and offense records as a quarter-back at North Central High School in Spokane, West Virginia . . . Acquired with Larry Bowa for Ivan DeJesus on January 27, 1982.

Height 6'1", Weight 190, Bats Right, Throws Right
Born 9-18-59, Place Spokane, WA
Home Tempe, AZ

This is one of the few counterfeits which can be definitively detected with the naked eye. Unfortunately, the characteristic which allows this diagnosis cannot be differentiated in black-and-white photos. In fact, that characteristic *is* a black-and-white photo. On this counterfeit, the small portrait of Sandberg at the upper-right on the back is printed in black-and-white, instead of the sepia-and-white with which genuine 1983 Fleer cards present the back photo.

The typography on the front will provide additional evidence of counterfeit status. Genuine cards will show the red "FLEER" and the black player's name and position as solid letters. On the counterfeit, these letters are made up of many tiny dots, rendering a fuzzy appearance.

Similarly, the black and white lines which frame the photo on a genuine card are clean and crisp. On the counterfeit,

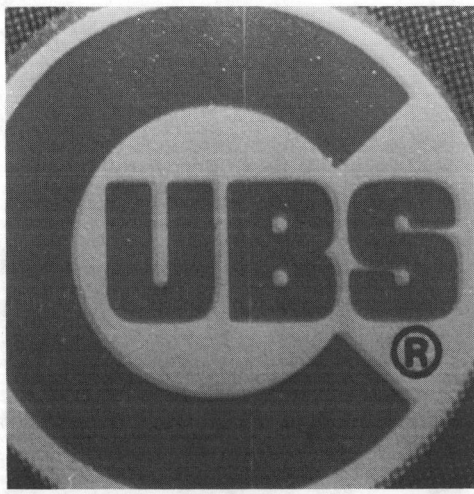

Genuine

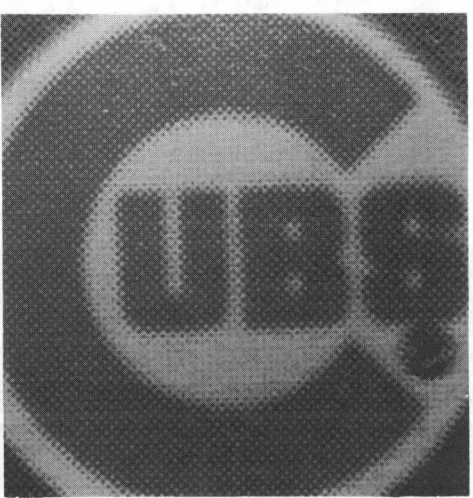

Counterfeit

the black line shows fuzzy edges, while the white line has tiny dark dots invading it.

Likewise, the red "Cubs" in the logo is solid on a genuine, but comprised of red dots on the counterfeit. The registration mark (®) under the "s" of "Cubs" is clear and readable on a genuine card, but inde-cipherable on the counterfeit.

Returning to the back of card, the observer will note that the Major League and Players' Association logos at bottom-right have wording that is illegible on the counterfeit, even when viewed under magnification.

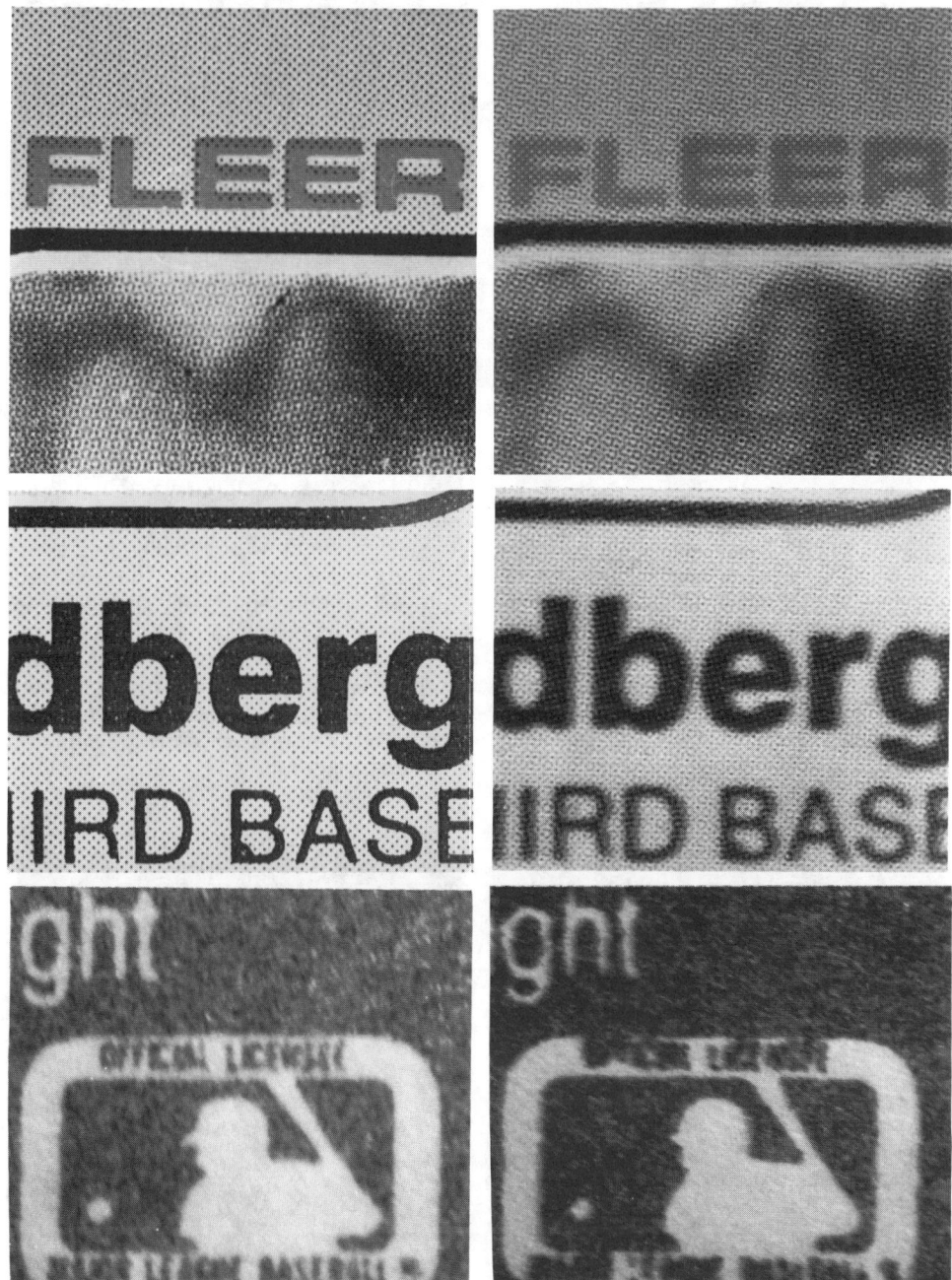

Genuine   **Counterfeit**

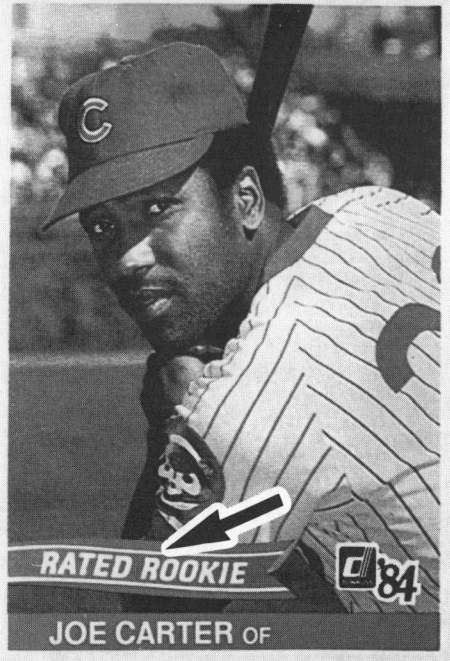

JOE CARTER OF

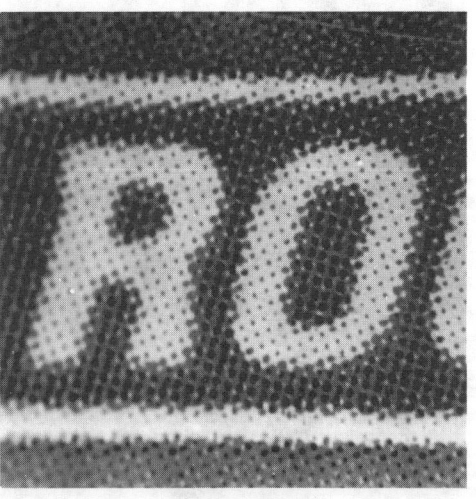

JOSEPH CARTER

Born: March 7, 1960   Home: Oklahoma City, Okla.
Hi.: 6'3"   Wgt.: 216   Bats: Right   Throws: Right

41

© 1983 Donruss
Printed in USA

RECENT MAJOR LEAGUE PERFORMANCE

Year	Team Name	Bat. Avg.	Games	At Bat	Hits	Runs	2B	3B	HR	RBI	Steal	Walk	SO
1983	Cubs	176	23	51	9	6	1	0	1	1	1	0	21
Career		176	23	51	9	6	1	0	1	1	1	0	21

*"Devotes
Led League

CAREER HIGHLIGHTS

Color: No. 1 prospect for '84... Batted .307 with 22 HR and 83 RBI at Iowa last year to earn a brief trial with Cubs in midseason...Led the American Association in total bases in '83 (265), was 2nd in stolen bases (40) and hits (190), 6th in HR and 11th in RBI...Hit .319 with 25 HR and 98 RBI in 110 games for Cubs Double A Midland farm in Texas League in '82...Cubs made him the No. 2 player in the nation selected in '81 amateur draft.

New Acquired: Signed by Cubs as their No. 1 choice in June 1981 amateur draft.

Contract Status: Signed thru 1984

Luckily, this particular counterfeit is rarely encountered, since it is good enough to fool most viewers without detailed study. The front of the counterfeit is much better than the back, which exhibits a yellowish cast to the green color bars and which has seen a too-heavy application of black ink, bloating the individual letters of the typography.

Unlike the '84 Donruss Mattingly counterfeit, which has poor replication of the logo, the Carter counterfeit has a very passable logo. Examination with a magnifying lens should be concentrated on the white letters of "RATED ROOKIE", the red stripes above and below that notation and the red stripe at bottom which bears the player's name and position. The white letters will be pure and clean on a genuine card, and the red stripes will be solid red. On the fake, there are many tiny blue dots in these areas. On the fake, the yellow letters of the name and position are fuzzy at the edges, rather than ending cleanly at the red background.

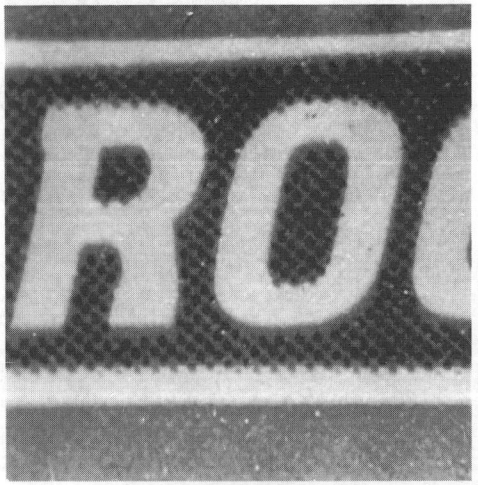

Genuine

Counterfeit

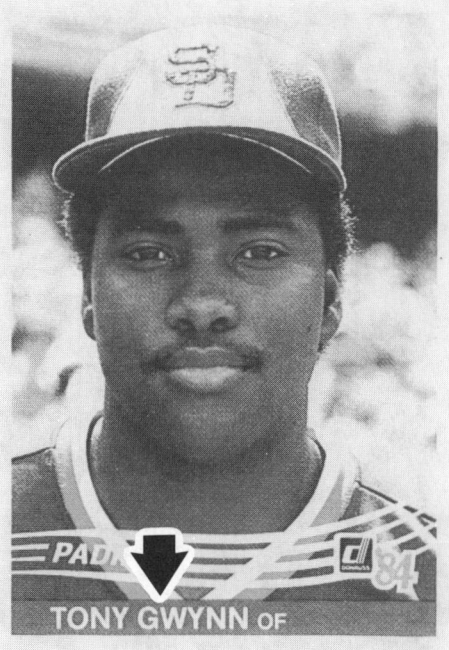

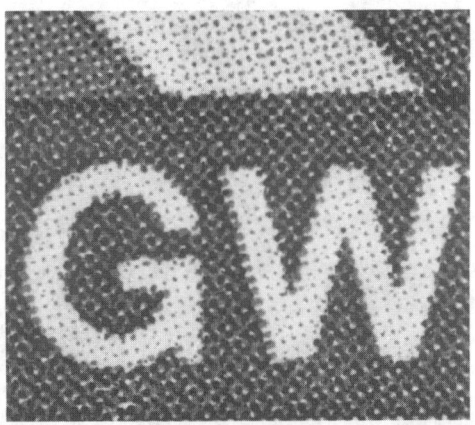

Like the '84 Donruss Ripken and Strawberry cards which may have been the work of the same counterfeiter, the graphic details at the bottom of the card front are the place to conduct an examination of Gwynn's card. To detect this counterfeit, study the yellow name and position with a magnifying glass. A genuine card will show these letters as solid yellow type. On the counterfeit, the letters show a pattern of many tiny dark-colored dots within.

The Donruss logo at lower-right can also be studied. On a genuine card, the white area behind the numerals will be free of any colored dots. On the counterfeit, the white background is full of hundreds of randomly placed dark colored dots. To the left of the numerals on a genuine card, the vertical lines of the "d" are smooth. On this counterfeit, those lines exhibit a sawtooth pattern. Similarly, many of the letters of "DONRUSS" in the logo are broken or indistinct. Those letters on a genuine card are well-formed and distinct.

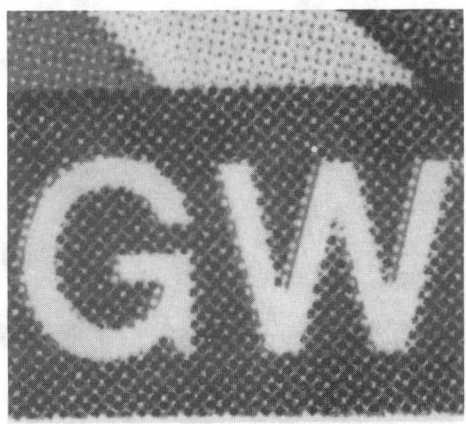

Genuine

Counterfeit

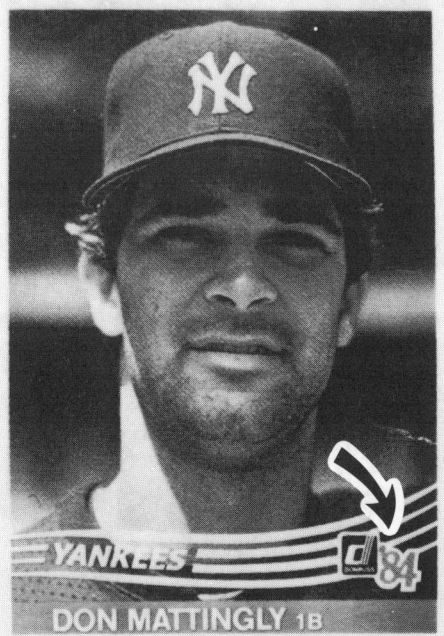

DON MATTINGLY 1B

DONALD ARTHUR MATTINGLY

248

Born: April 20, 1961   Home: Evansville, Ind.
Ht: 5'11"   Wgt: 185   Bats: Left   Throws: Left

©1983 DONRUSS
Printed in USA

RECENT MAJOR LEAGUE PERFORMANCE

*Denotes Led League

Year	Team Name	Bat. Avg.	Games	At Bat	Hits	Runs	2B	3B	HR	RBI	Steal	Walk	SO
1982	Yankees	.167	7	12	2	0	0	0	0	1	0	0	1
1983	Yankees	.283	91	279	79	34	15	4	4	32	0	21	31
Career		.278	98	291	81	34	15	4	4	33	0	21	32

CAREER HIGHLIGHTS

One of the very few Yankee farmhands who made it to the big leagues as a Yankee... Yanks tried to sign him for two seasons, last year, but he kept hitting... Was among last card in spring training, then was quickly called up after hitting .340 at Columbus... Was over .300 most of season with Yanks... Excellent defensively, both RF and 1B... In 4 previous minor league seasons, hit .349, .358, .316 and .315... His 35d at Greensboro in '80 won the South Atlantic League batting crown.

New Acquired: Signed by Yankees as free agent.

Contract Status: Signed thru 1984

One of the most widespread counterfeits, production was traced to a Florida print shop whose operator was told the cards were being reproduced by a relative of Mattingly's for use as party favors.

At first glance, especially with a genuine card available for comparison, this counterfeit should raise a warning flag. The front borders are more eggshell white than pure white and the surface has an unnaturally smooth gloss. Such subjective observations, however, can never be relied upon to positively identify a counterfeit.

Examination with a magnifying lens offers proof of this card's status through study of the Donruss logo at lower right. On a genuine card, the white outline around the black box and the "'84", along with the fancy "d" will be clear and clean. On the counterfeit there are many tiny black dots in these areas. Also, the counterfeit's rendition of the small "DONRUSS" in the logo box is fuzzy, with barely distinguishable letters.

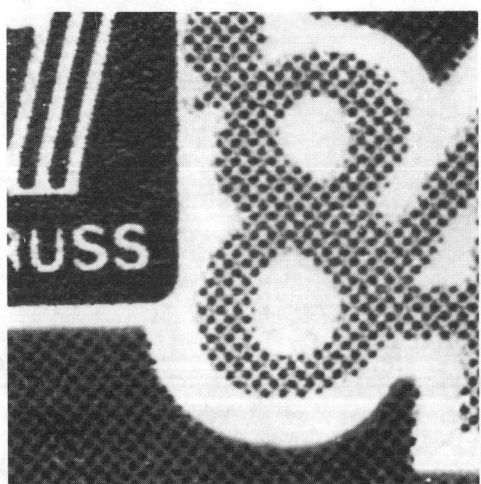

Genuine

Counterfeit

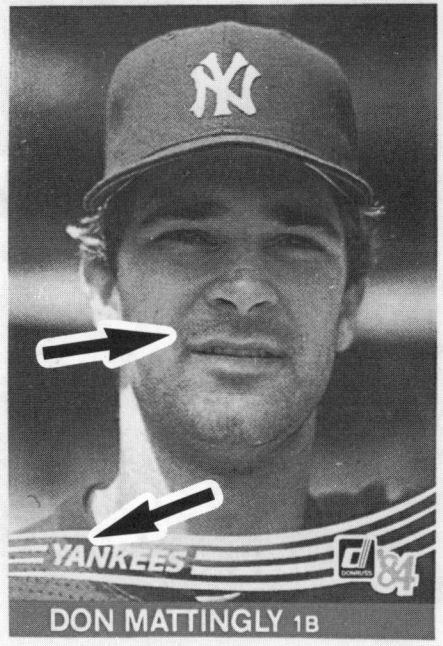

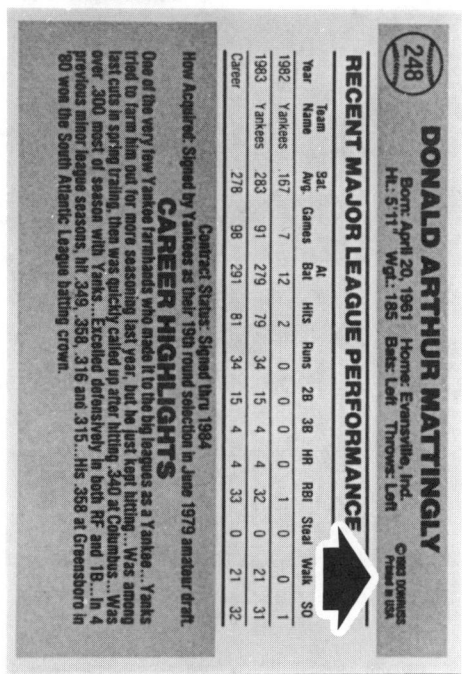

Much more dangerous than the other known '84 Donruss Mattingly counterfeit, this version also first surfaced in Florida, in November, 1991. It is among the most difficult counterfeits to detect, partially because its weight is within the tolerances of a genuine '84 Donruss card.

The back of a suspected card is the best area of examination, specifically the copyright notice at the upper-right. On a genuine card, all of the letters and numerals stand independently. The counterfeit shows many of these elements run together, touching one or both of the neighboring letters or numerals.

On front, examination with a magnifying

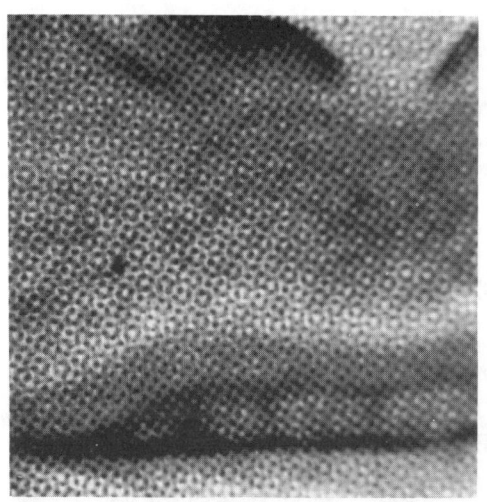

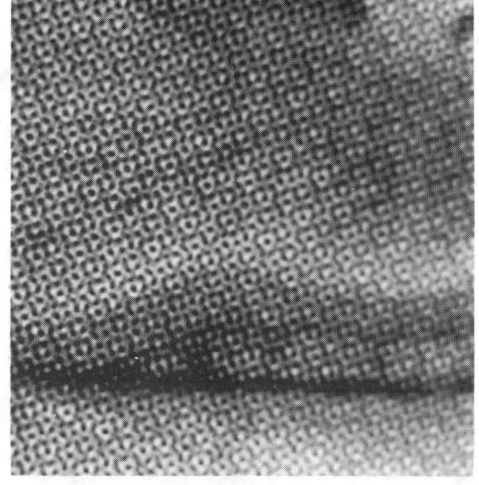

Genuine   Counterfeit

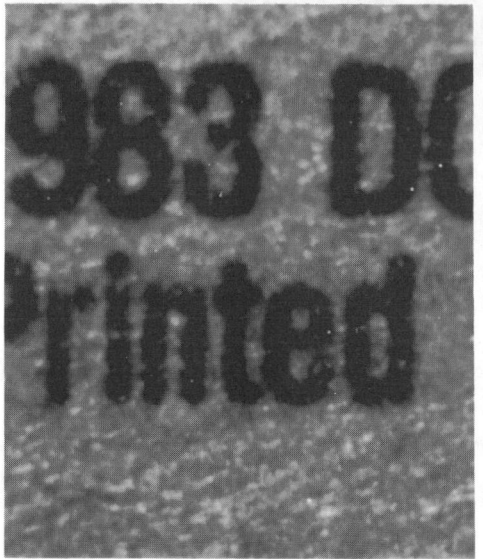 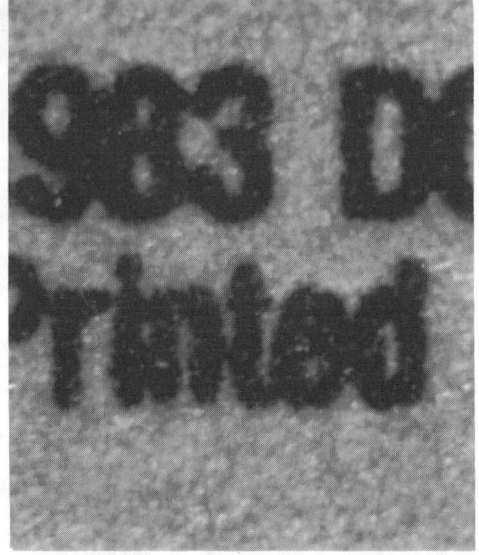

| **Genuine** | **Counterfeit** |

glass will reveal flaws in two areas of the counterfeit. The wavy gold lines which contain the team name, as well as the letters of "YANKEES" on a genuine card exhibit fairly clean edges. On the counterfeit, these edges are much rougher.

What appears to be a printing flaw on genuine cards can also be used as a diagnostic. All genuine cards examined show a black spot on Mattingly's upper lip, just above the tooth that is farthest to the viewer's left. In the reproduction process, the counterfeit rendered this dot as a broken pattern of smaller dots, making it virtually invisible to the naked eye.

Each of these areas requires careful study to differentiate between a good and a bad card, and it is especially useful to have a known genuine Mattingly available for comparison.

This dangerous fake can be readily identified by persons with access to a microscope by the presence of black printing dots where they do not exist on a genuine card. These areas include the highlighted areas of the player's neck and right ear lobe, and the wavy gold stripes to the left of the "Y" in "YANKEES".

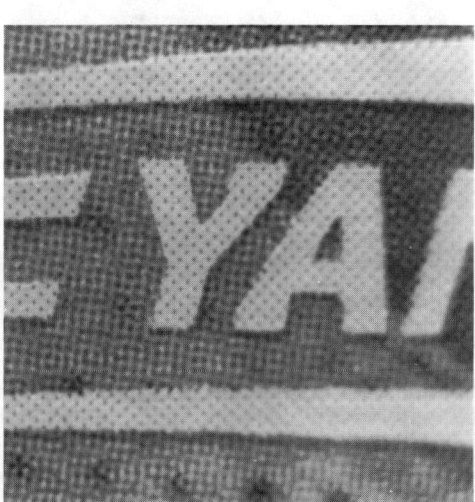 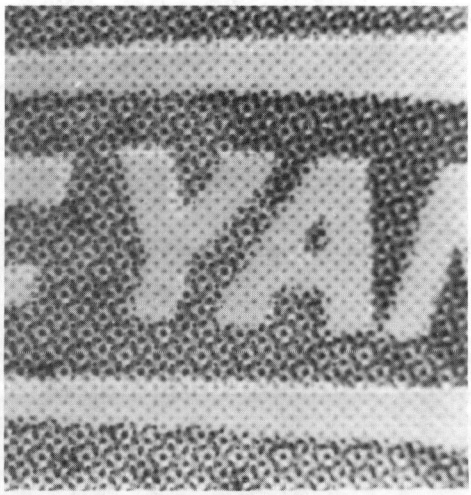

| **Genuine** | **Counterfeit** |

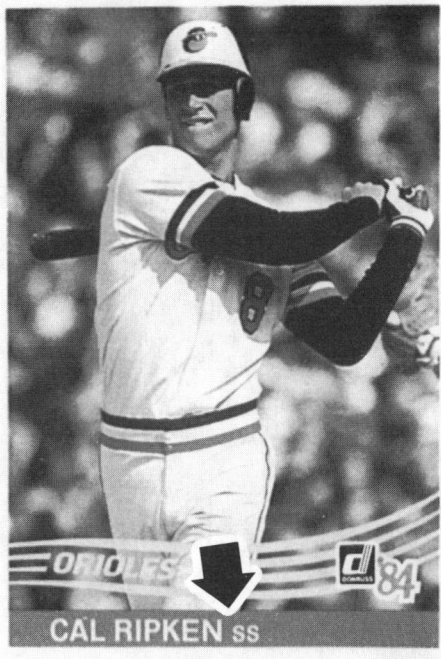

CALVIN EDWIN RIPKEN JR.
Born: Aug. 24, 1960   Home: Cockeysville, Md.
Ht: 6'4"   Wgt: 200   Bats: Right   Throws: Right

RECENT MAJOR LEAGUE PERFORMANCE

Year	Team Name	Bat Avg	Games	At Bat	Hits	Runs	2B	3B	HR	RBI	Steal	Walk	SO
1981	Orioles	.128	23	39	5	1	0	0	0	0	0	1	8
1982	Orioles	.264	'60	598	158	90	32	5	28	93	3	46	95
1983	Orioles	.318	'162	663*	211*	121*	47*	2	27	102	0	58	97
Career		.288	345	1300	374	212	79	7	55	195	3	105	200

106

Contract Status: Signed thru 1984
How Acquired: Signed by Orioles as their 2nd round selection in June 1978 amateur draft.

CAREER HIGHLIGHTS
Followed up his Rookie of the Year season of '82 with an MVP-calibre '83 campaign... Played every inning of every game last year, the only player in baseball to accomplish that...His avg. was 3rd highest in Oriole club history...Besides leading AL in runs, hits and doubles, was 5th in batting, 2nd in total bases (343) and 5th in slugging (.517)...Had 2 HR, 2 doubles, a single, 4 RBI and 13 total bases in 1 game (9/3) vs. Twins last year... Broke Oriole club records for HR and RBI by a SS...AL All Star in 83.

Though this fake is printed on somewhat heavier stock than a genuine 1984 Donruss card, it is visually very deceptive.

Like the '84 Donruss Darryl Strawberry card that was apparently the work of the same counterfeiter, the graphic details at the bottom of the card front are the place to conduct an examination. On the Ripken counterfeit, study of the yellow name and position with a magnifying glass will reveal evidence of forgery. A genuine card will show these letters as solid yellow type, with edges that end cleanly at the blue background. On the counterfeit, the letters show many tiny color dots within, and fuzzy edges at the background.

Flaws on the single counterfeit specimen examined may or may not prove to be diagnostic of the counterfeit printing. These include a pink "glob" slightly above and between the letters "A" and "L" of the name on front, and, in the Career Highlights on the back, a broken top to the second "a" of "baseball" on the second line, and a broken first "t" in "batting" on the fourth line.

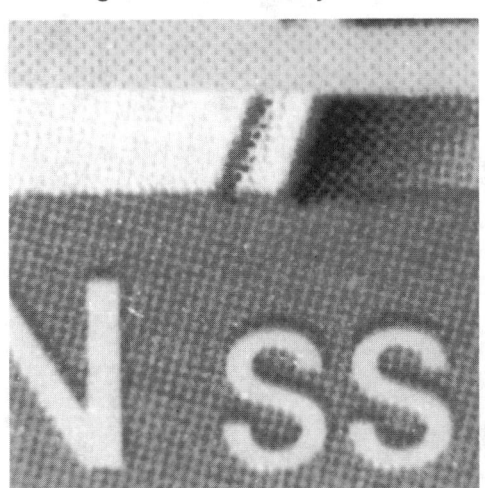

Genuine

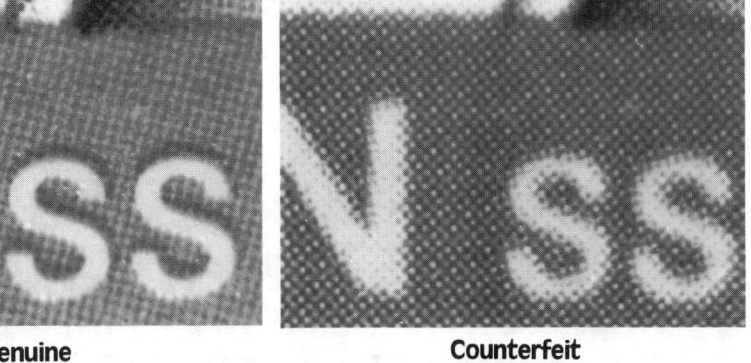

Counterfeit

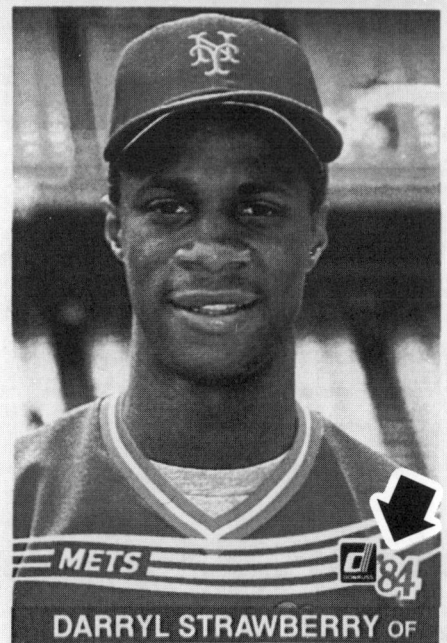

An extremely deceptive counterfeit, this is one of a handful of cards for which 5X magnification is barely adequate for detection of counterfeit "fingerprints."

As with the '84 Mattingly, examination of the logo area at lower right is recommended. On a genuine card printed with decent color registration, the white outline of the "'84" should be devoid of extraneous color dots. The counterfeit — under strong magnification — exhibits a smattering of tiny red and blue dots scattered throughout the white area. Simi-

larly, the player's name on a genuine card will be solid yellow, with only a very occasional intrusive red dot near the edges. On the counterfeit, the name is rife with tiny red and green dots.

On genuine cards that are printed in less than perfect registration, red, yellow or blue dots may occasionally be found in these areas, but they will always be in a pattern consistent with the nearest design elements, rather than scattered at random.

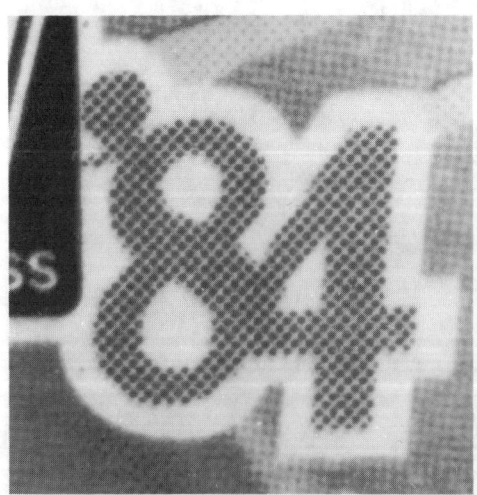

Genuine

Counterfeit

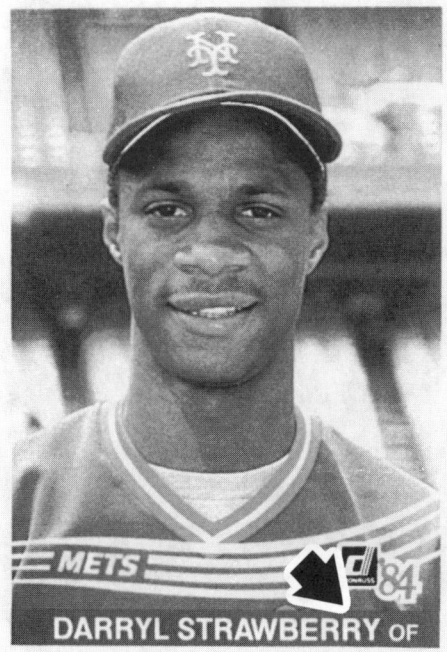

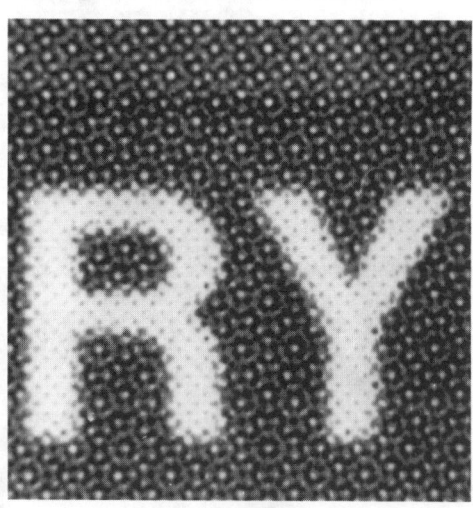

Though this fake is printed on somewhat heavier stock — about 12% overweight — than a genuine 1984 Donruss card, it is visually very deceptive.

Like the '84 Donruss Cal Ripken card that was apparently the work of the same counterfeiter, the graphic details at the bottom of the card front are the place to conduct an examination. To detect this counterfeit, study the yellow name and position with a magnifying glass. A genuine card will show these letters as solid yellow type, with edges that end cleanly at the brown background. On the counterfeit, the letters show a pattern of many tiny color dots within, and fuzzy edges at the background.

The "'84" of the Donruss logo at lower-right can also be studied. On a genuine card printed in normal registration, magnification will show an orderly pattern of black dots making up the numerals. On the counterfeit, this part of the logo is somewhat fuzzy as the result of the numerals being comprised of a haphazard arrangement of multi-colored dots.

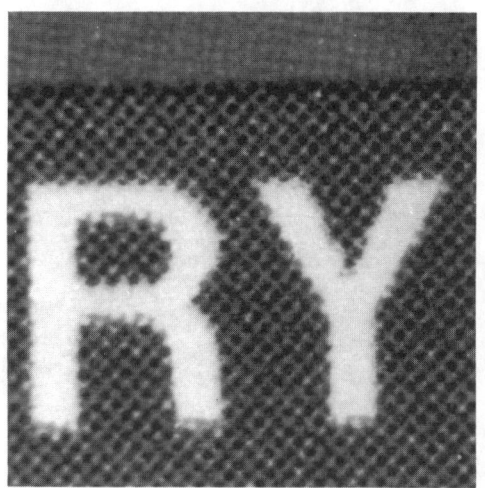

Genuine

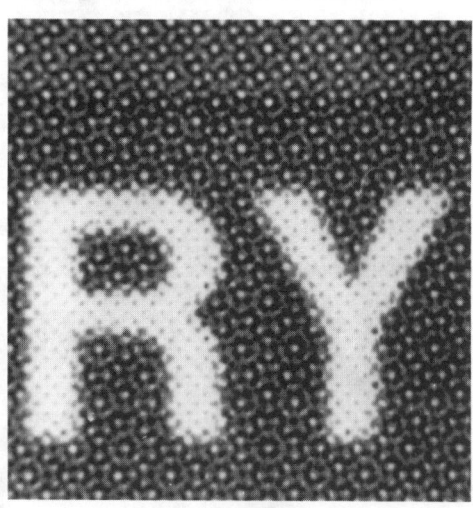

Counterfeit

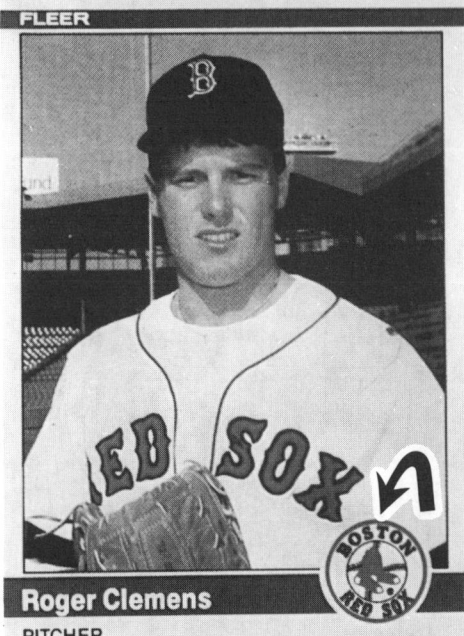

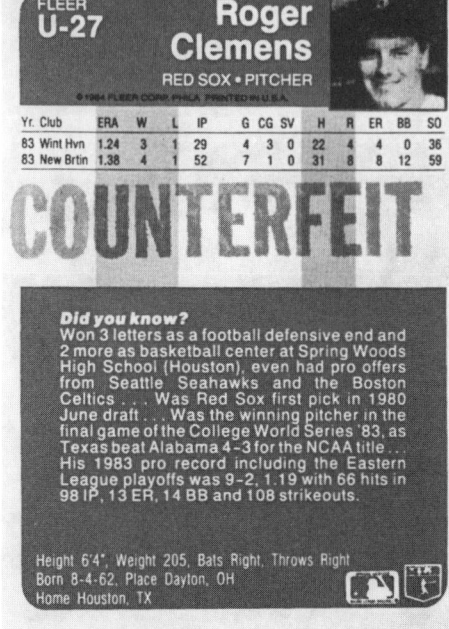

As with the known Gooden and Puckett counterfeits from this scarce and valuable edition, the Clemens counterfeit is most easily detected by close examination of the Red Sox logo on the front of the card.

Seen through a good magnifying glass, the counterfeit will exhibit a pattern of tiny blue dots both in the carmine hose themselves, and in what is supposed to be the pure white background of the baseball and the surrounding type circle. On a gen-uine 1984 Fleer Update card, the socks and the white area will be without these extraneous dots.

It is interesting to note that the Major League Players Association logo at the lower-right on the counterfeit's back has been "improved," with a new, bolder white outline to the shield.

A "COUNTERFEIT" stamp has been added to the back of the specimen photographed here.

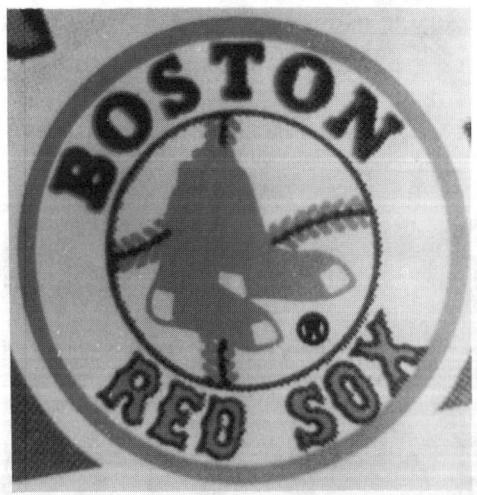

Genuine

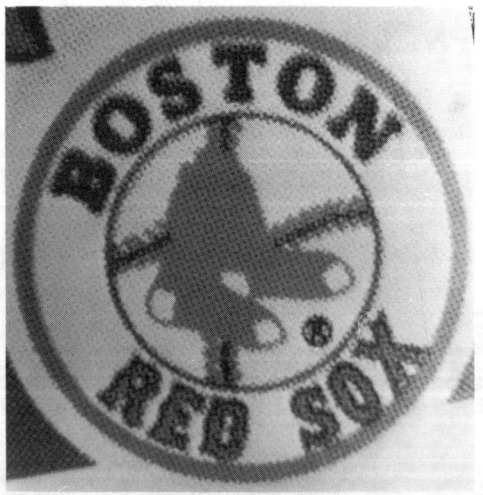

Counterfeit

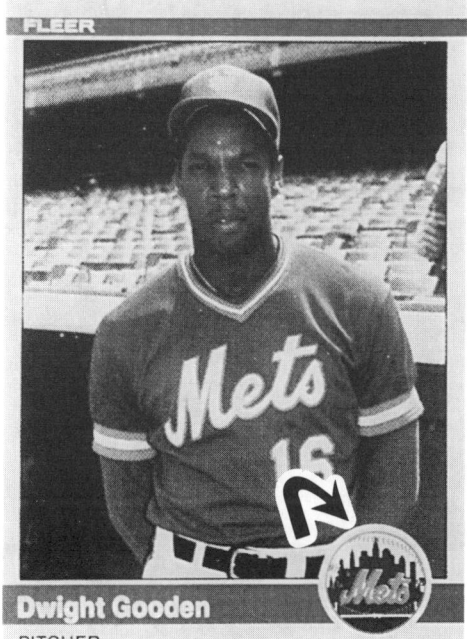

Dwight Gooden
PITCHER

At first glance a very deceptive counterfeit, a person with a keen eye for color might detect a more purple cast to the horizontal stripes on the front of this card, but ink color should never be used as a sole indicator of genuineness or lack thereof. Thankfully, with a good magnifying glass, even those whose chromatic acuity approaches color blindness can detect this counterfeit.

The key is the Mets logo at lower-right on the front. On a genuine card, the white background behind the skyline will contain no dot structure. On the counterfeit, the New York sky is filled with tiny dark dots. These dots can also be seen in the "METS" lettering on the phony, but not on the genuine card.

It is interesting to note that the Players Association logo on the counterfeit's back has been "improved," with a bolder white outline to the shield.

The specimen photographed here bears a "COUNTERFEIT" stamp that will not be seen in the marketplace.

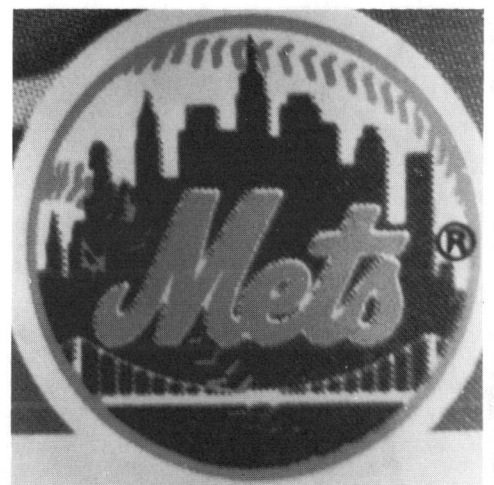

Genuine

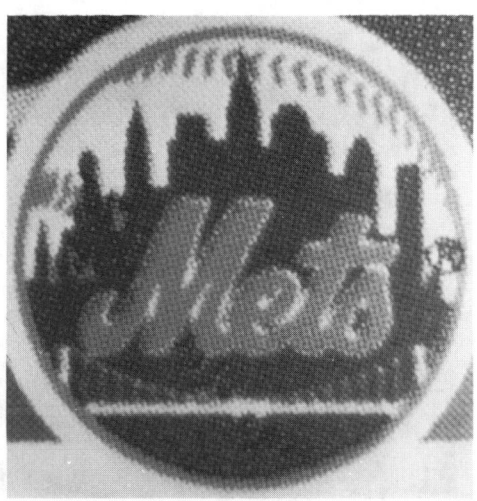

Counterfeit

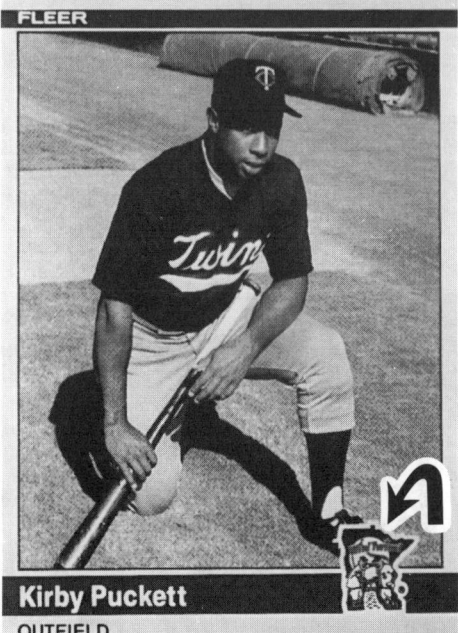

FLEER

Kirby Puckett
OUTFIELD

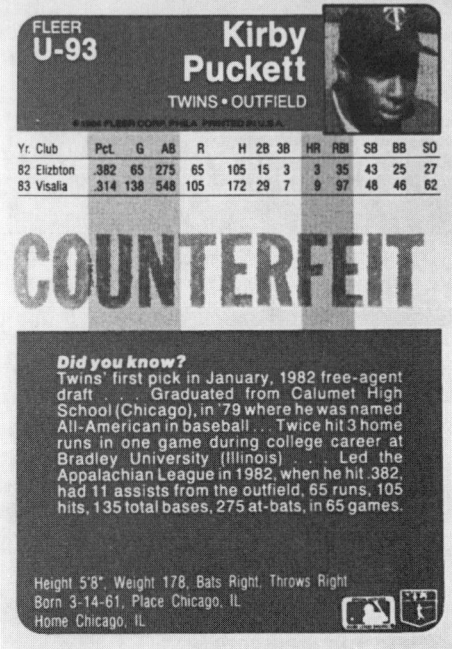

FLEER
U-93

Kirby Puckett
TWINS • OUTFIELD

© 1984 FLEER CORP. PHILA. PRINTED IN U.S.A.

Yr. Club	Pct.	G	AB	R	H	2B	3B	HR	RBI	SB	BB	SO
82 Elizbton	.382	65	275	65	105	15	3	3	35	43	25	27
83 Visalia	.314	138	548	105	172	29	7	9	97	48	46	62

COUNTERFEIT

Did you know?
Twins' first pick in January, 1982 free-agent draft . . . Graduated from Calumet High School (Chicago), in '79 where he was named All-American in baseball . . . Twice hit 3 home runs in one game during college career at Bradley University (Illinois) . . . Led the Appalachian League in 1982, when he hit .382, had 11 assists from the outfield, 65 runs, 105 hits, 135 total bases, 275 at-bats, in 65 games.

Height 5'8", Weight 178, Bats Right, Throws Right
Born 3-14-61, Place Chicago, IL
Home Chicago, IL

As with the known Gooden and Clemens counterfeits from this scarce and valuable edition, the Puckett counterfeit is most easily detected by close examination of the Twins logo on the front of the card.

Seen through a good magnifying glass, the counterfeit will exhibit a pattern of tiny blue dots in the white baseball and uniforms of the cartoon figures, and the red design details and letters of "WIN! TWINS!". On a genuine 1984 Fleer Update card, the white areas of the logo and the red letterings will be devoid of the tell-tale blue dots.

It is interesting to note that the Major League Players Association logo at the lower-right on the counterfeit's back has been "improved," with a new, bolder white outline to the shield.

A "COUNTERFEIT" stamp has been added to the back of the specimen photographed here.

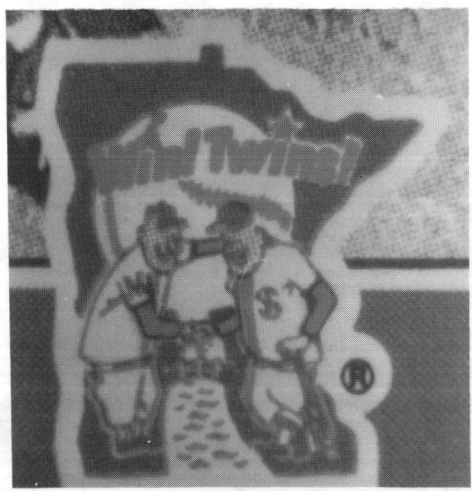

Genuine

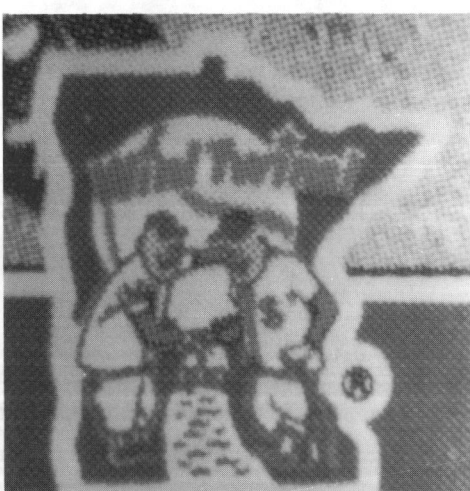

Counterfeit

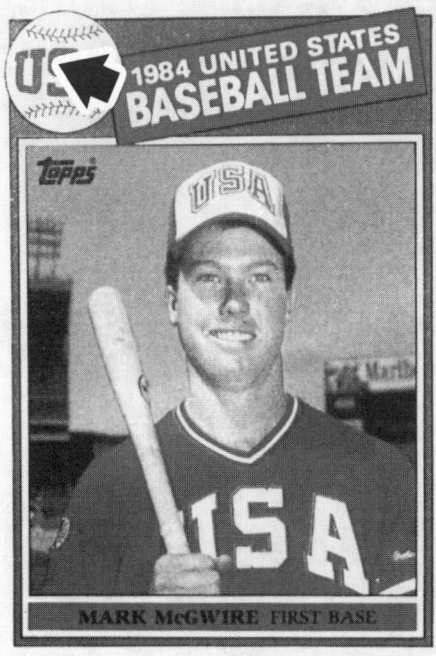

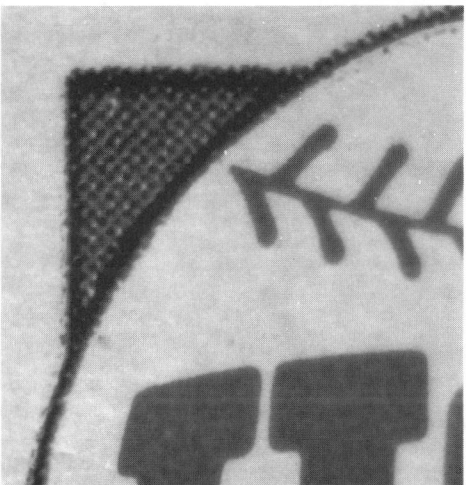

HEIGHT: 6'5" WEIGHT: 220 BATS: RIGHT THROWS: RIGHT
BORN: 10-1-63, CLAREMONT, CALIF.
HOME: CLAREMONT, CALIF. SCHOOL: USC

STATISTICS AT USC

YEAR	G	AB	R	H	2B	3B	HR	RBI	SB	SLG	BB	SO	AVG
1982	29	75	14	15	2	0	3	11	0	.347	20	15	.200
1983	53	191	46	61	9	0	19	59	0	.665	33	35	.319
1984	65	237	74	92	19	2	31	77	2	.878	30	50	.388
SCHOOL TOT.	147	503	134	168	30	2	53	147	2	.718	83	100	.302

*** 1984 USA BASEBALL STATISTICS ***

G	AB	R	H	2B	3B	HR	RBI	SB	SLG	BB	SO	AVG
5	21	4	4	0	0	0	0	0	.190	2	6	.190

Mark's 31 Homers in 1984 broke his own USC record. The most feared power-hitter in college ball, he was All-Pacific-10 pick, 1983 & 1984.

Without close inspection, this counterfeit is visually quite deceptive. Particularly dangerous is the fact that unlike most counterfeits, the weight of this forgery is nearly identical to that of a genuine '85 Topps card.

Using a magnifying glass to examine the details on the front will provide definite proof that this card is bogus. On a genuine card, such details as the lines around the blue frame and photo, and the black circle which outlines the baseball at upper left are printed in solid black. On the counterfeit, these lines are printed as composites of many tiny dots, resulting in a fuzzy appearance.

On the back of the counterfeit, the tiny red type at the bottom of the card is much less distinct than on a genuine card. Some of the words on the fake have letters that are no longer separated when viewed under magnification. All letters, in even the smallest type, on the genuine card retain their identity under magnification.

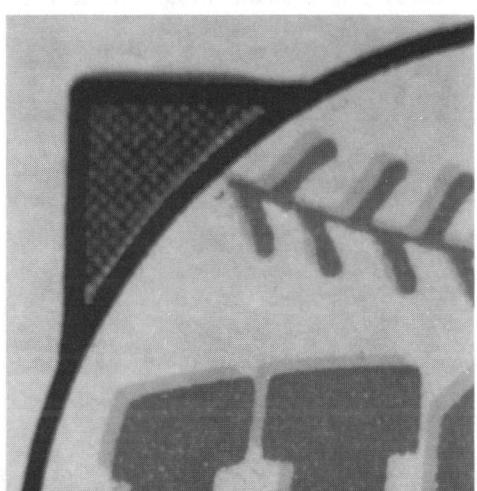

Genuine

Counterfeit

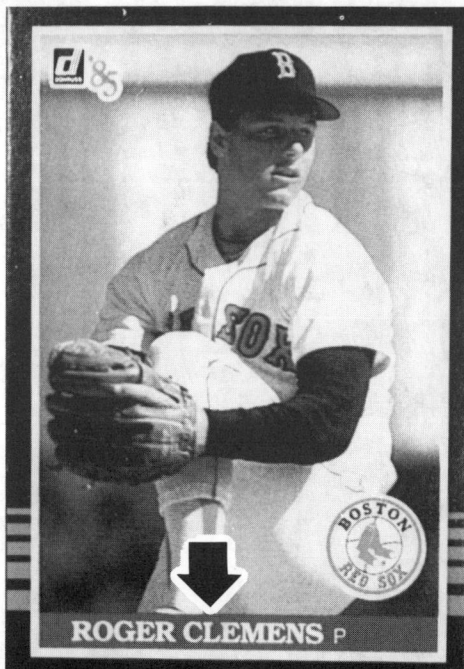

ROGER CLEMENS P

WILLIAM ROGER CLEMENS
Born: Aug. 4, 1962   Home: Houston, Texas
Ht.: 6'4"   Wgt.: 205   Bats: Right   Throws: Right

© 1984 DONRUSS
Printed in USA

RECENT MAJOR LEAGUE PERFORMANCE

Year	Team Name	ERA	Games	Inn. Pitched	Hits	Runs	Er. Runs	Walks	Strike Outs	Comp. Games	Shut Outs	Save	Won	Lost
1984	Red Sox	4.32	21	133	146	67	64	29	126	5	1	0	9	4
Career		4.32	21	133	146	67	64	29	126	5	1	0	9	4

*"Denotes Led League

Contract Status: Signed thru 1985
How Acquired: Signed by Red Sox as their No. 1 pick in June '83 amateur draft

CAREER HIGHLIGHTS
Struck out 15 batters vs. Royals 8/21/84, most by a Red Sox pitcher since '61...Had best strikeouts-per-innings ratio on Red Sox staff last year... Collegiate star at U. of Texas and was winning pitcher in Longhorns' 4-3 victory over Alabama in NCAA World Series final in '83... Had a combined 7-2 record and 1.33 ERA for his 1st pro season in '83 at Red Sox' Winter Haven and New Britain farms...Was 25-7 with 261 strikeouts in 275 innings in two years at U. of Texas.

273

Because this counterfeit is nearly 15% heavier than a genuine 1985 Donruss card, if examined outside of a card holder it is likely to be detected by an experienced dealer or collector who would find the cardboard stock considerably stiffer than that of a real card.

Visual evidence is best sought by close examination of the card company's logo and the player's name on the front of the card.

Seen through a good magnifying glass, the counterfeit will exhibit a pattern of tiny dark dots throughout the yellow letters of the name and position designation. On a genuine card, these yellow letters will be devoid of this dot pattern.

A similar situation exists in the Donruss logo at upper-left. On a genuine card, the white area behind the " '85" will be clear. On the counterfeit, the white area exhibits many tiny colored dots.

The black edges of this counterfeit readily show that it has been cut with a "guillotine" rather than "slit cut," as is the standard process with most sportscards.

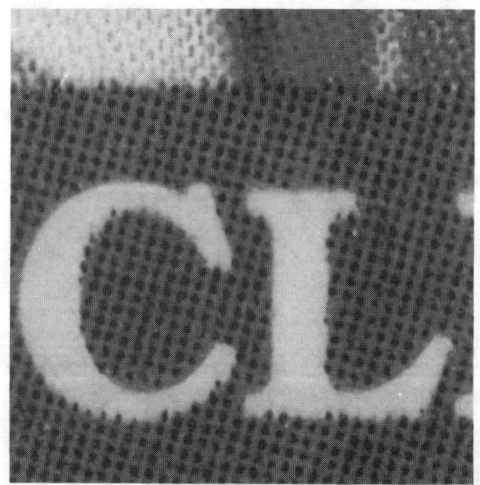

Genuine

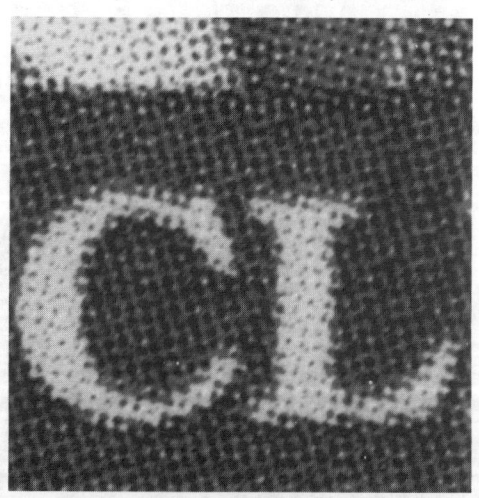

Counterfeit

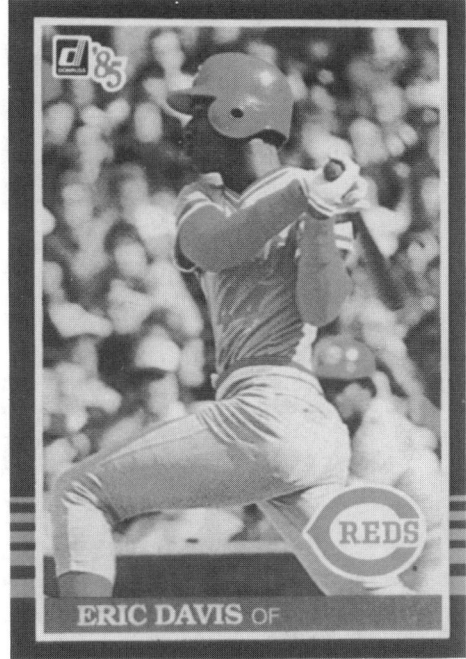

Because this counterfeit surfaced in 1987 — long before this book was contemplated — specific comparative detail photos are not available. Knowledge that the counterfeit exists, and the details provided in a contemporary *Sports Collectors Digest* news account, however, should help protect the consumer.

According to the SCD report, the counterfeit is printed on cardboard stock that is perceptibly thinner than a genuine '85 Donruss.

While it is a subjective criteria, the photo and general appearance of the counterfeit are said to be "fuzzy" in comparison to a genuine card.

More specifically, the report mentions that the counterfeit has a couple of imperfections in the Donruss logo at upper-left. On a genuine card, the white letters of "DONRUSS" are clearly distinguishable on the black background. On the counterfeit, the letters are blurred and mostly indecipherable.

The logo's "'85" on the fake is described as being black, rather than the gray identified with genuine cards.

Without a specimen at hand for examination it's impossible to say whether the errant dot structures usually found in graphics areas such as the player's name and position bar, and the team logo are present on this counterfeit.

The photo above is of a genuine, rather than a counterfeit, card.

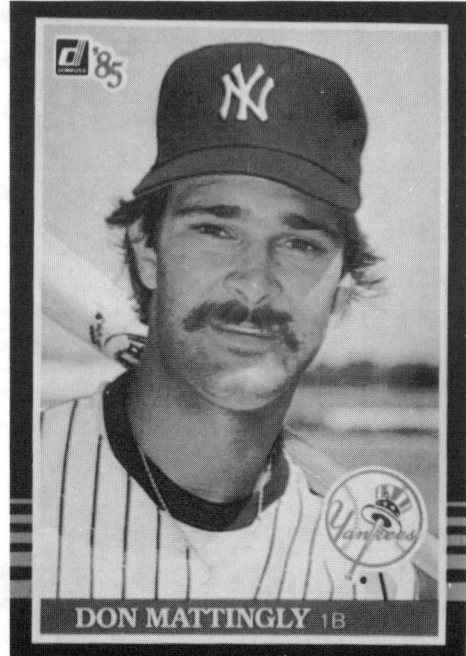

DONALD ARTHUR MATTINGLY

Born: April 20, 1961   Home: Evansville, Ind.
Ht.: 5'11"   Wgt.: 180   Bats: Left   Throws: Left

© 1984 DONRUSS
Printed in USA

RECENT MAJOR LEAGUE PERFORMANCE

*Denotes Led League

Year	Team Name	Bat. Avg.	Games	At Bat	Hits	Runs	2B	3B	HR	RBI	Steal	Walk	SO
1982	Yankees	.167	7	12	2	0	0	0	0	1	0	0	1
1983	Yankees	.283	91	279	79	34	15	4	4	32	0	21	31
1984	Yankees	.343*	153	603	207*	91	44*	2	23	110	1	41	33
Career		.322	251	894	288	125	59	6	27	143	1	62	65

Contract Status: Signed thru 1985
How Acquired: Signed by Yankees as their 19th selection in June '79 amateur draft

CAREER HIGHLIGHTS

Had sensational 1st full season in majors last year, leading AL in batting, ranking 2nd in slugging (.537), 1st in hits, 1st in doubles and 4th in RBI. Had most doubles by a Yankee since '39, most hits since '62. Hit over .390 in four different minor league seasons before winning a job with Yanks in '83.

295

Because this counterfeit surfaced in 1987 — long before this book was contemplated — specific comparative detail photos are not available. Knowledge that the counterfeit exists, and the details provided in a contemporary *Sports Collectors Digest* news account, however, should help protect the consumer.

According to the SCD report, the counterfeit is printed on cardboard stock that is perceptibly thinner than a genuine '85 Donruss.

While it is a subjective criteria, the photo and general appearance of the counterfeit are said to be "fuzzy" in comparison to a genuine card.

More specifically, the report mentions that the counterfeit has a couple of imperfections in the Donruss logo at upper-left. On a genuine card, the white letters of "DONRUSS" are clearly distinguishable on the black background. On the counterfeit, the letters are blurred and mostly indecipherable.

The logo's "'85" on the fake is described as being black, rather than the gray identified with genuine cards.

Without a specimen at hand for examination it's impossible to say whether the errant dot structures usually found in graphics areas such as the player's name and position bar, and the team logo are present on this counterfeit.

The photo above is of a genuine, rather than a counterfeit, card.

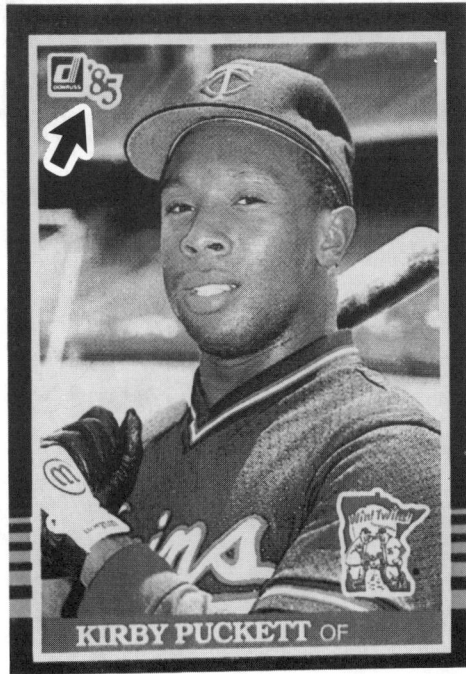

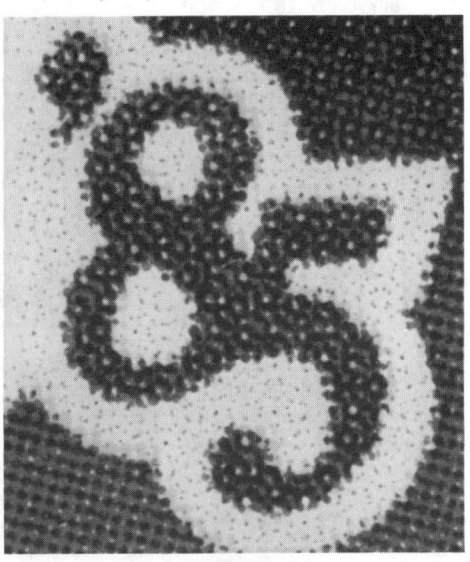

Because this counterfeit is more than 17% heavier than a genuine 1985 Donruss card, if examined outside of a card holder it is likely to be detected by an experienced dealer or collector who would find the cardboard stock considerably stiffer than that of a real card.

Visual evidence of counterfeit status is best sought by close examination of the card company's logo and the player's name on the front of the card.

Seen through a good magnifying glass, the counterfeit will exhibit a pattern of tiny dark dots throughout the yellow letters of the name and position designation. On a genuine card, these yellow letters will be devoid of this dot pattern.

A similar situation exists in the Donruss logo at upper-left. On a genuine card, the white area behind the '' '85'' will be clear. On the counterfeit, the white area exhibits many tiny colored dots.

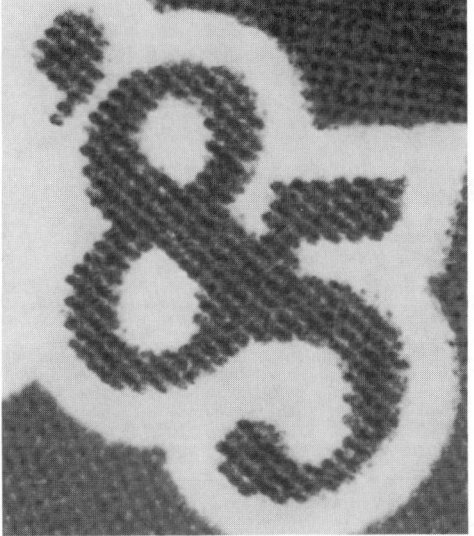

Genuine

Counterfeit

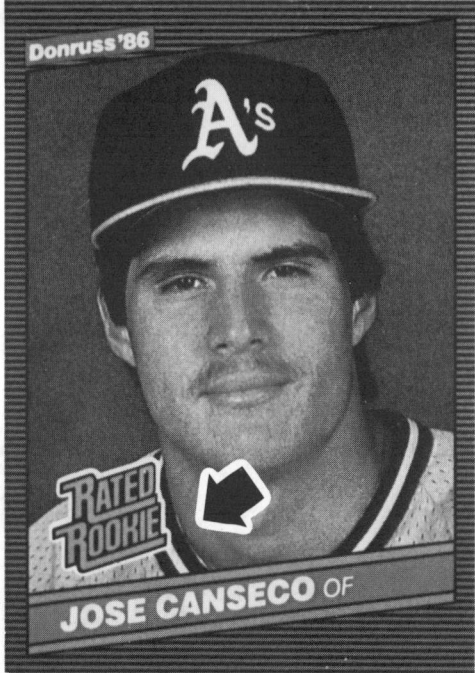

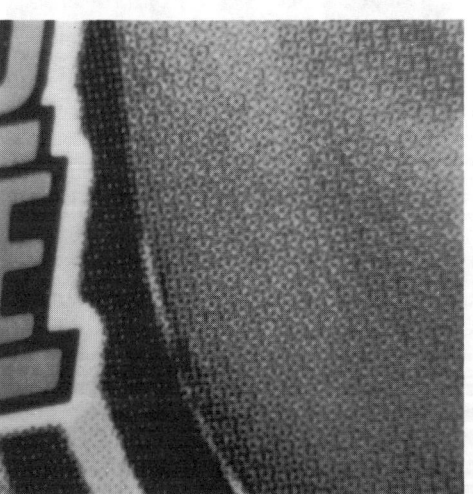

According to hobby lore, genuine Canseco rookies have a "white dot" ¼" above the player's right eye. Actually a pair of parallel scratches, that "dot" vanished when this very deceptive counterfeit was made. Unfortunately, that .dot also disappeared when Donruss printed its factory sets.

A similar indicator is the blue stripe under the lower-left corner of the red "Donruss '86" logo. On a genuine wax- or rak-pack card, that stripe extends almost to the "r". On the counterfeit — and on

genuine factory-set cards — the blue stripe ends under the "D".

The best test is to study with a magnifying glass the black "TM" to the bottom-right of the "Rated Rookie" logo. Barely visible on a genuine card because it is printed over a very dark green jersey stripe, the letters are solid black lines. On the counterfeit, these letters are rendered fuzzy with a dot structure and little except the right leg of the "M" is visible on the player's neck.

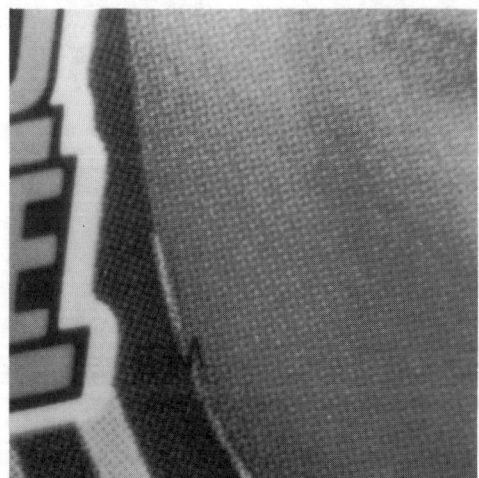

Genuine

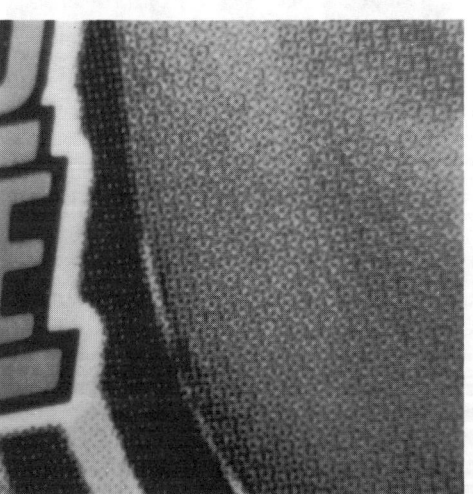

Counterfeit

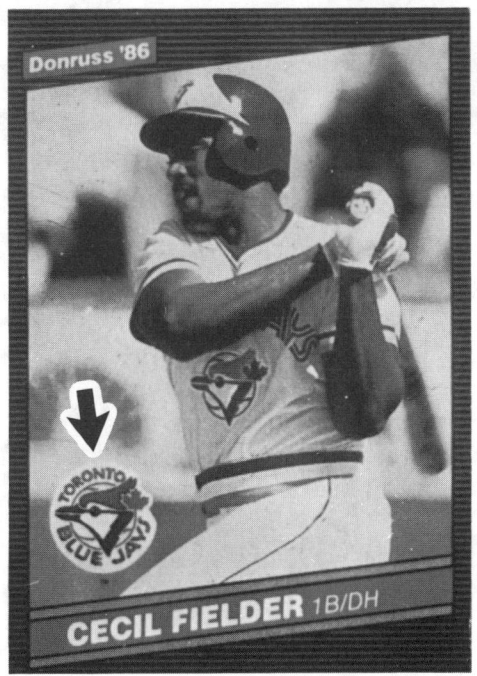

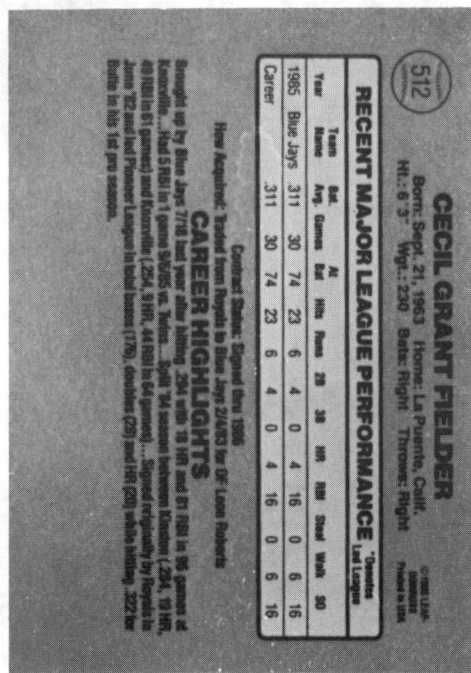

Side-by-side with a genuine card, this counterfeit should fool nobody. The white areas of the color photo on a good card have taken on a yellowish cast on the fake that should alert most viewers.

As always, however, color tint alone should not be relied upon to detect a counterfeit.

The Blue Jays team logo at the lower-left of the card can provide definitive proof under magnification. On a genuine card, the white areas of the circle and the ball will be pure white, and the maple leaf will be almost solid red. On the counterfeit, the white areas of the logo are invaded by a horde of tiny blue, yellow and magenta dots, and the maple leaf is covered with a pattern of dark dots.

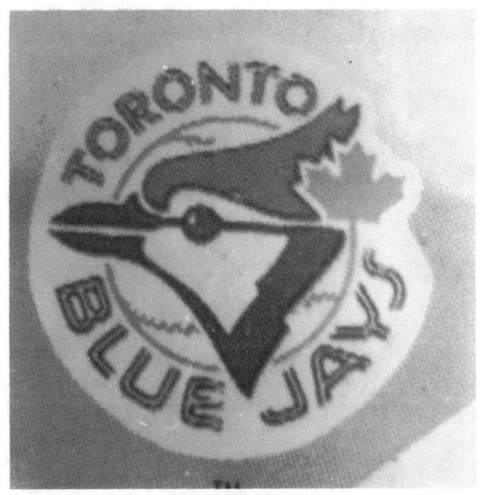

Genuine

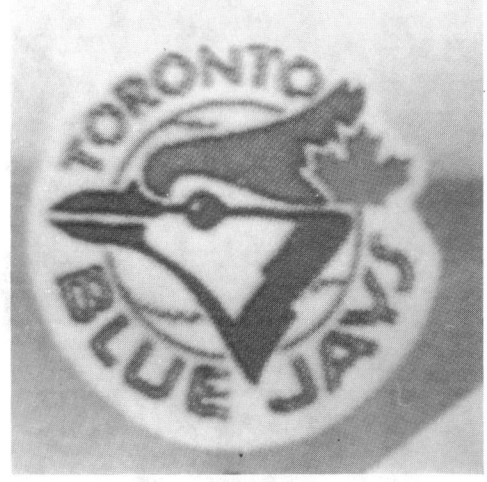

Counterfeit

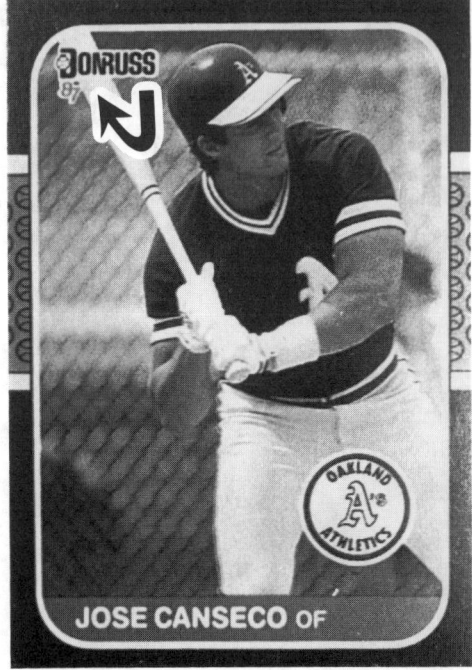

JOSE CANSECO of

JOSE CANSECO
Born: July 2, 1964   Havana, Cuba   Home: Miami, FL
Ht.: 6'3"   Wgt.: 210   Bats: Right   Throws: Right

RECENT MAJOR LEAGUE PERFORMANCE   *Denotes Led League

Year	Team Name	Bat. Avg.	Games	At Bat	Hits	Runs	2B	3B	HR	RBI	Steal	Walk	SO
1985	A's	.302	29	96	29	16	3	0	5	13	1	4	31
1986	A's	.240	157	600	144	85	29	1	33	117	15	65	175
Career		.249	186	696	173	101	32	1	38	130	16	69	206

CAREER HIGHLIGHTS
Contract Status: Signed thru 1987. How Acquired: Signed by A's as their 15th round selection in June 1982 amateur draft

Ranked 2nd in AL in RBI and 4th in HR last year...Batted a combined .333 with 36 HR and 127 RBI in 116 games for A's Huntsville and Tacoma farms in '84...On 9/22/85 became only the 27th player in history to hit a HR over the roof of 75-year old Comiskey Park in Chicago...Batted .276 with 15 HR and 73 RBI in 116 games for A's Modesto farm in '84.

With any genuine 1987 Donruss card available for comparison, this counterfeit would fool no one. The top and bottom jet black borders of an original card appear on this counterfeit in a charcoal gray tone. Similarly, the colors of the player photo have a washed-out appearance.

Examination with a magnifying glass reveals that many of the design details which are present on a genuine card as clear, solid elements are represented on the counterfeit as fuzzy creations comprised of many tiny dots.

On a genuine card the Donruss logo will be made up of solid black letters and red numerals and the white area around the logo will be free from dots. The counterfeit shows the letters and the baseball to be made up of many tiny black dots which create a fuzzy appearance and spill over into the white outline. Similarly, the red "87" on a good card is clean and sharp, while the counterfeit displays the number as a pattern of tiny dots.

Like the baseball in the Donruss logo, the balls in the left and right borders on a

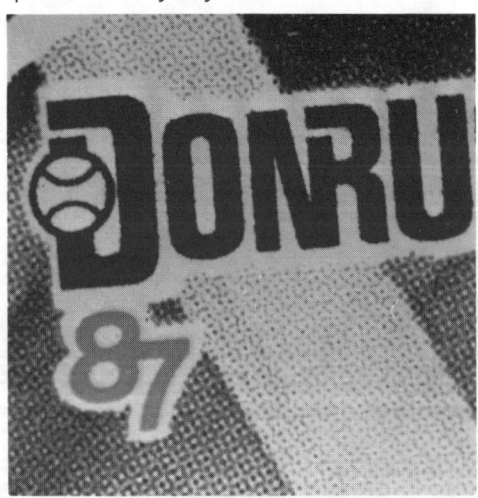

Genuine

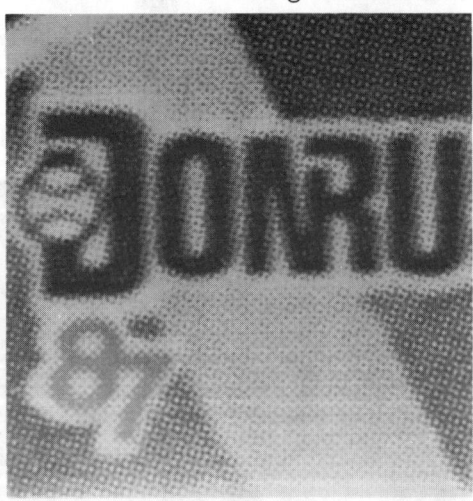

Counterfeit

genuine card will be shown as clean black lines. On the counterfeit, these balls are made up of small dots, giving them a fuzzy look.

The green stripe near the bottom of a genuine 1987 Donruss Canseco rookie card ends cleanly at the edges of each letter of the player's name and position. On the counterfeit, green dots intrude into the edges of each of these letters.

Because the A's logo on a genuine card is comprised of a dot structure to give it color, it cannot be easily used as a counterfeit detector.

The back of the counterfeit card displays black type that is heavier than on a genuine card, causing some of the letters and numerals to run together in the area of the biographical data and ''Career Highlights''.

It can be noted, though not used as a counterfeit detector, that this fake has the back printing in factory-set orientation. That is, when the card is flipped over, the number appears in the lower-left corner. This is also true of genuine factory-set Canseco rookies. The wax pack version shows the card number on back in the upper-right corner when the card is flipped.

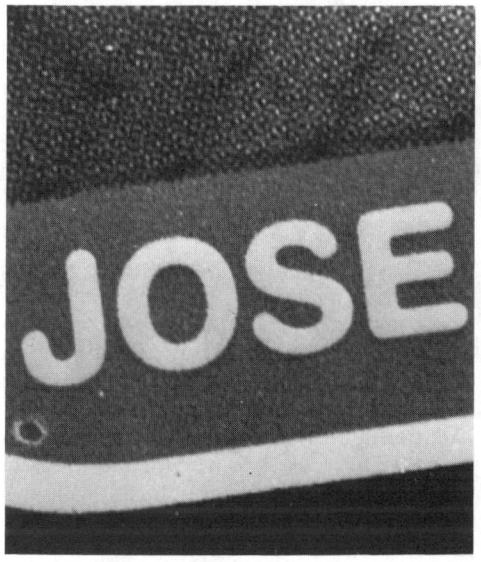

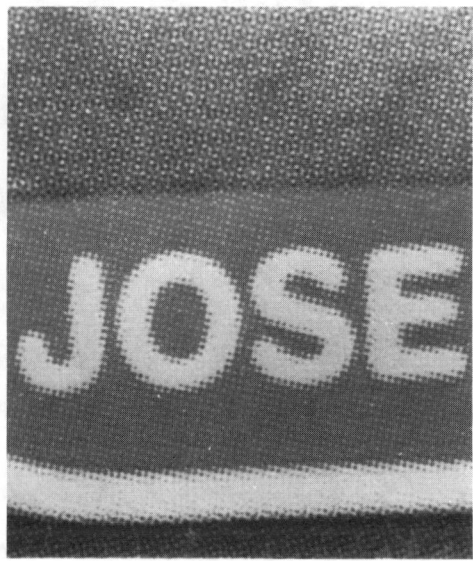

| Genuine | Counterfeit |

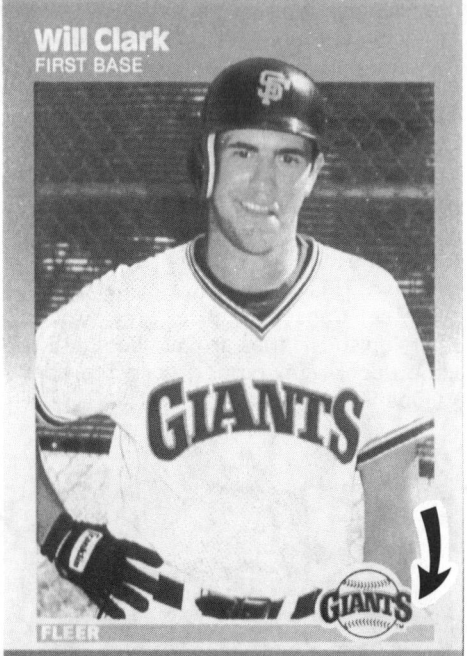

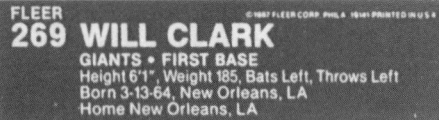

Yr. Club	Pct.	G	AB	R	H	2B	3B	HR	RBI	SB	BB	SO
85 Fresno	.309	65	217	41	67	14	0	10	48	11	62	46
86 Phoenix	.250	6	20	3	5	0	0	0	1	1	4	2
86 Giants	.287	111	408	66	117	27	2	11	41	4	34	76
ML Totals	.287	111	408	66	117	27	2	11	41	4	34	76

Probably not produced by the same person that counterfeited the bogus '87 Fleer Ruben Sierra card, this counterfeit Clark '87 Fleer rookie is easier to spot.

This counterfeit has a decidedly orange tone on Clark's skin. Also, the front of the card has an unusual, almost waxy, feel. However, since color judgement and "feel" are subjective, a close-up examination with a magnifying glass is essential. Such an exam reveals that some of the design details which are present on a genuine card as clear, solid elements are represented on the counterfeit as fuzzy creations comprised of many tiny dots.

This is evident in the seams of the ball and the black "TM" trademark indicator of the Giants logo at the lower-right.

A similar indicator can be seen where the white type with the player's name and position meets the blue background in the upper-left. On a genuine card the edges of the letters will end cleanly at the blue background. On the counterfeit, a line of tiny blue dots can be seen at the edges of the white letters.

On back, the lettering on the MLB and Players' Association logos at lower-left is rendered very indistinctly.

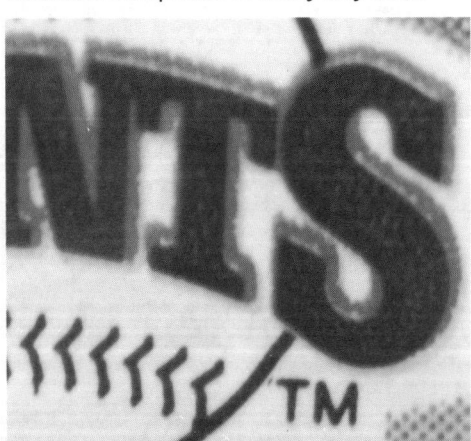

Genuine

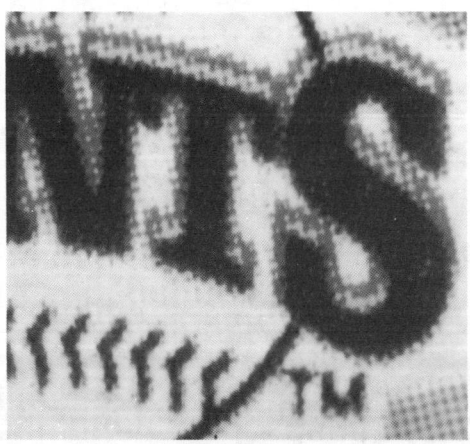

Counterfeit

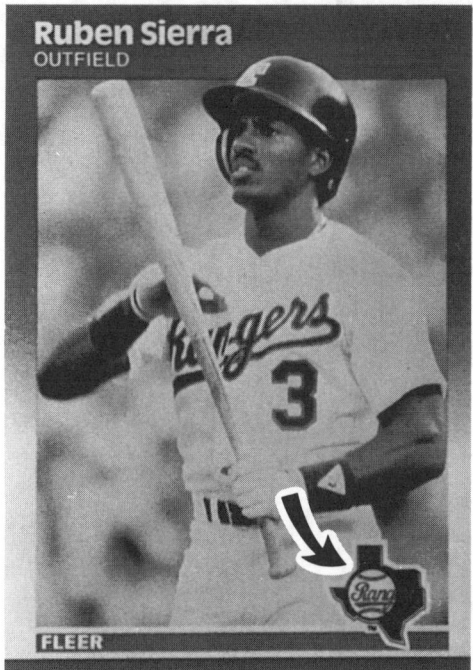

Yr. Club	Pct.	G	AB	R	H	2B	3B	HR	RBI	SB	BB	SO
83 Sarasota	.242	48	182	26	44	7	3	1	26	3	16	38
84 Burlington	.263	138	482	55	127	33	5	6	75	13	49	97
85 Tulsa	.251	137	545	63	137	34	8	13	74	22	35	111
86 Okla City	.296	46	189	31	56	11	2	9	41	8	15	27
86 Rangers	.264	113	382	50	101	13	10	16	55	7	22	65
ML Totals	.264	113	382	50	101	13	10	16	55	7	22	65

An excellent counterfeit. The hobby is fortunate the producer of the Ruben Sierra Fleer rookie card did not attempt to create bogus specimens of the more valuable cards in this popular set — at least so far as is known to date. In all likelihood, this card would fool most collectors and dealers because the color finish and focus are not markedly dissimilar from genuine 1987 Fleer baseball cards.

The place to look to be sure you're getting a genuine Sierra rookie — or at least not this particular counterfeit — is the Rangers team logo at lower-right on the front. On the genuine card, the white ball and the red stitching, along with the "Rangers" lettering, will be free of dots. The counterfeit has myriad dots in these areas, rendering the stitching as a pair of fuzzy curved lines, and generally muddying up the other elements of the logo.

Among recent counterfeits, the Fleer Sierra card is very seldom seen — unless a lot of people have unknowingly accepted them as genuine.

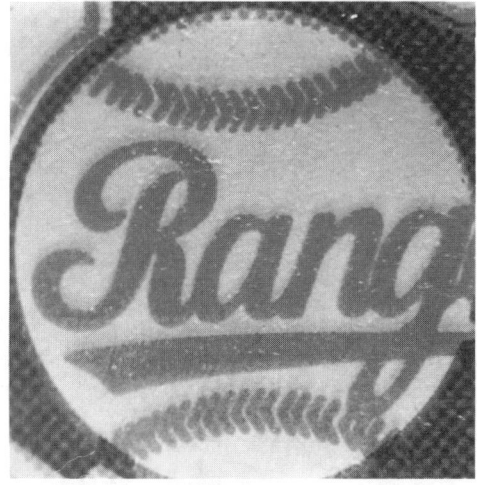

Genuine

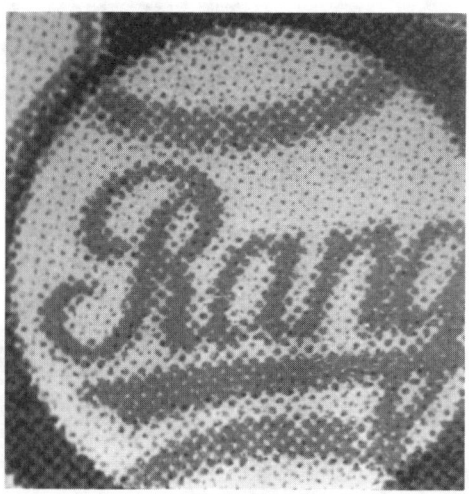

Counterfeit

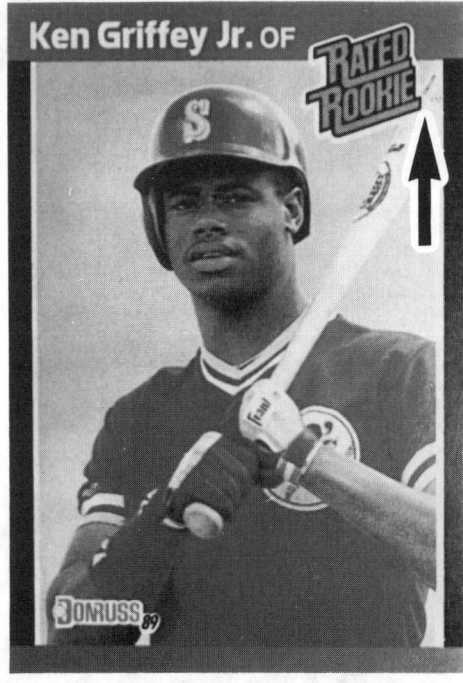

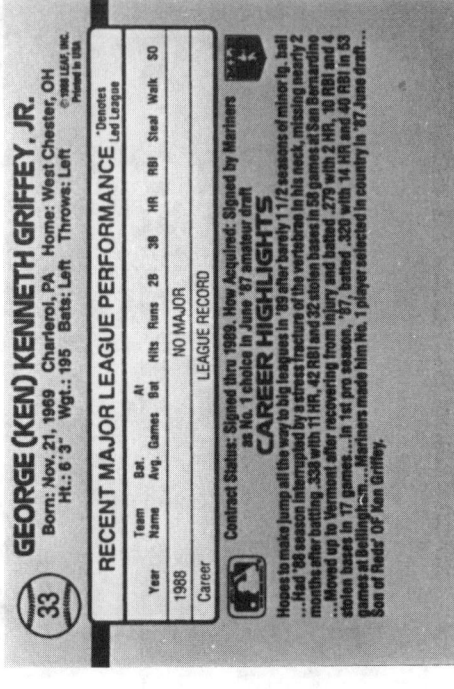

Unfortunately, the easiest way to spot this counterfeit doesn't show up well in a photograph, but we'll describe it anyway. Genuine 1989 Donruss cards have a "fifth color" ink — a flat black — that appears as a series of eight short horizontal bars in the black side borders to the left and right of the player photo. On this counterfeit, there are no bars visible.

When examined with a magnifying glass, the typographical elements on the front will provide additional evidence. Genuine cards will show the white letters of the player's name and position as having crisp edges which end cleanly at the purple background. On the counterfeit, there are many purple dots muddying up the edges of the letters.

On a real card, the blue "Rated Rookie", the red "Donruss" and the black "'89" are made up of solid colors. On the counterfeit, these elements are seen to

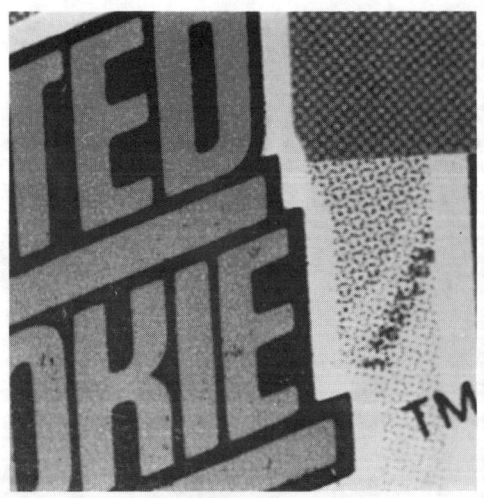

Genuine

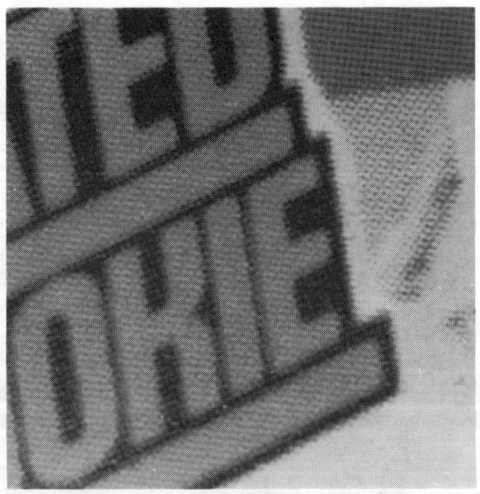

Counterfeit

be composed of tiny dots. Many stray dots also appear in the white vertical pin-stripes on the counterfeit's border.

The counterfeit also displays a very weak trademark ("TM") symbol to the right of the Rated Rookie logo. On a genuine card these letters are clean black lines.

The back of the counterfeit has Major League Baseball and MLB Players' Association logos that are considerably darker and less distinct than on a genuine card. The wording on the MLB logo at left is indecipherable on the counterfeit.

While such a judgement is subjective, it can be noted that the orange printing on the back of the counterfeit is more yellow than on a genuine card. It is also worth noting that the counterfeit features factory-set orientation of front and back. That is, when flipped over, the counterfeit will display the card number in the lower-left corner. Since a genuine factory-set Griffey card will display this same orientation, that trait cannot be considered a definitive indicator of a forgery. A wax-pack Griffey, when flipped from front to back, will show the card number at the upper-right.

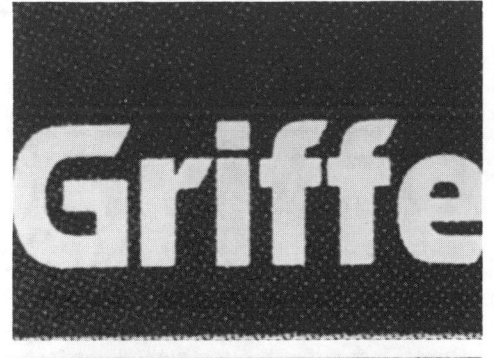
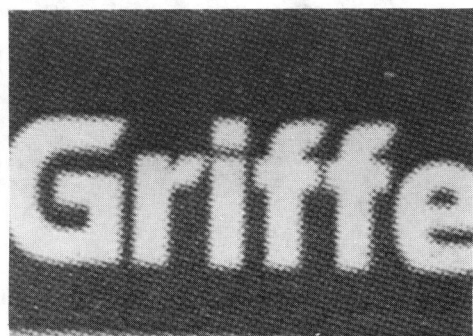

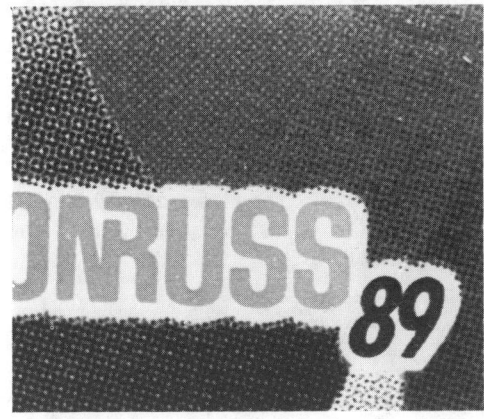
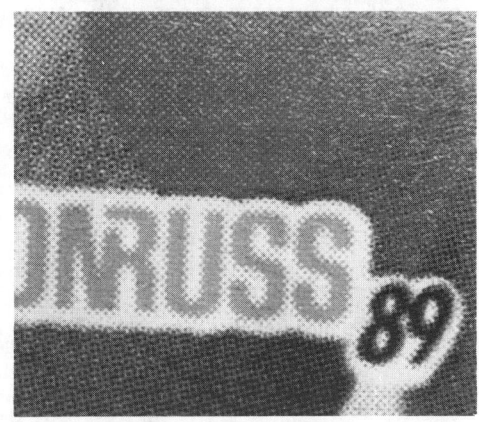

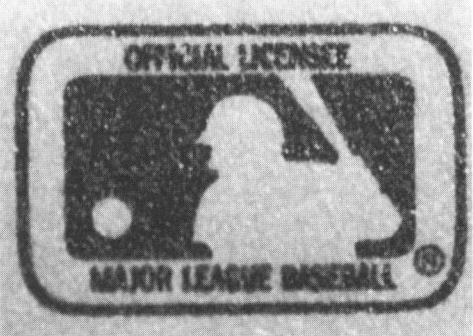
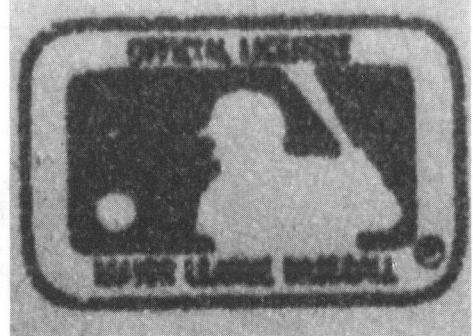

Genuine   **Counterfeit**

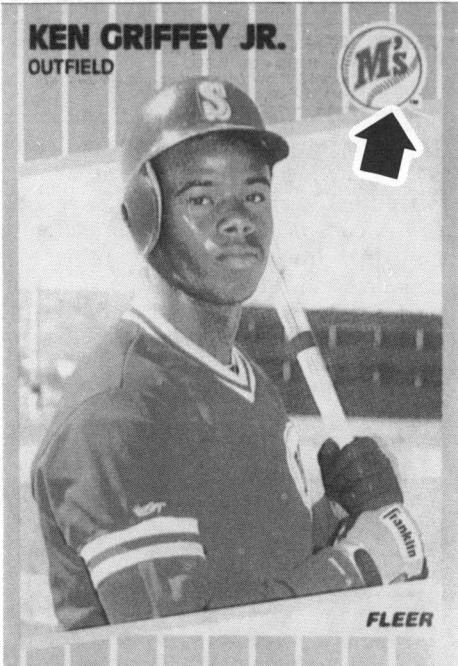

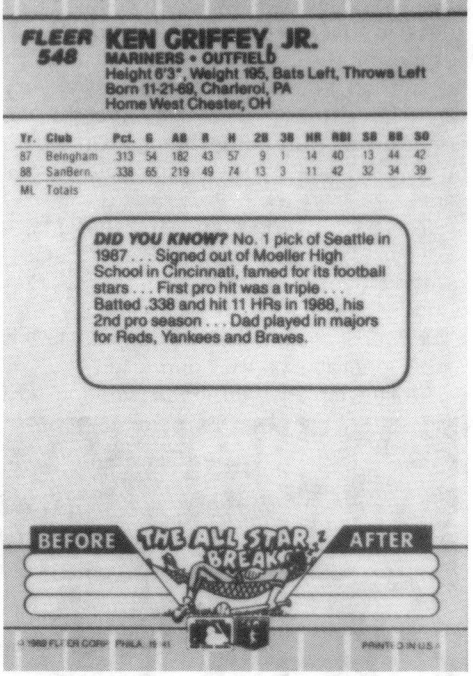

At first glance, this counterfeit might fool the average collector or dealer. Examination under magnification, however, will reveal many areas of the counterfeit which show evidence of re-screening.

On the front of the card, check the player's name and position at upper-left, the "FLEER" at lower-right and the team logo. On a genuine card, these details will be rendered in solid lines and colors. On the counterfeit, these elements are made up of many tiny dots, giving the edges of the letters a ragged appearance. This is especially noticeable in the team logo. On the counterfeit, the blue circle around the ball and the stitching are fuzzy dot structures, instead of the the clean lines found on the genuine card. The black "TM" near the logo on a genuine card is barely readable on the counterfeit.

The back of the counterfeit shows the Major League Baseball and MLB Players' Association logos with lettering that is indeciperhable. The Fleer copyright line at the bottom is also very broken on the counterfeit.

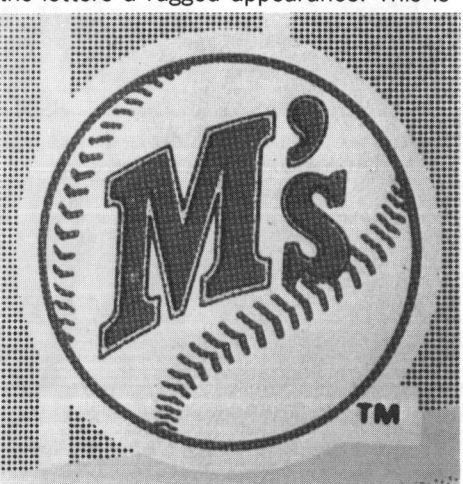

Genuine

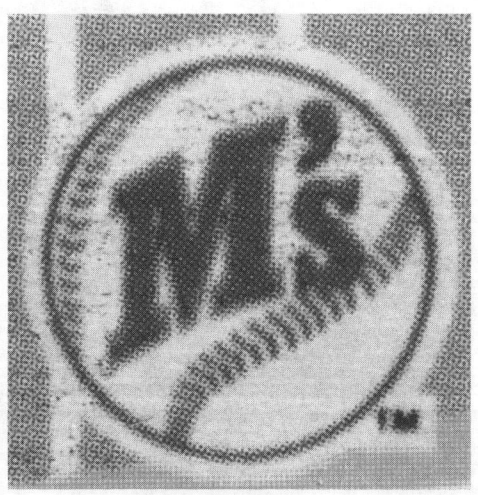

Counterfeit

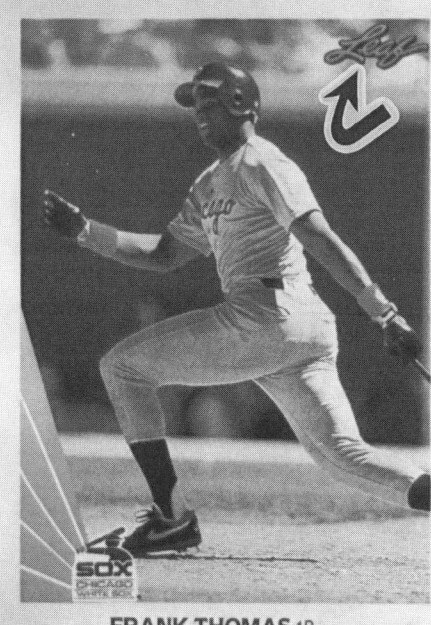

FRANK THOMAS 1B

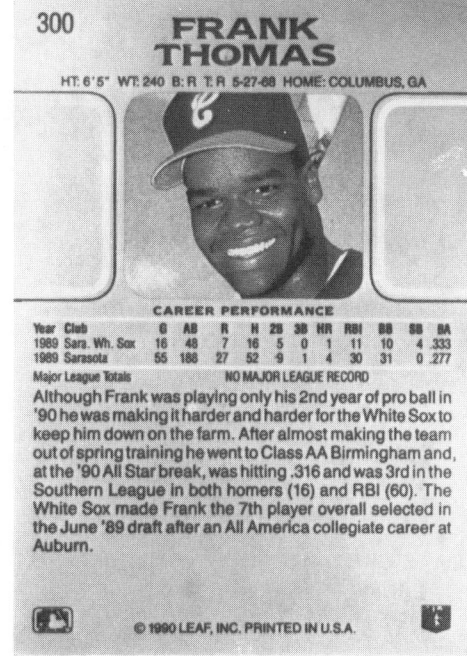

Printed on very thin cardboard, if presented outside of a plastic holder this counterfeit would deceive no one who has ever handled a genuine 1990 Leaf card.

This first known attempt to replicate one of the premium-quality five-color cards might stand a cursory visual once-over, but a close-up examination with a magnifying glass will reveal the counterfeit very easily.

Specifically, a study of the "Leaf" script White Sox in the upper-right corner will show a pattern logo at the lower-left will show of color dots within the letters on the counterfeit, instead of that the pure silver displayed on the genuine card. Similarly, instead of the "CHICAGO WHITE SOX" letters at lower-left being formed of clean red lines, as on the original, those words on the counterfeit are composed of many red dots.

As might be expected, this counterfeit weighs perceptibly less than a genuine Leaf card.

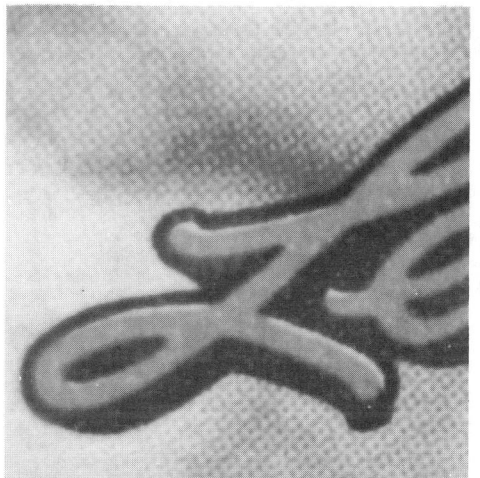

Genuine

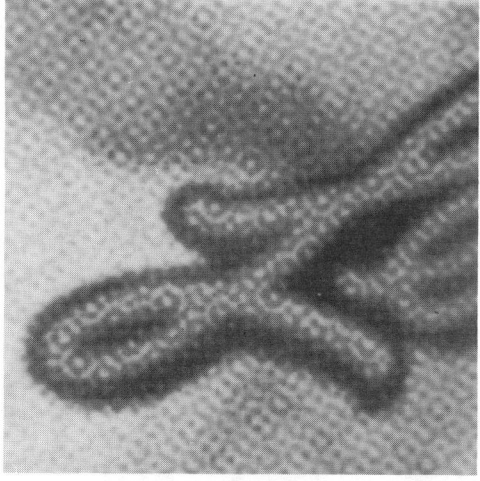

Counterfeit

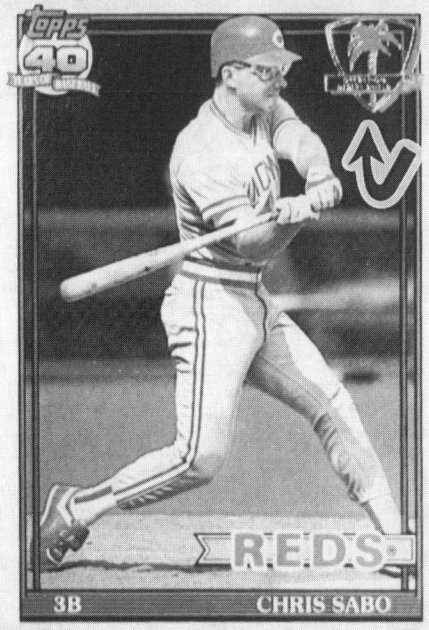

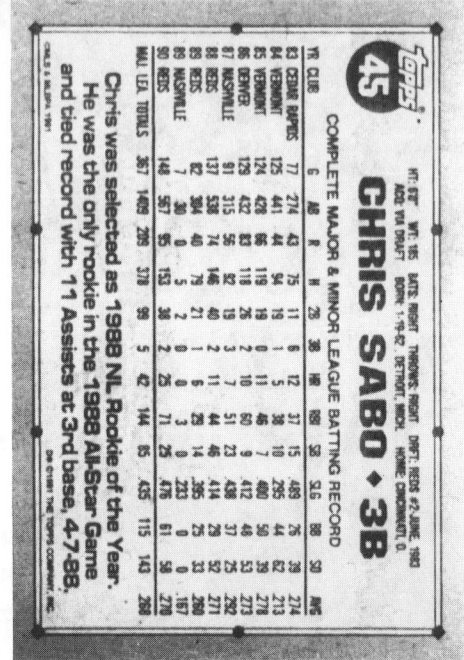

Here we are not dealing with a counterfeit card, but a bogus overprint. Color should never be used alone as a counterfeit detector, but on D.S. cards it's a good place to start. This fake overprint is a more yellow, brassy tone than the Topps-applied design.

Besides being larger than the genuine overprint, the phony lacks the fine details of the true version — the bands around the tree trunk and the coconuts cannot be seen. On the flag, the fake will show no stars, and the stripes are indistinct.

Probably the easiest point of difference to spot this fake overprint is at the bottom tip of the shield. On a genuine Desert Shield overprint, the tip of the shield is blunt, almost rounded. The tip of the shield on this type of counterfeit appears as a pair of sharp points.

It should be assumed that all cards in the 1991 Topps set can be found with the fake overprint, but naturally high-value rookie and star cards will be most often encountered.

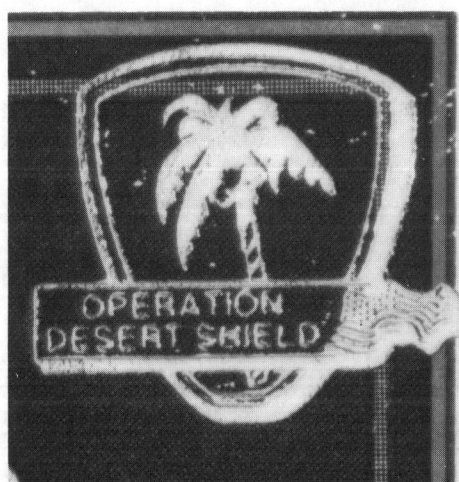

Genuine

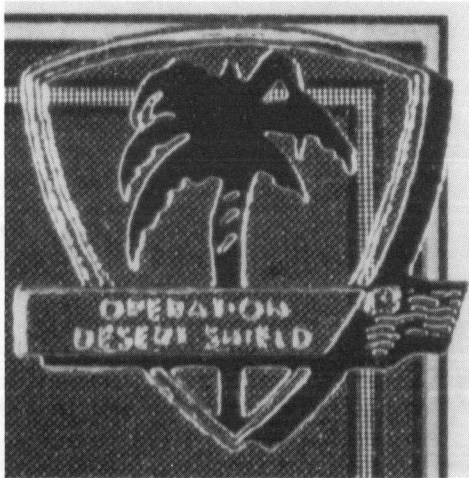

Counterfeit

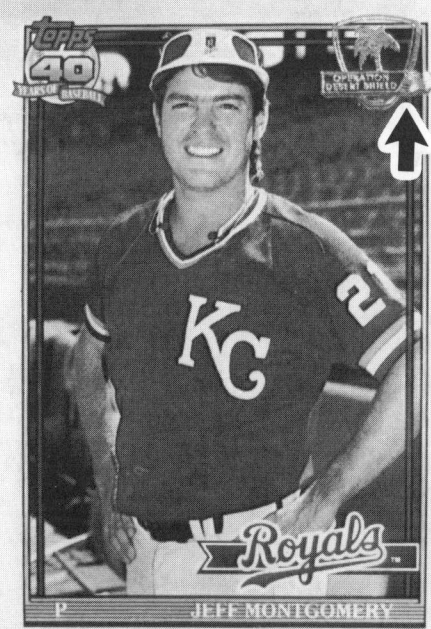

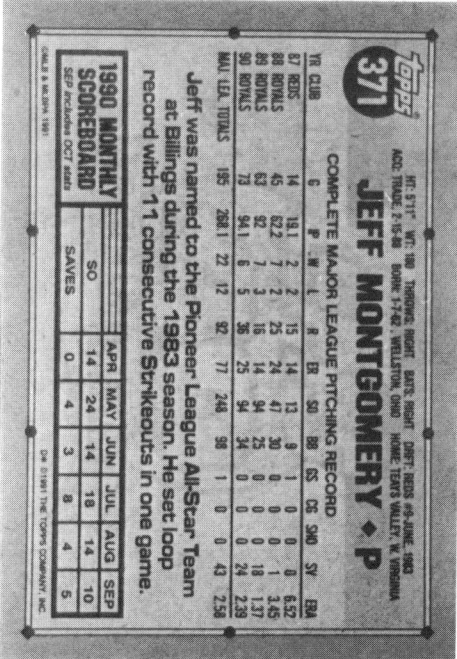

A more dangerous fake than the first variety, this type of counterfeit gold foil Desert Shield overprint features a round-bottom shield, much like the genuine.

While this counterfeit is labeled as a second version, it is possible that the work of more than one forger is being seen here. To date, however, all of these counterfeit round-bottom shield overprints share a common flaw — inability to reproduce the fine details of the U.S. flag seen on a genuine Topps overprint.

When viewed under strong magnifica-tion, a genuine Desert Shield overprint will show clearly detailed vertical rows of four, three, four and three dots (stars) at the left of the flag's field. All of the counter-feits seen to date have been unable to accurately depict the individual dot-stars, usually showing only two or three indis-tinct representations.

It should be assumed that all cards in the 1991 Topps set can be found with the fake overprint, but naturally high-value rookie and star cards will be most often encountered.

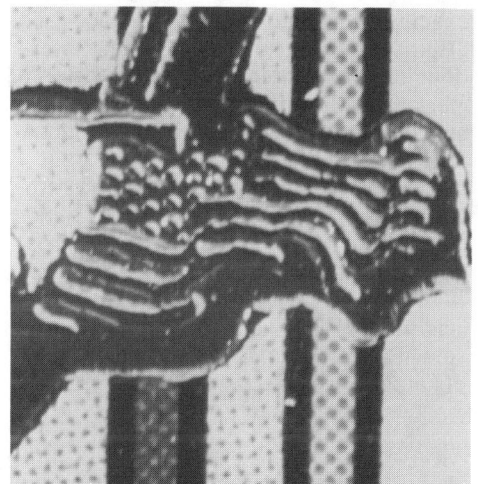

Genuine

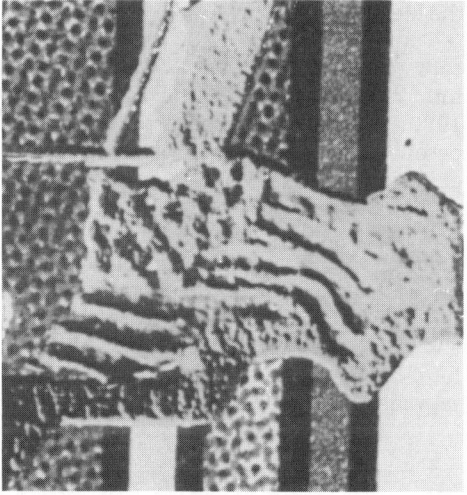

Counterfeit

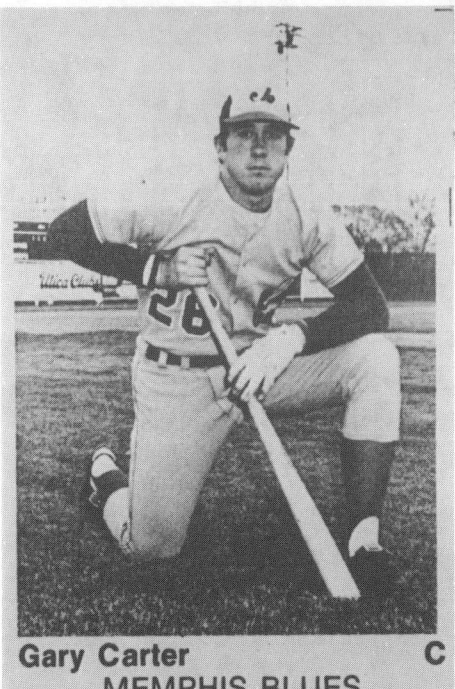

Gary Carter   C
MEMPHIS BLUES

GARY CARTER, C., MEMPHIS BLUES

Bn.—, —, —. Bats and Throws: Right

Despite his defensive prowess and great hitting ability, it is unlikely Gary Carter will be the regular catcher for the parent Montreal Expos, at least for awhile. However, his great versatility would gain him a spot in 1975 - he can play both third and the outfield as well! Carter's career has been one of rapid advancement: from the rookie league Cocoa Expos and West Palm Beach (1972) to Quebec City (1973), and now to Memphis. Carter hit 15 homers and .253 in 1973 at Quebec City.

International League	A.B.	H.	HR.	RBI.	AVG.
1974 Memphis	.386	105	21	74	.272

* T.C.M.A. 1975   **21**

These cards would more appropriately be found in the reprint section of this book, but because of long-standing hobby perceptions, the greatest number of suspicious hobbyists will be looking for them in the body of the counterfeit listings.

Originally produced in 1975, this black-and-white set includes 31 cards, several of which are pose variations of the same players. The only major star represented in the set is Gary Carter, then catcher for the Memhpis Blues.

Along with most 1970s minor league cards, little interest was shown by collectors in this issue until the early-to-mid 1980s, when Carter became a nearly perennial All-Star selection and began to compile Cooperstown credentials.

About that time certain East Coast dealers began to appear at shows with hundreds of the sets available at low prices. Examination of the paper on which the newly available sets were printed showed it to be much whiter and of a different texture than the originals, leading to widespread speculation that the set had been counterfeited.

More recent comparisons of the two types of cards, however, indicate that each was produced from the same negatives and/or printing plates.

In a subsequent conversation with one of the principals involved in the production of the set in 1975, it was revealed that an unspecified quantity of the I.L. sets had been printed at a later date. While the source would not specify exactly when the reprint took place, and attempted to make it sound as if it were done roughly contemporary with the original production, most hobbyists feel the second printing was more likely undertaken many years later.

Regardless of the timing, the controversy has prevented this particular minor league set from attaining any great degree of value. The *SCD Minor League Baseball Card Price Guide* lists the set at less than $40, while all other 1975 TCMA sets, none of which feature any future Hall of Famers, are listed between $70-195.

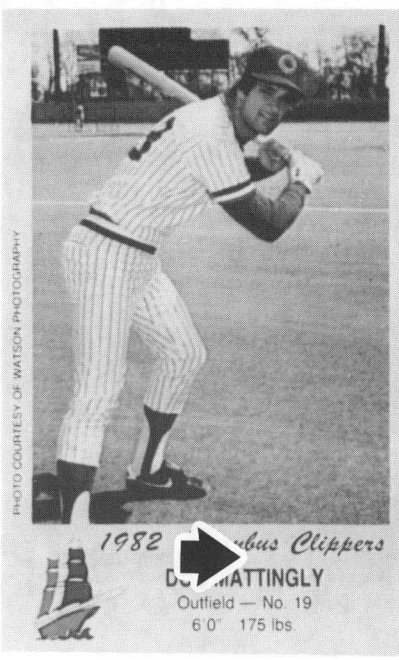

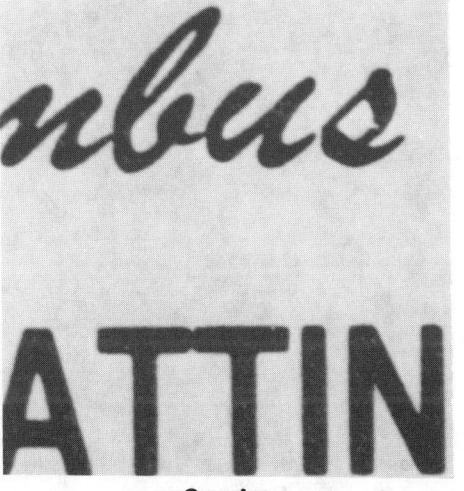

DON MATTINGLY
Born April 20, 1961

Played with Nashville in 1981 in the Southern League. Led the League with 35 Doubles and Hit .314.

CLIPPER TIPS

FOUR TERRITORY: That part of the playing field outside the first and third base lines extended to the fence.

CRIME TIPS

TIP: Play with your friends, only in fair territory — safe places. Never the streets, in vacant buildings, near construction areas.

Courtesy of Your Columbus Division of Police
Crime Prevention Unit and Hester Dysart

Visually, this is a very deceptive counterfeit if no known genuine set is at hand with which to compare a suspect set.

Because most people buy and sell minor league cards of this era in complete team sets, the counterfeiters were required to reproduce all 25 cards in the police set.

Counterfeit detection is hampered by the fact the original set was not all that well printed to begin with. Dot patterns come and go on originals, so they cannot be used to identify a phony.

Because it is the key to the set, detection should center on the Mattingly card. With a magnifying glass, examine the "u" of "Columbus" and the second "T" of "MATTINGLY" on the card front.

A stray hair has crept across the black negative, leaving a white hairline through those letters.

The counterfeits are printed on a much heavier card stock than the original, weighing as much as 25% more than genuine cards.

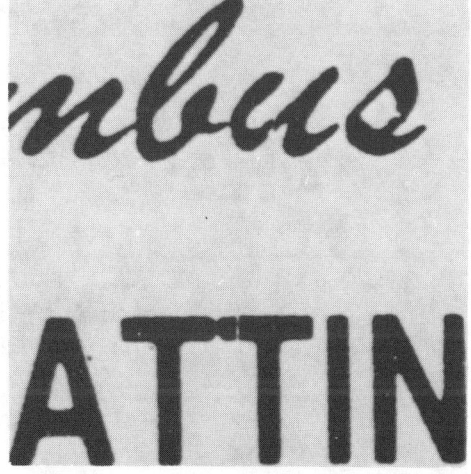

Genuine   **Counterfeit**

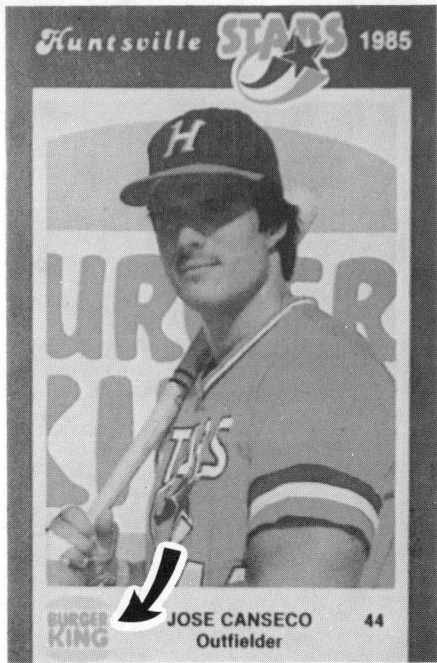

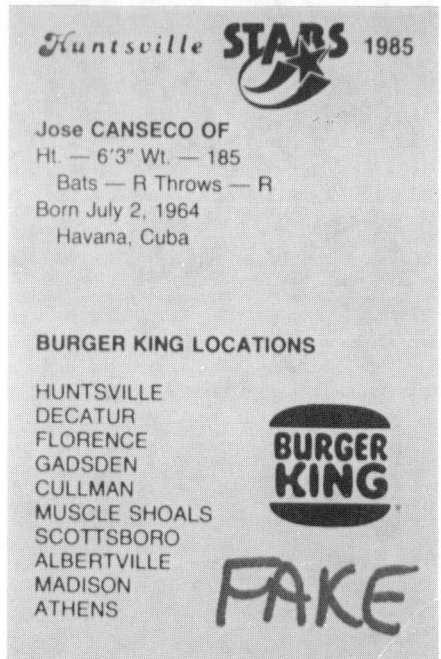

Any person offered a single Canseco card from this minor league set should be immediately suspicious. While there are several current stars in the set — Luis Polonia, Tim Belcher, Terry Steinbach — only the Canseco card was counterfeited.

The counterfeit is printed on much lighter cardboard than the genuine card, and the border is a much redder purple than the original. Of course, without a known genuine card to compare these details with, it is impossible to make a judgement on these elements alone.

Definitive analysis can be easily made by studying the Burger King logo. On a genuine card, the letters of "Burger King" will be solid red. On the counterfeit, these letters are composed of tiny red and yellow dots, creating a fuzzy appearance. On both the genuine and counterfeit card, the "bun" portions of the logo and the trademark to the right of the lower bun are made up of red and yellow dots.

The word "Fake" penned on the back of the card shown here will not be seen on counterfeits encountered in the market.

Genuine

Counterfeit

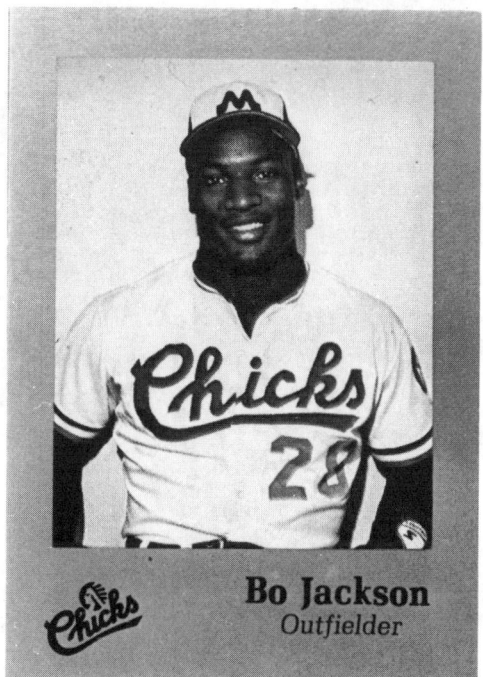

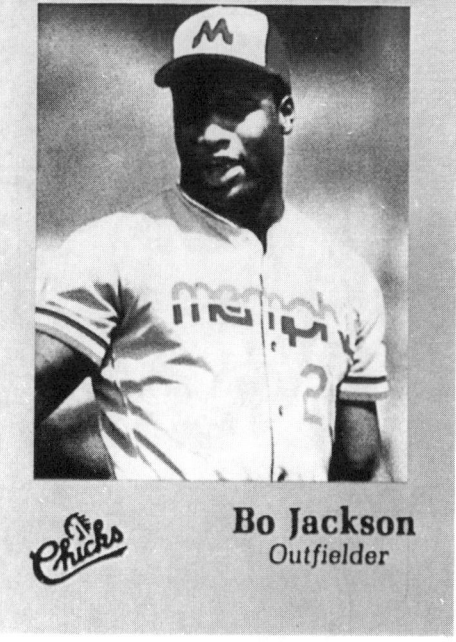

Genuine

Counterfeit

There is no challenge to identifying the counterfeit 1986 Memphis Chicks Bo Jackson minor league cards.

On the genuine card, issued as part of a team set, the color photo of Jackson shows him in the team's home white uniform, with "Chicks" visible across the chest.

The counterfeit depicts Jackson in a road uniform, with "Memphis" across the chest and can be found in both silver-border and gold-border versions, simulating the genuine issues.

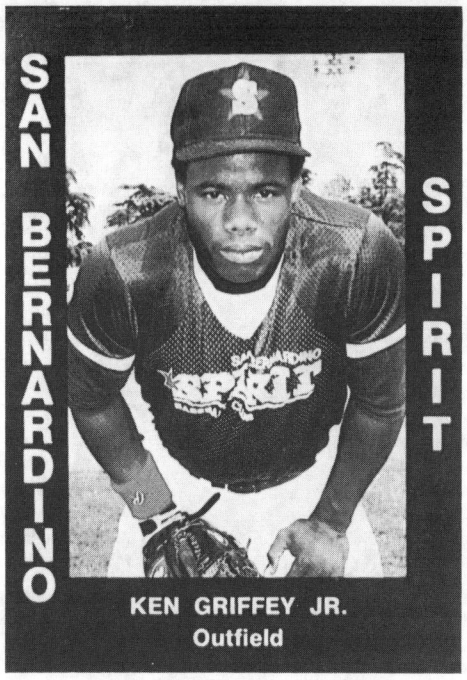

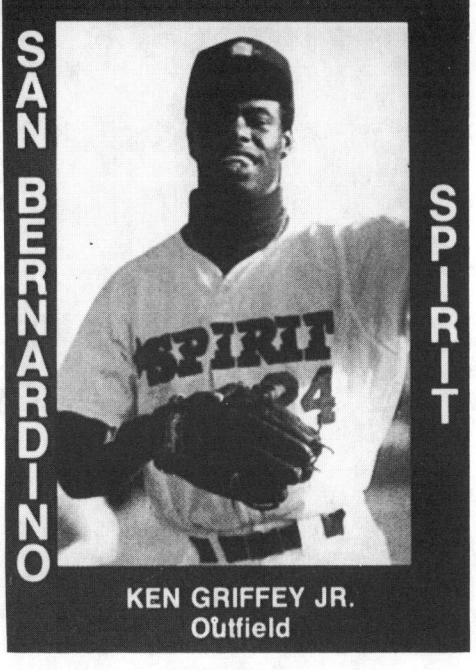

Genuine   **Counterfeit**

There is no challenge to identifying this version of the counterfeit 1988 Cal Cards Ken Griffey Jr. minor league card.

On the genuine card, issued as part of a San Bernardino Spirit team set, the color photo of Griffey shows him in the team's dark blue jersey, hunched over with his hands on his thighs.

The counterfeit depicts Griffey in a home white uniform, in a throwing pose.

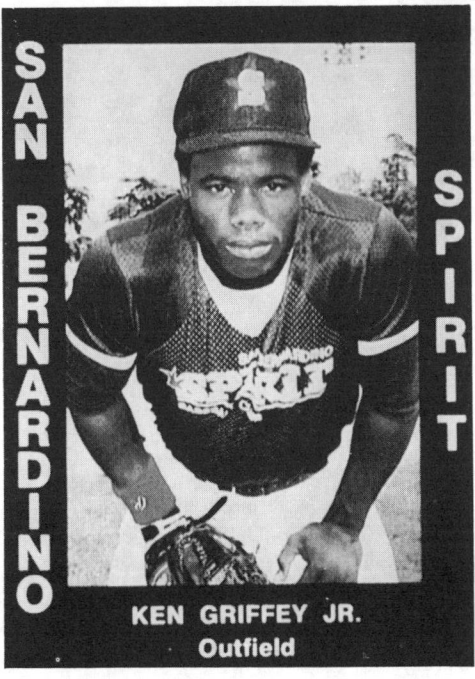

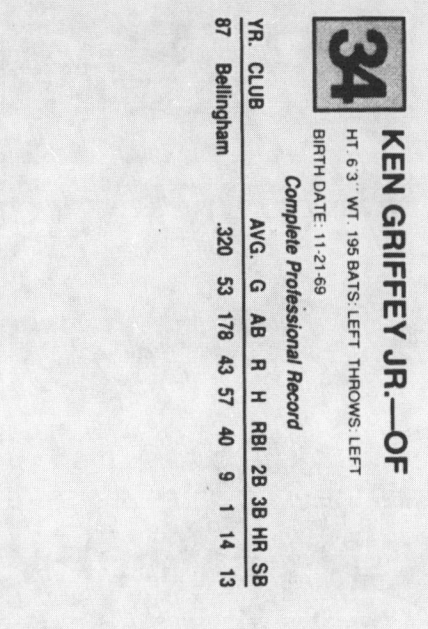

Definitely more challenging to identify than the other known forgery of the 1988 Cal Cards Griffey minor league card.

On the genuine card, issued as part of a San Bernardino Spirit team set, all of the white lettering down the sides and at the bottom of the card's front will be pure white when examined under magnifica-tion.

This counterfeit exhibits a dot pattern within these letters when viewed close-up.

Since the rest of the team set was not counterfeited, it pays to be especially wary when offered this card as a single, rather than part of a complete set.

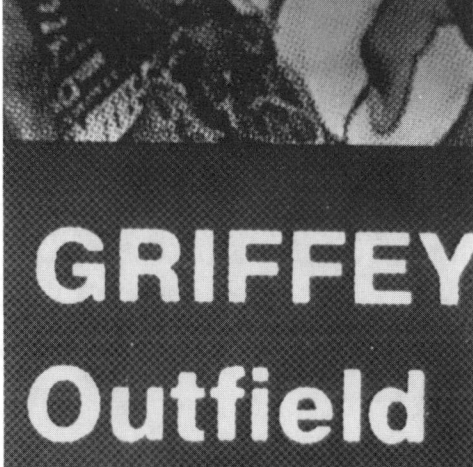

Genuine

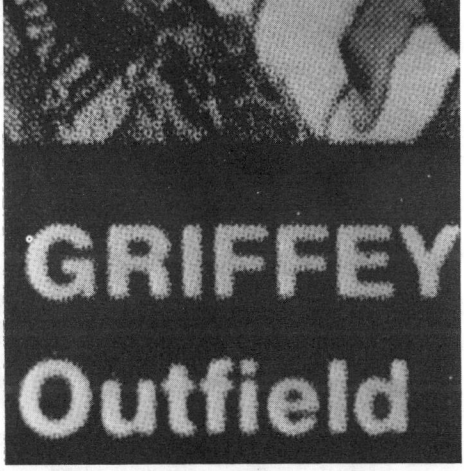

Counterfeit

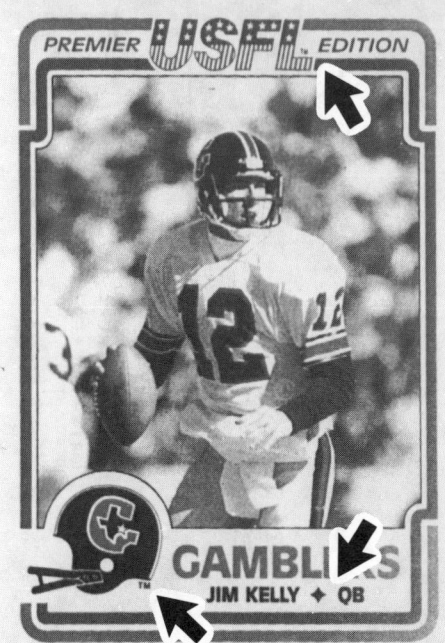

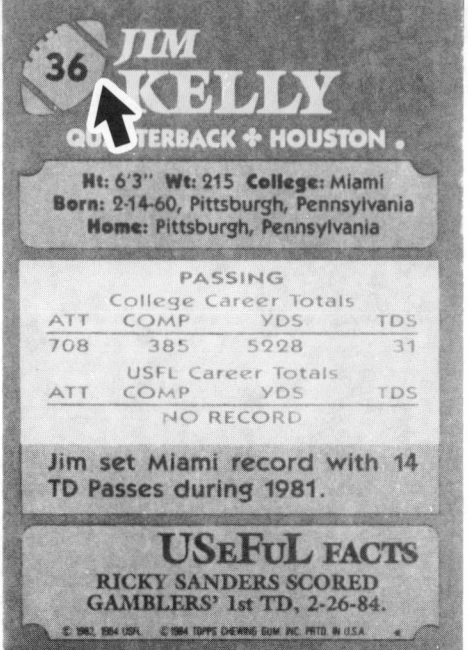

Appearing in the spring of 1992, this is the first known counterfeit of a Topps football card. With the value of Kelly's premiere card now pushing $200, the scarce USFL issue was a natural target for counterfeiters.

Visually, this is a very deceptive counterfeit. The technology by which this card was produced also represents a step forward in the fakers' never-ending quest to produce an indetectible forgery. Instead of re-screening a genuine card with a standard dot-pattern screen to produce new printing negatives, the counterfeiters of this card made their printing materials by re-screening a genuine card

with a parallel-line screen. The use of a parallel-line screen allows the reproduced printing materials to be more finely focused than if a traditional dot screen was used.

Helping to blunt the effect of better printing reproduction was the choice of cardboard stock on the counterfeit that is less glossy, more porous looking, than a genuine 1984 Topps USFL card. This, however, is a subjective observation and cannot be definitively used as an indicator of status.

Close-up examination of the card with a magnifying glass will show several elements on the counterfeit which are ren-

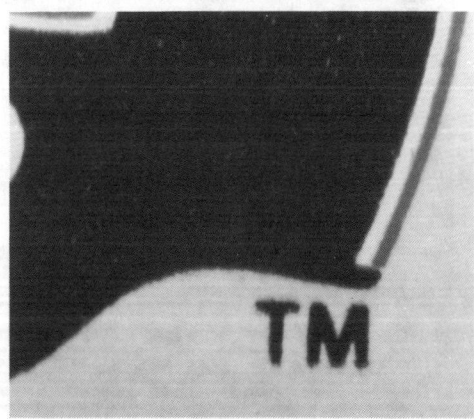

Genuine

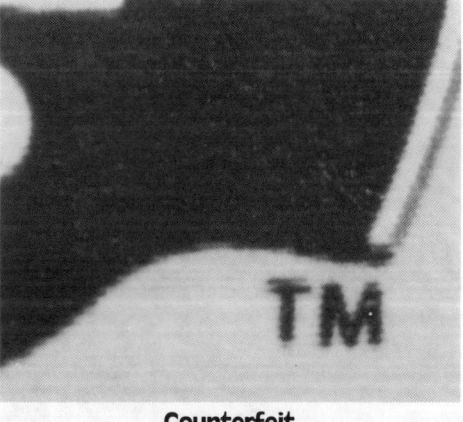

Counterfeit

dered as composed of very thin parallel lines — horizontal on the front of the counterfeit, vertical on the back — rather than the dot structure or clean, solid lines on an original card. This is evident especially in the finest printing, such as the "TM" trademark indicators near the USFL logo and the Houston Gamblers helmet. The thin black frame around the color photo is also seen as a series of lines on the counterfeit, rather than as a solid line on the original.

The red lettering in the blue boxes on the card back can also be seen under magnification as significantly different between the real card and the fake. The counterfeit shows a series of parallel lines in these letters, where the genuine card presents these letters as solid elements.

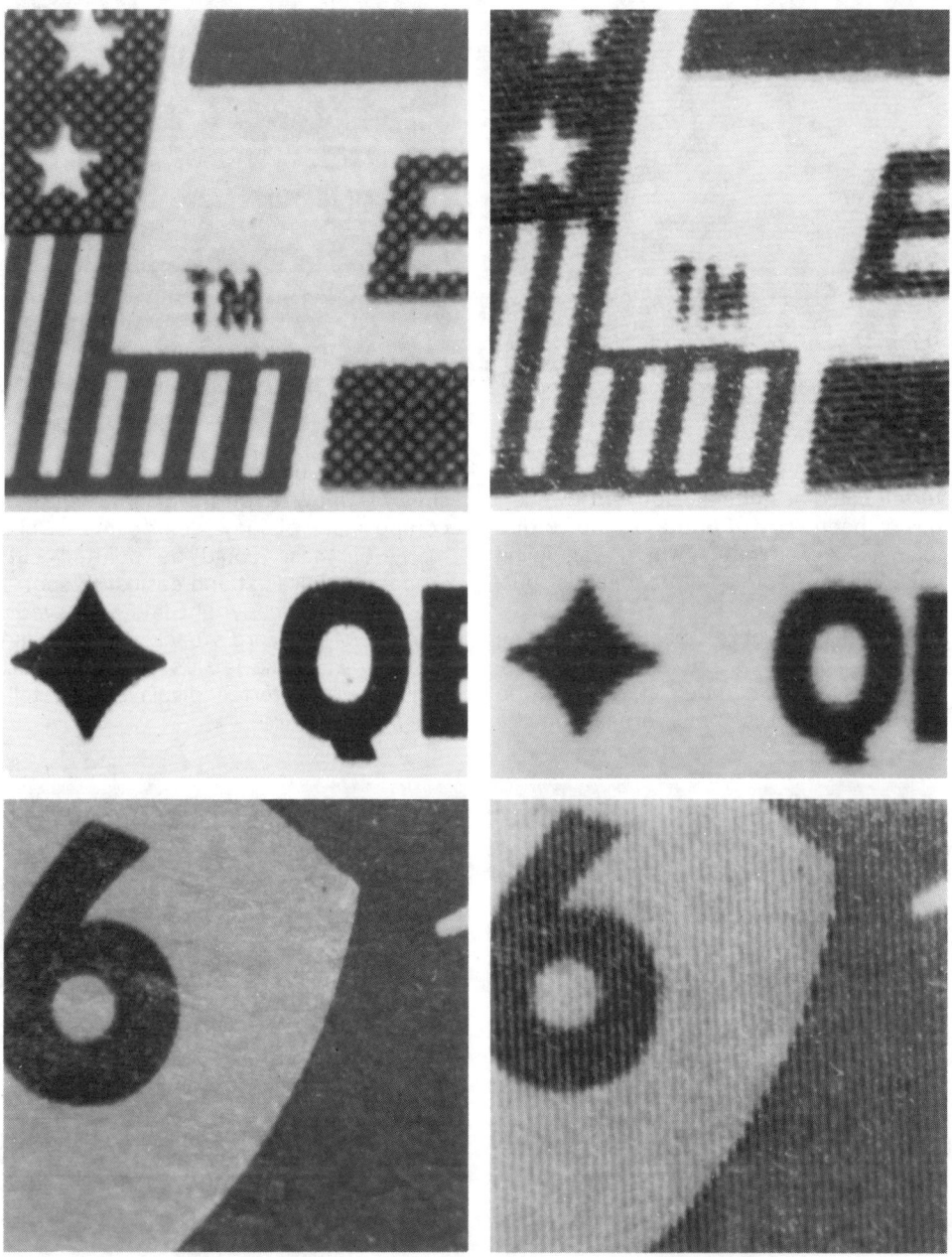

Genuine   Counterfeit

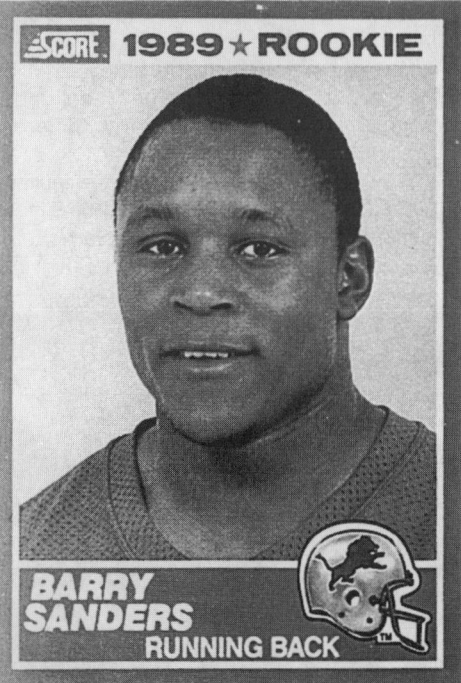

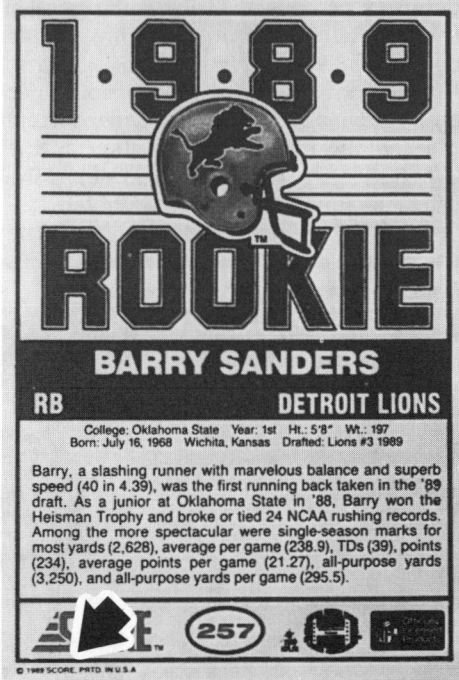

Viewed with the unaided eye, this counterfeit could be quite deceptive. However, having been warned of the existence of a fake, quick examination with a magnifying lens will protect any prospective purchaser.

In the process of re-screening a genuine Sanders rookie card to create printing materials for the counterfeit, many of the tiny design details that are seen on the real thing to be composed of clean, solid lines will show up on the counterfeit as a composition of tiny color dots. While many of these could be pointed out, among the quickest and easiest to spot is the tiny green copyright line at the bottom-left of the card's back. The genuine card shows these letters as clean lines, while the counterfeit displays their telltale dot structure.

Genuine

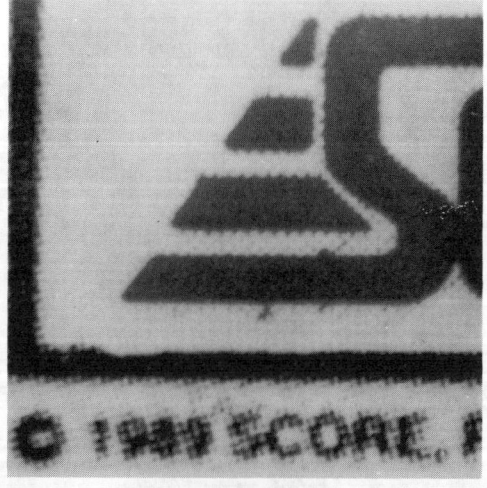

Counterfeit

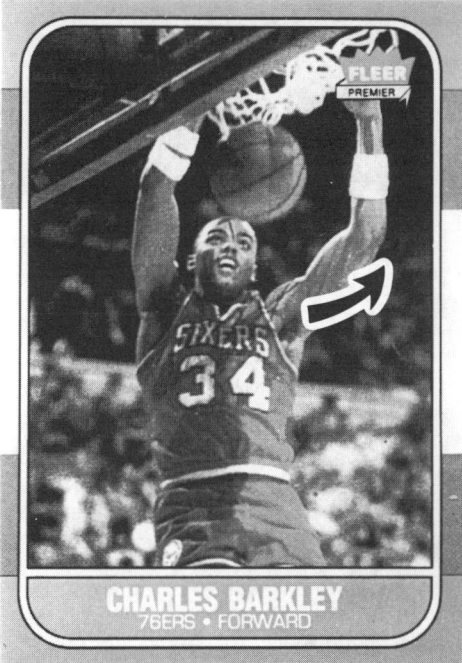

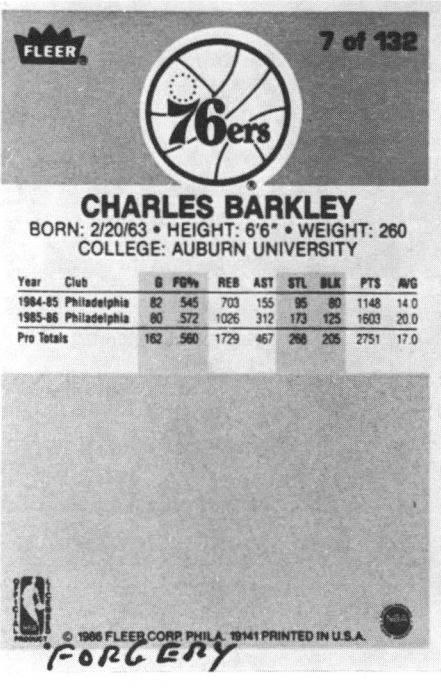

Year	Club	G	FG%	REB	AST	STL	BLK	PTS	AVG
1984-85	Philadelphia	82	.545	703	155	95	80	1148	14.0
1985-86	Philadelphia	80	.572	1026	312	173	125	1603	20.0
Pro Totals		162	.560	1729	467	268	205	2751	17.0

This is one of the toughest counterfeits for which to provide definitive points of difference between real and fake.

One difference centers on a flaw on the genuine card. At the player's left elbow there was an attempt made to clean up a print line extending roughly horizontally from the left bicep to within 1/16th'' of the right border. In re-screening a genuine card to create the counterfeit, the disguised print line disappeared. It's possible, however, that a later generation of the genuine Barkley card could have been printed with the touched-up print line totally removed.

Corroborating evidence can be sought at about the same point in the yellow right border. The counterfeit has a nick in the black frame line at left, exposing a pimple of yellow ink on the counterfeit that is not present on genuine cards.

On back, some of the loops of letters and numbers will be filled in or nearly so on the counterfeit. The ''FORGERY'' penned on the back of the photographed card is unique to this specimen.

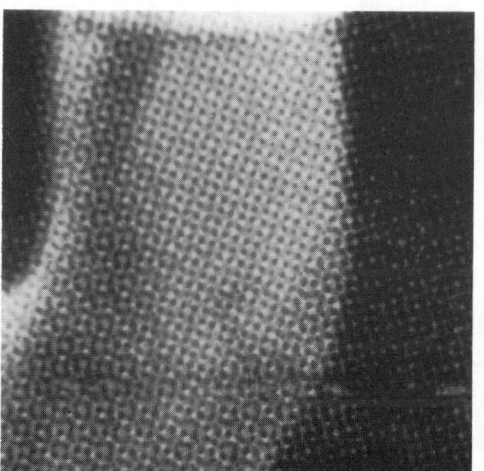

Genuine

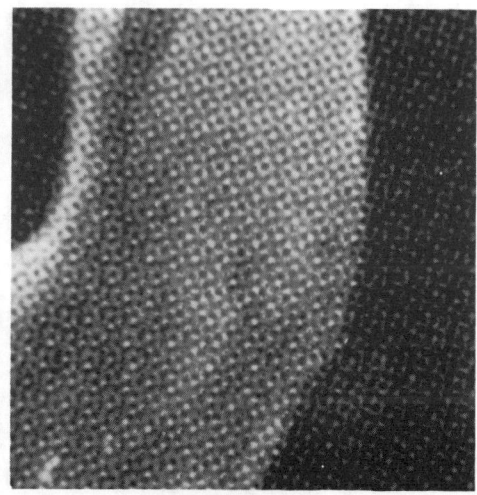

Counterfeit

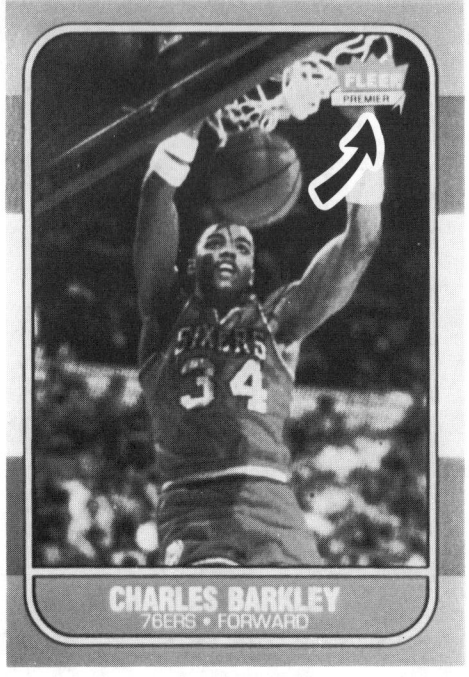

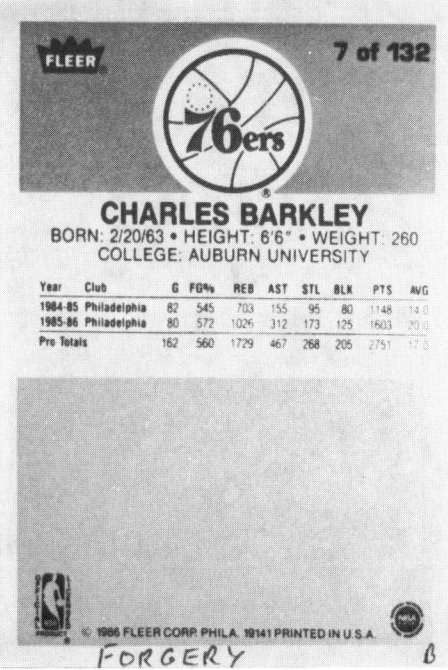

FORGERY   B

This is by far the easier of the known types of 1986-87 Fleer Barkley counterfeits to spot. This card exhibits its fatal flaw within the crown-and-banner "FLEER PREMIER" logo at the upper-right.

On a genuine card, the word "PRE-MIER" will show its letters as clean, solid black lines. On this counterfeit, the letters (as well as the black borders of the banner) are composed of many tiny black dots.

Like many (but not all) of the 1986-87 Fleer basketball counterfeits, the fine details of the NBA Players Association logo on the back of the card did not reproduce well; the seams of the basketball are missing, and there is a lack of distinctness to the letters around the ball.

The "FORGERY B" penned on the back of the photographed card is unique to this specimen.

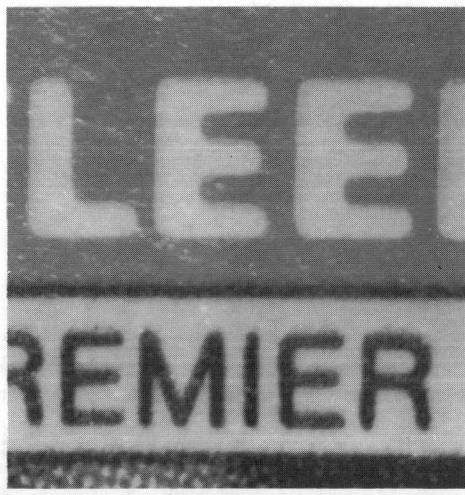

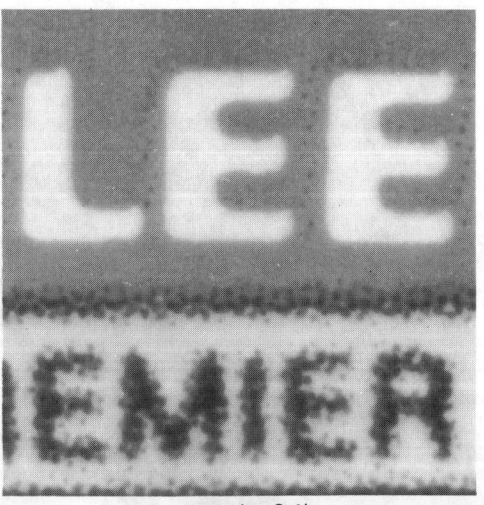

Genuine   Counterfeit

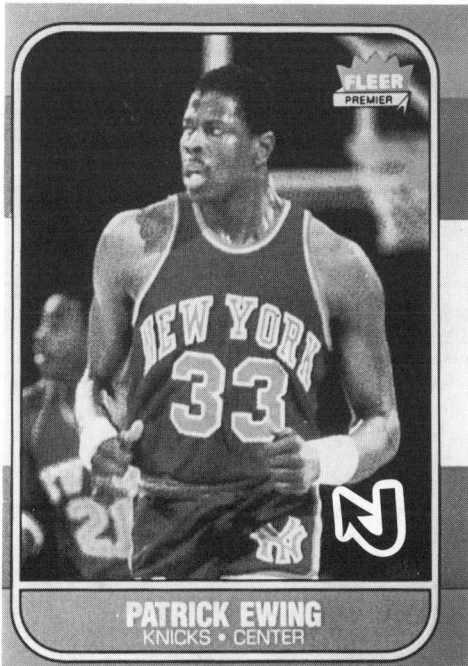

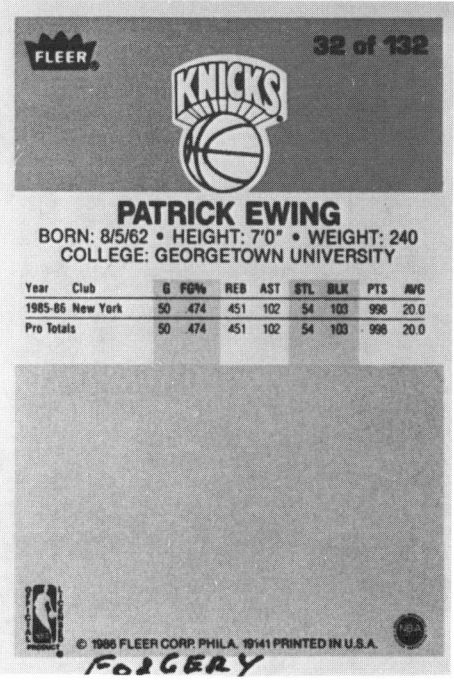

The better of two known Fleer counterfeit Ewing cards. The key to quick, easy detection is worn by the Knicks star, on each wrist. On a genuine card, examination under magnification will reveal hundreds of tiny blue dots giving a subtle hint of color to the wristbands worn by Ewing. This particular counterfeit has no such dots on the wristband. As is frequently the case, this difference cannot be detected by the naked eye, a good magnifying lens is necessary.

A tiny white dot to the left of the "P" in "PATRICK" on the counterfeit card's front can also be used as a counterfeit indicator.

Unlike most of the 1986-87 Fleer basketball counterfeits, the Fleer logo on front, and the NBA and Players Associations logos on the back of this version are virtually indistinguishable from those on a genuine card.

The counterfeit card shown here has had the word "FORGERY" and letter "A" penned on the back.

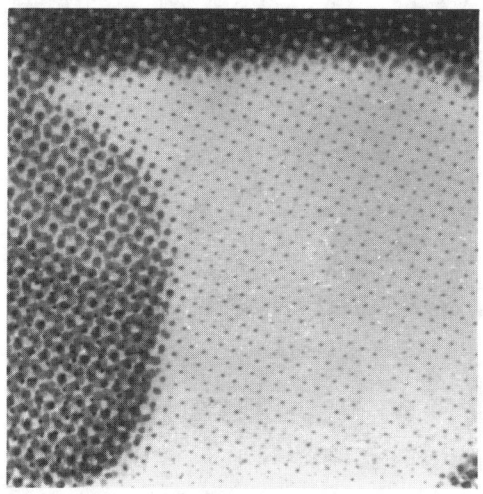

Genuine

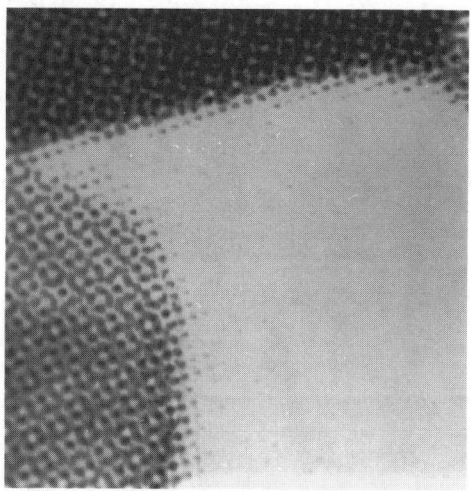

Counterfeit

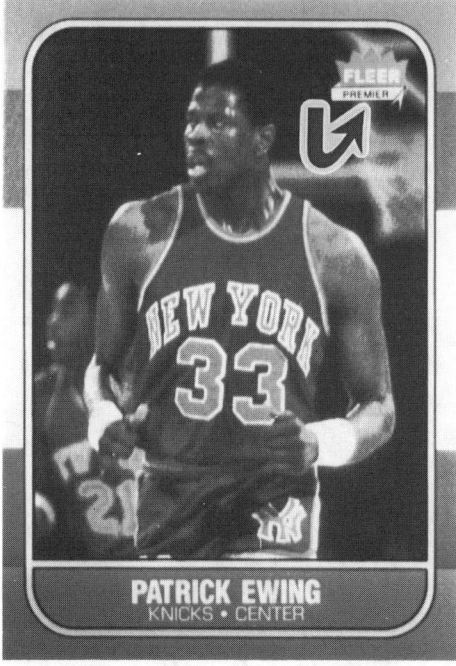

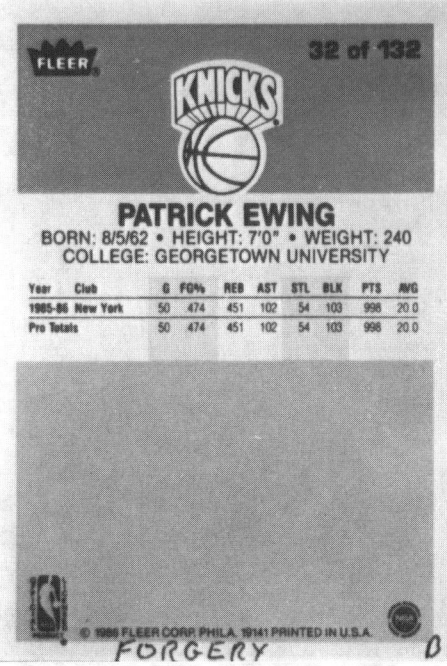

The second type of Ewing counterfeit is best detected by magnification-assisted examination of the crown-and-banner "FLEER / PREMIER" logo in the upper-right corner of the card's front. Instead of the solid black "PREMIER" and lines bordering the yellow banner of the logo, this counterfeit evidences those elements in a myriad of tiny black dots, creating an overall fuzzy appearance.

Unlike the other Ewing fake, this card does have the blue dots in the wristbands.

The back of this counterfeit has a very bad rendition of the NBA Players Association logo at lower-right; virtually none of the letters around the ball are decipherable, and several of the letters of "PLAYERS" inside the ball-logo are filled in with excessive blue ink. The registration mark (®) beneath the NBA logo at lower-left is similarly unidentifiable.

The specimen shown here has had the word "FORGERY" and the letter "B" penned on.

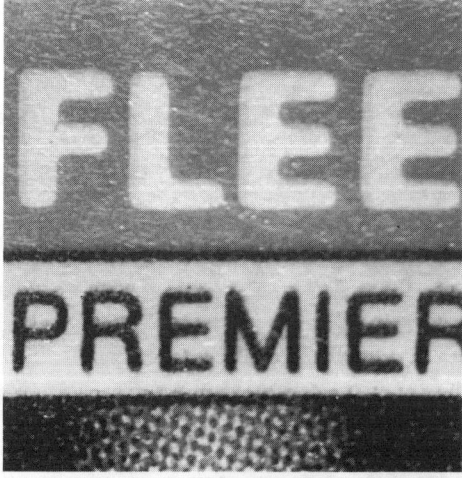

Genuine

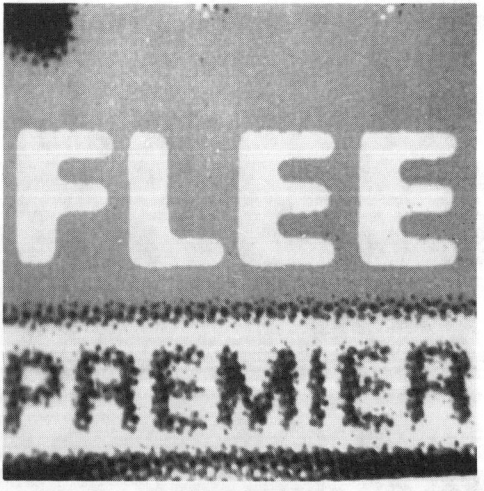

Counterfeit

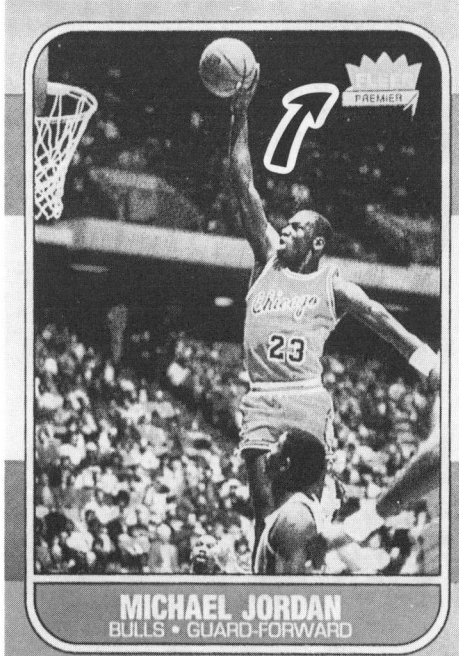

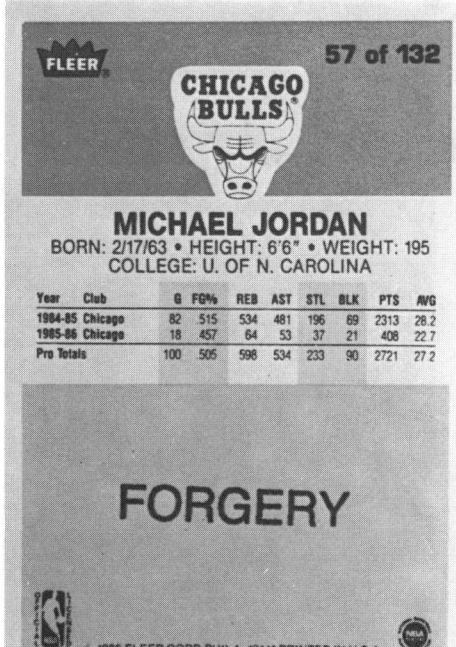

The first of three known counterfeits of the Jordan rookie card is easily and unequivocally detected by examination of the "FLEER / PREMIER" logo in the upper-right corner of the card's front. On a genuine card, the red crown, yellow pattern and black "PREMIER" are made up of solid colors. On this particular Jordan counterfeit, those elements are seen under magnification to contain dot structures, the result of a genuine card having been rescreened to create the necessary printing elements for the counterfeit.

The blue color of the fake card's back is lighter than on a genuine Jordan rookie, especially in the area of the Fleer crown at upper-left. On a genuine card, the crown is actually purple, the result of combining blue and red ink. This Jordan counterfeit shows only the blue ink used in the crown.

The counterfeit card shown here has had the word "FORGERY" stamped on it; do not expect to see such a warning on cards you may be offered for sale.

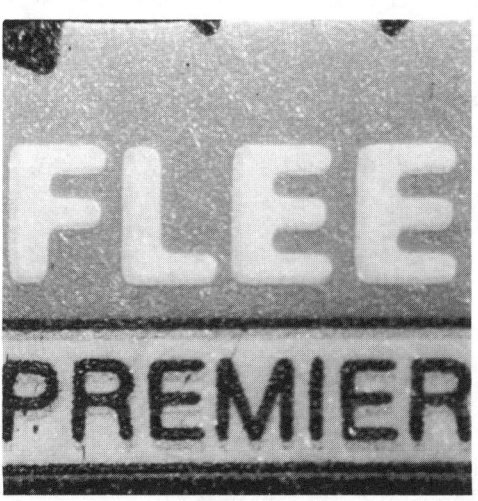

Genuine

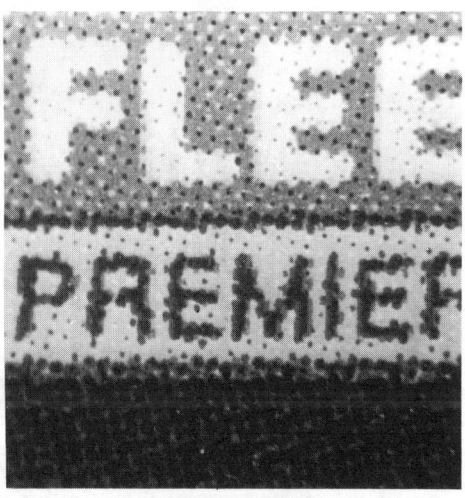

Counterfeit

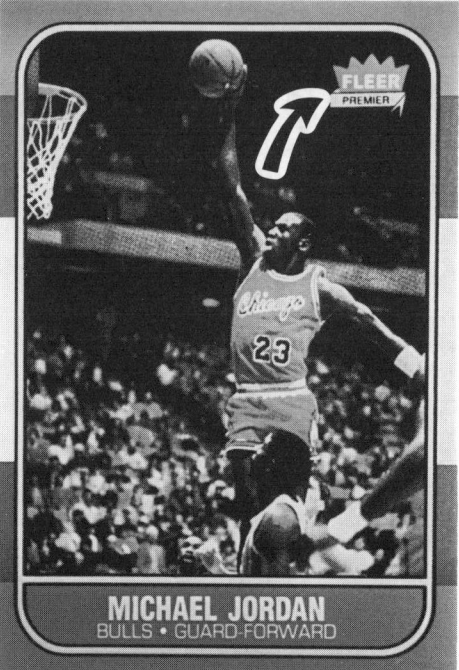

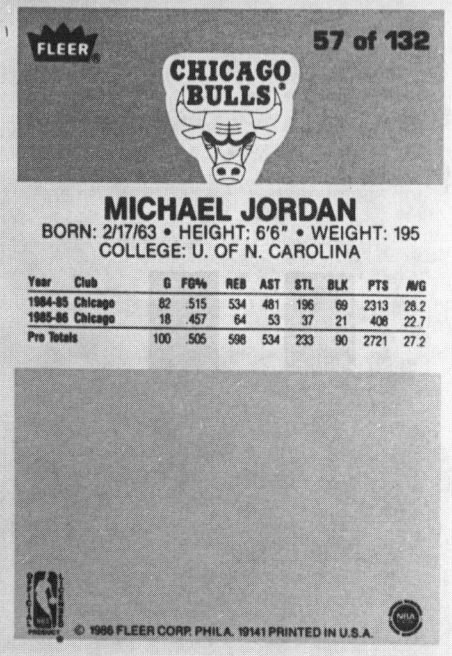

The second identified Jordan rookie counterfeit is somewhat more deceptive than the first, but the area of scrutiny is the same, the ''FLEER / PREMIER '' logo in the upper-right corner of the card's front. On a genuine card, the black lines which border the yellow panel, and the word ''PREMIER'' itself are made up of solid colors. On this particular Jordan counterfeit, those elements are seen under magnification to be made up of many tiny black dots, giving the word a fuzzy appearance under magnification.

Unlike the Jordan counterfeit identified as (1), the red crown and yellow panel of the logo do not contain any dot structure on this version.

Like most of the 1986-87 Fleer basketball counterfeits, the NBA Players Association logo at the lower-right on the back is very muddy on this counterfeit. The ''seams'' of the basketball, usually visible on a genuine card, are all but absent on this phony, as are most of the details of the lettering in and around this logo.

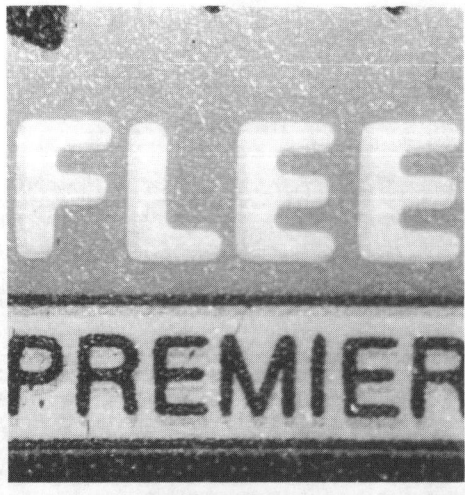

Genuine

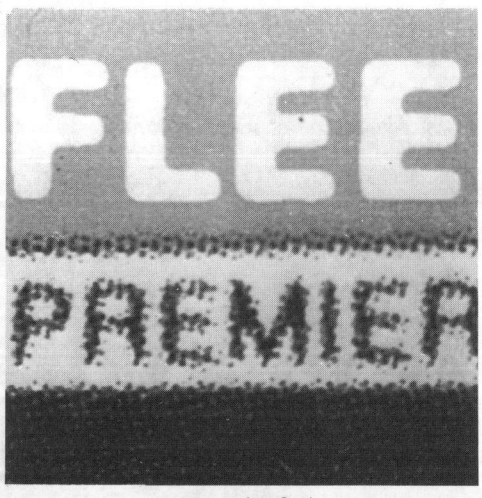

Counterfeit

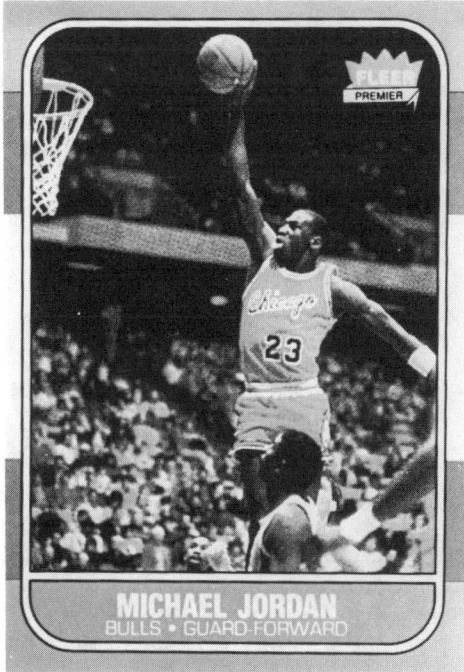

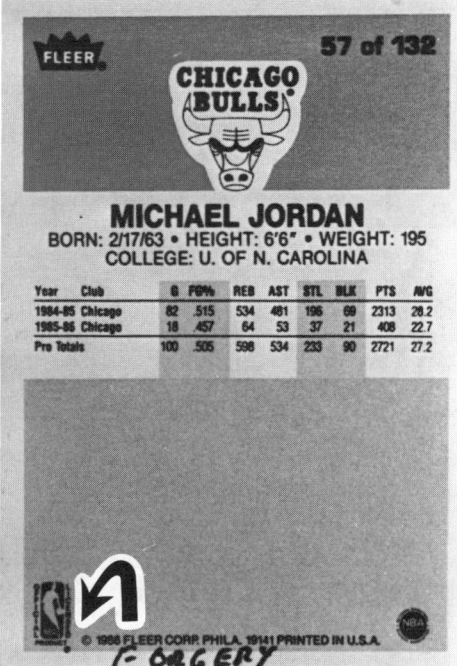

One of the most deceptive of the known counterfeit Jordan rookie types. The crown-and-banner "FLEER / PREMIER" logo on the card's front, which is so useful in detecting the other two known Jordan counterfeits, cannot be so readily used as an indicator on this card.

The most reliable signposts of this card's counterfeit status are found on the back, where a too-liberal use of the blue ink tended to clog the fine details of the logos and typography. This is most noticeable in the ® registration mark beneath the NBA logo at lower-left. On a genuine card, the "R" is readily seen; on the counterfeit, it is an indecipherable blob. By contrast, the Players Association logo at lower-right is much better defined on this counterfeit than on most of the fake 1986-87 Fleer basketball cards.

Again, the word "FORGERY" penned in the bottom border of the photographed card is unique to this specimen.

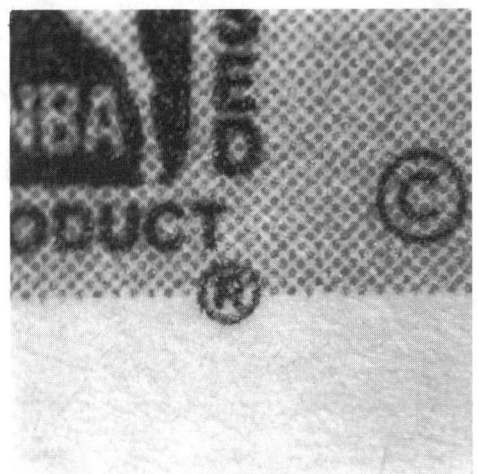

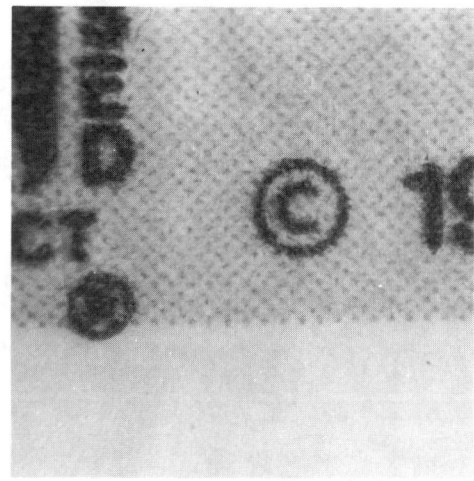

Genuine   **Counterfeit**

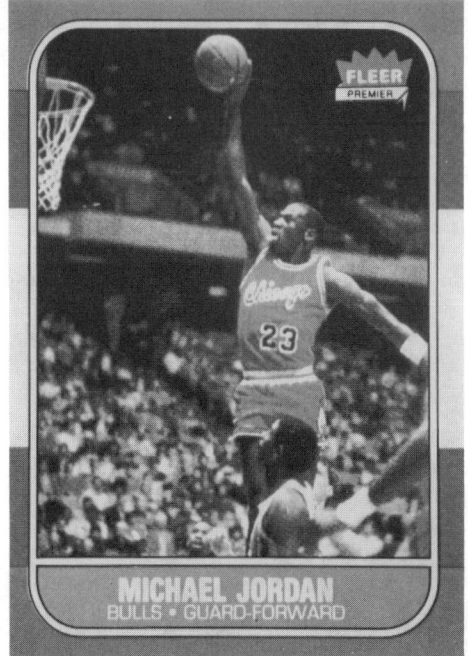

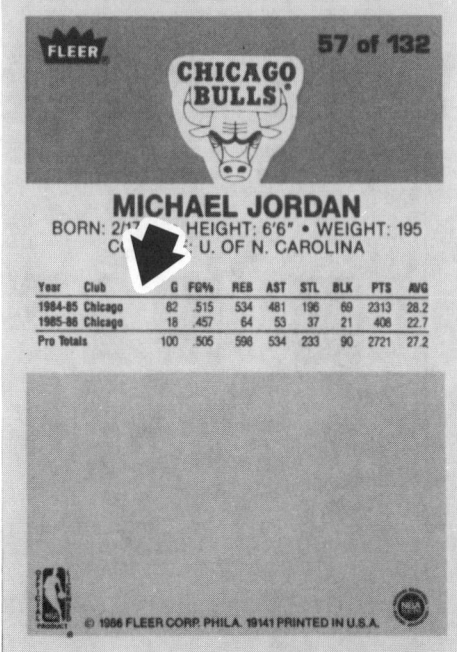

The fourth type of identified counterfeit Jordan rookie card is quite deceptive, especially on the front. A virtually perfect job was done in rescreening the photo and mating it to the border graphics. Persons who have viewed a lot of Jordan rookies might recognize the rescreened photo of the counterfeit as being too fuzzy, but there are no specific details which can be cited to allow for specific identification of the rescreened photo.

The gloss on the front of this counterfeit is not consistent with genuine 1986-87 Fleers, but we can't show that in a photo, and it's too subjective a judgement to make in identifying a counterfeit, anyway. Microscopic comparison of the blue ink in the bottom panel beneath the photo would show a totally different ink coverage, but such a variance is also too fine to present in a black-and-white photo.

The best identifier for this particular counterfeit appears on the back. Most noticeably, the two vertical pink bars in the middle of the card, which contain the stats for games, field goal percentage, steals and blocks are much too light on the counterfeit, in comparison to other Fleer cards, even though the rest of the red ink coverage on the back is about normal for the issue.

Examination with a magnifying glass will also reveal differences in the blue numbers and letters of the stats. On the counterfeit, it appears the blue ink has bled into the porous paper of the card back, causing many feathery edges to the numerals and letters. There is also a too-heavy application of the blue ink, clogging the lower loops of the "g"s in "Chicago" and the zeros of the percentage sign. Surprisingly, the fine details of the NBA Players Association logo in the lower-right corner were well-reproduced on the counterfeit.

It might be noted that genuine Jordan rookies could exist with either a too-lightly-inked red printing on the back or an overinked blue printing, appearing sim-ilar to this counterfeit. It is very unlikely the two conditions would be found together on a genuine card, however. It would be better to err on the side of safety by not purchasing any card which exhibits either of these characteristics.

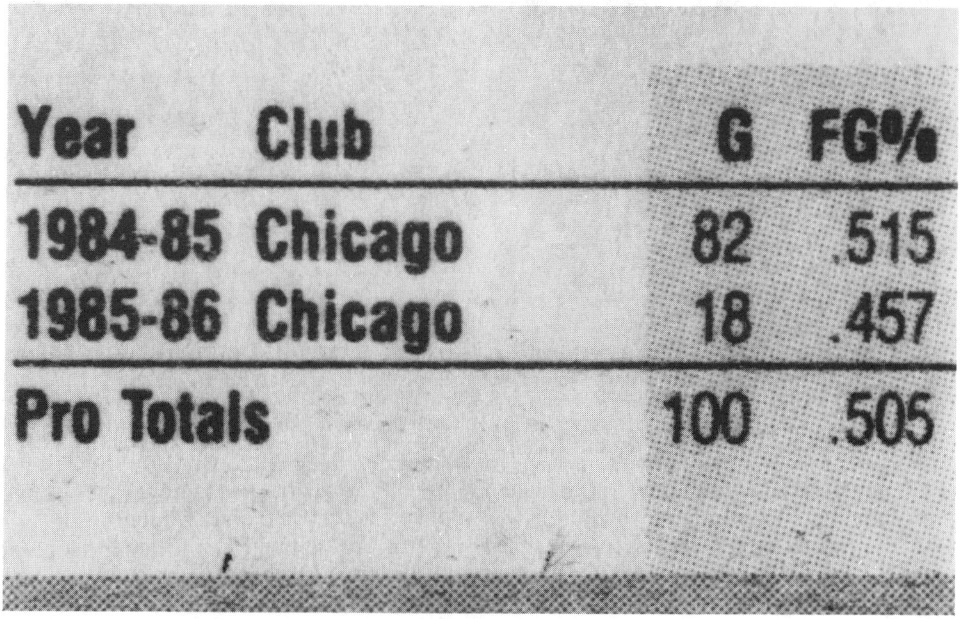

Year	Club	G	FG%
1984-85	Chicago	82	.515
1985-86	Chicago	18	.457
Pro Totals		100	.505

Genuine

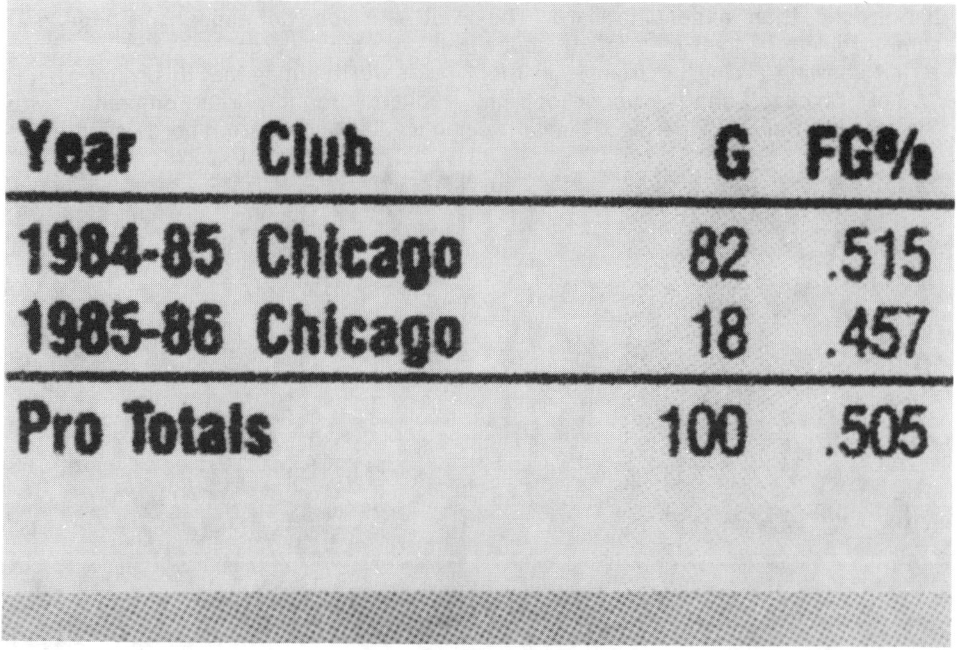

Year	Club	G	FG%
1984-85	Chicago	82	.515
1985-86	Chicago	18	.457
Pro Totals		100	.505

Counterfeit

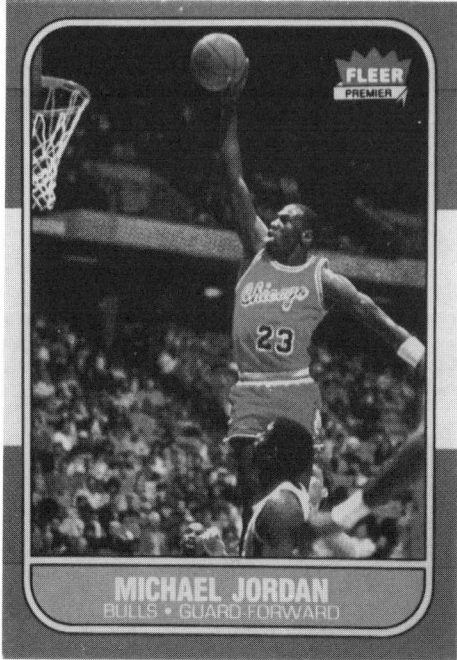

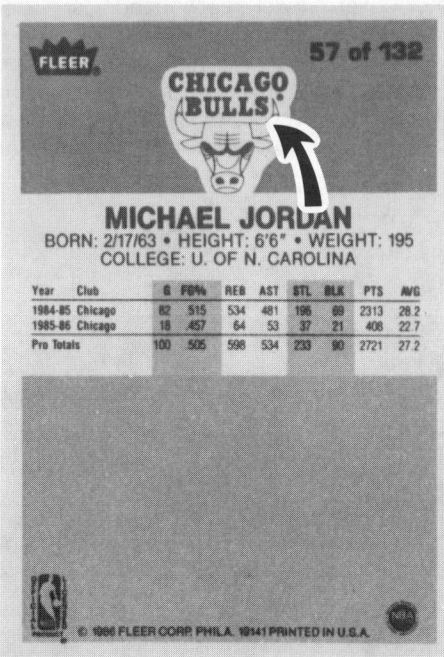

57 of 132

CHICAGO BULLS

MICHAEL JORDAN
BORN: 2/17/63 • HEIGHT: 6'6" • WEIGHT: 195
COLLEGE: U. OF N. CAROLINA

Year	Club	G	FG%	REB	AST	STL	BLK	PTS	AVG
1984-85	Chicago	82	.515	534	481	196	69	2313	28.2
1985-86	Chicago	18	.457	64	53	37	21	408	22.7
Pro Totals		100	.505	598	534	233	90	2721	27.2

© 1986 FLEER CORP. PHILA. 19141 PRINTED IN U.S.A.

Going eyeball-to-eyeball with the bull on the back is the best way to detect this fifth known type of Jordan rookie card counterfeit, which surfaced in Chicago in Dec., 1992. Specifically, a too-liberal application of blue ink on the card back has virtually closed up the eyes on the logo animal, leaving much less white background than a genuine card. The same problem has resulted in the counterfeit showing a clogged triangle in the "A" of "Chicago" and the upper loop of the "B" in "Bulls" in the logo. Similarly,

the "0"'s of the percentage sign above the stats are filled on this counterfeit.

Also on the back, scan the NBA logo at lower-left. On a genuine card, the letters "NBA" are well-formed; on the counterfeit they are not. The size of a blue dot on the "face" of the player on that logo may or may not be diagnostic of this counterfeit — it does not appear this large, if at all, on genuine cards.

It is worth noting that this counterfeit is frequently found printed off-center, with noticeably uneven front borders.

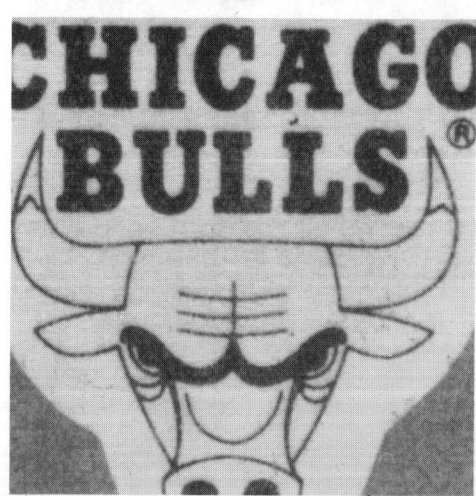

Genuine

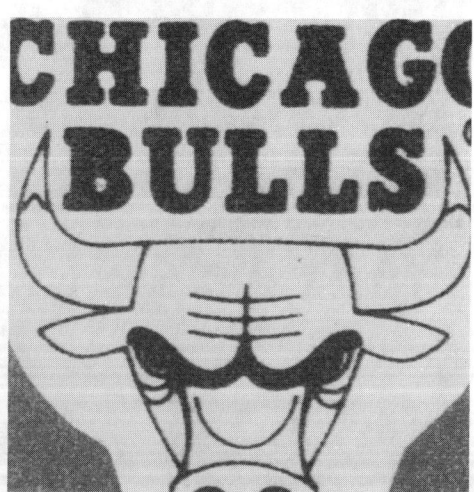

Counterfeit

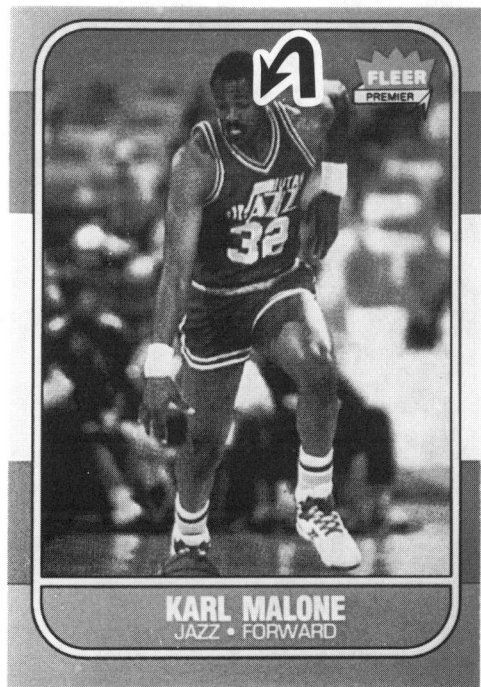

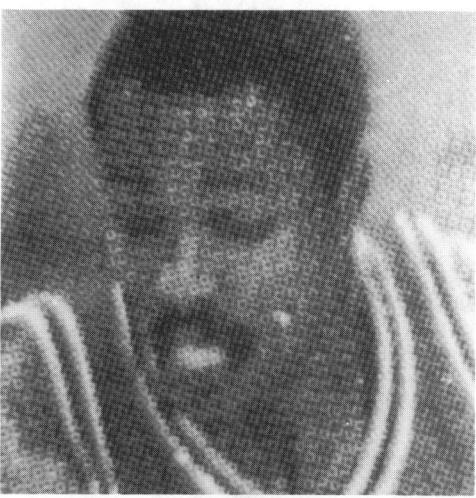

Unlike the majority of 1986-87 Fleer basketball counterfeits, the Fleer crown-and-banner logo cannot be used to detect this counterfeit.

On the front, the best place to check the card is the point of the player's left cheek. On the counterfeit examined, a white spot is visible to the naked eye. However, the reader should be cautioned that insufficient specimens of this type counterfeit have been examined to determine whether this white dot can be used alone as a diagnostic.

On back, the registration (®) and copyright marks (©) near the NBA logo can be used as a double-check. On a genuine card, the "R" and the "C" and the circles around them will be distinct and complete. On the counterfeit, the "R" looks more like a misshapen "K" and the "C" and its circle are incomplete in spots.

The "FORGERY" penned on the back of the photographed card is unique to this specimen.

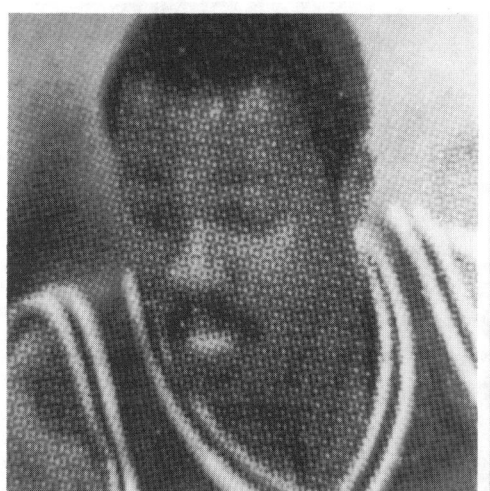

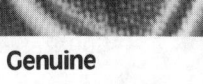

Genuine   Counterfeit

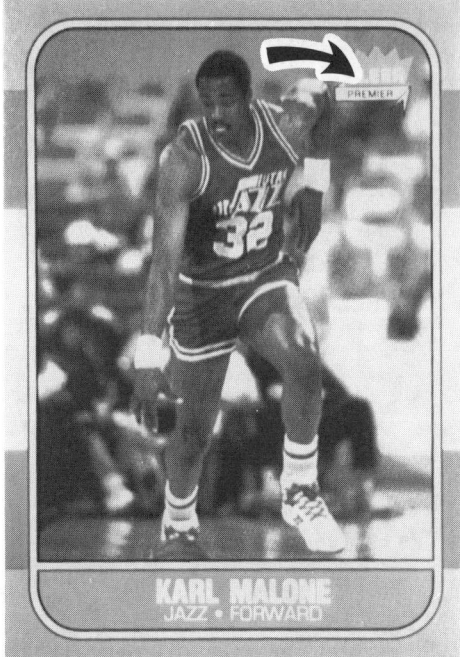

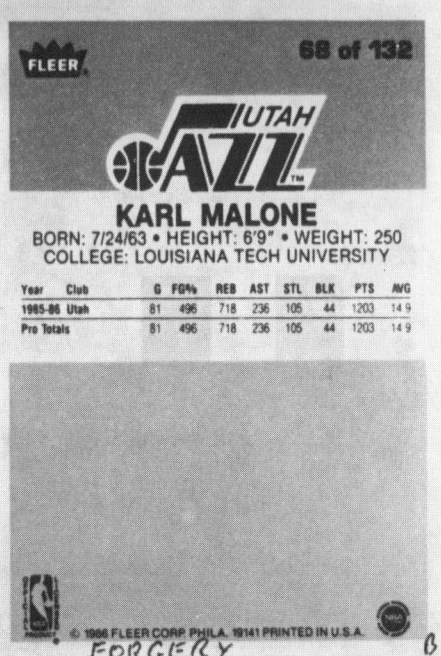

This is by far the easier of the known types of 1986-87 Fleer Malone counterfeits to spot. This card exhibits its fatal flaw within the crown-and-banner "FLEER PREMIER" logo at the upper-right.

On a genuine card, the word "PRE-MIER" will show its letters as clean, solid black lines. On this counterfeit, the letters (as well as the black borders of the banner) are composed of many tiny black dots.

Like many (but not all) of the 1986-87 Fleer basketball counterfeits, the fine details of the NBA Players Association logo on the back of the card did not reproduce well; the seams of the basketball are missing, and there is a lack of distinctness to the letters around the ball.

The "FORGERY B" penned on the back of the photographed card is unique to this specimen.

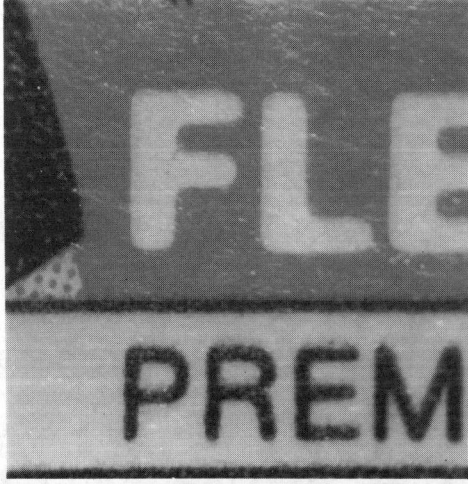

Genuine

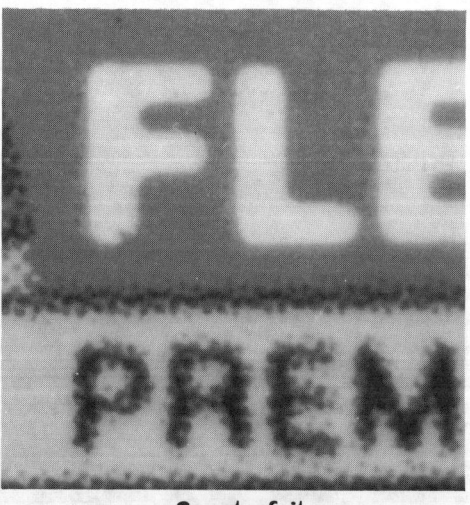

Counterfeit

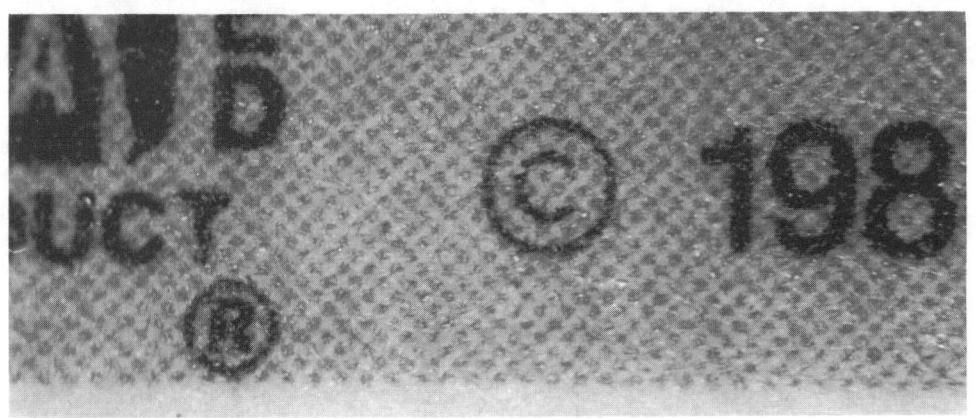

Genuine

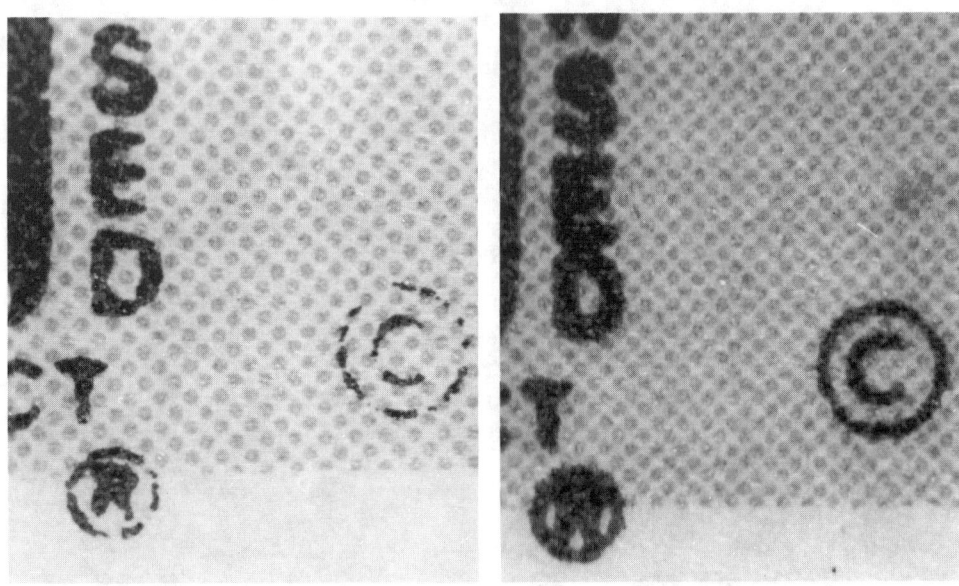

Counterfeit   Counterfeit

Counterfeit 1986-87 Fleer backs

Because most of the known 1986-87 Fleer basketball counterfeits exhibit diagnostics that are more easily seen, described and/or photographed, little was said about the card backs.

In most cases, the counterfeits of this Fleer issue bear markedly flawed design details on the card backs. This is the result of the counterfeiters having to reproduce design details that are already very small.

On genuine Fleer cards, the registration (®) and copyright (©) marks at the bottom-left of the backs will virtually always be perfectly clear and legible upon close examination with a magnifying glass. Both the letters and the circles will be complete.

On most of the counterfeits, these marks are rendered as either incomplete (most often the ©) or over-inked, blurred images (®).

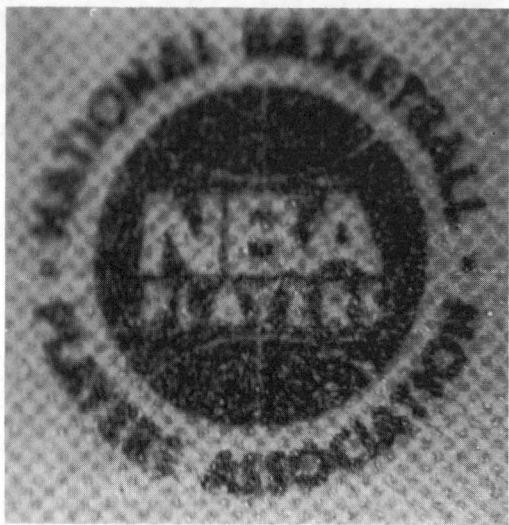

Genuine

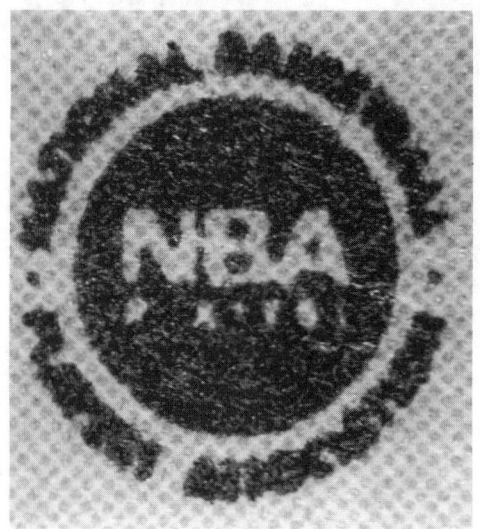

Counterfeit

Counterfeit

On the right side of the card back, the logo of the National Basketball Players Association can be found. On genuine cards, the letters within and around the basketball symbol can be easily distinguished with the use of a magnifying glass. Likewise, the "seams" of the basketball will be readily visible.

Most of the counterfeits can do little but reproduce this logo as a purple blob. The letters around the ball are indecipherable, and usually there are several missing or misshapen letters among "PLAYERS" inside the ball. In most cases there will be little or no trace of the ball's seams.

Because this appears to be a set that will be subject to future counterfeits as the value of the scarce genuine cards rises, hobbyists will be well advised to study these card-back design details whenever considering purchase of a high-value card from the 1986-87 Fleer set.

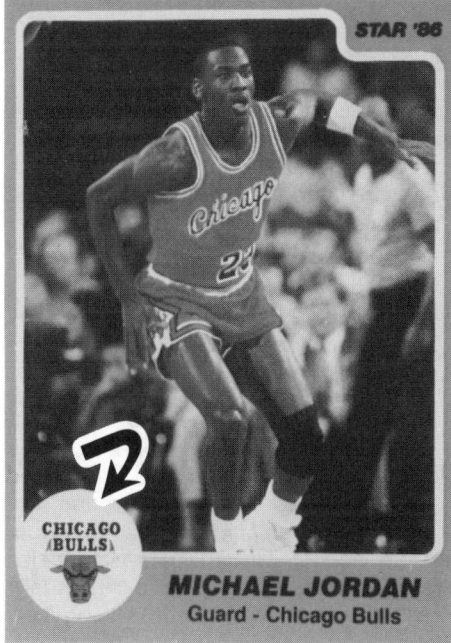

MICHAEL JORDAN
Guard - Chicago Bulls

Like the photo on many counterfeit cards, the picture on Star Co. basketball issues is somewhat fuzzy.

Virtually since the time of their initial release, these cards have been beset by rumors of reprinting or counterfeiting to such an extent that many collectors and dealers have opted to avoid the cards rather than take a chance.

As this book went to press, an FBI investigation into the matter of suspected counterfeiting of Star basketball cards was being wrapped up. According to the special agent assigned to the case, there was no evidence to indicate counterfeiting.

The publisher's independent investigation came to the same conclusion.

To be sure, there are differences in the two "types" of Star cards found in the hobby market. There are visible and measurable differences in the paper stocks. There are discernible differences in shades of ink used and the volume of ink coverage from card to card. There are differences in the physical dimensions of the cards. There are most assuredly differences in packaging. On some cards, such

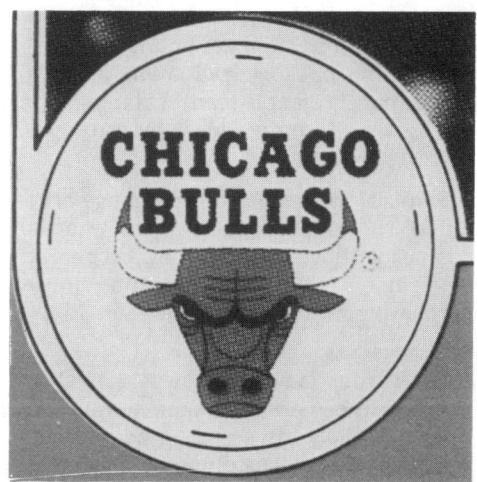

Genuine

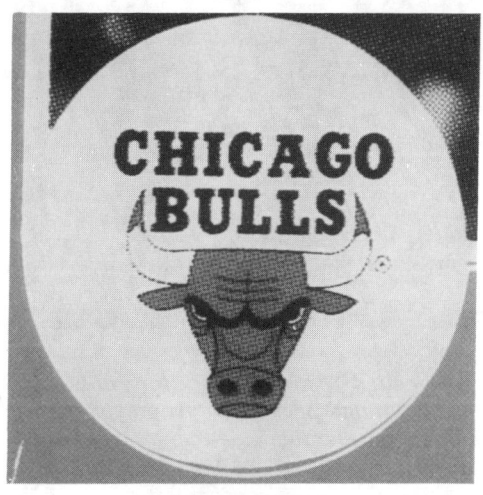

"Counterfeit"

as the 1986 Chicago Bulls team set, there are even design differences.

None of which proves that these cards have ever been counterfeited.

Rather, it is more likely that some of the cards present in the card hobby are pre-production press samples and/or factory rejects — cards intended to be scrapped which were salvaged by parties unknown and recycled into the market.

Star basketball cards were printed on multi-team sheets, the existence of which in the market is not all that uncommon. If these sheets were initially rejected by Star quality control because part of the printing was not up to standards, or because of difficulties with cutting into the team sets in which they were originally sold, there still remained on many of those reject sheets team sets and single cards which could be cut out and sold.

With the exception of the '86 Bulls set, examination of known genuine and supposed counterfeit Star cards was unable

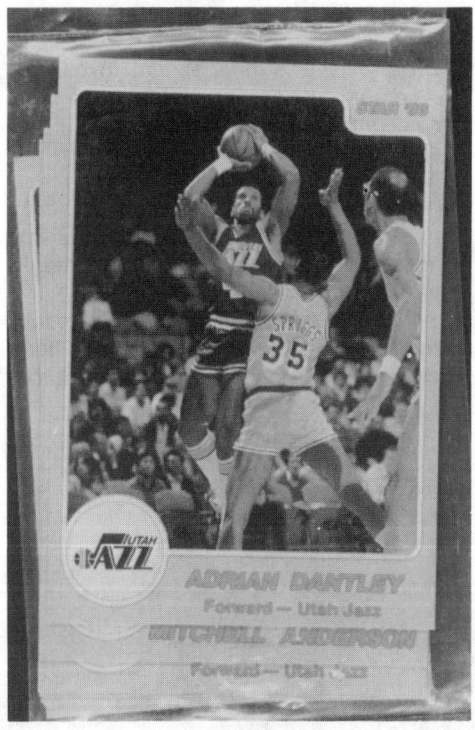

So-called "counterfeit" Star cards are usually found packaged in a polybag that allows considerable movement of the cards within.

to turn up any physical evidence that the "counterfeits" were not printed from the same plates as the genuine cards.

The differences in paper stock and ink coverage could be consistent with discrepancies found in any volume printing operation. The differences in physical size clearly indicate that some cards were cut from sheets in a fashion other than that which was used for normal production of these issues.

At present, it appears there are only a few ways to reliably differentiate "good" Star cards from "rejects."

As mentioned, on the '86 Bulls set, there exists a card type which lacks the black pinstripes around the bull's-head logo and the white frame around the photo. The four black hash marks at top, bottom and sides of the logo are also missing on the type of card usually described as counterfeit. It is very likely this missing black lineage was the reason the sheets on which these cards were printed were slated for the scrap pile. This defect has not been noted on other '86 Star sets.

Quite often, the "reject" cards are offered, as were the originals, in pliofilm bags. It is noteworthy that original Star sets were packaged in bags which were sized to offer little opportunity for card movement therein. The bags in which the "reject" cards are usually offered are roomy enough inside to allow the cards to slide around, and the package can be "thumbed" to see cards other than those on top and bottom. Now that a large number of persons within the hobby are familiar with this packaging variation, it is possible that "reject" team sets may be repackaged to more closely approximate the original.

Some of the suspect cards, those attributed to pre-production press checks, can be identified because they are printed on thinner, cheaper paper than those cards which were intended for sale to the public.

Where this leaves the two "types" of cards in the market is open to speculation. It is likely the so-called counterfeits will never be fully accepted by collectors.

Star cards with discernible defects and those packaged on the secondary market will probably never bring the same prices that "original" Mint cards will command. Hobby questions about the cards will continue to haunt the issue to the point that future price appreciation cannot reasonably be anticipated.

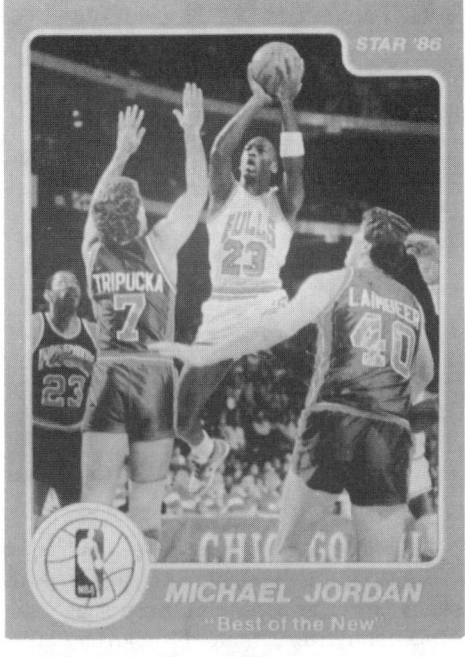

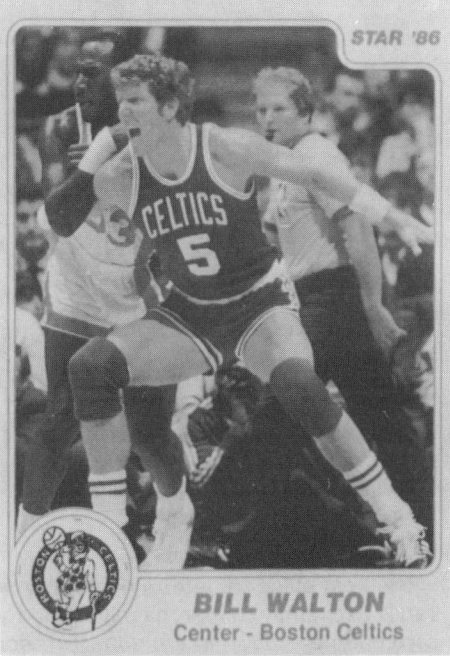

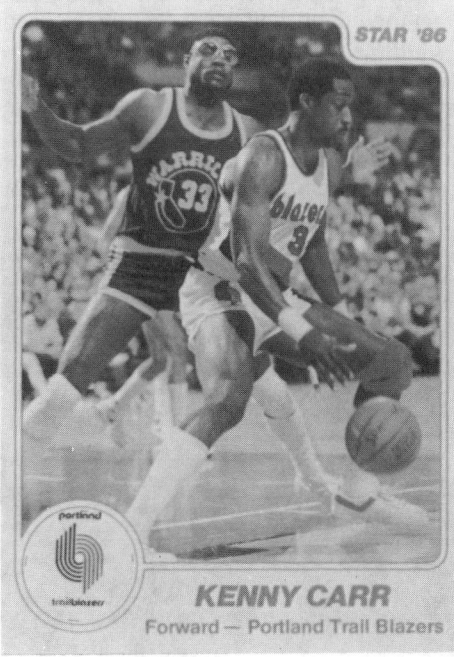

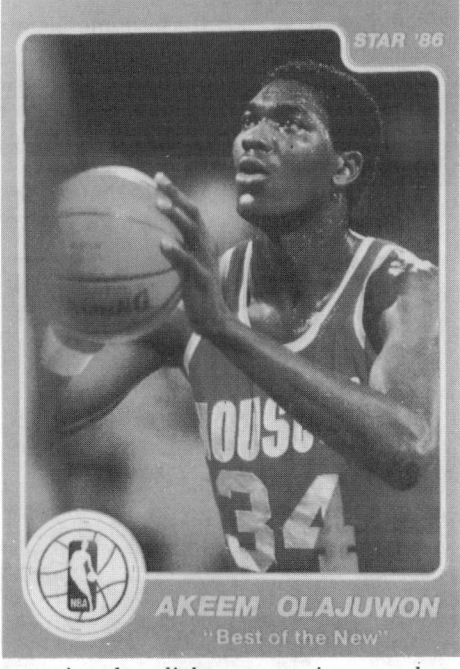

As a general rule, the "reject" Star cards are printed on lighter paper in somewhat darker ink. Without an "original" card for comparison, however, the difference may not be discernible.

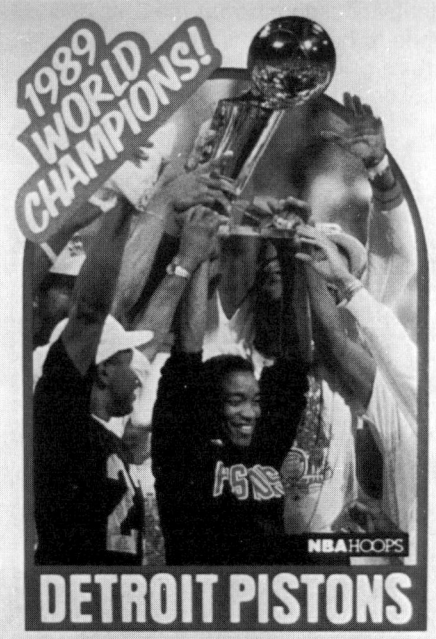

Visually a very deceptive counterfeit.

The best place to determine good from bad is to examine under magnification the card number ''353'' in the upper-left corner of the card's back.

On a genuine card these numerals are clean and white. On the counterfeit, the numerals' edges appear fuzzy. On close examination, stray print dots of blue, red and yellow can be found scattered throughout the numbers on the fake.

It is also interesting to note that the fine type at the bottom of the card back is actually cleaner on the counterfeit. On a genuine card, many of the letters in those lines are run together. Surprisingly, on this counterfeit, most of the letters stand distinctly apart. This cleaner typography on the counterfeit is apparently the result of the counterfeiters having these lines re-set. In doing so, however, the copyright line at the bottom was rendered somewhat longer than the line on the genuine card, This line measures 44.5mm on a real card, while on the counterfeit, the line measures 46mm.

Genuine

Counterfeit

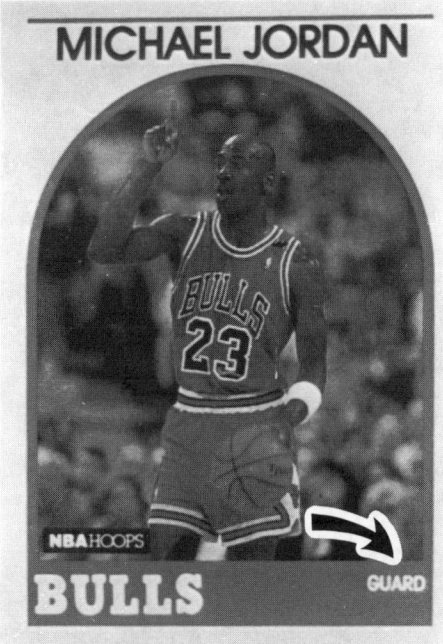

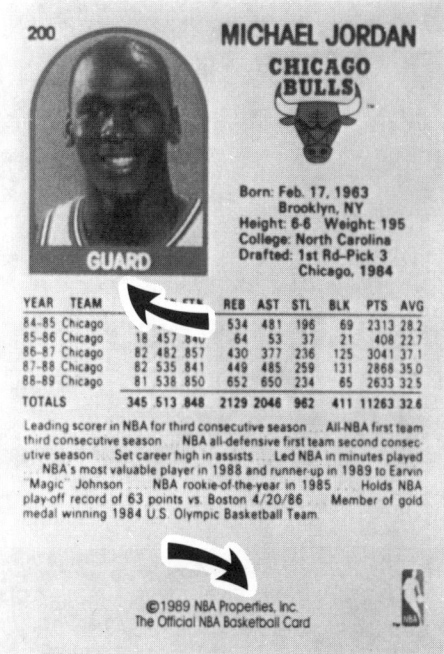

This is a very deceptive counterfeit, perhaps the work of the same parties responsible for the Type 2 Hoops David Robinson counterfeit.

On this card, the best areas for examination are the white words "GUARD" at the lower-right of the front, and under the portrait on the back. In each case, the counterfeit shows letters that are joined rather than separated as on a genuine card.

Under magnification, the "GUARD" on front of a counterfeit will show the "G" and "U" connected near the crossbar of the "G". On back, the counterfeit has the

"R" and "D" connected near the top. On a genuine card, only the "A" and "R" are connected, near the bottom, on both front and back.

Another indicator of status can be found in the copyright notice on the back. On a genuine card, many of the letters and numbers in both lines are run together. Surprisingly, on this counterfeit, the letters and numbers do not connect, except at the "rt" of "Properties", and the "ff" of "Official". This cleaner typography on the counterfeit is apparently the result of the counterfeiters having these lines re-set with a new, slightly lighter,

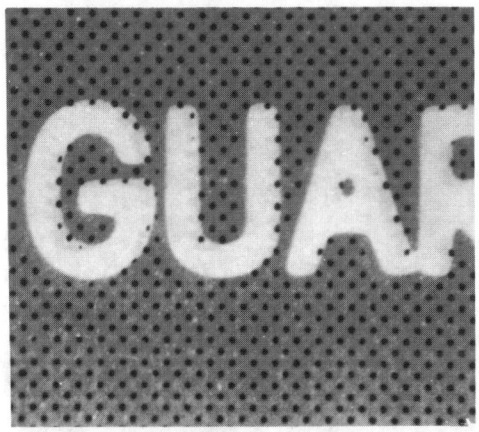

Genuine

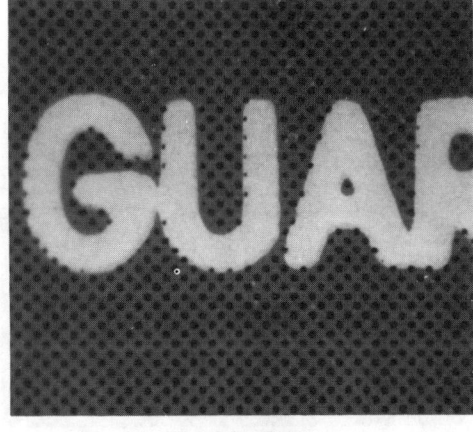

Counterfeit

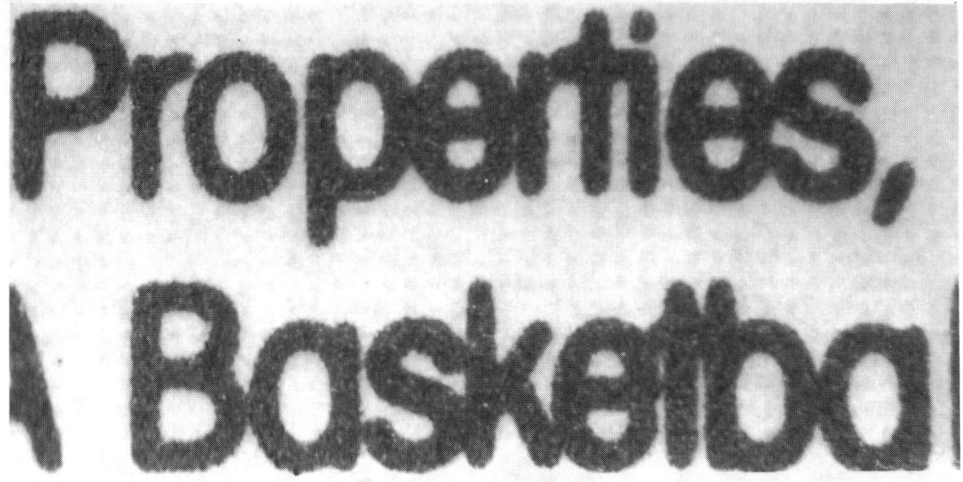

Genuine

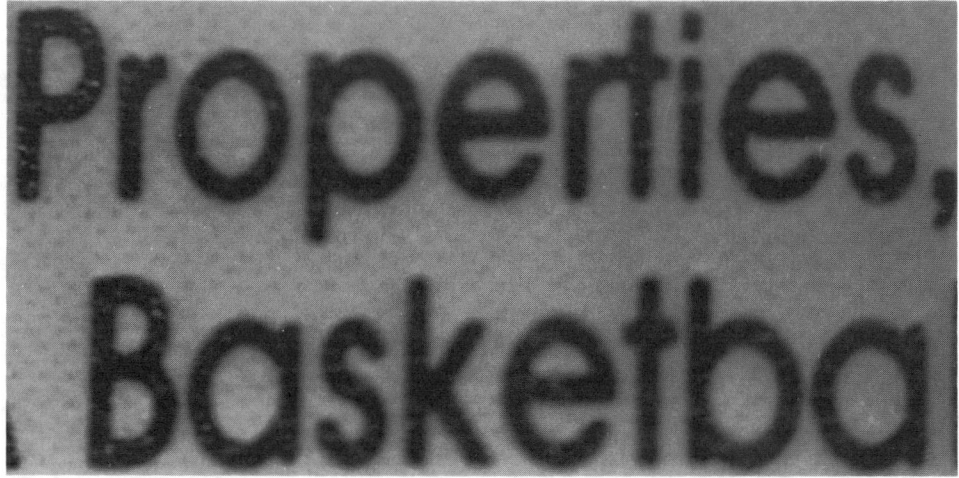

Counterfeit

typeface. In doing so, however, the resulting copyright lines are somewhat longer than the lines on the genuine card. The bottom line of a genuine card, "The Official NBA Basketball Card", will measure 23mm. On the counterfeit, the line measures 24mm.

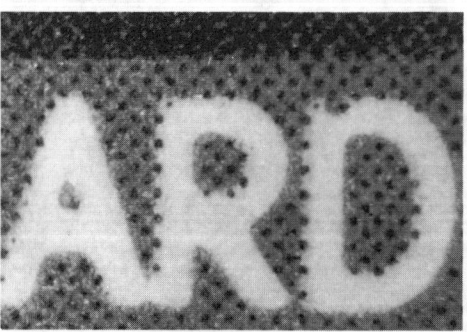

Genuine

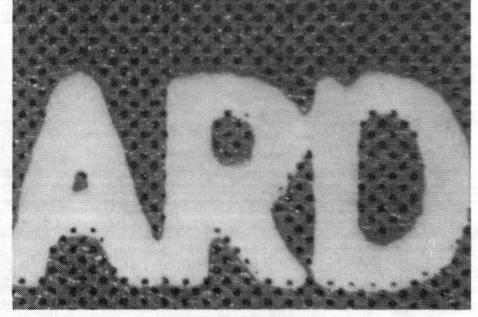

Counterfeit

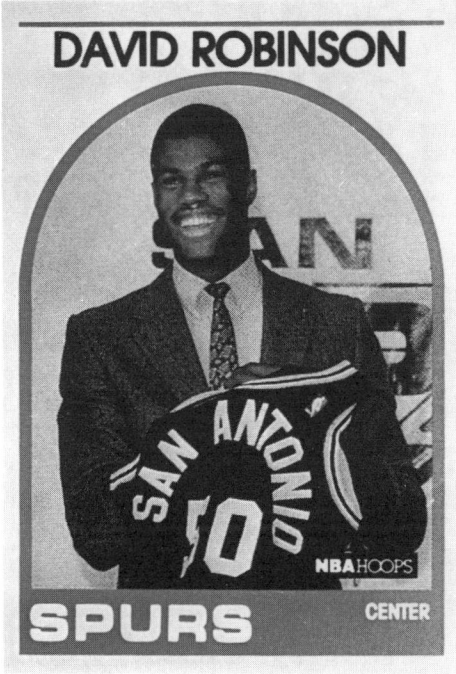

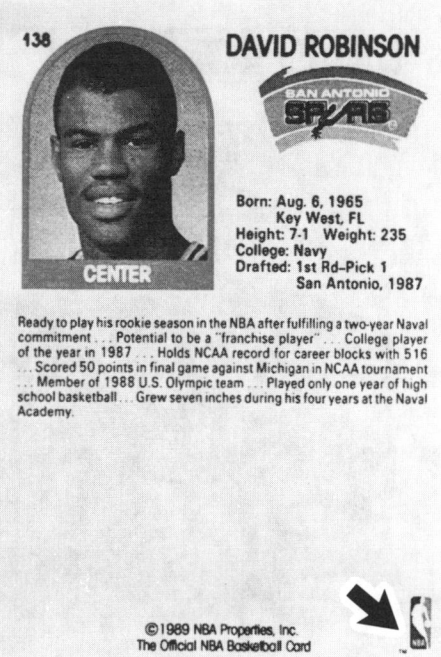

The "lesser of two evils," the first type of two known fake Hoops Robinson rookies should be easily spotted on the basis of its overall appearance. The colors — front and back — are darker and coarser than on a genuine card. However, as color can never be reliably used by itself to establish the status of a questioned card, a closer look is necessary.

In this case, the closer look is best concentrated on the back of the card; specifically on the NBA logo at lower-right. On a genuine card the white "NBA" initials and the black "TM" will stand out clearly as distinct individual letters. On this type of counterfeit, these letters (especially the white "NBA") are blurred and virtually indistinguishable.

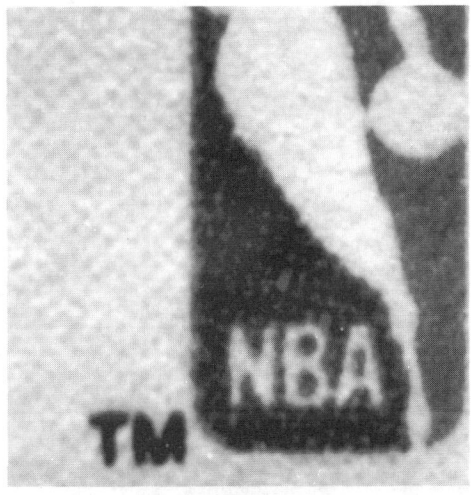

Genuine

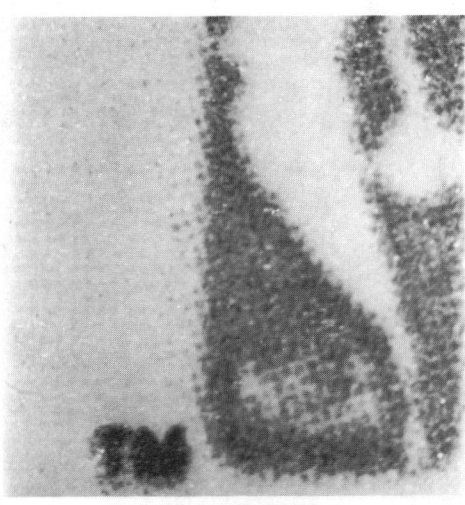

Counterfeit

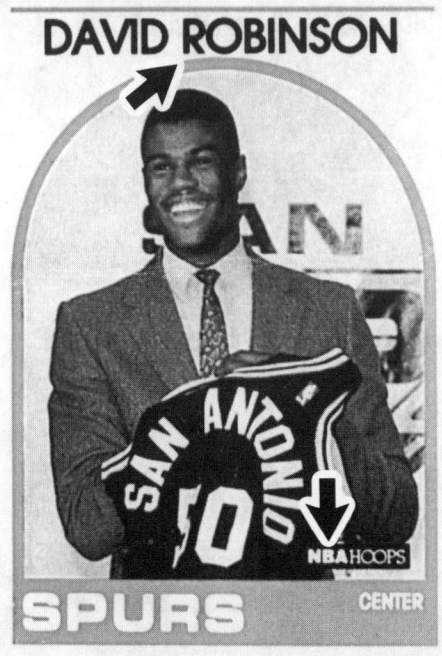

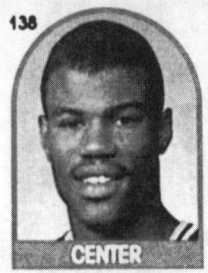
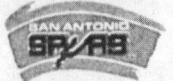

DAVID ROBINSON

Born: Aug. 6, 1965
Key West, FL
Height: 7-1   Weight: 235
College: Navy
Drafted: 1st Rd–Pick 1
San Antonio, 1987

Ready to play his rookie season in the NBA after fulfilling a two-year Naval commitment . . . Potential to be a "franchise player" . . . College player of the year in 1987 . . . Holds NCAA record for career blocks with 516 . . . Scored 50 points in final game against Michigan in NCAA tournament . . . Member of 1988 U.S. Olympic team . . . Played only one year of high school basketball . . . Grew seven inches during his four years at the Naval Academy.

© 1989 NBA Properties, Inc.
The Official NBA Basketball Card

By far the scarier of two known types of counterfeit Hoops Robinson rookies, it will take a good magnifying lens to identify this particular fake.

There is an irregularity in one of the letters of the player's name at top that is worth mention. Specficially, the counterfeit shows a tiny white notch near the top of the slanting leg of the "R".

A second indicator — again requiring high magnification to detect — is seen in the "B" of the "NBA Hoops" logo in the lower-right corner of the photo. On a gen-uine card, that letter (and all the others) will be pure white against the black background. On the counterfeit, the holes formed by the loops of the "B" will show red ink — it looks like nothing so much as blood oozing out of the two "bullet holes" in the "B". Depending on the printing registration of the specific example of the counterfeit being viewed, a few other extraneous red dots may be visible at the edges of some of the other letters in this logo.

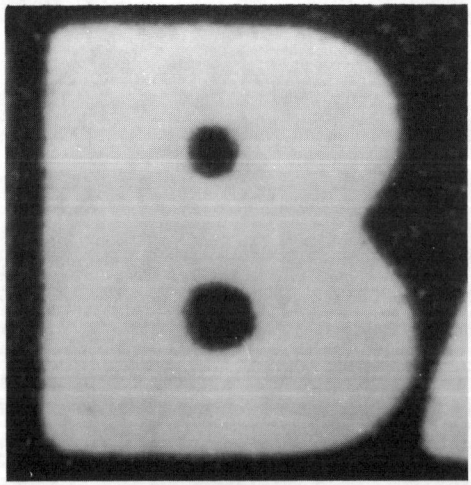

Genuine

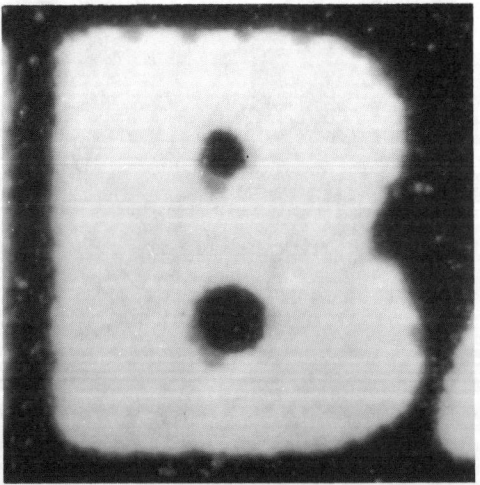

Counterfeit

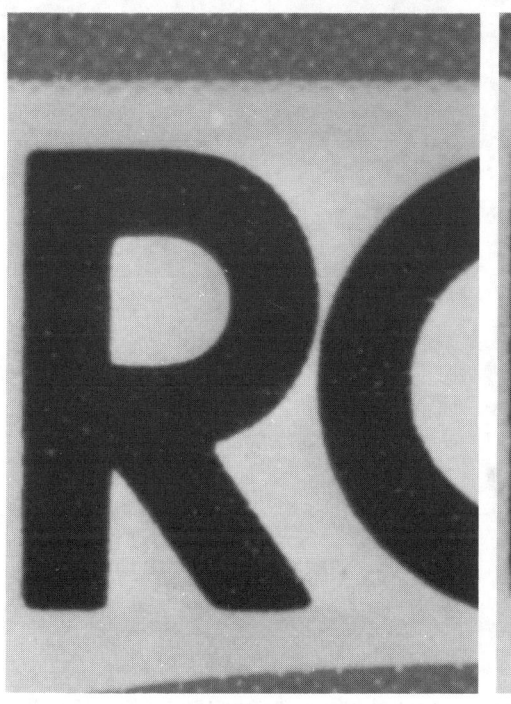

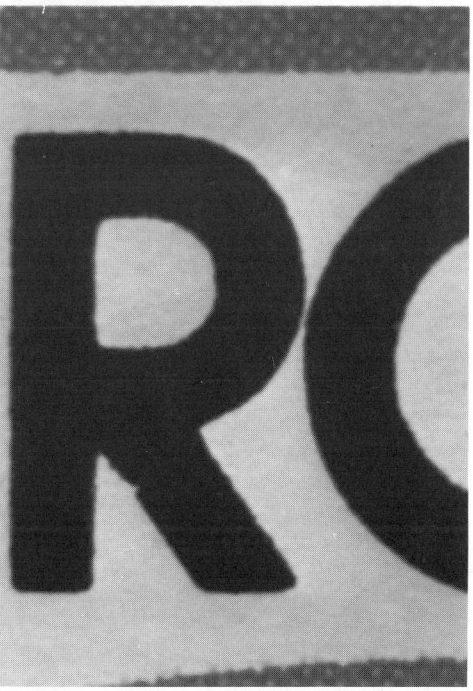

Genuine   Counterfeit

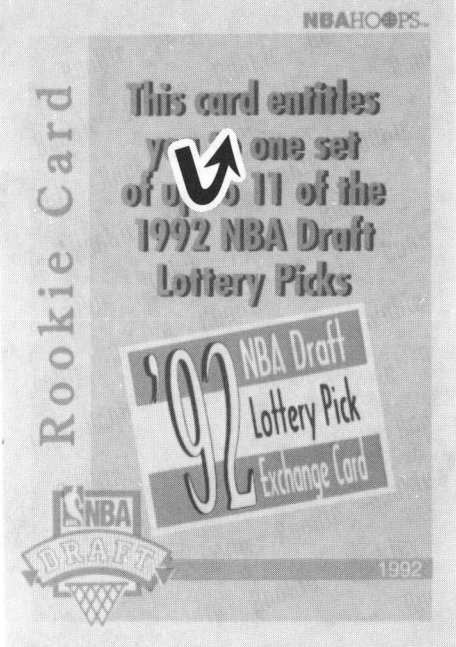

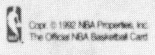

While the "value" of this card expired on March 31, 1993, when redemption ended, it is nonetheless worth including this counterfeit, if only to warn hobbyists that not only player cards can be faked for profit.

Inserted into random wax packs, this exchange card could be redeemed for a set of 10 NBA draft lottery picks player cards, which retailed for $150 or so at the time the redemption period ended. At least the counterfeiters thought so.

This counterfeit can be detected with the naked eye by examining the five lines of blue words at the top of the card front. On the genuine card, the "loops" of such lower case letters as "a, d, o" and "e" show the gray background behind the letters. On this counterfeit, the loops on such letters are solid black.

Also indicative of counterfeit status is the fact that the ® registration mark near the NBA logo at lower-left on the back is a black dot, while the circled "R" is clearly visible on the genuine card, when seen through a magnifying glass.

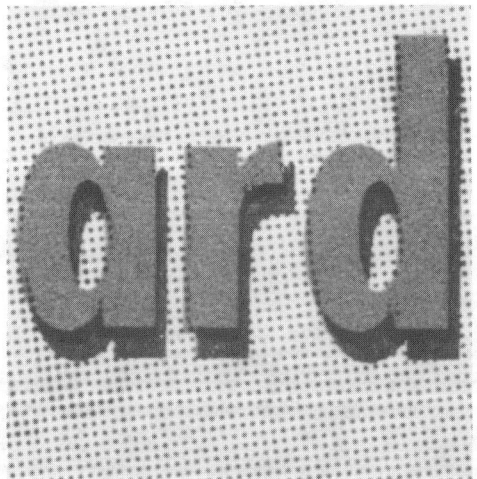

Genuine

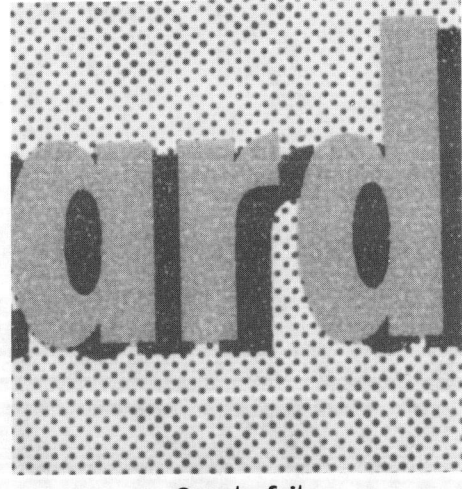

Counterfeit

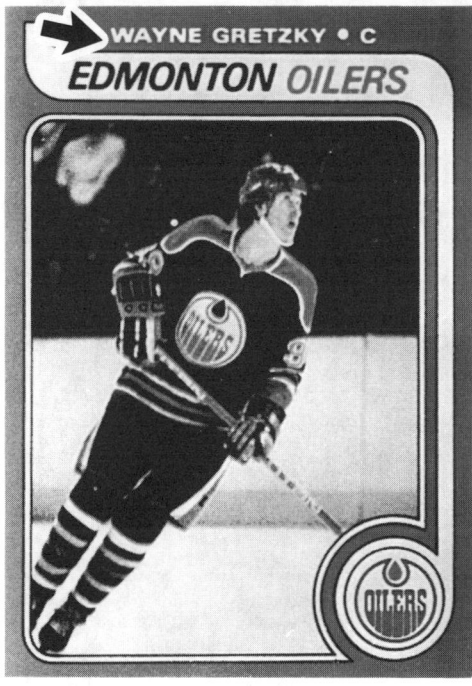

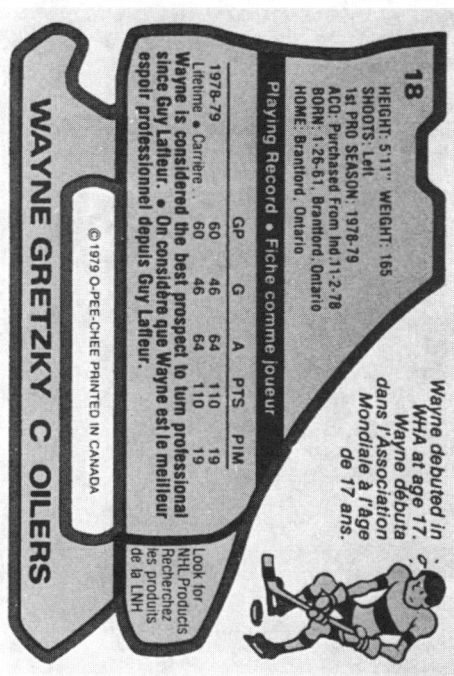

Viewed with the naked eye, the Gretzky rookie counterfeit can be considered fairly deceptive. That illusion vanishes with the application of a magnifying lens to the front of the card. Many of the design elements on the front of the counterfeit can be seen under magnification to be composed of tiny dots, rather than the solid lines and colors of the genuine card.

This is easily noted in such areas as the black frame lines around the photo and designs, the black "EDMONTON", the orange "OILERS" and flame of the team logo, and the white letters of the player's name and position.

The ice in the photo can also be used to determine the status of a questioned card. On the genuine card, the ice is clean and white. On the counterfeit, there are thousands of tiny blue dots visible on the ice.

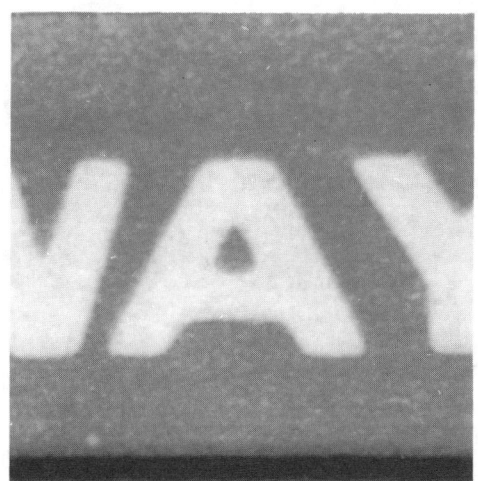

Genuine

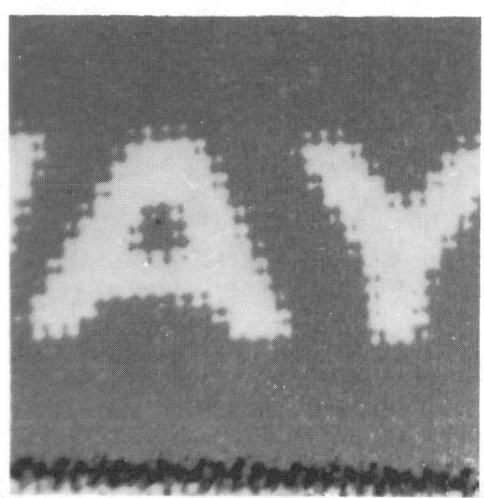

Counterfeit

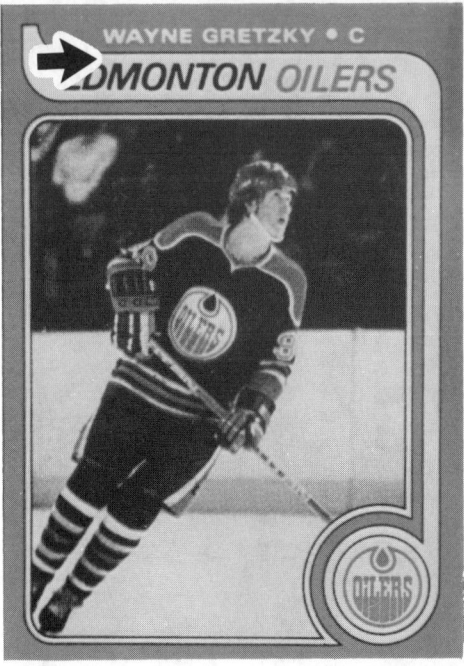

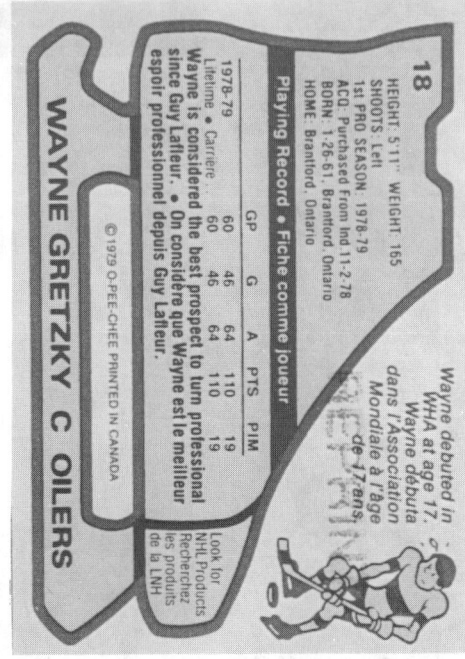

This version of the Gretzky rookie counterfeit was faked in exactly the same way as the forgery identified as (1). This card is even less deceptive in that it is printed on extremely thin semi-gloss cardboard.

Many of the design elements on the front of the counterfeit can be seen under magnification to be composed of tiny dots, rather than the solid lines and colors of the genuine card.

This is easily noted in such areas as the black frame lines around the photo and designs, the black "EDMONTON", the orange "OILERS" and flame of the team logo, and the white letters of the player's name and position.

The ice in the photo can also be used to determine the status of a questioned card. On the genuine card, the ice is clean and white. On the counterfeit, there are thousands of tiny blue dots visible on the ice.

The stamped "REPRINT" on the back of the card is unique to the specimen photographed.

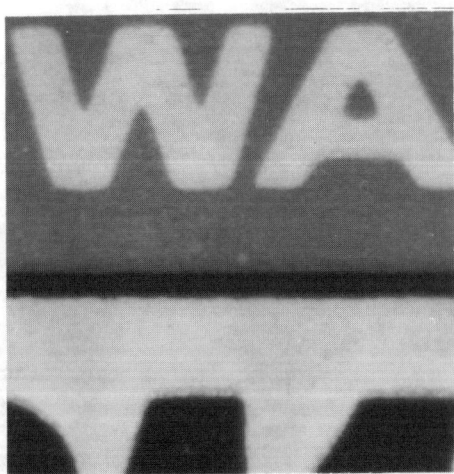

Genuine

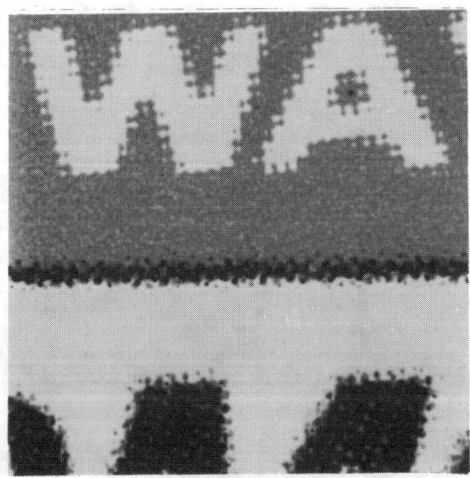

Counterfeit

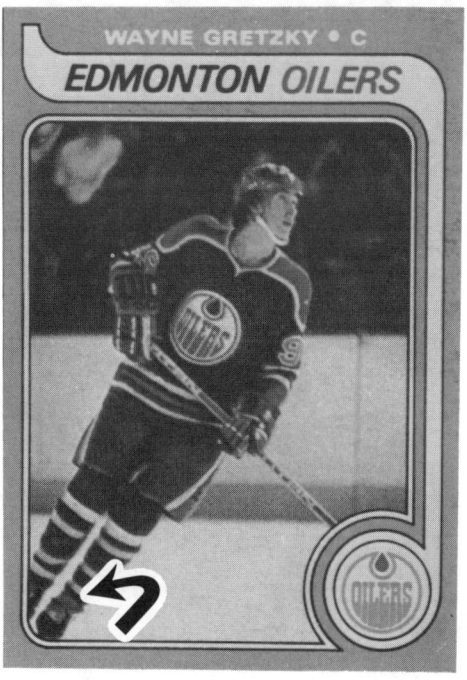

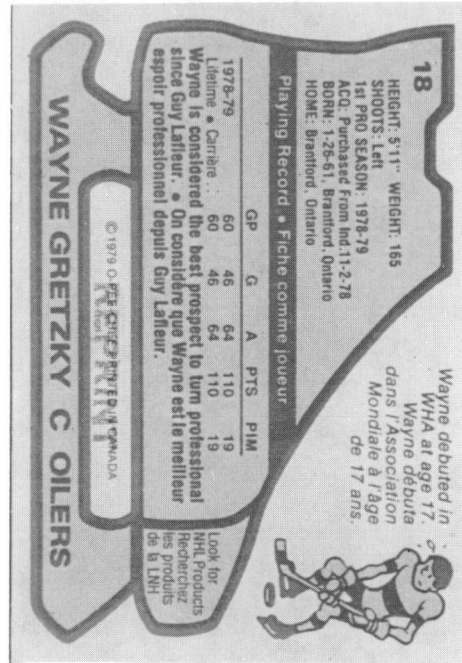

Viewed with the naked eye, this Gretzky rookie counterfeit has a dull, almost linen-look finish on the front. The card is also considerably lighter in weight than a genuine OPC card of 1979-80.

In terms of print quality, however, it is a dangerous counterfeit. Separate printing materials were made for the photo and the graphic elements of this counterfeit. This eliminated many of the tell-tale signs found on counterfeits that are made by merely re-screening negatives from genuine cards.

This counterfeit can be detected by using a magnifier to examine the ice surface. On a genuine OPC Gretzky rookie, only a few colored printing dots will be seen on the ice, near the player's left skate. On this counterfeit, virtually the entire surface of the ice is spattered with color dots.

The word ''REPRINT'' stamped on the back of the card photographed here is unique to this specimen.

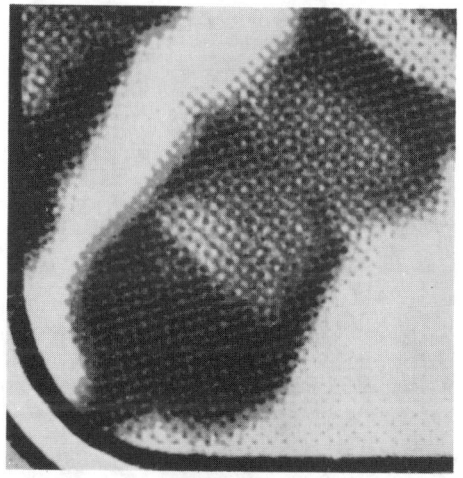

Genuine

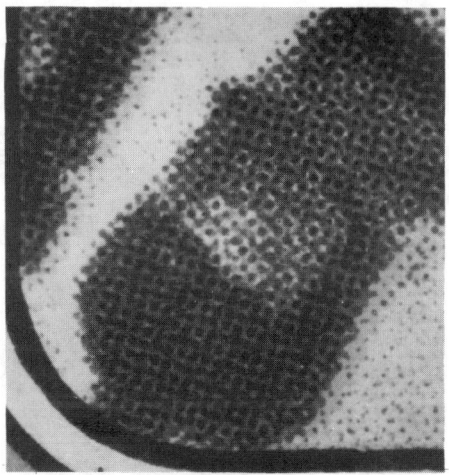

Counterfeit

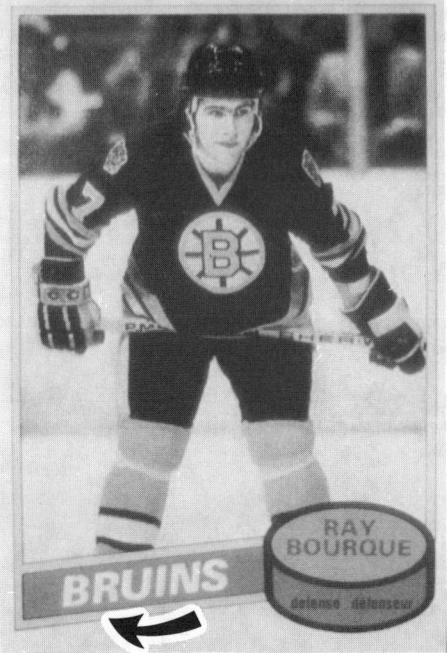

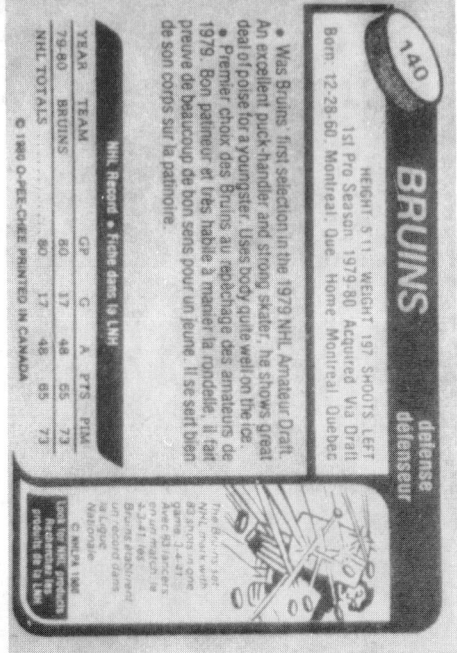

This is one of a group of six OPC counterfeits that surfaced in March, 1992, all apparently the work of the same forger.

The best places to check this card are the team name and the English/French position designations at the bottom-front. Examination with a magnifying glass is, as usual, required.

On a genuine card, "BRUINS" will be pure white against a solid green background. This counterfeit has a large number of tiny blue dots within the white letters, and the green background will have a pattern of yellow dots throughout.

On the real card, the "defense defenseur" will be printed in solid black against a solid magenta background. The fake shows these words in black dot composites against a background that includes a dot pattern over its entirety.

The back of the counterfeit exhibits a much brighter yellow ink than a genuine card, though this type of subjective opinion should not be used by itself to judge the status of a suspect card.

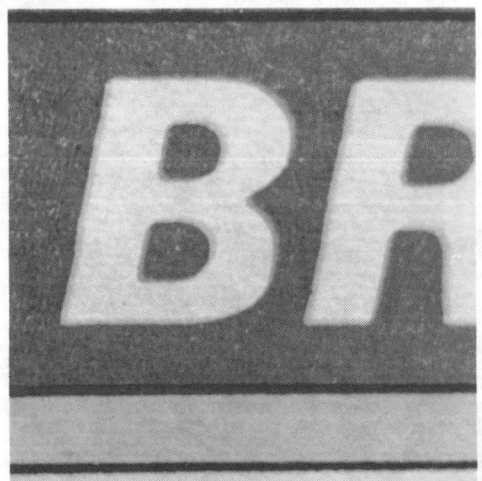

Genuine

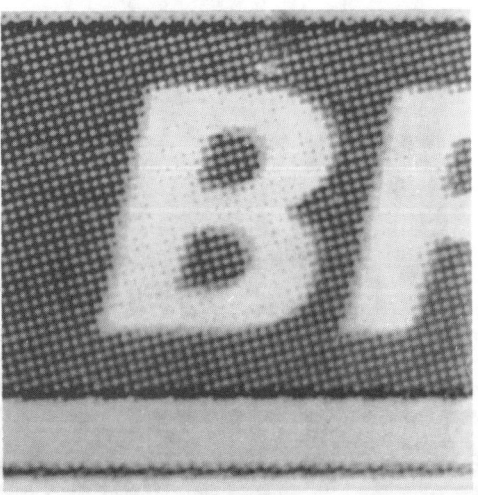

Counterfeit

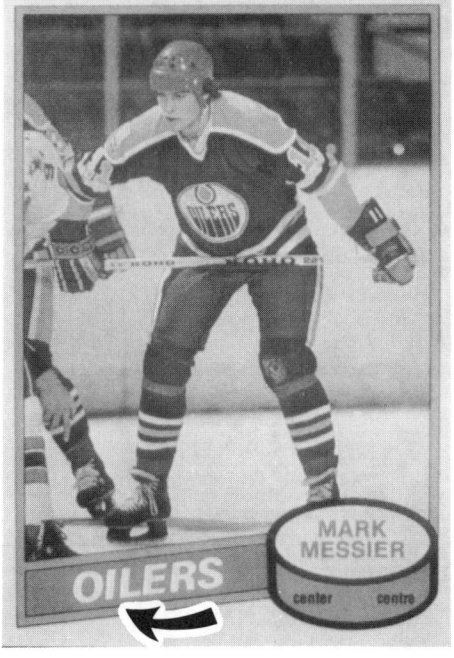

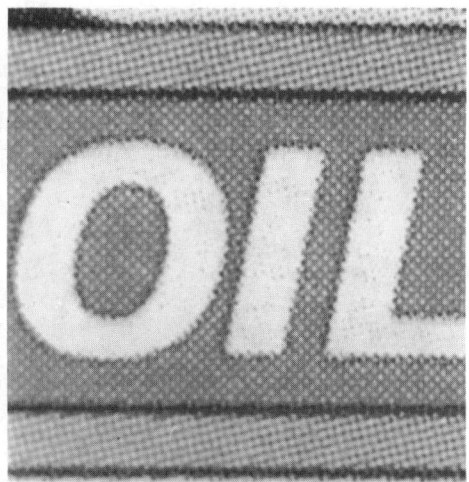

This is one of a group of six OPC counterfeits that surfaced in March, 1992, all apparently the work of the same forger.

Examination with a magnifying glass will show than on a genuine card, the team name "OILERS" at lower-left will be pure white against a solid red background. This counterfeit has a large number of tiny blue dots within the white letters, and the red background shows a pattern of white dots throughout. Even more noticeable, there is an outline of tiny black dots around the letters of the team name on the counterfeit that is not present on a genuine card.

Also, on the real card, "center centre" will be printed in solid black against a solid blue background. The fake shows these words in black dot composites against a background that includes a white dot pattern over its entirety.

The counterfeit's back is much brighter yellow than a genuine card, though such a subjective opinion should not be used by itself to judge a suspect card.

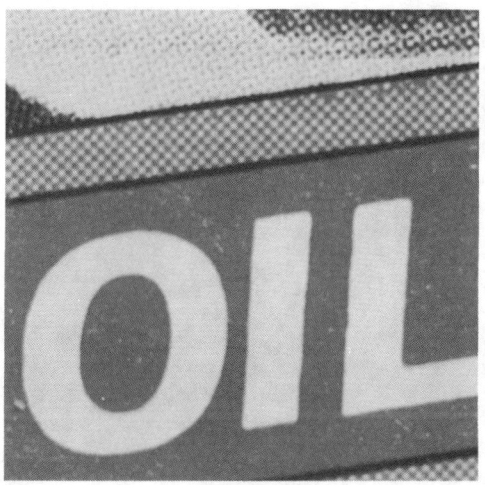

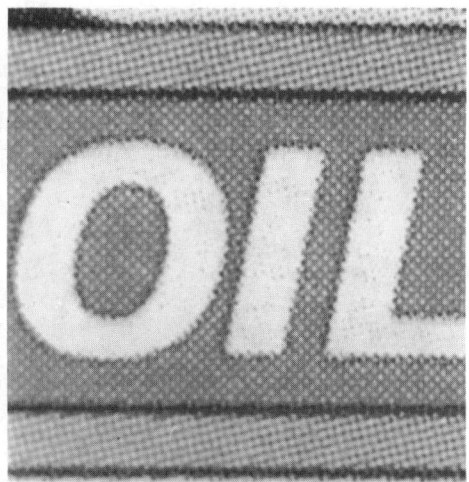

Genuine   **Counterfeit**

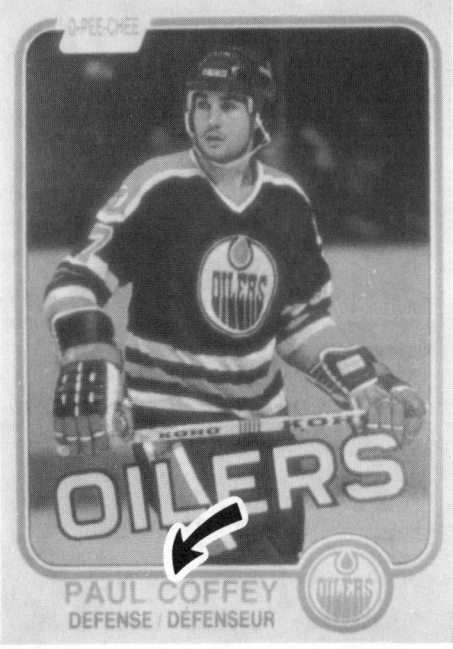

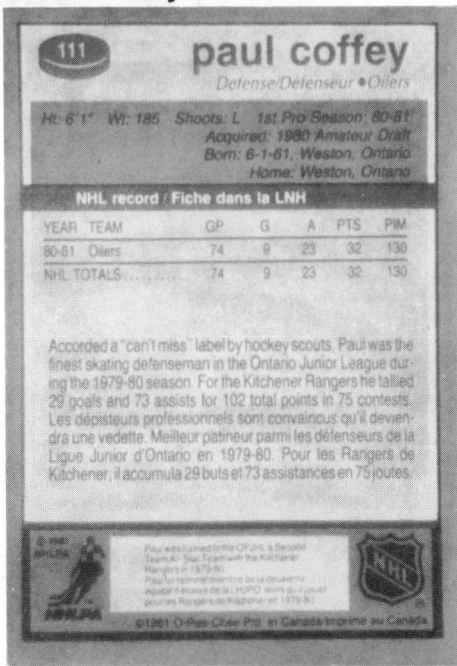

This is one of a group of six OPC counterfeits that surfaced in March, 1992, all apparently the work of the same forger.

A quick and easy determination of this card's status can be made by using a magnifying glass to study the player's name and the portion of the Oilers logo printed in blue on the front of the card.

On a genuine card, the letters of the player's name and the blue portions of the team logo will appear as solid letters, with edges that end cleanly against the white background.

On the counterfeit these elements show up as compositions of many tiny blue dots, giving the edges a fuzzy appearance.

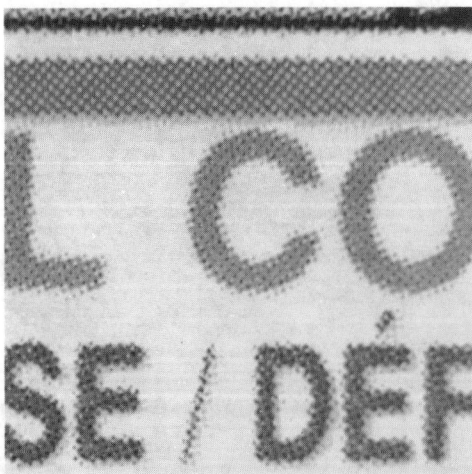

Counterfeit

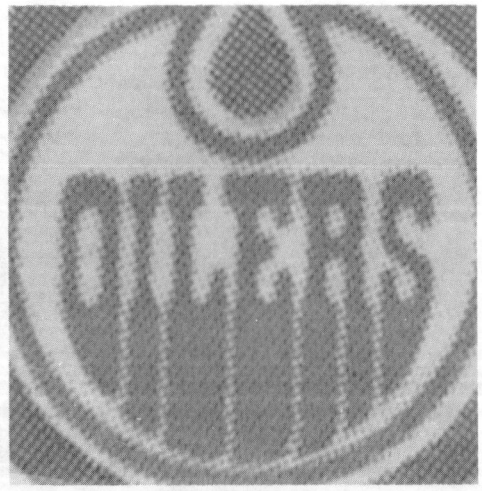

Counterfeit

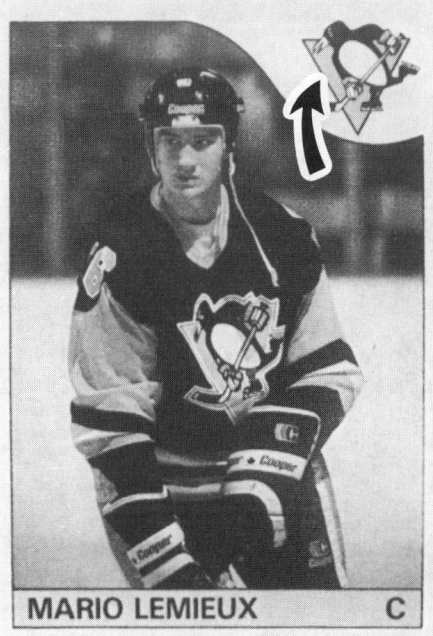

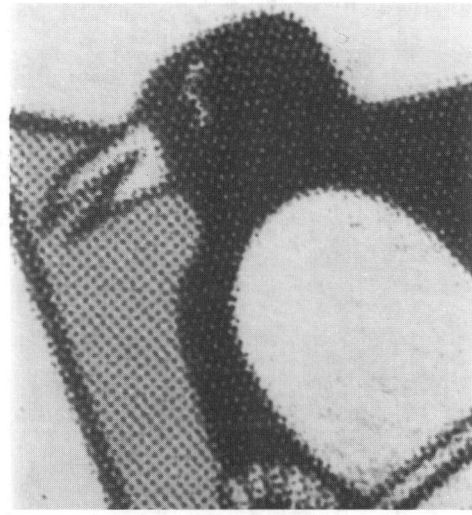

This appears to be part of a group which includes five other OPC counterfeits that surfaced in the spring of 1992, all apparently the work of the same forger.

A quick and easy determination of this card's status can be made by using a magnifying glass to study the player's name and position and the Penguins logo on the front of the card.

On a genuine card, the letters of the player's name and position will appear as solid black letters, with edges that end cleanly against the orange background. On the counterfeit these letters show up as compositions of many tiny black and orange dots, and the edges have a fuzzy appearance.

Likewise in the logo, the genuine card shows the penguin in sharp black and white areas, while the counterfeit shows many light dots in the black areas, and colored dots in the areas that are supposed to be solid white.

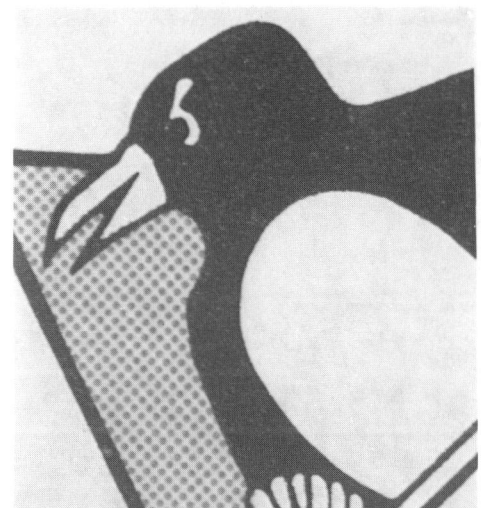

Genuine

Counterfeit

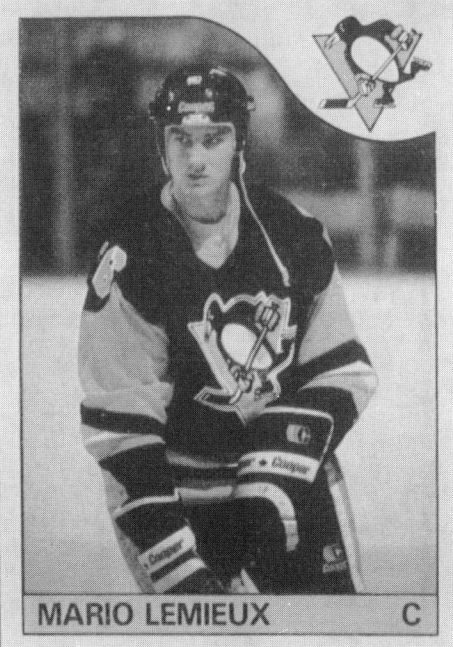

MARIO LEMIEUX   C

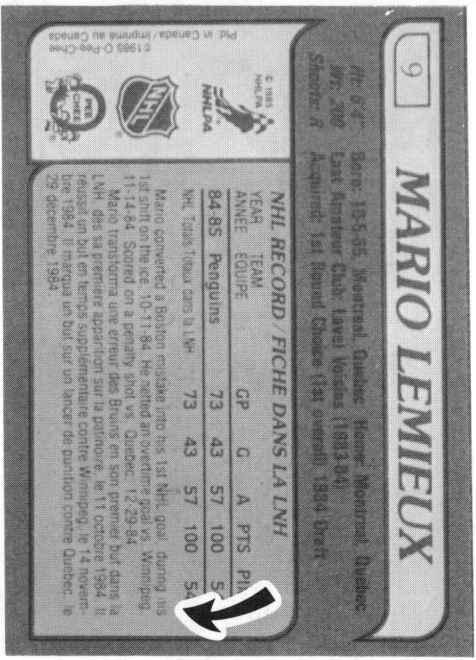

Technically a well-done counterfeit, this card shows evidence that separate printing materials were made for the graphic elements and the photo. Several small flaws on the fake, however, give it away.

Easiest to spot is a broken "h" in the "his," the final word in the first line of the career summary. On this counterfeit, the top of the letter is missing.

Also notice on the back the pattern of red dots which make up the background of the stats/career summary box. On a real card, these dots are arranged in diag-

onal rows. On this counterfeit, the dots run in nearly vertical rows. The maroon back color on the fake is much deeper than on a genuine card, with the result that the three lines of biographical information are less distinct on the fake.

On the front of the counterfeit, examination of the logo penguin's upraised skate will show a half-moon white line near the toe. Most genuine Lemieux rookies show only a tiny white dot in this area.

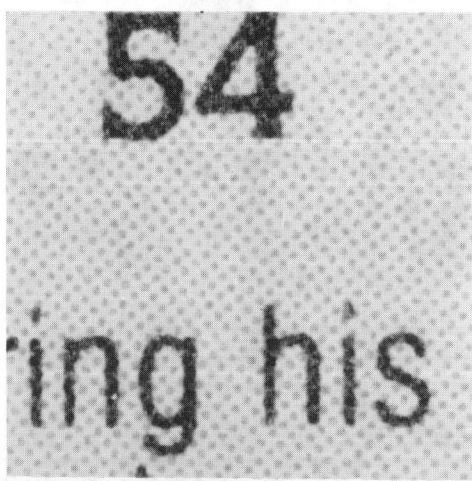

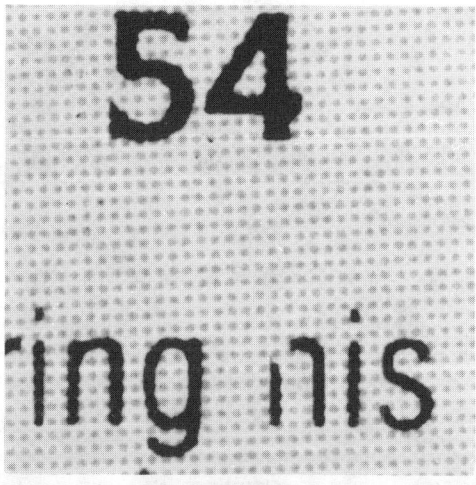

Genuine   **Counterfeit**

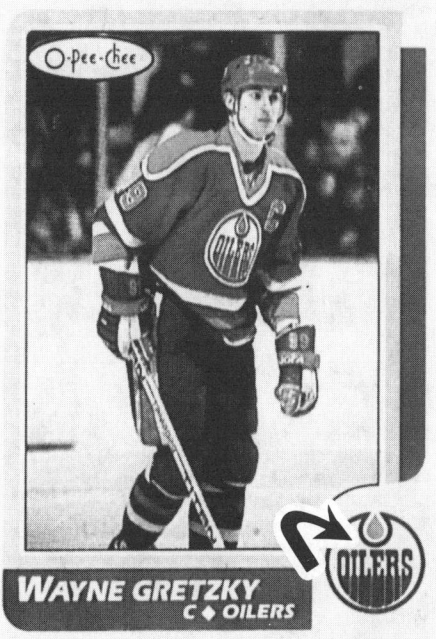

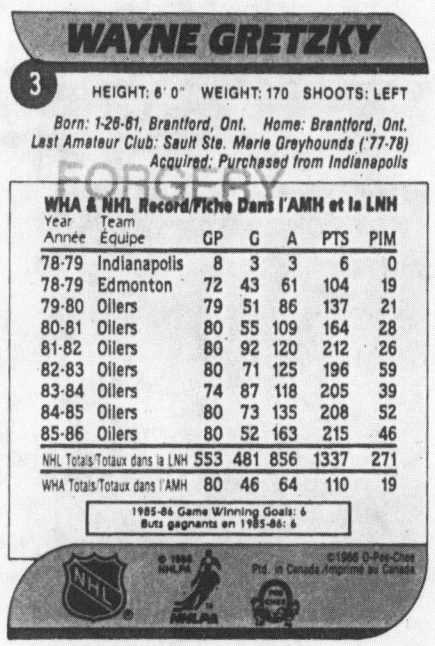

The card back shows:

Year Année	Team Équipe	GP	G	A	PTS	PIM
78-79	Indianapolis	8	3	3	6	0
78-79	Edmonton	72	43	61	104	19
79-80	Oilers	79	51	86	137	21
80-81	Oilers	80	55	109	164	28
81-82	Oilers	80	92	120	212	26
82-83	Oilers	80	71	125	196	59
83-84	Oilers	74	87	118	205	39
84-85	Oilers	80	73	135	208	52
85-86	Oilers	80	52	163	215	46
NHL Totals/Totaux dans la LNH		553	481	856	1337	271
WHA Totals/Totaux dans l'AMH		80	46	64	110	19

Only with a quick glance by the unaided eye would an experienced hockey card enthusiast be taken in by this counterfeit.

Because an original card was re-screened to create printing materials for the counterfeit, the resulting bogus card shows printers' dots in all sorts of places where they will never appear on the genuine version.

The re-screening has resulted in tiny blue dots in what are supposed to be the card's pure white borders and in the player's name, position letter and team in the in the bottom blue stripe. There are also big black dots making up the O-Pee-Chee brand name in the logo at upper-left. Those letters should be clear, clean black lines.

Similarly, the blue and orange Oilers logo at lower-right is composed of color dots rather than solid structures.

The stamped "FORGERY" on the back of the card photographed is unique to that specimen.

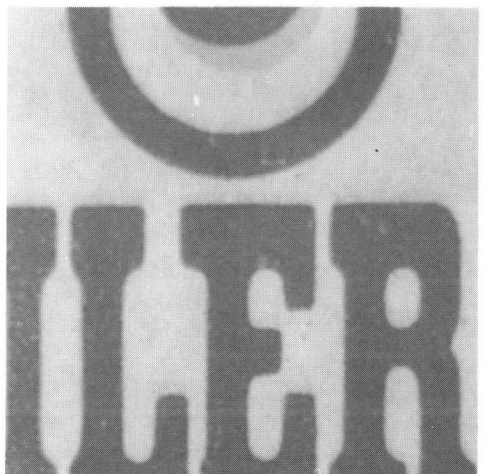

Genuine

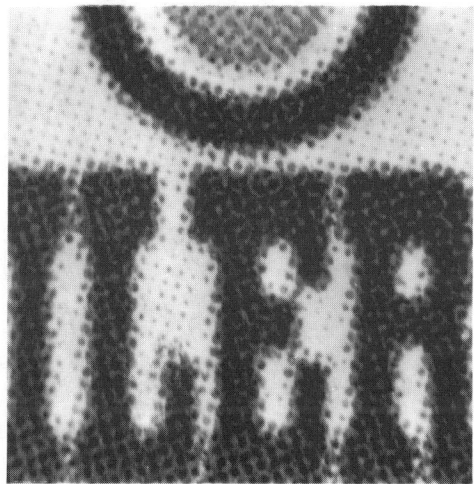

Counterfeit

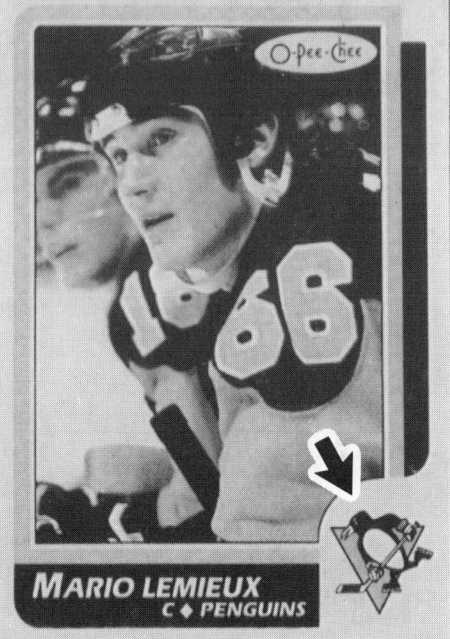

The re-screening has resulted in tiny blue dots in what are supposed to be the card's pure white borders, the penguin's chest and the player's name in the bottom black stripe. There are also multi-colored dots making up the O-Pee-Chee brand name in the logo at upper-right. Those letters should be clean black lines.

Probably the work of the same counterfeiter who produced the 1986-87 OPC Gretzky fake. Only a quick glance by the unaided eye would fool an experienced hockey card enthusiast.

Because an original card was re-screened to create printing materials for the counterfeit, the resulting bogus card shows printers' dots in all sorts of places where they will never appear on the genuine version.

The stamped "FORGERY" on the back of the card photographed is unique to that specimen.

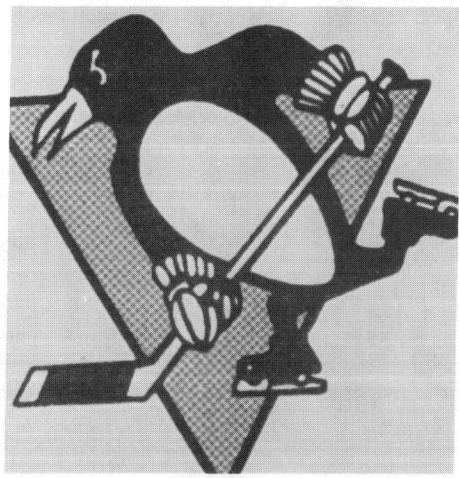

Genuine

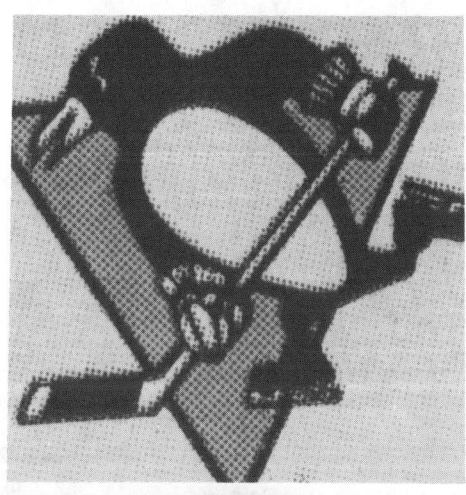

Counterfeit

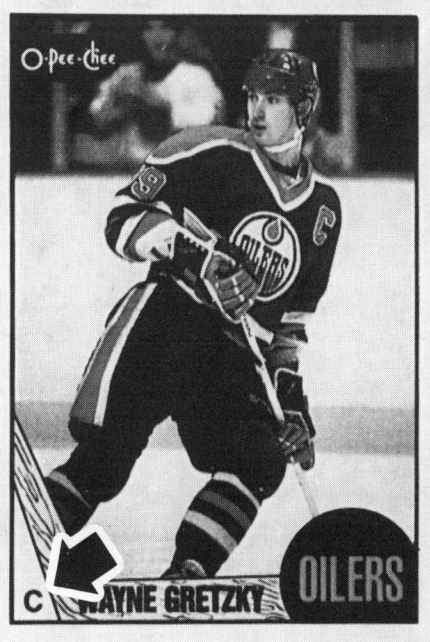

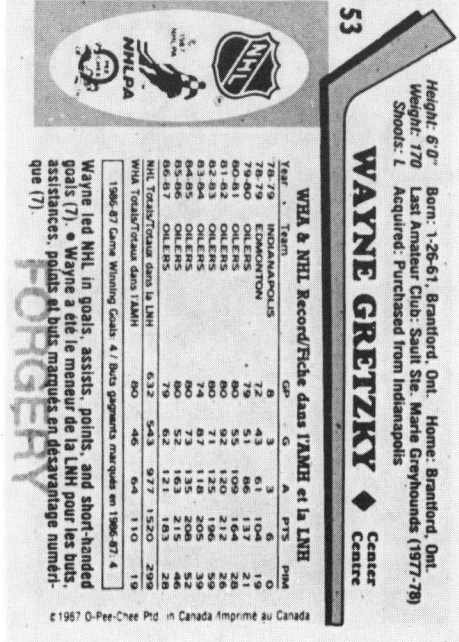

Not a particularly deceptive counterfeit, except perhaps when viewed with the unaided eye in a plastic holder. A tip-off to the card's counterfeit status should come from the unnatural glossy finish on the front of the card.

More objectively, a close examination of the card front with a magnifying glass will reveal the counterfeit on the basis of printing dots where they will never appear on a genuine card — in the white border. This is the only counterfeit examined to date which exhibits a dot pattern in what

is supposed to be a white border. The yellow triangle at lower-left which has the player's position indicated also exhibits background dots on the counterfeit that are not present on the genuine card.

Perhaps the easiest extraneous dots to spot are in the black oval OPC logo at upper-left. On the genuine card the white letters of the brand name should be pure white. On the counterfeit, these letters have been invaded by red and blue color dots.

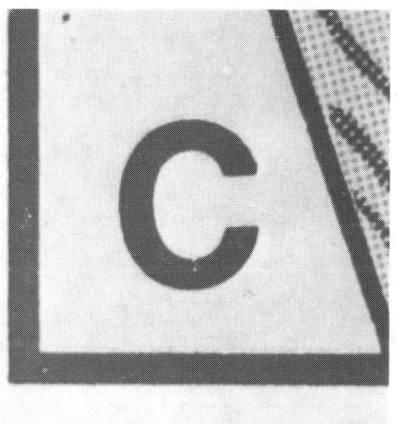

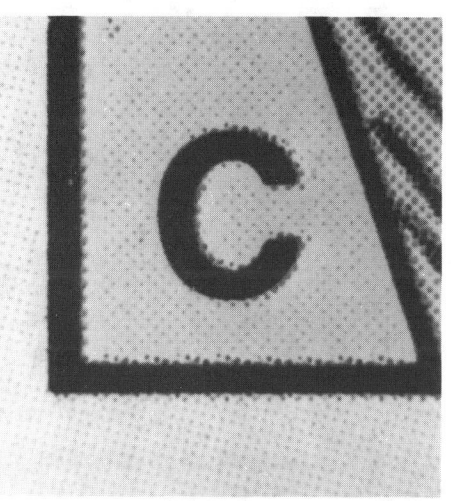

Genuine

Counterfeit

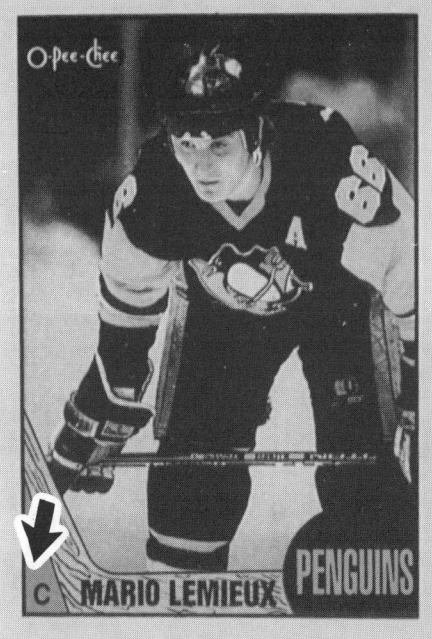

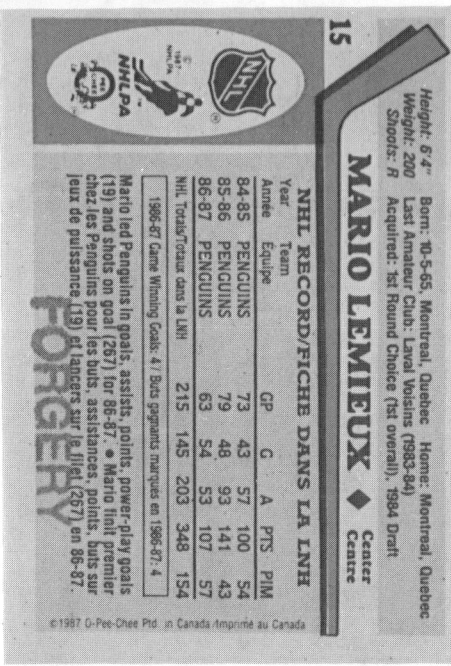

Probably made by the same persons and process as the 1987-88 OPC Gretzky counterfeit.

A tip-off to the card's counterfeit status should come from the unnatural glossy finish on the front of the card.

More objectively, a close examination of the card front with a magnifying glass will reveal the counterfeit on the basis of printing dots where they will never appear on a genuine card — in the white border. This is one of the few counterfeits examined which exhibits a dot pattern in what is supposed to be a white border. The red triangle at lower-left which has the player's position indicated also exhibits background dots on the counterfeit that are not present on the genuine card.

Perhaps the easiest extraneous dots to spot are in the black oval OPC logo at upper-left. On the genuine card the white letters of the brand name should be pure white. On the counterfeit, these letters have been invaded by red and blue color dots.

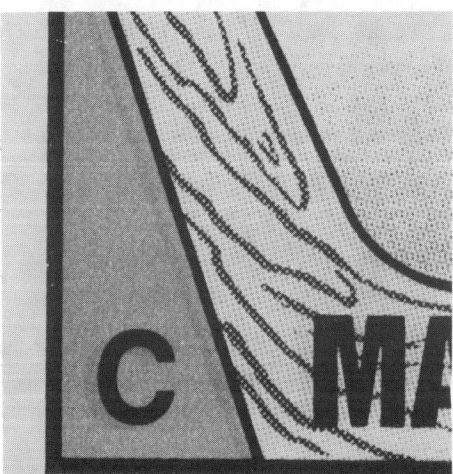

Genuine

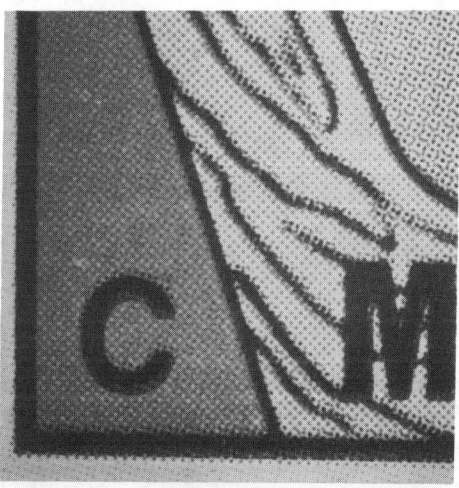

Counterfeit

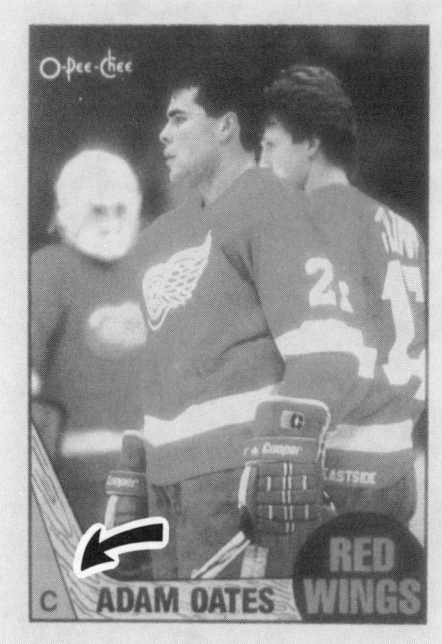

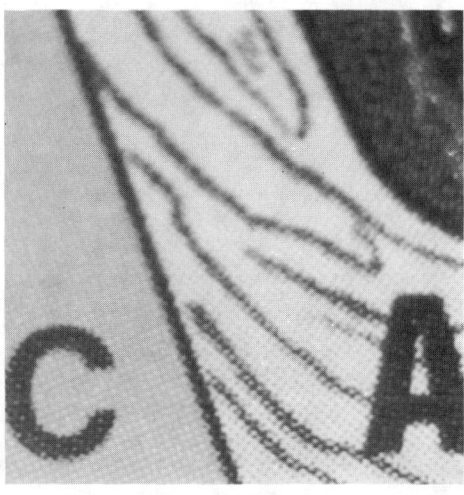

Any of the typography on the front of this card can be used to detect the counterfeit.

This is one of a group of six O-Pee-Chee hockey counterfeits that surfaced in March, 1992, all apparently the work of the same forger.

Examination with a magnifying glass will show that the letters of the company logo, and the player's name, team and position abbreviation on a genuine card are printed in solid colors with clean edges. By contrast, the counterfeit shows these letters as composed of many tiny dots, which creates the effect of ragged edges where the letters meet the background color.

This counterfeit is printed on much lighter stock than a genuine 1987-88 OPC hockey card. Those very familiar with OPC cards might instantly notice that the back of the fake is much whiter than a genuine card, though this type of subjective opinion should not be used by itself to judge the status of a suspect card.

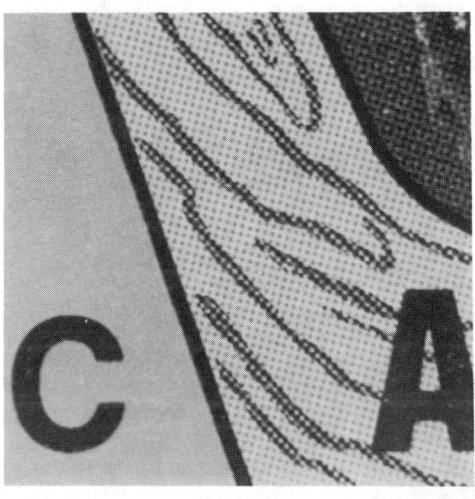

Genuine

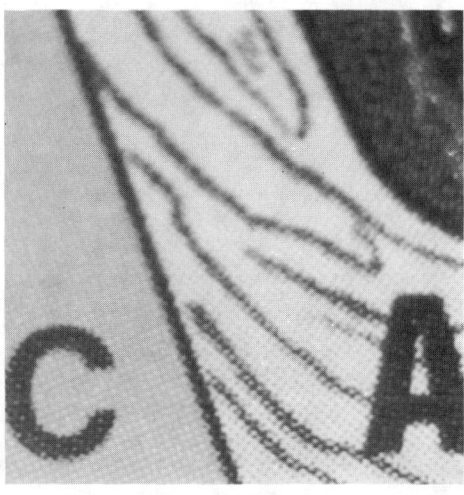

Counterfeit

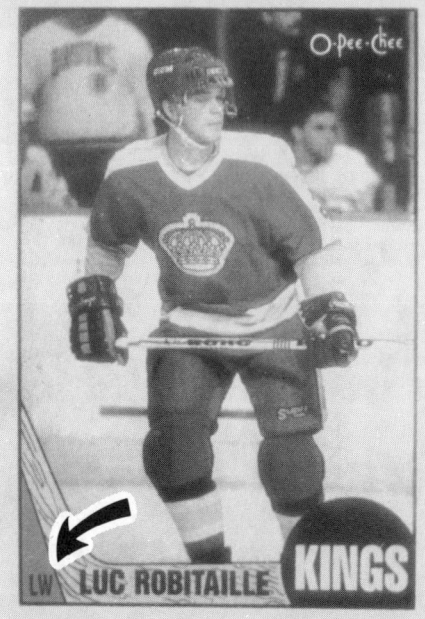

Any of the typography on the front of this card can be used to detect the counterfeit.

This is one of a group of six O-Pee-Chee hockey counterfeits that surfaced in March, 1992, all apparently the work of the same forger.

Examination with a magnifying glass will show that the letters of the company logo, and the player's name, team and position abbreviation on a genuine card are printed in solid colors with clean edges. By contrast, the counterfeit shows these letters as composed of many tiny dots, which creates the effect of ragged edges where the letters meet the background color.

This counterfeit is printed on much lighter stock than a genuine 1987-88 OPC hockey card. Those very familiar with OPC cards might instantly notice that the back of the fake is much whiter than a genuine card, though this type of subjective opinion should not be used by itself to judge the status of a suspect card.

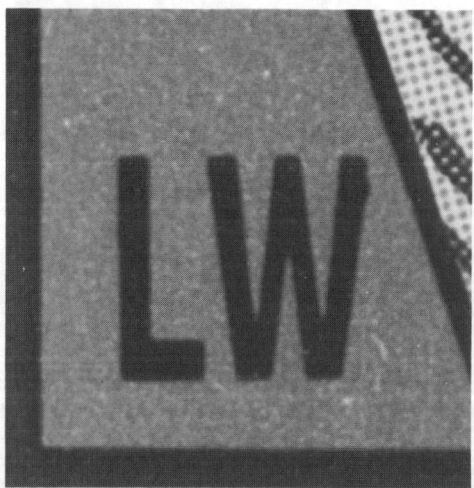

Genuine

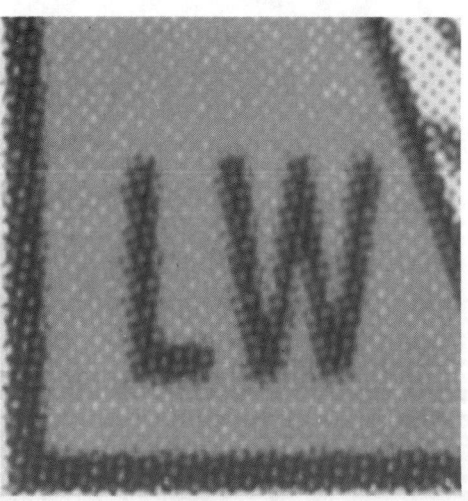

Counterfeit

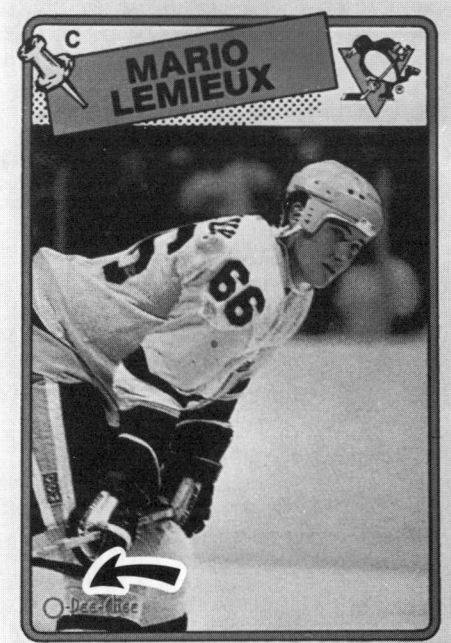

One of a quintet of very skillful counterfeit 1988-89 OPC hockey cards.

Unlike some of the counterfeits of earlier OPC cards, which show printers' dots in all sorts of places where they will never appear on the genuine card, this group requires close examination of specific areas with a good magnifying glass to spot the counterfeiter's mistakes.

On this card, the best area for examination is the blue O-Pee-Chee logo in the lower-left corner. Off-register placement of the blue letters (they are low and to the right) has left a visible group of "shadow" letters composed of blue dots above and to the right. These shadow structures are the remainder of the original logo that was re-screened from a genuine card to create printing materials for the counterfeit.

While it cannot be used as a diagnostic, it is worth noting that genuine specimens of 1988-89 OPC are quite often found with one or more edges fairly roughly cut, while all counterfeits seen have well-cut edges all around.

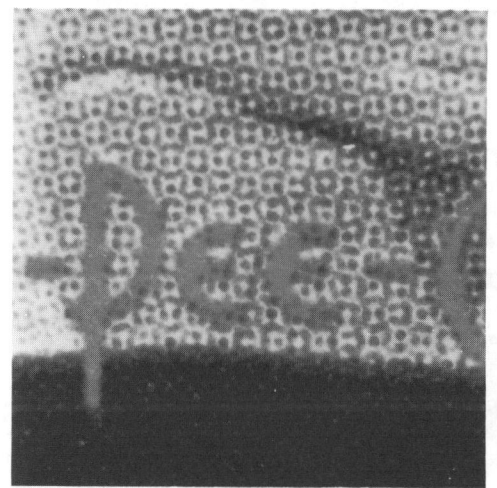

Genuine

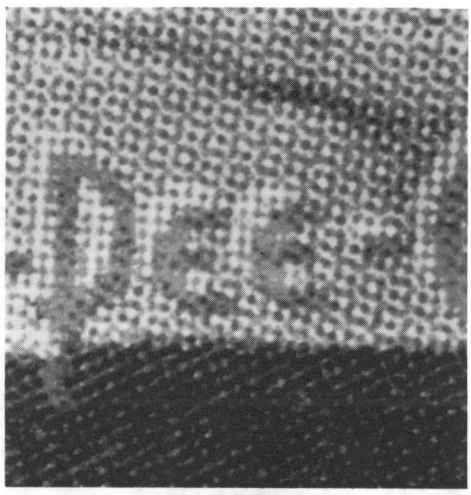

Counterfeit

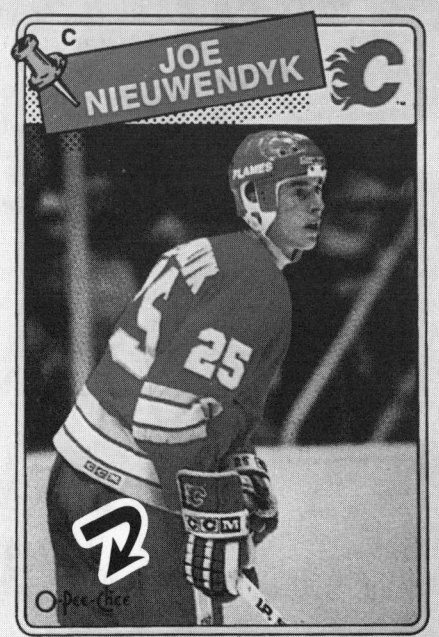

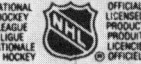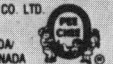

JOE NIEUWENDYK

C ✦ CALGARY FLAMES

HEIGHT: 6'1"   WEIGHT: 175   SHOOTS: LEFT
Last Amateur Club: Cornell Univ. (1986-87)
Acquired: 2nd Round Choice (27th overall), 1985 Draft
Born: 9-10-66, Oshawa, Ont. Home: Whitby, Ont.

NHL RECORD/FICHE DANS LA LNH

Year Année	Team Équipe	GP	G	A	PTS	PIM
86-87	FLAMES	9	5	1	6	0
87-88	FLAMES	75	51	41	92	23
NHL Totals/Totaux dans la LNH		84	56	42	98	23

GAME WINNING GOALS/BUTS GAGNANTS 1987-88: 8

Won 1988 Calder Trophy. Led NHL in PPG (31). Recorded 4 Hat Tricks in 87-88. Led all Rookies in G, A, PPG, & GWG ● Gagnant du Trophée Calder en 1988. Meneur de la LNH pour les buts marqués en attaque à 5 (31). Il réussit 4 tours du chapeau en 87-88. Chez les recrues, meneur pour les matches, assistances, buts marqués en attaque à 5 et buts gagnants.

PLAYOFF RECORD/FICHE DURANT LES ÉLIMINATOIRES

	GP	G	A	PTS	PIM
1988	8	3	4	7	2
Career/Carrière	14	5	6	11	2

This is one of five very dangerous counterfeit 1988-89 OPC hockey cards. This group requires close examination of specific areas with a good magnifying glass to spot the counterfeiter's mistakes.

On this card, the best area for examination is the black O-Pee-Chee logo in the lower-left corner. Rather than being printed as clean, solid black letters, the "O-Pee-Chee" on the counterfeit is composed of letters made up of many small black dots.

The same is true for the black dots in the upper-left of the picture, which are supposed to represent the "shadow" of the red name box. On an original card these dots would be rendered as single black dots. On this counterfeit, they are made up of many smaller dots.

While it cannot be used as a diagnostic, it is worth noting that genuine specimens of 1988-89 OPC are quite often found with one or more edges fairly roughly cut, while all counterfeits seen have well-cut edges all around.

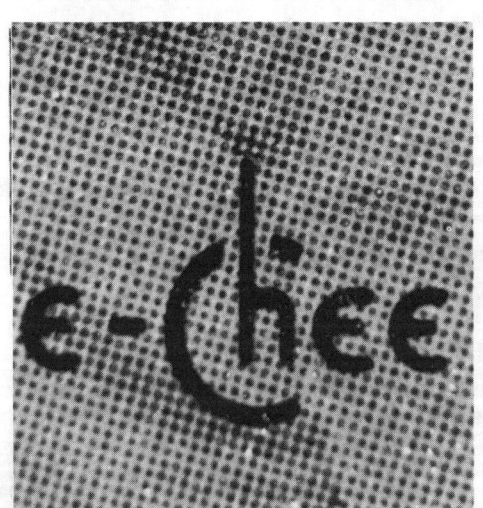

Genuine

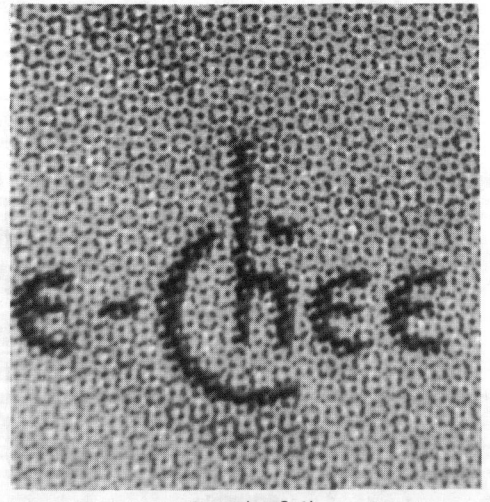

Counterfeit

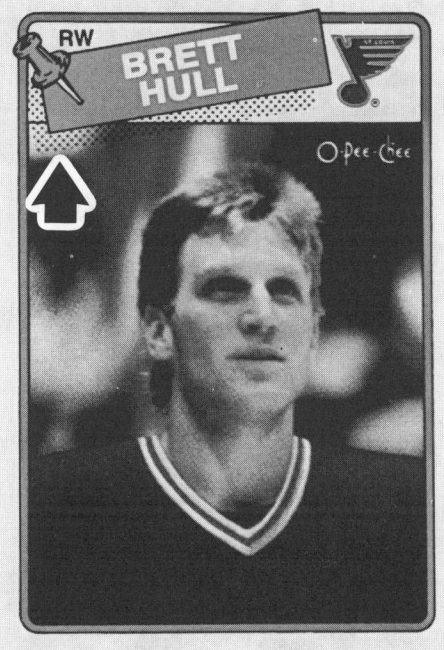

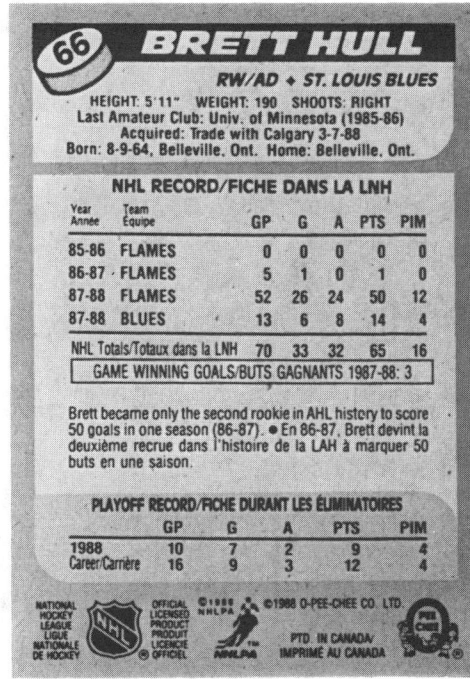

This is one of five very dangerous counterfeit 1988-89 OPC hockey cards.

Unlike some of the counterfeits of earlier OPC cards, which show printers' dots in all sorts of places where they will never appear on the genuine card, this group requires close examination of specific areas with a good magnifying glass to spot the counterfeiter's mistakes.

On this card, the best area for examination is the pattern of black dots in the upper-left of the picture, which is supposed to represent the "shadow" of the blue name box. On an original card these dots would be rendered as single solid black elements. On this counterfeit, each dot is made up of many smaller dots.

While it cannot be used as a diagnostic, it is worth noting that genuine specimens of 1988-89 OPC are quite often found with one or more edges fairly roughly cut, while all counterfeits seen have well-cut edges all around.

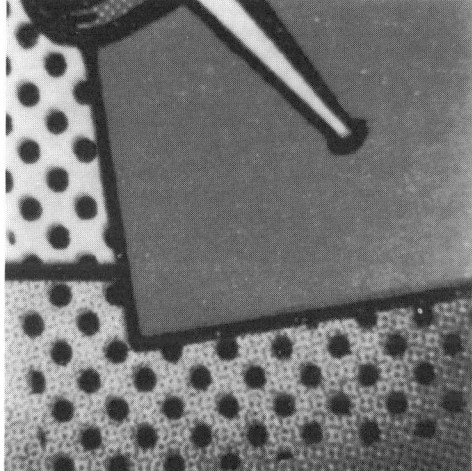

Genuine

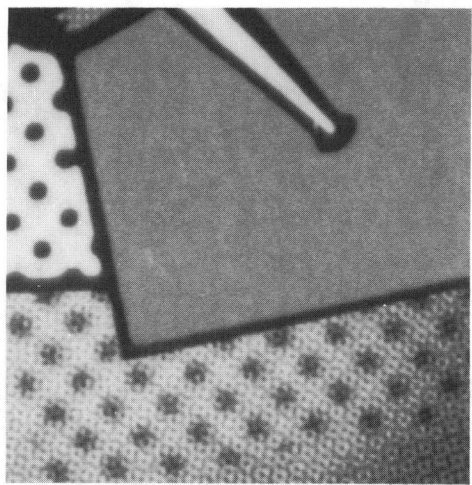

Counterfeit

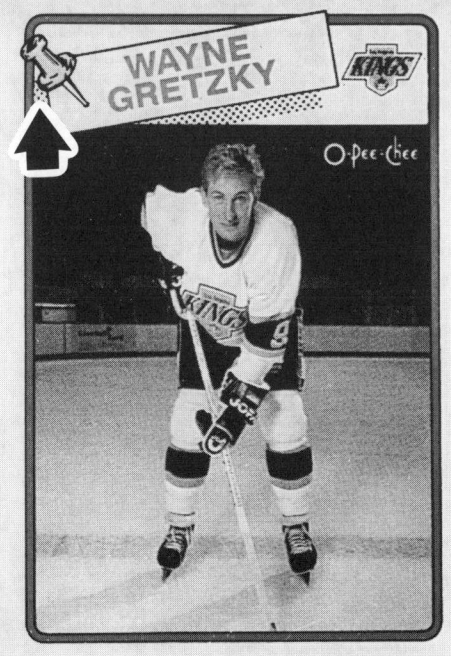

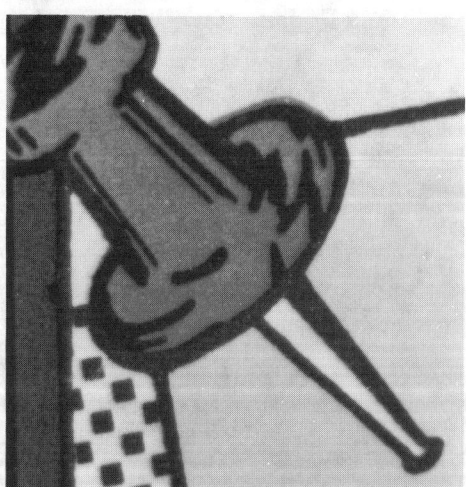

This is hardest to spot among a quintet of dangerous counterfeit 1988-89 OPC hockey cards.

On this card, the best area for examination is the series of square black dots intended to represent a shadow beneath the yellow name box. Specifically, the uppermost squares to the left of the push-pin should be studied under magnification. On the counterfeit, many of the squares are poorly formed, but the real key is the top square in the row third from the left of the name box; it has a bar that extends to the left, touching the black photo-frame line. On a genuine card, there is no such bar, though the square itself does touch the frame line. Also note on the genuine card that there is a partial black square printed into the purple border, above and to the left of the previously mentioned square.

While it cannot be used as a diagnostic, it is worth noting that genuine 1988-89 OPC are often found with one or more roughly cut edges, while all counterfeits seen have well-cut edges all around.

Genuine

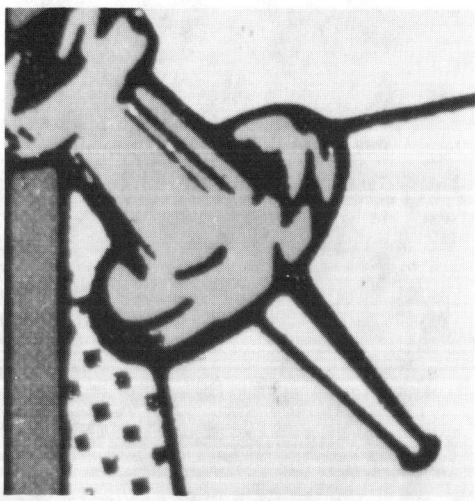

Counterfeit

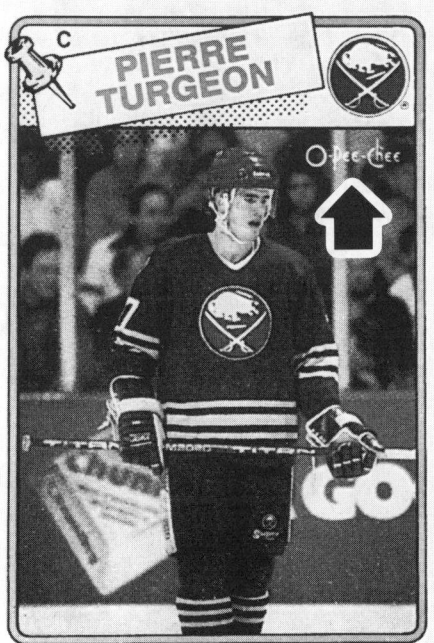

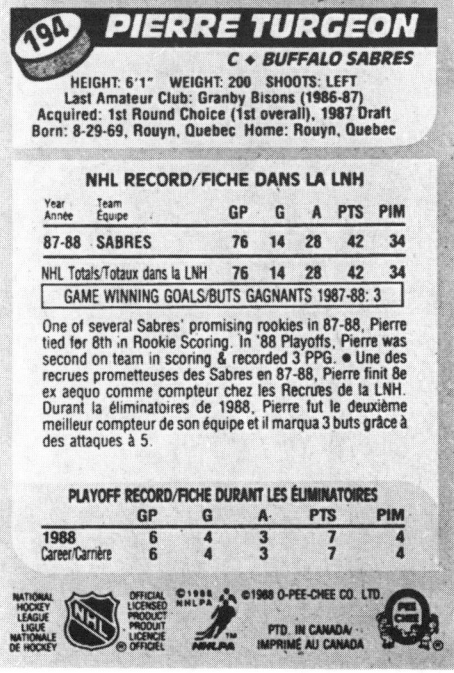

This is one of series of five very dangerous counterfeit 1988-89 OPC hockey cards.

Unlike some of the counterfeits of earlier OPC cards, which show printers' dots in all sorts of places where they will never appear on the genuine card, this group requires close examination of specific areas with a good magnifying glass to spot the counterfeiter's mistakes.

On this card, the best area for examination is the white O-Pee-Chee logo in the upper-right corner of the photo. On a genuine card, the letters of the brand name should be clean and white when viewed under magnification. On this counterfeit, the letters will be seen to be infected with many small printers' color dots.

While it cannot be used as a diagnostic, it is worth noting that genuine specimens of 1988-89 OPC are quite often found with one or more edges fairly roughly cut, while all counterfeits seen have well-cut edges all around.

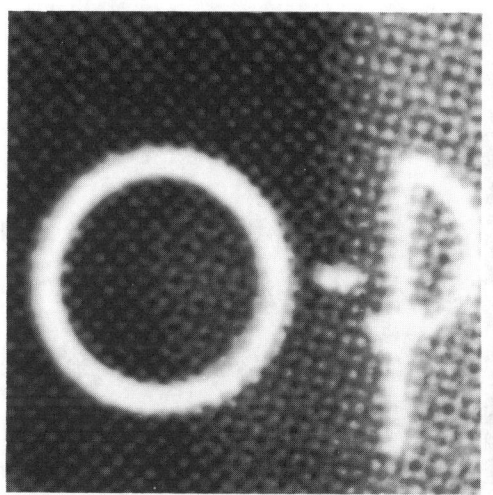

Genuine

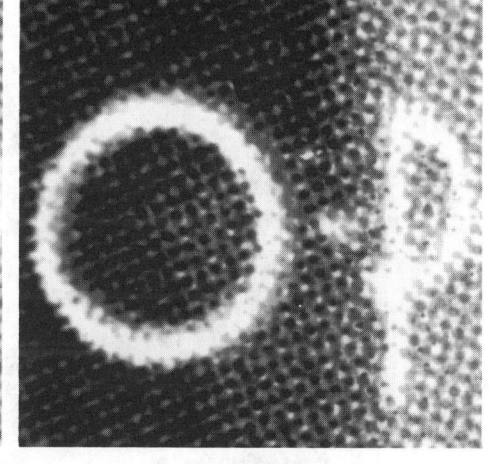

Counterfeit

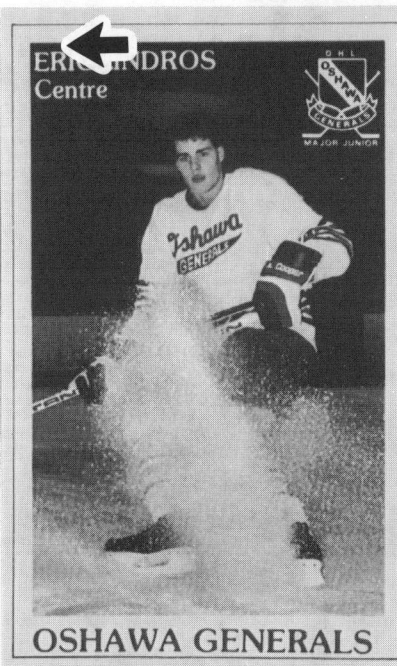

OSHAWA GENERALS

P.L.A.Y. Card #31
**POLICE LAWS AND YOUTH
DRUG TIPS
from
DURHAM REGIONAL POLICE**

Join the Generals in their fight
against drug abuse.
Drugs are for healing not dealing.

**NATIONAL Sports Centre
Five Points Mall
Ritson & Taunton.**

**Board of Police Commissioners
for the Regional Municipality
of Durham.**

Whitby Lions Club.

**Magill Business Forms
95 Athol St. Oshawa**

Cards of Lindros and four teammates were added to the 1989-90 Durham Regional Police set as an update. The update sheets were printed with two cards each of the other four Generals and eight Lindros cards. This means there are essentially eight different versions of the Lindros card, each with tiny differences on front and/or back in terms of photo cropping and legibility of typographic elements.

Luckily, this particular counterfeit has a "fingerprint" that exists on none of the genuine cards.

The use of a magnifying glass will reveal that on the counterfeit card there is a thin (1 mm or so) band of light blue dots on each side of the photo on the card's front. Even if a genuine card were printed with the blue color badly out of register, there would only be a row or two of extra blue dots on one or two sides of the photo.

While the counterfeit is printed on fairly thin cardboard stock, it is only marginally lighter than the stock of the genuine card.

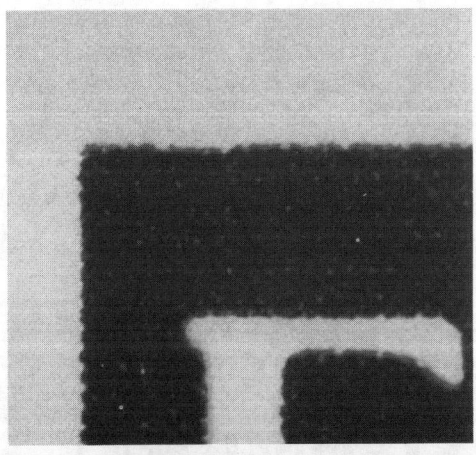

Genuine

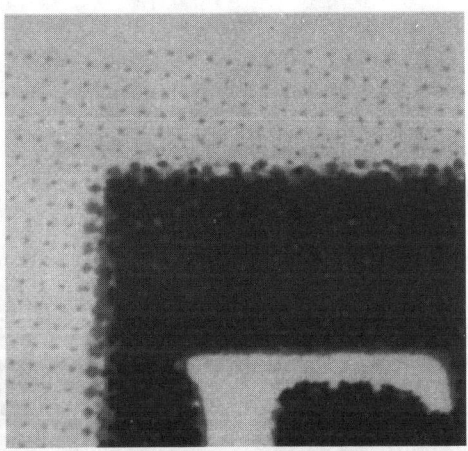

Counterfeit

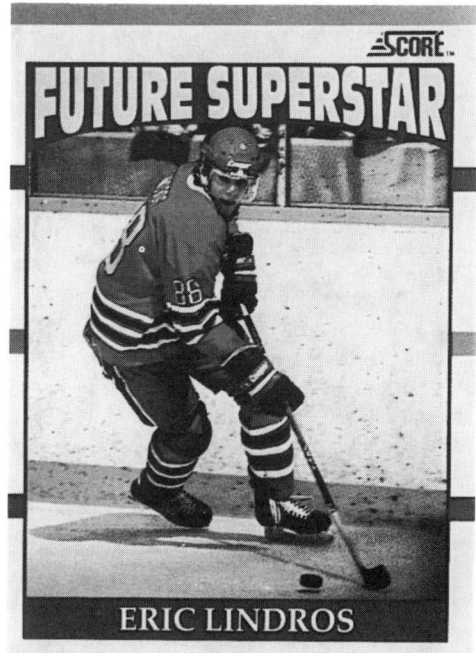 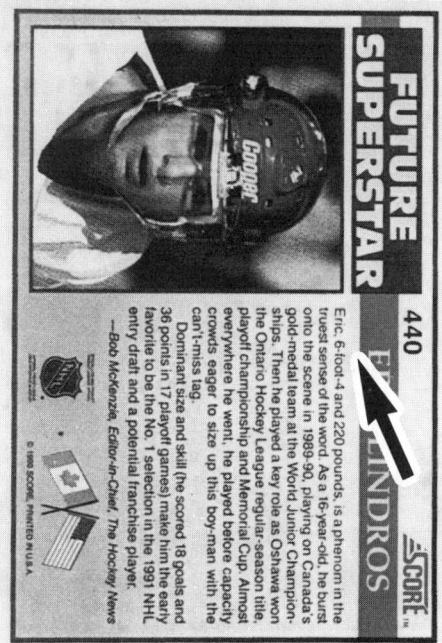

Visually a fairly deceptive counterfeit, this is one example of a fake that is so far out of bounds on card weight as to raise immediate suspicions — it is over 40% heavier than a genuine card. This difference is easily perceived when handling the card outside of any type of plastic holder.

There is also a very easily detected visual indicator of this card's counterfeit status. The black type on the back of card is rendered on this counterfeit in a series of tiny dots, rather than as the clean black lines found on a genuine card. This flaw is not visible to the naked eye, requiring the aid of a magnifying glass. The rescreening of the type on a genuine card has produced indecipherable legends above and below the NHL shield.

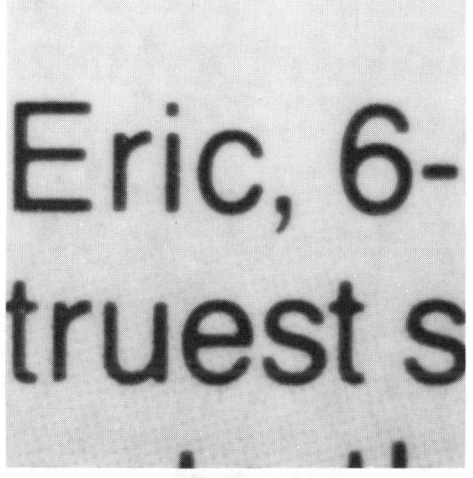 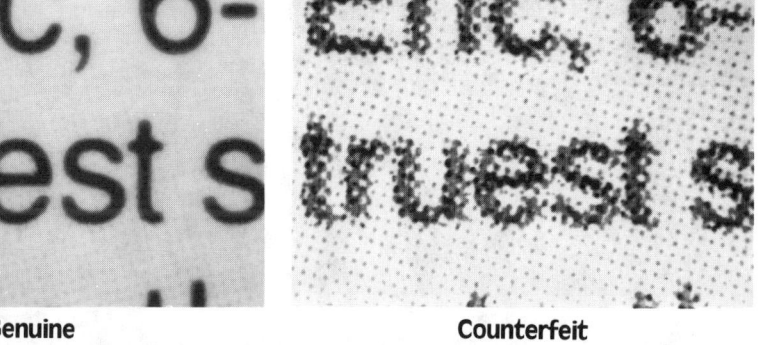

Genuine   **Counterfeit**

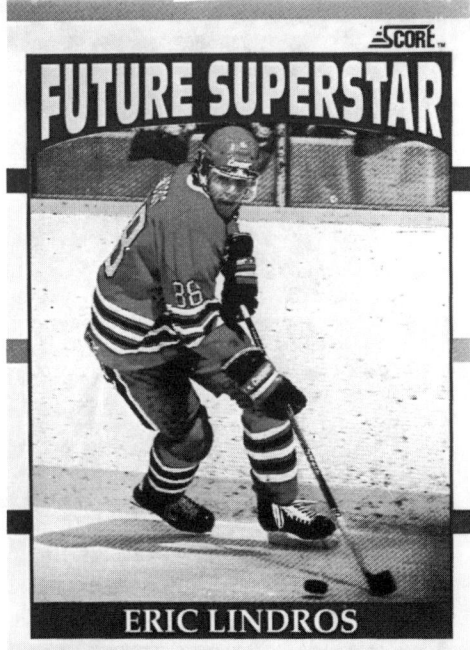

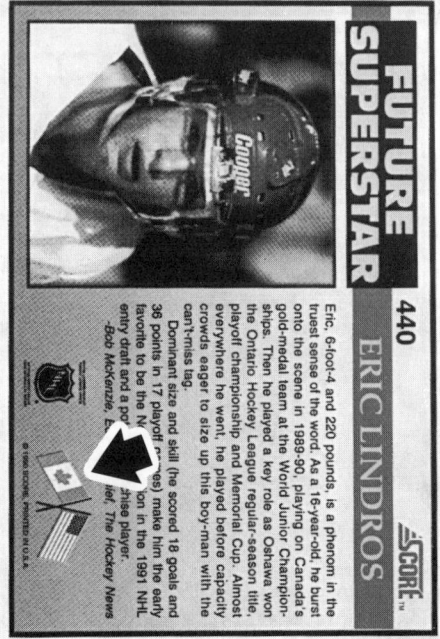

The second known type of Lindros counterfeit is also a very deceptive card.

While this counterfeit, too, varies in weight, the slightly more than 10% difference (the counterfeit is lighter than a genuine 1990-91 Score hockey card) is not significant enough to be discerned except by very precise scales.

Fortunately, there is an easily detected flaw, again on the back of the card. Whereas the red bars and maple leaf of the Canadian flag will be printed on a genuine card in solid red, the counterfeit card displays these elements with a pattern of tiny yellow dots in the red areas.

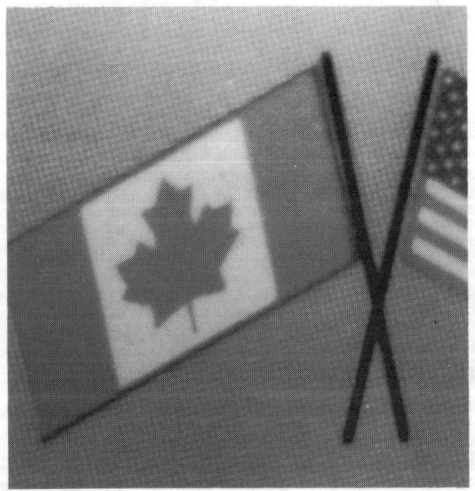

Genuine

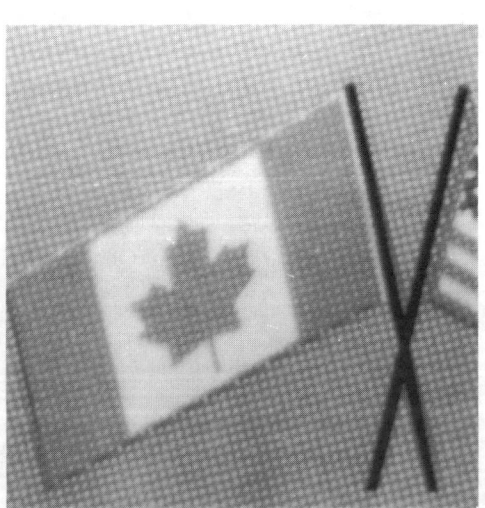

Counterfeit

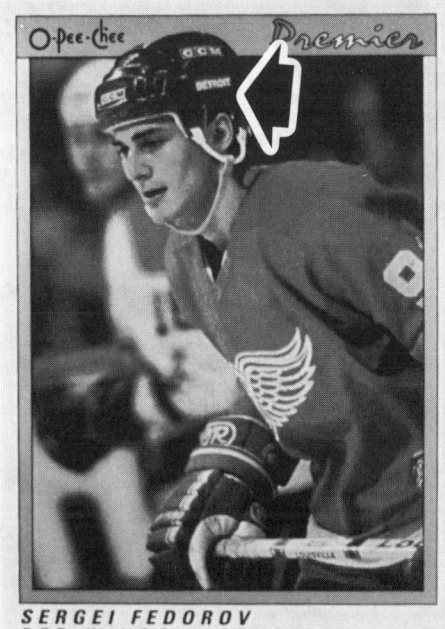

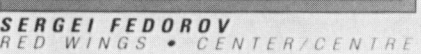

SERGEI FEDOROV
RED WINGS • CENTER/CENTRE

To an experienced hockey card collector, something is "not right" about the look of the three known counterfeited cards in this set. However, since such things as the richness of color and the shade of the gold band at top are subjective, they cannot be reliably used as definite indicators of genuine or counterfeit status.

Rather, flip the card over and with a magnifying glass, examine the O-Pee-Chee logo to the lower-left of the Red Wings logo. On a genuine card, the boy at left will be a "blond", having three shocks of white hair, separated by black lines. On the counterfeit, the boy has all-black hair. Similarly, the boy lazing in the "O" of a genuine card has a complete black line defining the outline of his left leg. On the counterfeit, part of that line is missing.

Another indicator is found in the letters of the NHL logo at lower-left. The white letters in the outer ring are readable on a genuine card, but indecipherable on the fake. Again, use a good magnifier.

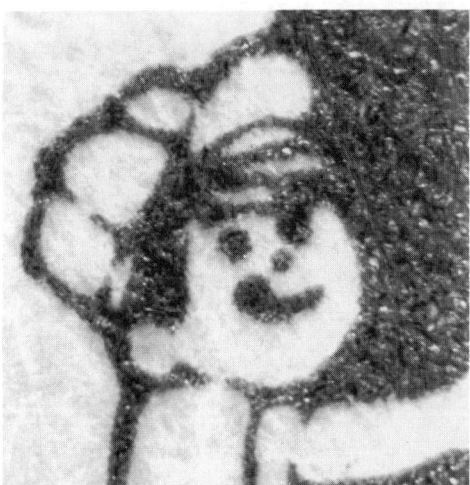

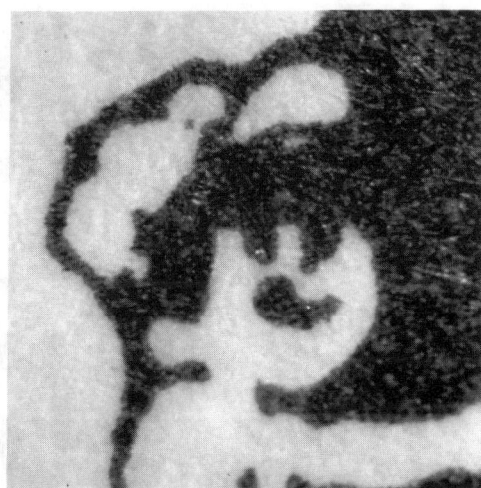

Genuine   **Counterfeit**

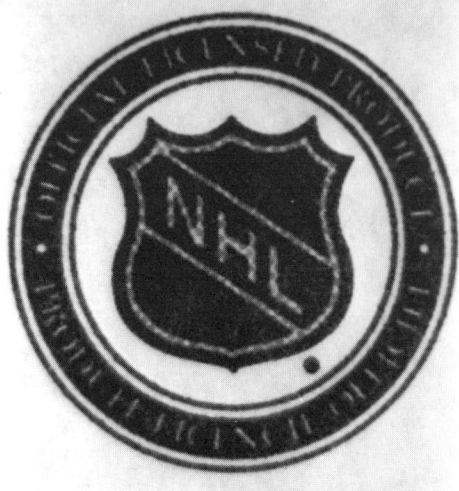

Genuine

Counterfeit

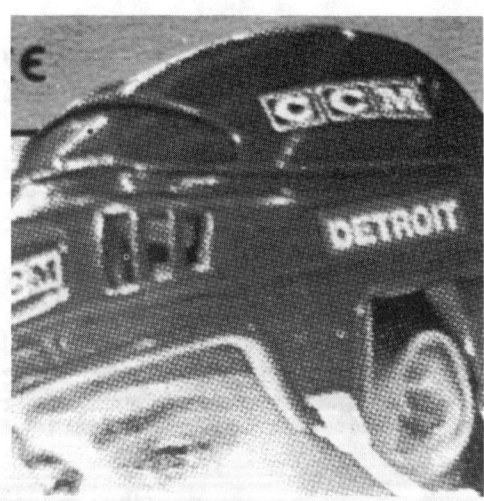

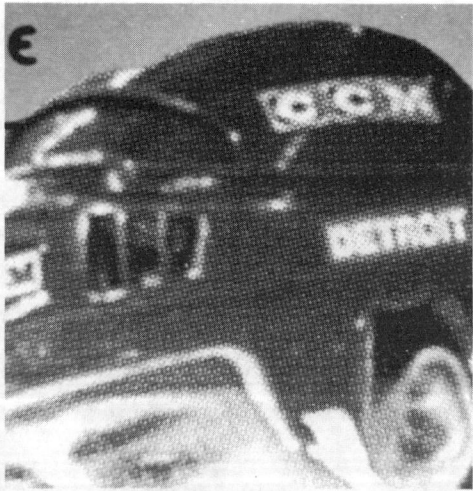

Genuine

Counterfeit

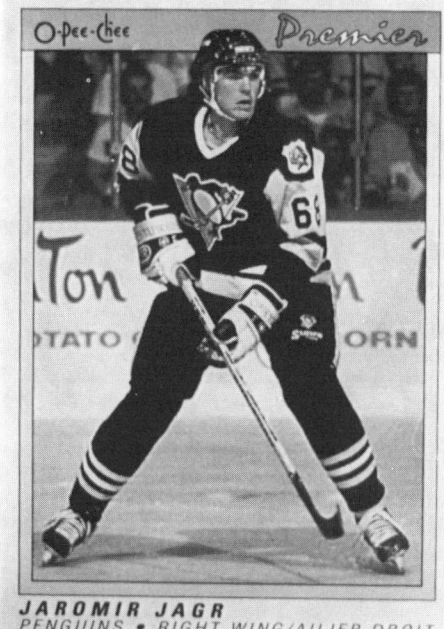

JAROMIR JAGR
PENGUINS • RIGHT WING/AILIER DROIT

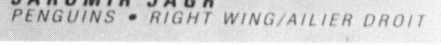

To an experienced hockey card collector, something is "not right" about the look of the three known counterfeited cards in this set. However, since such things as the richness of color and the shade of the gold band at top are subjective, they cannot be reliably used as definite indicators of genuine or counterfeit status.

Rather, flip the card over and with a magnifying glass, examine the O-Pee-Chee logo to the lower-left of the Penguins logo. On a genuine card, the boy at left will be a "blond", having three shocks of white hair, separated by black lines. On the counterfeit, the boy has all-black hair. Similarly, the boy lazing in the "O" of a genuine card has a complete black line defining the outline of his left leg. On the counterfeit, part of that line is missing.

Another indicator is found in the letters of the NHL logo at lower-left. The white letters in the outer ring are readable on a genuine card, but indecipherable on the fake. Again, use a good magnifier.

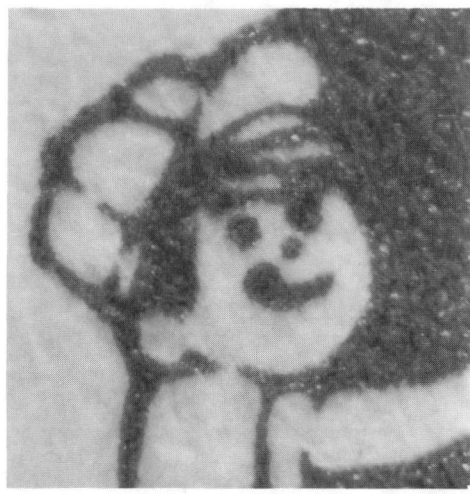

Genuine

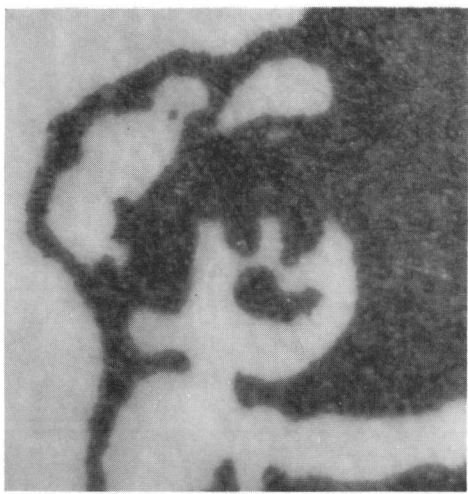

Counterfeit

 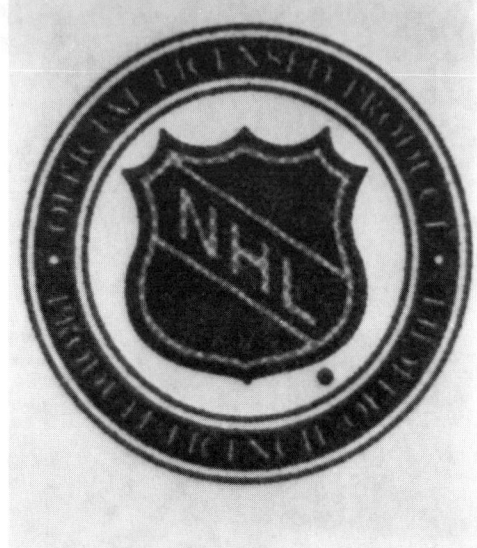

Genuine   Counterfeit

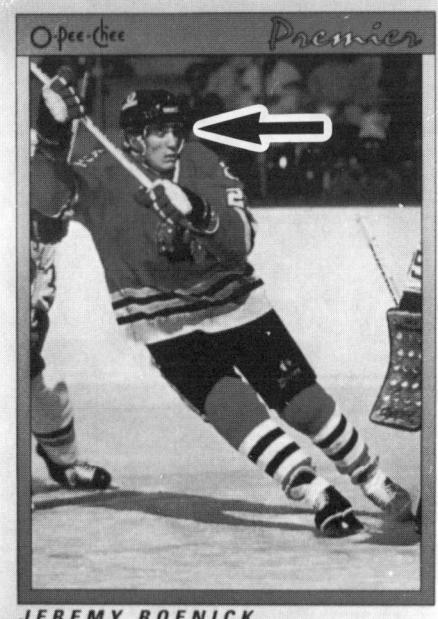

JEREMY ROENICK
BLACKHAWKS • CENTER/CENTRE

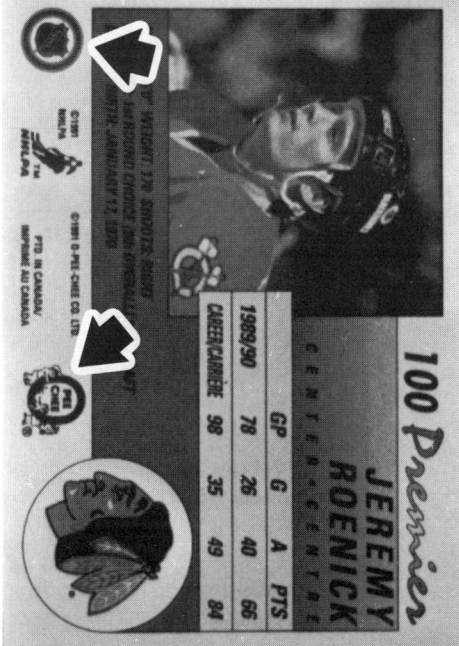

To an experienced hockey card collector, something is "not right" about the look of the three known counterfeited cards in this set. However, since such things as the richness of color and the shade of the gold band at top are subjective, they cannot be reliably used as definite indicators of genuine or counterfeit status.

Rather, flip the card over and with a magnifying glass, examine the O-Pee-Chee logo to the lower-left of the Blackhawks logo. On a genuine card, the boy at left will be a "blond", having three shocks of white hair, separated by black lines. On the counterfeit, the boy has all-black hair. Similarly, the boy lazing in the "O" of a genuine card has a complete black line defining the outline of his left leg. On the counterfeit, part of that line is missing.

Another indicator is found in the letters of the NHL logo at lower-left. The white letters in the outer ring are readable on a genuine card, but indecipherable on the fake. Again, use a good magnifier.

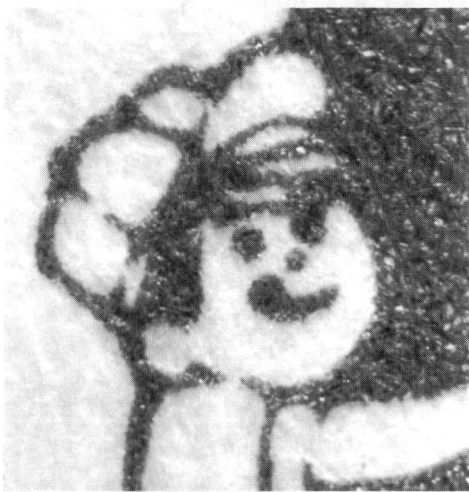

Genuine

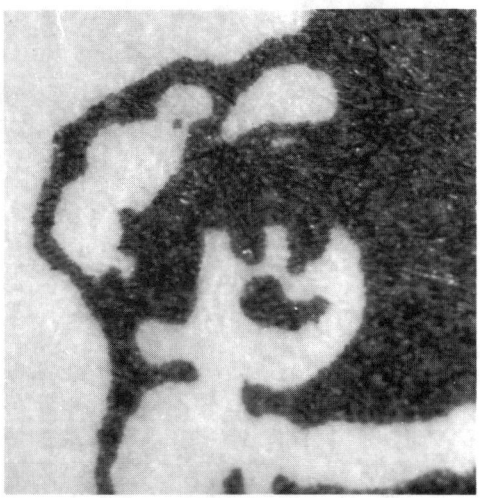

Counterfeit

Genuine   Counterfeit

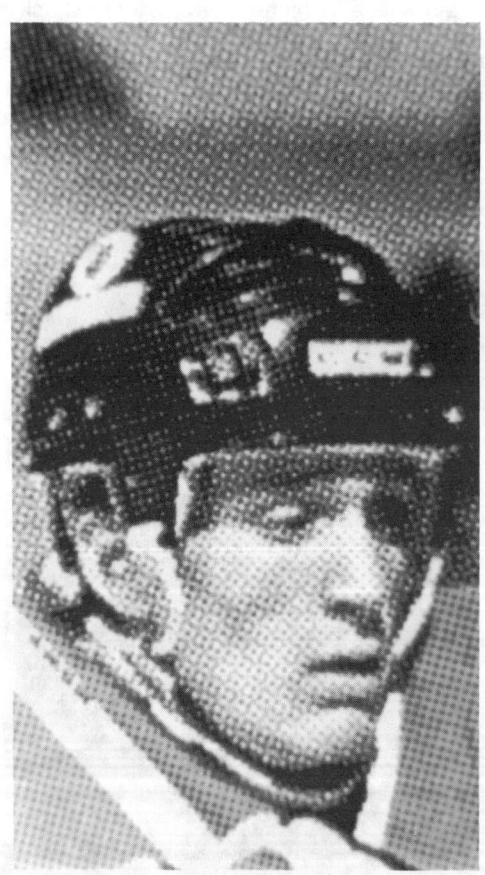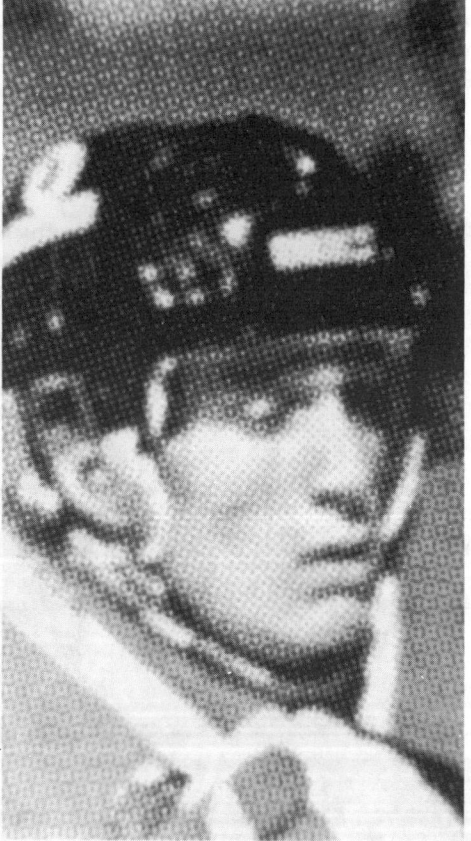

Genuine   Counterfeit

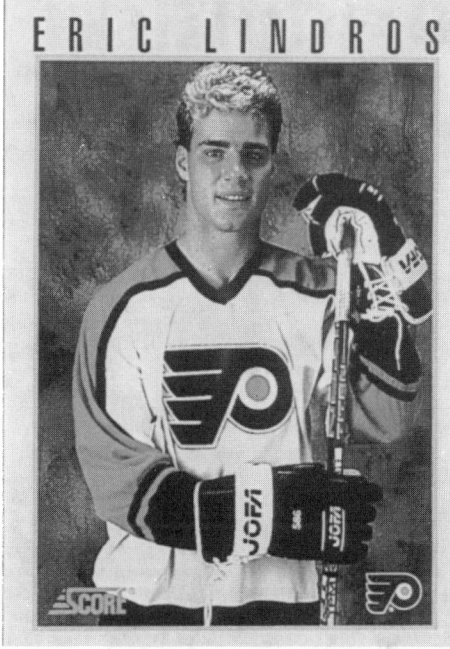

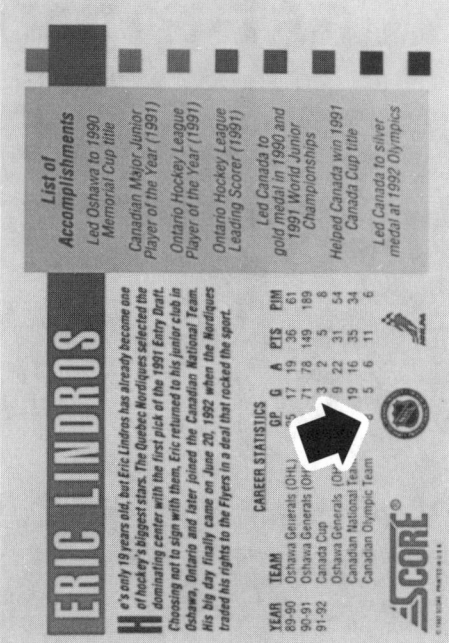

One of the first Eric Lindros cards, Score's creation given out when he announced his signing with Philadelphia, and later inserted into 1991-92 "American" wax boxes as a chase card, has been counterfeited.

Luckily this fake is fairly easy to spot with the use of a magnifying glass. The counterfeit was created by re-screening an original card, with the result being a fuzziness of all graphics details and typography that is not found on a genuine card.

One of the easiest places to detect the

counterfeit is on the back, in the NHL shield logo at bottom center. Examined with a glass, the tiny white lettering is easily readable on a genuine card, but completely indecipherable on this counterfeit. Ditto for the copyright line at lower-left.

Note also the graduated color bar at top, with the skater's name. On a genuine card the color bar and white letters of the name have no outline. On the counterfeit the bar and letters appear to have a dark outline.

Genuine

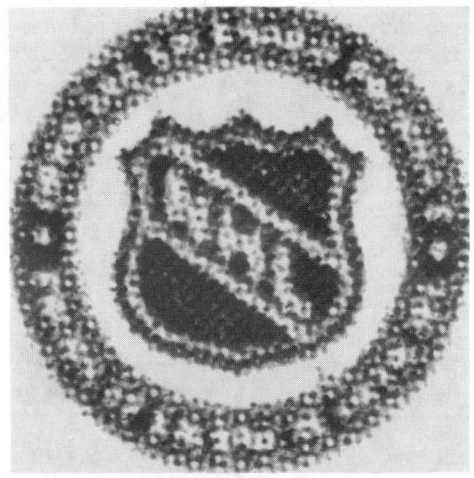

Counterfeit

Last-minute addition

1989 Score Troy Aikman

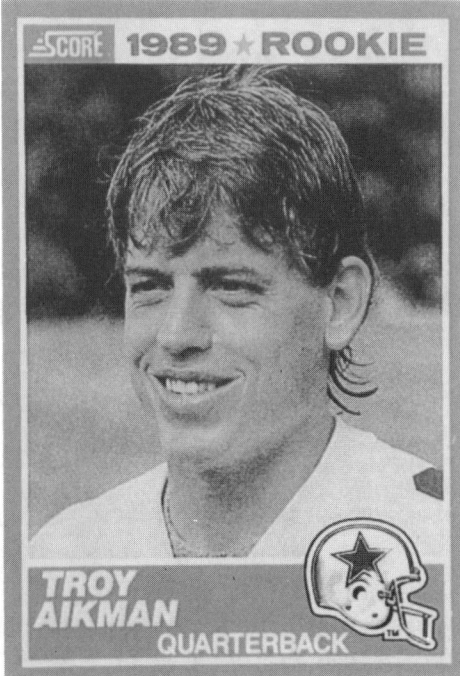

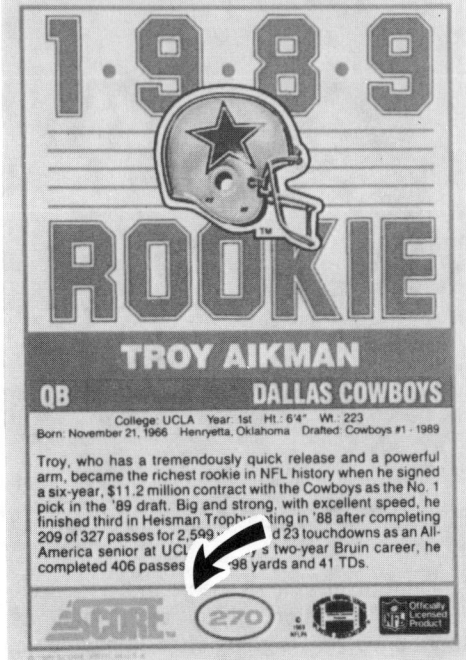

You can get the number on this counterfeit relatively easily — look at the card number on back. The red "270" on a genuine card is made up of numerals with edges that end cleanly at the white background. This counterfeit shows the number as a composition of many tiny red dots, giving its edges a fuzzy appearance when viewed under magnification.

Similar rescreening of the other red graphic elements on the cards is noted — check the Score logo on back and the star at top front.

Note also the counterfeit's general loss of detail in each of the "TM" trademark indicators near the Cowboys helmets on front and back, and the Score logo. While it is a subjective criteria, the photo on the counterfeit is fuzzy and darker in comparison to a genuine card.

The counterfeit specimen examined was also notably undersized, measuring a full 1/16th" shorter and narrower than the standard 2-1/2x3-1/2".

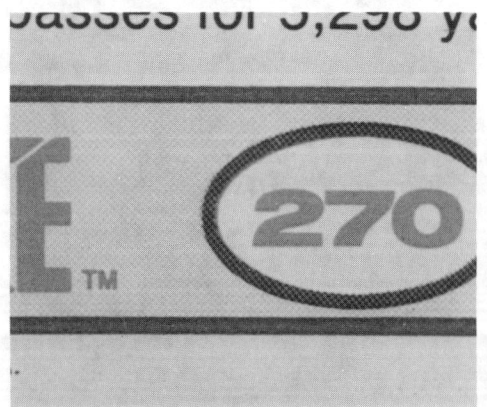

Genuine

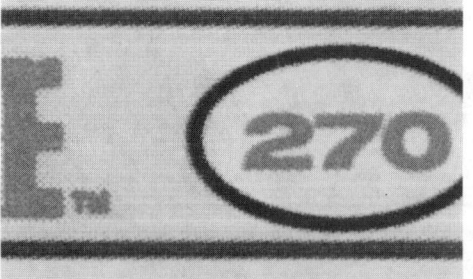

Counterfeit